PAUL GILK
THE LOGHOUSE
N 3920 COUNTY E
MERRILL, WI 54452

Picking Fights with the Gods

Also by Paul Gilk

Green Politics Is Eutopian

Nature's Unruly Mob: Farming and
the Crisis in Rural Culture

Polemics and Provocations: Essays
in Anticipation of the Daughter

The Kingdom of God Is Green

A Whole Which Is Greater: Why the
Wisconsin "Uprising" Failed
(with David Kast)

As "Seedy Buckberry"

Get Poor Now, Avoid the Rush

A Windfall Homestead: The Life and
Times of Henry Buckberry

Picking Fights with the Gods

A Spiritual Psychoanalysis of Civilization's Superego

Paul Gilk

Paul Gilk (6/6/2018)

WIPF & STOCK · Eugene, Oregon

PICKING FIGHTS WITH THE GODS
A Spiritual Psychoanalysis of Civilization's Superego

Wipf & Stock
An Imprint of Wipf and Stock Publishers
199 W. 8th Ave., Suite 3
Eugene, OR 97401

www.wipfandstock.com

PAPERBACK ISBN: 978-1-61097-538-4
HARDCOVER ISBN: 978-1-4982-8605-3
EBOOK ISBN: 978-1-4982-9983-1

Manufactured in the U.S.A.

For Maynard Kaufman, Kat Becker, Tony Schultz, Barb Kass, Mike Miles, Tenzin and Stacey Botsford—the seven people I know who are doing the most for the revival and renewal of rural culture, and for the resurrection of *pagus*.

By definition a revolution is illegal; it can advance to the new only by violating the old.

Will and Ariel Durant, *The Age of Reason Begins*, page 220

Once we have made explicit the biblical basis of the claimed right of Christian discovery and dominion . . . it then becomes possible to call this oppressive religious aspect of federal Indian law into question, directly challenge it, and eventually overturn it. However, so long as the Old Testament background . . . continues to remain hidden from view, it will continue to be taken for granted and successfully used as a covert weapon against indigenous nations and peoples.

Steven T. Newcomb, *Pagans in the Promised Land*, pages xxi-xxii

We are all trying to live in an age of accelerating change with a static theology. Since the phrase *rapid social change* serves often merely as a euphemism for *revolution*, the issue could be put even more bluntly: we are trying to live in a period of revolution without a theology of revolution.

Harvey Cox, *The Secular City*, page 107

The greatest error of which historical Christianity is guilty is due to the circumscribing and deadening notion that revelation is finished and that there is nothing more to be expected, that the structure of the Church has been completely built and that the roof has been put on it. Religious controversy is essentially concerned with the problem of the possibility of a new revelation and of a new spiritual era. All other questions are of secondary importance. . . . The revelation of the Spirit cannot be just simply waited for; it depends also upon the creative activity of man; it cannot be understood simply as a new revelation of God to man; it is also a revelation of man to God. This means that it will be a divine-human revelation.

Nicolas Berdyaev, in *Christian Mystics* by Matthew Fox, page 263

The healing process is in fact synonymous with the uncovering of truths repressed or never known.

Walter Wink, *The Bible in Human Transformation*, page 71

Generally an advance in human theory carries with it many remnants of the theory displaced.

Will Durant, *The Reformation*, page 862

Unlike many of his contemporaries among the deities of the ancient Near East, the God of Israel shared his power with no female divinity, nor was he the divine Husband or Lover of any. He can scarcely be characterized in any but masculine epithets: king, lord, master, judge, and father. Indeed, the absence of feminine symbolism for God marks Judaism, Christianity, and Islam in striking contrast to the world's other religious traditions. . . .

Elaine Pagels, *The Gnostic Gospels*, page 48

The human male alone is not the image of God, only the male and the female together. And this duality in the image must somehow be matched by a duality in the original. It is this fact that requires us to speak of the exclusion rather than the mere absence of the feminine from God's character.

Jack Miles, *God: A Biography*, page 265

But to achieve this reintegration of the repressed feminine, the masculine must undergo a sacrifice, an ego death. The Western mind must be willing to open itself to a reality the nature of which could shatter its most established beliefs about itself and about the world. This is where the real act of heroism is going to be. A threshold must now be crossed, a threshold demanding a courageous act of faith, of imagination, of trust in a larger and more complex reality; a threshold, moreover, demanding an act of unflinching self-discernment. . . .

This is the great challenge, yet I believe it is one the Western mind has been slowly preparing itself to meet for its entire existence. I believe that the West's restless inner development and incessantly innovative masculine ordering of reality has been gradually leading, in an immensely long dialectical movement, toward a reconciliation with the lost feminine unity, toward a profound and many-leveled marriage of the masculine and the feminine, a triumphant and healing reunion. And I consider that much of the conflict and confusion of our own era reflects the fact that this evolutionary drama may now be reaching its climactic stages.

Richard Tarnas, *The Passion of the Western Mind*, page 444

Contents

Acknowledgments

FIRST, CAROL ANN OKITE. Carol Ann has had a hand in the preparation of all my books. Even though she's insisted I learn elemental editing on the computer (Wipf and Stock requires the electronic submission of manuscripts), Carol Ann has bailed me out of innumerable keyboard difficulties, often with my hand-me-down laptop popped open on her kitchen table. Thank you, Carol Ann. Thank you very much.

Second, T. B. Scott Public Library in Merrill, Wisconsin. On the third floor, there's a behind-the-stacks, long, narrow table bolted to the north wall, its big windows overlooking the Prairie River as it tumbles through an adjoining park. It's from that perch (when I'm not at Carol Ann's) that I edit until my head feels like cooked oatmeal looks. (And then there are the librarians who so graciously rescue me when the computer plays a totally one-sided game of electronic chess with its operating idiot.) Once again, my heartfelt thanks.

Finally, with some ambiguity, I want to express genuine but cranky gratefulness to Quakers and Catholic Workers. These folks—the radical fringe respectively of Protestantism and Catholicism—are groping (or just hunkered down) at the boundary of orthodoxy. Since Trinity is a heavy cross to bear, it is—apparently—even harder to set down. That is, I'm not seeing much, even among Quakers and Catholic Workers, indicating a decisive break with or breakthrough from orthodoxy, though they've largely gotten beyond murderous Protestant mythology and the magical Catholic fascination of playing dolls with saints.

As the epigraphs in this book indicate, I believe the world is in a crisis of unprecedented magnitude, a crisis not only irresolvable by the core constructs of religious orthodoxy and civilizational principles, but a crisis *created by* religious orthodoxy and civilizational principles. This is a crisis that will only get worse—much, much worse—until we repent of our orthodoxy and civility. It's time we learned to live on Earth. When that occurs, it will be the greatest acknowledgment of all.

Introduction

I OCCASIONALLY READ ALOUD a new essay to my wife, Susanna. I do this—especially with the shorter ones—not only to get her response to the written ideas, but to test the flow of speech as spoken. While Susanna may not be my most severe critic, I've learned not to anticipate a gush of praise, either.

Her criticism seems to fall in two clusters. First, she says, I make a pretense of "reviewing" somebody's book or essay only to hop up on my favorite soapbox and shamelessly begin to blow my own bubbles. Second, I may lead off with praise or a compliment for the author I'm about to attack, but in no time flat I've got—or am attempting to get—my "opponent" in a mud puddle for a real mud brawl. Not nice.

In some ways, I plead No contest. Let the jury decide. But that's not the end of it. Maybe girls just don't understand how boys show affection for other boys by wrestling one another to the ground and rubbing each other's head in dirt. Bumps, bruises, and assorted abrasions are all part of the huggy tussle. (Or is it time to grow up?)

So, in these essays, I pick fights with Karen Armstrong, Andrew Bacevich, Thomas Berry and Wendell Berry, Marcus Borg and John Dominic Crossan, Joan Chittister, Noam Chomsky, Robert Funk, René Girard, Chris Hedges, Elizabeth Johnson, my dear friend Maynard Kaufman, Michael Lerner, Leopold Kohr, Thomas Merton, Lewis Mumford, Ched Myers, Saint Augustine, Teilhard de Chardin, Garry Wills, and (as if that's not enough) Aristotle the Greek—or, as Louise Ropes Loomis, in her Introduction to *Aristotle: On Man in the Universe*, says he was called by an old woman in Ireland, Harry Stottle.

A couple decades ago, I wouldn't have picked fights like this: who was I, after all, a mere jackpine savage (an undereducated one, at that), to take on these gods of philosophy, literature, and spirituality? Who was I to question the unquestionable? But, if I've matured sufficiently to indulge in such feisty presumption—which is, of course, open to question—I'd better get cracking before I'm too old and much too feeble to wrestle with these venerable geezers.

I've been slow to mature. That's just a fact of personal ontogeny. It's taken me a long time to come to conclusions. Partly that's a peasant's way of being in and observing the world, partly it's due to a haphazard education, including an idiosyncratic "self-education" undertaken by kerosene lamp and candlelight in the woods of northern Wisconsin, a deliberate and crucially needful balance between the neolithic and the civilized, a refusal to be fully civilized and an inability to achieve—as yet—an ethical and ecological merging of *pagus* and *civis*, which is the task of all serious Green movements.

But this idiosyncratic, backwoods immersion in the psychomythic history of cultural origins led me to Taoist places I probably would never have discovered had I led a more conventional life, for the conventional is a zone from which the idiosyncratic is roughly excluded and consistently denied entry. So what slowly dawned on me, as I suspect it has dawned on others who've undertaken "withdrawal from the world" by various means of homemade meditation, is that "the world" not only isn't what it's cracked up to be, its mythological self-regard is a construct whose perpetuation will kill us—is killing us. I not only take that seriously, I also take it personally.

So the mud fights—allowances, please, for irrepressible boyish behavior—are a way to goad my friends, both personal and intellectual, into deepening their critiques and broadening their analyses. Of course this implies I believe I'm seeing something they're not seeing or willing to consider. I understand that can feel irritating and condescending. But, after forty years of haphazard thought and irregular study, I'm at least entitled to a little eccentricity. Learning to see Trinity, for instance, in mythic terms of cultural evolution is not as easy as it sounds. Prevailing forms of thought, especially those with divine sanction, have boundaries not easily crossed, much less dissolved.

II

There are a number of ways to describe the preoccupations in my previous books, as well as in these essays. Perhaps the two main obsessions are rural culture and human gender.

We obviously live in a time when the city-systems of civilization, including their economic and military infrastructures, have achieved global dominance. Rural culture (whatever we mean by the term or however it might be defined) has receded to a nondominant state or condition—a "recessive gene," as Maynard Kaufman might put it. I say "receded" because even superficial knowledge of human history—and I mean to include what we usually think of as "prehistory"—shows that the rural was not only "dominant" before the rise of civilization, it was total. There was no urban, no city, no civilization in the precivilized world. The enormous bulk of our evolutionary history was lived in *pagus*. (And, as we shall see, *pagus* has itself become the "predator beast" to our *civis* sensibility.) In other words, if we were to graph "rural" and "urban" in human history, "urban" would be exceedingly tiny, a mere fingernail clipping on an immense chart, exactly the opposite of its current near totality.

And yet, it seems, almost all of us not only accept the present magnitude of urbanization as desirable, even as normal or normative, we (on the other side of that acceptance) could care less that the rural has been so surpassed and debilitated. (If only its disappearance would proceed more quickly!) Aligned with this acceptance of the urban is a conviction that city life is "progressive," that it is and has been the means by which and the medium through which the human "races" have more or less successfully mingled and women have more or less achieved "equality" with men. Corresponding to this positive or "progressive" conviction is a negative or "regressive" belief that rural culture—until it was finally overpowered by industrial urbanization—held humanity back from racial integration and women's liberation. The countryside, in other words, has been the locus of immobility and backwardness, the place where cultural change rarely if ever was permitted to occur. The city, with its progressive energy and dynamic expansion, set us free. Civilization globalized creates the conditions for universal human liberation.

There are ways—credible ways—by which to make exactly that case. There are threads of truth in the construct, even if the construct itself is shot through with ambiguity, contradiction, and qualification.

My argument, however, despite positive features within civilization, is that "progressive" attributes are largely what we might call "externalities" or "unintended consequences." The civilizational project did not begin or proceed with anything resembling "progressive" intent, either in behalf of gender equality or racial integration; its core institutions—"traumatic" in the language of Lewis Mumford, "diseases of Class and War" in the expression of Arnold Toynbee—continue to embody and carry forward the original institutional traumas and diseases. Civilization has not shed the one-percent violence of its founding even as the means of control have become much more sophisticated and complex.

Achieving "progressive" attributes has always involved struggle, and the durability of those attributes has usually been resisted. What prevents or obstructs us from recognizing this deeper truth is our vast historical ignorance. Enclosing this ignorance is a shroud of protective mythology. The shroud constitutes, enables, generates, and exonerates civilizational convictions and behavior. It is this mythological shroud these essays are attempting to penetrate and expose.

If civilized humans have achieved independence from and supremacy over the rural via conquest of indigenous cultures, enclosure of peasant commons, squeezing of small-scale farming, and the installation of economies-of-scale industrial agribusiness as a food-producing replica of the industrial factory, then we have arrived at a place of total civility and even a true utopia. But since utopia has presented us with (among other things) weapons of mass destruction and a rapidly intensifying climate change due to the externalities of the industrial economy this utopia itself has produced, should, perhaps, cause us to re-examine the warnings of Toynbee and Mumford. These essays consist of such a re-examination. Either civilization has made a glorious breakthrough into permanent utopia or civilizational dystopia is in process of engulfing us in episodic shocks and catastrophes as it blows itself apart.

III

One last little warning. I'm more or less equally hard—"fair and balanced"—toward both "liberals" and "conservatives." If "conservatives" have their heads stuck in the authoritarian vise of God the Father, "liberals" have theirs (in addition to being scared of righteous authoritarianism) mesmerized by the pious mythology of civilizational superiority. If "conservatives" are stuck in cosmic fear and earthly vindictiveness, "liberals" ooze cosmic evasion and earthly condescension. Liberals are mostly middle-class professionals whose generous ethical sentiments remain woefully lacking in eutopian cultural vision and eutopian economic grounding. However, the respective mythologies of "liberal" and "conservative" overlap and interpenetrate. These mythologies have mutually reinforcing roots. We might say one is explicitly religious and the other explicitly civilizational. But—the truth is—they're so entangled they're nearly inseparable.

It is the shifting fusion and frequent cross-dressing of these mythologies that makes one tempted to think of them almost as gendered beings, just as contemporary political wit recognizes Republicans as Daddy Party and Democrats as Mommy —Donald versus Hillary. In the following essays, it's Dorothy Dinnerstein who comes closest to lifting the mythological curtain—closest, that is, to Joachim of Floris, who provided us with the essential construct by which the entire curtain is being raised, the Emperor exposed with bony legs and threadbare underwear, and a lovely new cast of characters about to take the stage.

Or, perhaps, our predicament could be expressed like this—

Once upon a time
we thought End Times
belonged to God,

      but

    now

   we see

  it's

ours.

1

What's Become of Rural Culture?

On an afternoon in July of 2009, my wife Susanna and I stopped by Stoney Acres Farm, near the little town of Athens in north-central Wisconsin. We were there to see Kat Becker and her husband Tony Schultz—and, of course, their little, red-haired son Riley, ruddy-faced, hanging out with his Grandpa Ed, who was working on a walk-in produce cooler in the barn. We had to visit Julie the pig, proud mom of (I think it was) nine little piglets, and then the CSA (Community Supported Agriculture) garden plots, amazingly vigorous despite the unseasonably cool weather.

Tony and Kat gave us a dozen farm eggs, and we gave them a copy of my newly published *Nature's Unruly Mob: Farming and the Crisis in Rural Culture*. Tony, sniffing the *Mob*, immediately did two things. He handed me a copy of the Summer 2009 *Defender*, newsletter of the Family Farm Defenders (familyfarmdefenders.org, for those inclined to cyber space), with his "Pinning Down Pastoral" in the coveted centerfold position. Then he asked if I'd write an article for the Stoney Acres newsletter on the subject "What is Rural Culture?" As an afterthought, glancing again at my book's title and shaking the *Mob* in my face, Tony (who's tall and muscular) demanded to know, "And where in here do you define 'rural culture'?"

I was stumped. I'm not sure there's even an attempt at "rural culture" definition in the entire book. I hadn't realized one was—maybe—needed. So I shrugged and diverted attention to young Riley, whose fistful of crumpled cornbread might've been shareable if only I could be sufficiently coaxing. I tried. My attempt was not successful.

II

I have a compulsive writing habit. It was fueled, and its direction shaped, by a naïve and innocent question I'd begun asking in the early 1970s: "Why are small farms dying?" Born in 1946, I'd grown up on a small homestead farm in northern Wisconsin. By the early '70s, living in St. Louis, I was seriously missing many aspects of farm life in the largely wooded countryside of my youth. I realized small farms were disappearing. I wanted to know why. My urban friends were not particularly helpful in exploring an answer to that question. Their minds didn't seem to work well when asked to think in an agrarian direction or rural mode. So I shifted toward historians.

The most comprehensive were Lewis Mumford and Norman O. Brown—Mumford the world historian and Brown the classics professor turned explicator of Freudian psychoanalysis. Here's a compacted version of what I learned.

III

Gathering and grubbing are the oldest forms of human food procurement. Hunting came later and was largely a male phenomenon: the band of brothers out on the chase, while the sisters gathered by the encampment, doing a lot of food, shelter, and clothing things, plus child care.

Hunter-gatherers—that's the term we probably all were taught for precivilized, nonagricultural people. That's our primary image of Native American cultures, for instance, people who lived in wigwams, tipis or longhouses, who hunted wild animals with snares, nets, spears, or bows and arrows, who gathered wild plants—roots, berries, nuts, fruits, stems, leaves—whatever. Birchbark canoes and wild rice.

If hunters were male, gatherers were female. Historians say horticulture derives from the diligence of attentive gatherers—a process of long-term but concentrated female sensibility. When sufficient food was available to the no-longer-nomadic villagers (because horticultural and garden abundance made being nomadic unnecessary), the domestication of animals besides the dog got seriously underway. It's likely that youthful male hunters captured young, wild critters and brought them back alive, perhaps as a challenge or taunt or joke to play on the women. Here, feed this! And when a digging stick got hooked behind an ox (either in comic jest or as part of a cosmic ceremony—the two may not be all that far apart), a primordial plow was invented, and men began to participate in a new and deeper way in what was not just horticulture and gardening but horticulture in small fields with animal domestication and plowing—that is, agriculture. Women, in other words, may have accidentally domesticated men—or at least they may have begun to domesticate men, right along with plants and other animals in the new stable village. Hunters became farmers in the footsteps of the women, shedding in the process a certain propensity or capacity toward violence. This thinning of the readiness for violence will figure into the eventual takeover of the village by nomadic raiders.

It is the village agricultural abundance of the late Stone Age on which civilization squats and sits. Without food in abundance (we'll slide for the time being around the slippery word "surplus"), civilization could not exist. Civilization is what happened when hit and run raiders became permanent expropriators. Coming to terms with the meaning of civilization—"meaning," I say, not "definition"—was one of the hardest parts of my haphazard and idiosyncratic education, for I had been taught (and I uncritically believed) that civilization was an unmitigated good, the cultural and moral opposite of "savage," "primitive," "pagan," "undeveloped," or "backward." Civilization was the catapult by which the human race had hurled itself, once and for all, beyond the quagmire of primitivity.

But when I realized that civilization came into existence with the armed and violent expropriation of the production and persons of the agrarian village—that civilization rests on a base of murder and expropriation—I was thrown into a metaphysical, spiritual, and religious crisis. If God gives and sustains empires and kingdoms, as Saint Augustine taught, and if kingdoms and empires are only specific forms of the overarching project of civilization, and if civilization was explicitly governed, up until the industrial revolution, by hereditary aristocracy, then either Augustine was dreadfully wrong or God is a cunning, cruel, and brutal aristocrat who has contempt for the "commoner."

Confronted with that choice, I went for the one that said Augustine was an apologist for empire—as, in fact, he was. We should also say that he probably couldn't help being an apologist, for a combination of Greek philosophy, Old Testament "history," and a nearly total absence of the kind of historical scholarship we now possess and rely on, made Augustine's assertions mythological, even as he thought them historical. (The great bulk of Christian writing in the history of the church continued to confound mythology for historical fact, as fundamentalism especially still does.) Nevertheless, Augustine was an apologist for the empires God supposedly gives and sustains, and his apologetics have been key and crucial elements within Christian theology ever since. Those apologetics are operative to this day. One nation under God. The divine right of kings. Manifest destiny. The indispensable nation.

IV

So what did I learn from my investigation into why small farms were dying? First, I learned that women's gathering ramifying as gardening and horticulture is the deepest root of agriculture. Second, the first "farm crisis" occurred when armed and violent men (renegade hunters? bored nomadic herders? marauding "pastoralists"?) took over the agrarian village by brute force and imposed what would become aristocratic civilization, expropriating as much of the farmers' production as possible and imposing a fierce regimentation with both military and slavery manifestations. This dynamic describes the relationship between aristocrat and peasant (which is, of course, the way civilization operated for five thousand years) until the emergence of the industrial revolution, at which point the second "farm crisis" began to kick in.

If the *first* farm crisis can be described as the violent expropriation of agricultural abundance (the so-called "surplus" of the agrarian village) for purposes of civilization-building and aristocratic luxury (all in a mode resulting in a systematically impoverished peasantry), the *second* farm crisis developed as a consequence of commercial capitalism combined with industrialization. *Industrial civilization discovered it no longer needed a peasantry*, so it began to systematically dispossess the country folk in favor of what we now call commercial agriculture or agribusiness, the maximized rationalization of agricultural production, food (or commodity) production essentially devoid of cultural considerations. Subsistence as a mode of life, as a cultural form, dies with the suppression of the indigenous and the peasant.

If agrarian culture had its evolution checked, thwarted, and impounded on the occasion of the first farm crisis, it actually ceased to exist with the dispossession of the peasantry and the squeezing out of small-scale farming. In this country, the Jeffersonian agrarian vision was slowly but steadily strangled by the Hamiltonian industrial-financial garrote machine. The year 1896 represents something of a watershed. The People's Party (or so-called "populists") lost in the presidential election of that year, and the exhausted farm community began its demographic disintegration, no longer able to mount a serious political challenge to the capitalist industrializing and urbanization of America. The machine had been rolled into the garden, and the machine was winning.

The civilized elite have typically expressed a rather undisguised contempt for the cultural backwardness of rural life. To kill and dispossess the indigenous, to crush the peasantry, to practice agricultural slavery, and to undermine and eliminate small-scale farming were righteous forms of civilized missionary work. I say this without sarcasm—or nearly so. It's simply not possible to understand the demise of rural culture without recognizing the power and persistence of aristocratic, civilized contempt for rural culture—or the extent to which this traditional contempt permeated the sensibility of the urban and commercial middle class. (See especially the chapter "The Puritan Movement" in R. H. Tawney's *Religion and the Rise of Capitalism*.) Civilized people are invariably pleased with their civility, and nothing is more frightening than the threat of retrogressive "backwardness." This dynamic pervades our lives all the way from Wal-Mart consumerism to reflexive support for American global dominance. This, too, is part of our metaphysical inheritance from Saint Augustine, the civilized institutions God gives and sustains. One nation under God.

V

So if rural culture is dead or dying, when's the funeral? The question may seem snide, sardonic and snotty, but (aside from curiosity malls called museums) there are no farewell ceremonies for the unworthy, the undeserving, or the merely outdated utilitarian. Native American hunters may put tobacco down at the site where a deer is killed, but employees at a slaughterhouse hardly have time to spit while working on the kill line.

We could leap ahead by an indeterminate quantum of time and ask whether there might be resurrection in store for rural culture. Buried in that question is another question: whether rural culture *deserves* resurrection. This is in many ways the crucial question: not just "Why are small farms dying?" but "Will rural culture revive?" or

"*Should* rural culture revive?" Sometimes to answer a difficult question, it's useful—even necessary—to trace the roots of the problem first. The answer may come less as a lushly blooming insight than as gestalt of root structure, with dirt intact and worms wiggling.

We might ask, "Why has rural culture been so unworthy, contemptible, unfit, and dispensable?" Is it simply obsolete? Is it merely the primitive cultural compost out of which progressive civility has matured? The mud beneath the lotus? In my opinion, there's a lot of traction to be found in that exploration—only we've got to be prepared to examine, and even relinquish, our comfortably unconscious civilized prejudices if we're serious about following this query through to an honest answer. It was hard enough for a self-interested farm boy to make this journey. It's not an easy or pleasant job for people wearing ideological uniforms or dressed in the immaculate robes of spotless religious doctrine. Just finding the will to begin is itself a major effort.

It may be time for a little peasant dirt.

VI

A dictionary was only a place to brush tangles out of poorly spelled words until I was about thirty years old. One day I decided to look up "peasant." It was a good dictionary, an old *Webster's*, half a foot thick. Many entries had brief, opening sections giving the languages through which a word had passed before becoming lodged in contemporary English. What I presume was the oldest known form or usage of the word was also given, often in Latin. Occasionally there were cross-references. "Peasant" had a cross-reference, including its oldest Latin form. Peasant's cross-reference was *pagus,* meaning "country district." In brackets, the cross-reference said "[See Pagan]." So I looked up "pagan."

What I saw blew my mind. *"Pagan" had the identical Latin root as "peasant."* Both peasant and pagan derived from *pagus.* The dictionary, at that moment, was a magic portal into a semantic wardrobe through which I unexpectedly entered Narnia: peasant and pagan were twin children of mother *pagus,* country kids of a country mom! I felt the curtain rise (or the fog lift) on an entirely new vista of intellectual, religious, and historical comprehension. I was stunned.

Now I already knew (good old *Webster's*) that *civis* was the Latin connecting root between "city" and "civilization." So it didn't take a genius to see why the Augustinian *civis* of God (*De Civitate Dei*) was so determined to pin a tail of evil on country *pagus.* A neutered and urbanized Christianity provided Empire a *religious* rationale for rural suppression. The fall of man had triggered the fall of Creation, and fallen nature was where the Devil went to do his dirty work. God was a *civis* man; the Devil lurked in *pagus.* I suddenly felt I was getting an eagle's view of a hugely meaningful historical, religious, and mythological watershed conveyed in plain etymology, a glimpse of where and how Christianity had become the ceremonial sidekick of *civis* and the sanctimonious inquisitor of *pagus*.

What was needed now was not only a deeper historical understanding of agriculture, but also a grasp of how Christianity's Constantinian/Augustinian accommodation was, in the centuries to come, going to suck the earthy life out of rural spirituality as a consequence of the armed expansion of Christendom, complete with crusades and inquisitions, Reformations and Counter-Reformations, resulting in the eventual enforced atrophy of rural culture on a global scale. I needed to fit this dictionary revelation into a larger perspective.

VII

Lewis Mumford and other historians suggest that male hunters had a condescending and even contemptuous attitude toward the bloodless plant food garnered by gatherers and gardeners, and an even fiercer negative view of early farming—its drudgery, its boredom, its allegedly small-horizon of village domestication: not meaningful activity for real men who needed to stretch their legs, exercise their muscles, outwit large mammals on a serious hunt, and maybe even aggressively bump up against a rival band of hunters contesting turf.

One theory regarding the origins of the first aristocrats goes like this: Male herders weren't above a little reckless pillage now and then—as long as it was somebody else's village. One day one of the brighter (or perhaps just old and gimpy) brigands turned to his pals and said, "You know, we could just camp out by this farming village and make those stupid farmers bring us stuff every day, make them build us a fortress and, rather than swoop in for a raid once a year or so, we'll be the most powerful and protected raiders in the world. We can conscript a few of their sturdy boys to join our happy band as we expand our raiding area and, with some of their pretty girls, we'll have all the juicy sex we want." A lust for war and war egged on by lust.

So, hunters had contempt for "women's work," except for arousing bedtime stories, and early farming (at minimum, the gardening aspect) was primarily the work of women. When nomadic hunters/herders/bandits settled in as civilized aristocrats, this contempt deepened in three ways, at least. First, there was contempt that so many farmers were helpless in the face of so few bandits. (Farmers had, over time, emotionally distanced themselves from predatory killing, but bandits still had eyes of hawks.) Second, imposed economic destitution and compulsive labor as a consequence of systemic expropriation made agricultural life even less desirable and more contemptible. The peasant was a despised peon. Third, secret fear of peasant rebellion (they may be stupid, but they're strong and there's a lot of them) agitated macho aristocratic bravado and inspired wanton cruelty, thus making peasants not merely inferior humans, but an inferior species, not really or fully human—stupid, dirty, masochistic, and passive—objects of derision and therefore deserving random acts of capricious violence.

If that seems farfetched, consider the linkage between "peasant" and "pagan" in a good dictionary and then meditate on the fact that, first, the peasant Jesus was legally murdered by the civilized elite in Jerusalem but, three centuries later, when Christianity formally merged with the Roman Empire, the deepest and most pervasive moral enemy of Christian faith was not the civilized, aristocratic bandit class (the class that killed Jesus) but the "pagans," that is, the country dwellers. ("Perfidious Jews" was the chosen scapegoat. Just as a "villain" comes from a village or "heathen" from the heaths.)

With Christianity, explicitly so from the fifth century onward, what's good and desirable is linked not to the agrarian "kingdom of God," as articulated scores of times in the first three gospels, but to Augustine's "City of God," the crowning symbol of God's residential preference and the place to which the elect will someday get to go. God in this latter construct is depicted as King of kings in a sacred hierarchy pervading the entire social order; but only the cream of the crop will achieve eternal salvation. With City of God theology, the peasant Jesus becomes an aristocratic Prince residing in heavenly estate with his Father, God the King. Salvation comes (or is at least facilitated) when people are liberated from their paganism, that is, from their intimate affiliation with "country district" and ecological groundedness, including the spiritual or religious practices expressing or reflecting that groundedness. Civilized imperialism (the relentless expansion of aristocratic greed and power) discovered that religious imperialism (with its spiritual agrarian egalitarianism carefully pruned away) provided a huge steroid boost to imperial energy. We might even say that Augustine helped rescue the Roman Empire from total collapse by transforming its predatory core into a newly christened *Holy* Roman Empire. Civilization now became, in Christian theology, an elevated step—a hugely elevated step—closer to the otherworldly God. "Not of this world" (e.g., John 18:36) was a death blow to the *pagus*, just as it was to the "kingdom of God" proclamation. *Civis* was under God's protection. *Pagus*, at minimum, was under divine surveillance.

It took centuries to achieve, but a quasi-aristocratic standard of living, an ersatz ruling-class lifestyle appetite, and an urban self-concept slowly but steadily saturated human consciousness as the social and economic ideal to be achieved in the Western world. (And then, of course, the industrial revolution ratcheted the process beyond anyone's expectation or imagination by going global.) That the West has been the agency for world conquest and economic globalization is due precisely to the metaphysical strength Western civilization obtained when Christianity abandoned its evolutionary/revolutionary vision of the "kingdom of God," in which everybody might learn to practice radical servanthood and radical stewardship, and instead became an explicitly imperialist religion aiming at ruling-class luxury and aristocratic idleness, if not in this world, then certainly in the next. A deep disorientation and penetrating bewilderment entered into the heart and soul of rural culture as peasants were persuaded to abandon or coerced into abandoning their "pagan" understandings and pushed into accepting a set of religious doctrines, creeds, and images heavily shaped by affiliation with civilized empire, whose God was King of kings and whose Son was Prince of Heaven. The cruel paradox of "democracy"—despite Jefferson's "agrarian vision" intention—is that it did not result in the liberation and empowerment of impounded rural culture but, instead, in its virtual extermination and extinction. Democracy is apparently only for the civilized middle class. The *city* of God.

VIII

Perhaps, to get a clearer view of why rural culture is so debilitated, and why there are so few state or federal policies designed for its revival or reconstruction, we need to look at a rough but critical parallel. That is, as the entire world lies under the shadow of nuclear ecocide and under the growing ecological wreckage of catastrophic climate change, state and federal policies addressing these End Times calamities are feeble, weak and paltry, hardly more than insincere symbolic gestures. What does this mean? What does this tell us when the ecological basis of our evolutionary existence is threatened with toxic corruption by our instruments and behavior and we refuse to pay attention? (See the small book—small but tough—by Naomi Oreskes and Erik Conway, *The Collapse of Western Civilization: A View from the Future*.)

Well, I take this refusal to mean that our mental configuration—our daily consciousness, our religious beliefs, our anticipations of the future, our considerations of the past, our lifestyle habits and consumer addictions—is such that we are intellectually anesthetized by the civilized/heavenly ideal that has been the truck of both church and state for centuries on end. (By "ideal" I mean something far deeper, more pervasive and penetrating than an occasional lofty thought. This heavenly/civilized "ideal" is the air we breathe, the money we spend, the images we take in from the television screen, the very language we speak.) We have surpassed nature to such an extent, we have removed ourselves from life lived within nature to such a degree, that we are mentally, morally, and ethically on the edge of being *incapable* of recognizing the ecocidal pickle we're in, even as the facts build inescapably around us. Or, insofar as we may *recognize* the danger factually or "objectively," we don't truly *feel* it because either civilization will protect us or God will save us. So there's really nothing to worry about. James Watt, Ronald Reagan's Interior Secretary, put it succinctly when he urged coal companies to strip mine because "Jesus is coming."

Now James Watt didn't mean Jesus is coming to live ecologically an Earth. His wasn't a call for recognizing the ethical importance of the "kingdom of God." What Watt meant was the Second Coming, Armageddon, End Times, Jesus with a sword in his mouth as described in the Book of Revelation, true believers taken safely home to happy eternity in heavenly bliss, and Earth destroyed. That an Interior Secretary would not instantly be fired for such antiecological psychosis (he might have been entitled to religious hallucinations as a private citizen, but not when those delusions shaped public policy) is a token, emblem, and symbol for how far public policy has climbed out on the utopian twigs of never-never land. It is an indication (rather like Agriculture Secretary Earl Butz's famous "Get big or get out" dictum to American farmers in the 1970s) of how normative this religious/civilized psychosis has become. IBM's new slogan is "Building a better planet." The "better planet" of IBM has its intermediate link to End Times via computerized ICBMs. Building better instruments for planetary holocaust.

There are only a handful of major options here, each of which may have its kick at the can. First (or last) is real ecocide, the bombs and missiles unleashed, mammalian extinction achieved. Righteous male violence carried to its ultimate rationalized blasphemy. Mutually Assured Destruction. Radioactive male bonding. The deliberate destruction of evolutionary creation achieved by male emptiness, arrogance, fear, and pride. *The instruments are in place to make it happen.* Second is restoration on a global scale of explicit aristocratic class, with Blackwater mercenary clones, nomadic raiders in fancier gear, putting down "peasant" rebellion with an iron fist. *Democracy dies, and with it dies the prospect for a deeper and more loving human soul, at least for the foreseeable future.* Third is resurrection of the precivilized agrarian village, the overthrow (both political and spiritual) of bandit aristocracy, the recapitulation of Jesus' vision of the "kingdom of God," life and human self-governance transformed toward the twin ethical principles of radical stewardship and radical servanthood.

We might call this latter option libertarian democratic ecological socialism. *But this one depends on our energetic willingness to go there.* It'll not be a gift from throne or altar, God or king. If we can get there, it's because the "kingdom of God" is ingesting *civis* into its *pagus* body and transforming metal weaponry into tools fit for use in the eutopian garden.

IX

It's so stupidly obvious to say so, but we are all individual human beings, flames of living consciousness, each of us on a sliding scale of inevitable mortality, headed for death; and, as far as I can tell, our job is to cultivate and nourish the deepest reservoirs in our souls—to live as deeply, as wisely, as humbly, as simply, and as engaged as possible, to get down to where we truly have our feet on Mother Earth, where we feel ourselves aligned with Earth's recovery and with the Spirit of Peace, capable, finally, of helping transform nuclear swords into solar plowshares, utopian spears into eutopian pruning hooks. *Then* our grandchildren and great-grandchildren will inhabit a depth and breadth of spiritually wholesome ecological culture we now only dream about. But such dreaming is part of our recovery, too.

X

I'm going to go on a wee bit more about religion; and, in my imagination, I believe I can hear some people shouting, "Oh, God! Not more of that boring, stupid, irrelevant, distracting crap. Get real. Talk about something of substance, will you?" Sorry, but in my view, the failure (or refusal) to look at the role religion plays in our predicament is a really big mistake. Humor me. Keep reading.

With Jesus and his "kingdom of God" proclamation, we have a dynamic that was provisionally but falsely resolved. That is, the first three gospels in the New Testament—Matthew, Mark, and Luke—show a Jesus of lower-class village origins, a man of the peasantry, whose transformative speech was composed of anecdotes, stories and parables, speech at once pointed and elusive, witty and sharp, exactingly germane to the present moment, yet also a wellspring of ever-flowing wisdom to be carried away by the listener and savored for a long time to come. This Jesus eventually goes to the city to mock and confront its rulers, both its Jewish upper class and its Roman overlords. They kill him in the most brutal and public way. ("It is better to have one person die on behalf of the people, rather than have the whole nation ruined," as Caiaphas explains to the Sanhedrin in John 11:50.)

In the gospel of John, we have a Jesus somewhat like the synoptic Jesus, only much more long-winded, given to mystical speeches about himself and his divinity—a Jesus, it seems, fitted to John's purpose of converting gabby gentile Greeks to the new "Christian" message. And in the remainder of the New Testament, we largely have analysis, assertion, moral and theological exhortation, finishing up in Revelation with a lurid sort of hallucinatory science fiction depicting the End of the World.

As the Jesus story settled into established religion, it became less and less a shared life lived in the visionary (but intensely ethical) liberation of spiritual fullness and more a compacted set of private convictions oriented toward eternal happiness after a miserable life and dreaded death. The "kingdom of God" became a smaller and smaller fly buzzing more and more distantly in an ever-bigger web of otherworldly theological formulation and ecclesiastical power structure.[1]

1. This assessment needs qualification. Marcus Borg, in his *Evolution of the Word*, describes (on page 9) ancient Rome as "an especially large domination system, controlling much of Europe, the Middle East, and North Africa. Its military was both powerful and efficient. Its legions were highly trained professional soldiers and engineers who built a system of all-weather roads, so they could move quickly to quell resistance in any part of the empire.

"It was even more economically exploitative than its predecessors. Not only were conquered provinces required to pay annual tribute to Rome (a form of taxation collected by local authorities), but Roman economic policy promoted the commercialization of agriculture. Small plots of land that had been farmed for centuries by families to produce food for their own use were combined into large estates owned by the wealthy to produce crops for sale and export. Having lost their land, many in the rural class became tenant farmers, sharecroppers, or day laborers, producing not their own food, but commercial crops like grains, olives, and grapes. Outside the Jewish homeland, the commercialization of agriculture also resulted in large-scale migration to cities, where former agricultural laborers became part of the urban working poor—a situation that becomes important for understanding the

We tend to think the Constantinian accommodation in the early fourth century a sudden and unexpected overthrow of "pagan" civilization by Christian faith, a faith fiercely set against Roman imperialism. If so, Constantine saw otherwise. He recognized a corresponding and complementary imperialism in Christian doctrine, and he seized the opportunity to incorporate Christianity's *religious* imperialism into his immediate *political* need, as well as into a larger imperial design. When the youthful, pious Thomas Merton wrote in his 1950 Introduction to *The City of God* that Augustine's fifth-century book "contains the secret of death and life, war and peace, hell and heaven," he (Merton) was in his rapturous enthusiasm recognizing that *civis* had smashed *pagus*, that the mission of the church had entered the cockpit of Empire: "Was St. Augustine planning a temporal theocracy," Merton asks, "a Holy Roman Empire in *The City of God*? It is abundantly clear that the City he described is the Kingdom of Christ which, as Jesus told Pilate, is 'not of this world.' Nevertheless, that does not mean that Augustine would necessarily have frowned on a temporal theocracy," [2]

urban context of Paul's activity."

On page 25, Borg tells us more about the "urban context." He says there "was no sanitation. Today's visitors to the remains of ancient cities of the Roman Empire often marvel at their water systems, including even toilets, but these were luxuries for the wealthy. In the tenement areas, where most of the population lived, water had to be carried, most often up several flights of stairs. Human waste was dumped into gutters. These conditions and crowding meant that contagious disease was rampant. Life expectancy was low, about thirty years for those who survived the high mortality rates of infancy and childhood.

"The urban working population could be sustained only by continuing migration from rural areas. Roman agricultural policy virtually compelled migration to cities. Small peasant farms that had provided basic sustenance to the families that had lived on them for centuries were being combined into large estates that now produced grains and other agricultural products for export. Many of the rural class, now without their own land, moved to cities to find work. Most did so out of desperation, not because they desired city life.

"Migration to cities destroyed the extended family and village relationships that marked traditional rural communities. Newcomers to cities, even if they arrived with their family, were severed from the familiarity and common concern of village life. They were, in an important sense, alone and on their own. Moreover, cities were populated by many ethnic and linguistic groups, in contrast to the homogeneity of village life. Ethnic estrangement and conflict were frequent.

"Thus life was difficult for most of those who lived in cities. Earning enough money to pay for food and shelter was always an issue. Disease and death were constant threats. Community was no longer something that one was born into, but was either absent or newly formed."

Borg goes on to say that "Paul's purpose as apostle was to create and nurture urban communities of Christ-followers—from among Gentiles in particular." In the context of the synoptic gospels especially, we see Jesus proclaim the "kingdom of God" not to alienated urban dwellers but to peasants primarily. This enables us to recognize that the radical difference between the speech of Jesus and the speech of the apostles is hugely contextual; that is, Jesus may have been speaking to oppressed and exploited peasants; but they *were* peasants. Paul is exhorting the totally disenfranchised, the landless, the alienated and desperate city dwellers—including, probably, a small slice of the merchant class, and even a few of the modestly wealthy. Perhaps this helps us understand how quickly Jesus became an otherworldly savior—the only hope was for a decent life after death—rather than the initiator of transformative spiritual revolution on Earth. The "kingdom of God" apparently became unimaginable in a context of urban despair.

2. Merton, "Introduction," xv, xiv.

"The whole of history since the ascension of Jesus into heaven," Merton says, "is concerned with one work only: the building and perfecting of this 'City of God.' Even the wars, persecutions, and all the other evils which have made the history of empires terrible to read and more terrible to live through, have only had this one purpose: they have been the flails with which God has separated the wheat from the chaff, the elect from the damned."[3] As Augustine says, God Himself gives all earthly kingdoms. God is in control as King of kings.

It is much more than historical curiosity that Merton can say the topic first engaging Augustine's attention was "Christianity versus the official pagan religion of imperial Rome."[4] This glaringly oxymoronic use of the word "pagan" is common to such pious commentary; but it's not merely a conventional semantic mistake repeated out of scholarly habit. Peasants may have "pagan" religions (etymologically, peasants can't help but have "pagan" religions), but imperial power always has a religion that undergirds, supports, and justifies its *civis* status. Empires don't have "pagan" religions. Empires have *civilized* religions. Rome was no exception. To say otherwise—to say Rome had a *pagan* religion—is sheer semantic nonsense, irrespective of how venerable that nonsense may be.

This devious scapegoating of "pagan" was intended not merely to condemn the earlier non-Christian religion of imperial Rome, but also to justify Christianity's shotgun marriage to Empire. In order to gloss over the shocking implications of this sacrilege—the ragtag followers of Jesus merging officially with Jesus' unrepentant murderer, without so much as a Truth and Reconciliation Commission—the murderer's system gets magically transformed from evil to good by identifying its older, evil phase as "pagan" and its new, holy phase as "Christian." The elemental sophistry of this slight of hand is stunning. That it has stuck for so long is also stunning. That it continues to stick is stunning. But we would be foolish not to recognize the function this sophistry has served in the maintenance of orthodox Christianity as an enabler of civilized imperialism. Since it's God who gives kingdoms and empires, we are to be obedient and thankful. God wants us all to be civilized.

So, via our topic in this little essay ("What's become of rural culture?"), we can see the first impoundment of rural culture occurring with the rise of civilization itself, roughly five thousand years ago. And while it's true that the industrial revolution provided the means and circumstances for what I've called, with little or no irony, the second farm crisis (the liquidation of the peasantry), the stage for this latter crisis was set less by eighteenth-century perfecting of steam engines than by Constantine, Augustine, and all the incrementally but increasingly abstract theological formulations transforming Jesus from grounded *pagus* sage to aloof prince of heavenly *civis*. Christianity is a *civilized* religion. Peel away the complex layers of theological explanation for the crucifixion, get down to the core image of the crucifix itself, and what do

3. Merton, "Introduction," xii.
4. Merton, "Introduction," x.

we see but a dead peasant on a stick—a peasant not hoisted with his own petard but nailed to a post by the Powers and Principalities as a brutal illustration of the fate for any would-be "kingdom of God" advocate.

It's not accidental that the West has been the agency for world conquest, colonialism, doctrines of religious supremacy, and enforced globalization in behalf of Christian civilization. With the merging of Christianity and Rome's Empire, we have the centralizing principle (civilization) taking on board a reformulated religion (Christianity) containing all the necessary elements for insinuating itself into peasant culture (the "sower of seeds" and other such parables with explicit agrarian imagery) and then—having taught peasants that pagan is a filthy word, loaded with spiritual corruption—jerking the rug out from under rural life when the industrial means were finally at hand by which that rug could be jerked. Nature may be God's (fallen) creation, but to hold this (fallen) creation in excessive esteem, to cultivate what Albert Schweitzer called reverence for life, is to dabble with false spirituality, with paganism, and, finally, with the Devil. If *civis* is good and godly, *pagus* is bad and wicked. These are the semantic weights we bring to our present evaluation of rural culture, to the "definition" asked for by Tony Schultz.

XI

"Unless you are born again from above," says Jesus in John 3:3, "you cannot see the kingdom of God." "Above" is a potent word, much like John's other much-used phrase "not of this world." If God is "above," Elsewhere, and if the "ascended" Jesus has gone to this elusive Elsewhere, a disembodied heaven where the City of God elect will someday get to go, too, then this world is only a Kennedy Space Center launch pad for Christian Endeavor, counting down to End Times.

I have hammered these concepts into bolder relief than they appear in political speech, in magazines or newspapers; but, like Thomas Merton's God, I am merely flailing the manufactured wheat from the ecological chaff, revealing underlying tendencies within our civilized trajectory. That's not to say there is no countertendency at work. There is. Grounded folk sensibility is not dead. Neither evolution nor cultural evolution is finished. But it's crucial to recognize that most Christians remain in the immobilizing grip of the Constantinian accommodation. Not capable of realizing that it's "the Devil" who gives kingdoms (see Matthew 4:8-9 or Luke 4:5-6) or that civilization means systemic exploitation and oppression (see I Samuel 8), most religious people are reflexively fearful of and viscerally repulsed by anything "pagan" or "peasant." The wickedness of the pagan is part of what makes the "kingdom of God" unattainable on Earth. "Pagan" is emblematic of a fallen creation, and the kingdom of God is unattainable in a fallen creation. Wholesome life on a fallen Earth is a pagan idea. Civilization is God's device for controlling pagan fallenness until End Times. It is the historically accrued and politically channeled energy of this metaphysical containment that provides the temporal momentum for the civilized status quo as fed by the (now beginning to sag) energy supply of oil, gas, and coal. The City of God is our ideal and destination. But liftoff is leaking. The extraterrestrial rocket is beginning to falter. Therefore in desperation to maintain the energy by which to perpetuate our civility, we are fracking Mother Earth. We are empathy deficient eco-sadist Mother Frackers. Building a better planet. Chemistry for better living. Civilization needs lift-off energy to achieve its heavenly destination, or at least sustain its utopian replica here below.

We are in the moderately advanced stages of a slow-motion global train wreck of gigantic ecological proportions. Whether the outcome will be radioactive death, climate change catastrophe, brutal aristocratic restoration, or the resurrection of the agrarian village married to the "kingdom of God" is, in large but immeasurable part, up to us. The Spirit of Peace may be yeastily at work in the collective human soul, but you and I have our own bread to bake. The oven is getting hotter; and, as Harry Truman might once have said, those who can't stand the heat should get out of the kitchen and into the garden. We each have our own row to hoe.

2

An Ethical Audit of Overconsumption

IT'S PUZZLING TO THE point of amazing how difficult it is to talk about class or class distinctions. Or, if we do get to the topic, "class" quickly becomes packaged in quantitative terms, usually by income. The wealthy (we don't say "upper class," for that's politically obnoxious and perhaps even obscene) are those whose incomes may be $250 thousand per year, or $500 thousand per year, or maybe $1 million per year. Of course we occasionally hear of people who "earn" multimillions per year or people whose "net worth" is in the billion-plus range. (It takes, you know, a thousand million to be a billionaire. I personally think that's a lot of money. But the most I ever earned in one year in my working life was in the $13 thousand range. So I'm not sure I really understand what a "lot" is or what the bottom dollar may be to the one-percent insider.)[1]

It also seems as if almost everybody thinks (or wants to think) of himself or herself as "middle class." Upper middle class or middle middle class or, if absolutely necessary, lower middle class. But always middle class. Nobody wants to be called lower class or thought of as lower class. Lower class is sort of how a litter box smells when it's overused—something to be dumped in the woods or dropped into the trash. Out of sight, out of mind.

And "working class"? That term has become really puzzling and awkward. "Working class" is an embarrassment, as if it applied to people in process of scraping the cat stuff off the soles of their scuffed-up shoes before daring to enter the back door of the middle class. Working class hints of unsavory union affiliations, cheap beer, tobacco smoke, trailer houses—with maybe a rogue uncle who was (if you can believe it) a *socialist*. But that's the sort of thing we just don't talk about. Period.

Now I was raised on a small homestead farm in northern Wisconsin. Big garden, work horses, cows, chickens, a big hay mow, barn gutters cleaned with shovel and

---

1. "Earn," at least in contemporary usage, is a rather elastic word, even as its roots lie in an old German term meaning "harvest." Its somewhat more modern meaning is to merit or deserve, to receive that to which one is entitled. In both evolutionary and spiritual terms, however, we might say (from our humble perspective) that living creatures *deserve* to live and that they are *entitled* to a habitat appropriate to their healthy survival. But at what point does the assertion of human "earning" violate fundamental ethics? Have Americans, as roughly five percent of the world's population, magically "earned" the right to consume between twenty-five and forty percent of the world's annual production? If we have such a right, who exactly conferred it on us? Are we God's chosen consumers?

wheelbarrow. Despite the fact that we ate exceedingly well, we were "poor," I guess, but so was everybody in the neighborhood. We had friends, relatives, the woods, a small river to fish and swim in and skate on in the winter, a one-room school just down the gravel road. There were enough "poor" people in enough agrarian neighborhoods that it could be said, at least up and into the 1960s, that we had a rural culture. The annual county fair was, to some extent, a celebration of this culture. This was a fairly new rural culture, with most farms dating back only two or three generations. My family's farm had been old-growth white pine forest as recently as the 1880s and 1890s. My father began clearing the land of brush, stumps, and rocks in the early 1930s. Our township had over two dozen small farms of similar vintage.

Perhaps this is the place to tuck in, as a cultural backdrop, a compacted observation of preindustrial European society. This passage comes from *Samuel Johnson*, a biography by the English novelist and poet John Wain:

> European society in the earlier eighteenth century had a stability, a continuity of habit and tradition that in our change-ridden age is virtually unimaginable. For two or three thousand years—we can afford to be vague about the beginning, as we approach so nearly to the end—Western society had organized itself in a way that must have come to seem eternal. Everywhere, the bulk of the population worked on the land, and the agriculture to which they gave their working lives was predominantly a subsistence agriculture. Farms supplied their neighborhoods. Apart from a few luxury items such as tea, coffee and ginger, most people even in the more comfortable middle class went through their lives without consuming or owning anything that had to be imported. As for the labouring class, they never saw, handled, ate or drank anything that came from more than a few miles off. Life was rooted and immobile to an extent that deeply affected everyone's outlook on it. To understand the eighteenth-century mind, as it shows itself in art, in politics, in conversation, in relationships, one has to start from that premise.[2]

Wain goes on to say that, during Samuel Johnson's lifetime (1709-1784), England in particular was

> . . . emerging from its feudal past and into its plutocratic future. In a feudal society, wealth and influence are reckoned in terms of ownership of land. In a plutocratic society, such as we have now, wealth and influence are reckoned in terms of money. The change was and still is heavily camouflaged by the fact that land is a valuable commodity, so that the owner of land is also rich in terms of money, which is why the aristocratic land-owning families have managed to stay near the top of the heap. Nevertheless, the jump from a feudal to a plutocratic society has been made. Land is no longer the means of producing wealth; even if oil or coal are found on one's land, the business

2. Wain, *Samuel*, 41.

of extracting and marketing them must be handed over to an industrial and commercial machinery of which the landowner, *per se*, knows nothing. Land is exchangeable for wealth, but that is not the same thing as being the means of its production.[3]

Wain's remarks allude to the beginning of history's second major "farm crisis"—the first such crisis occurring at the dawn of civilization, when nascent aristocrats (i.e., armed bandits) forced gardeners and farmers into peasant servitude by systematically expropriated the village "surplus" in the initial stage of what became a multimillennial "development" project of civilizational self-aggrandizement. With the industrial revolution, however, civility no longer needed peasants, serfs, slaves or even small farmers; so began the extraction of agricultural "surplus" by means of machinery, chemicals, fossil fuels, and genetic engineering. This was (and is) the second "farm crisis." The first of these crises overpowered the village, expropriating its production and labor. The second exterminated the village itself as methods for industrial food production were invented and deployed.

There were thirty farms in my township when I was a kid, and now, sixty years later, none. Zero. Not one that is actually a functioning farm. Farm culture and the working class died, we might say, hand in hand. The socialist uncle and the populist People's Party uncle ate from the same bowl of "anachronistic" dust. They died of "out-sourcing" and "economies of scale." They were victims of plutocratic hit squads. They were victims of civilized mythology and middle-class hubris. They were totally expendable.

By the time I was an adolescent, rural culture was no longer generated by evolving folk life. Its community, craft, and self-provisioning roots were being hacked off and discarded. "Culture" was what you could buy at the store, what the endless advertisements told you was cool to have or smart to own, how formal institutions (like consolidated schools) were shaping youth in anticipation of a nearly perfect plastic and steel future. Grumpy old citizens were told to get with the program and become smart, new consumers.

So a new designation was needed, something overarching, a larger concept to tell us who we were becoming, some snazzy term to shape our emerging identity. That new something was "middle class." We all were, or we all could become, "middle class." We could be trained for jobs; we could earn money; we could buy stuff. The better the job, the more money we could earn and, therefore, the better and bigger stuff we could buy. Class became one's "level" of education, job, money, and stuff.

Outside this designation were unfortunate "clients" who needed help. Welfare recipients. Bohemians, beatniks, and hippies. Criminals. Perhaps even terrorists. A lot of people with artistic inclinations needed help, as did many of those with a deeper understanding of history or a premonition of ecological disaster. Perhaps even a nervous

3. Wain, *Samuel*, 42–43.

handful of religious people who recognized the cultural and ecological significance of the ancient "kingdom of God" proclamation, with its troubling servanthood and stewardship ethics.

"Middle class," in other words, is more a commercial fiction than an authentic cultural construct. It's largely a bloated post-World War Two suburban and commercial demographic generated by a variety of economic and psychological forces. Cheap oil. Big cars. Tract homes. Consolidated schools. The interstate highway system. Industrial prosperity. A willful shutting out of the horrors of both world wars and a stubborn refusal to consider what those horrors (plus the nuclear arms race) imply for the future. First World achievers apparently have no time for End Times.

Before World War Two, perhaps only three or four generations ago, middle class was more narrowly defined. It was almost exclusively made up of professionals (doctors, lawyers, teachers, clergymen), tradesmen, the owners or top managers of prosperous but not necessarily large business concerns. All in all, and despite its overbearing self-satisfaction, this middle class had a certain cultural solidity along with its smugness; it knew a little something about art, music and literature, and guided— even pushed—its children into cultural literacy.

Above the middle class were the truly wealthy, with remnants, at least in Europe, of hereditary aristocracy. (This aristocracy had traditionally subsidized the classical arts out of the immense "surplus" it "harvested" or "earned" from the peasantry.) Below the middle class was the urbanizing working class, overwhelmingly blue collar, but with a bit of pink filtering in. And below the working class—?

It's always a puzzle whether to include agricultural laborers, peasants, and small farmers in the working-class designation. As a boy I saw that a substantial proportion of small farmers voted Republican either because they were politically flattered into thinking of themselves as "small businessmen" or because they were opposed to craft and industrial unions out of envy and resentment. Small farmers had virtually no marketing cooperatives by which to bargain collectively; they had to accept what the market offered, which typically wasn't much. They believed unions caused price hikes for industrial goods (including farm machinery), and it was galling to know factory workers who not only earned more money than they did but who had weekends off, paid vacations, and other "fringe benefits." (Farming, although it has seasonal variation, is a seven-days-a-week occupation.) Farmers saw themselves pitted, not so much against big business (which existed in a privileged universe beyond reach, not unlike how peasants perceived the preindustrial aristocracy), but against blue-collar workers with their goddam unions: it's always easier to resent those closest to home, those most like oneself. Many (perhaps most) of these agrarian "small businessmen" died, as it were, with their barn boots on; but their sons and daughters, almost without exception, drifted into the new income-defined "middle class." Some of these sons and daughters even found it expedient to join unions.

In a sense, it *is* difficult to talk about class in any way than by income when all classes, in a cultural sense, are largely defined by consumerism, with status determined by purchasing power, when art, music, and literature are considered commercial "products" in a totally commercialized "culture." In the 1970s, for instance, "consumer" replaced "citizen" in much of the media, just as a whole host of activities previously considered *cultural* were increasingly designated *industrial*. Agriculture, medicine, entertainment, banking, sports, nursing homes, and even education underwent identity change from culture to industry. Things that had never been "industrial" were becoming (or had become) "industrialized," not because iron, coal and steam were crucial to their practice, but because culture was being subsumed by the all-consuming commercial, shedding anything that couldn't be obtained or measured by money, anything ethical or spiritual that might interfere with measurement by money. (I've kept waiting for religion to industrialize, but churches are sluggish. Perhaps they have a superstitious dread of coal smoke.) All this underscored Jacques Ellul's assertion that everything in the modern, industrial, bureaucratic world was being swallowed by "technique."[4]

"Technique" seems to be one of the defining features (just as Ellul said) of the modern globalizing experience, but it's a feature hardly anybody seems able to define or pin down. Here is where the historical groundedness of Lewis Mumford and the psychoanalytical brilliance of Norman O. Brown are so wonderfully helpful. If civilization was born in utopian violence, with systemic theft and focused oppression, asserting justification by reference to the will of a fierce male God, oozing with aggression and vigilant in suppression, always dreaming of perfect mastery, of rising above and possibly even ridding the world of the "backward," then civilization globalized

4. I utilized Ellul's "technique" analysis in *Nature's Unruly Mob* (see especially chapters 8 and 9); but, even in 1986, I realized there was something ghostly and ungrounded in Ellul's use of the term. Now, in 2011, rereading the opening pages of *The Technological Society*, I see that Ellul recognizes (he says so explicitly on page 3) that "Technique certainly began with the machine" and that "without the machine the world of technique would not exist." But he immediately goes on to say, on page 4, that "Technique has now become almost completely independent of the machine" and that it "transforms everything it touches into a machine."

Lewis Mumford rescues this drifting concept and brings it securely ashore. The details are fleshed out in Mumford's essay "Utopia, the City, and the Machine," especially when combined with the recurring "megamachine" analysis in both *The Myth of the Machine* and *The Pentagon of Power*. In essence, the "machine" Mumford discloses is *the utopian power structure imposed as slavery with the rise of civilization*. Enslaved human beings, organized by civilizational power, constituted the first mass machine. I presume what Ellul was driving at with "technique" was the overwhelming and virtually irresistible power of utopian civilization in its current mode of industrial/electronic/financial globalization, so that slavery is now commercially voluntary and "democratic."

The problem with Ellul's "technique" is that it's often as elusive as the Christian Devil. (The term "civilization" does not appear in the Index of *The Technological Society*.) Where Ellul proceeds in a mode of (sometimes brilliant) metaphysical abstraction, Mumford methodically works out a kind of historical *habeas corpus*. That is, he shows us where the actual bodies are buried, how the oppressive structures were constructed, and he warns us what the consequences are likely to be if we don't surpass the utopian mesmerization generated by civilization and learn to live on Earth with eutopian groundedness.

in industrial/electronic form is finally able to put in place its demonic, Apollonian imposition of perfect mastery, displacing or crushing all the slowly evolved forms of craft and culture that can now be heroically surpassed with near-perfect, uniform, industrial substitutes, exquisitely engineered and electronically controlled. Genetic cloning and electronic droning. Apollo, like Lucifer, is not some dark, ugly, stinky devil who might sneak up on you in the dead of night and scare you half to death with magical voodoo mumbo-jumbo, but is instead a Sun God, the bearer of light, someone or something that beckons you toward a golden utopia of perfect control and total mastery. (In both *The Myth of the Machine* and *The Pentagon of Power*, Mumford returns again and again to linkage between the Sun God and what he calls the civilized "megamachine.")

The present "assault on the middle class" by right-wing politicians (Scott Walker is our current Wisconsin contribution), screaming about debt and deficits, social programs that must be cut, is a warning shot from behind-the-scenes wealth and power (the Koch brothers, et al.), telling us that implicit aristocracy is reasserting itself, that the consumerist utopianism of the "middle class" is facing forced constriction. I presume this means, at least in part, that the truly wealthy, despite their corporate propaganda to the contrary, are alarmed by climate change, nuclear disasters, and the general assault on world ecology by rampant consumerism. (Or is it simply their stupendous greed and pride at work? Can they really be that selfish and stupid?) Spiritual selfishness among the neo-aristocracy rules out, as far as their greed is concerned, Green socialism as an economic and ecological corrective. So they are making moves politically toward the restoration of an increasingly explicit aristocracy, and that restoration necessitates a serious shrinkage of "middle-class" consumer habit and lifestyle prerogative. As the upper class goes Chartreuse in the direction of Ayn Rand, it will fiercely fight to enlarge its traditional prerogatives of wealth and power, even as it forces the great bulk of the human population—certainly including much of the rather comfortable "middle class"—into a life of hugely constrained consumption. This in itself, in some ways, is not a bad deal: *if* it serves to jolt the "middle class" into keener ecological and political awareness, *if* it provokes a real Green response.

Overconsumption is not simply an upper-class phenomenon. "Middle-class" affluence also needs to shrink. Almost nobody in America (except the truly impoverished, and many of those folks live on junk food and crappy electronics) can claim exemption from a thorough ethical audit of overconsumption. We have little understanding of what "sustainable" or "healthy" really mean. In that sense, the overwrought, nearly hysterical budget pruners are obliquely correct: there *does* need to be a reduction in consumption. Where they're absolutely wrong is in refusing to focus on empire hubris, "strategic interest" aggression, and neo-aristocratic wealth concentration. Their assertive religious and political piety is devoid of humble spiritual ethics. Reduced consumption is for others, not for themselves. But unless we move clearly, cleanly, and decisively toward Green socialism, and away from the hubristic supremacy of military-industrial empire, while systematically undoing neo-aristocratic wealth accumulation and self-righteous aggression in the process, we will end up—fairly soon—with something resembling the two-class aristocrat/peasant universe of preindustrial civilization or, alternatively, the authoritarian, plutocratic regimes of many contemporary Islamic states, popular upheavals ("Arab Spring") notwithstanding. And that would represent not only colossal democratic bankruptcy but also (and even more seriously) a disastrous *spiritual* failure to embrace what the gospels call the "kingdom of God"—for embracing the ethical prescriptions of radical servanthood and radical stewardship is, in the end, the acid test of any so-called "Christian civilization." Without servanthood and stewardship, democracy dies or is merely the "democracy" of the gated elect. The next step in democracy requires the embrace of stewardship and servanthood. This is how spiritual ethics will leaven the political loaf.

But all this raises the question of how the "middle class" can resist being submerged into the lower class, and even whether it will be able to resist submersion. Its fate is in doubt in part because its *cultural* underpinnings are so weak and artificial. Its "class" is largely a consumerist, commercial fiction built on "democratic" excesses in an empire economy of utopian unsustainability. Defined by income and largely finding its provisional identity via consumerism, "consuming" its "culture" via online shopping, electronic games and other disposable entertainment, what happens to this "middle class" when its purchasing power is radically reduced? When its income gets kicked out from under its expectation of entitlement? When its politicians are ideologically glib but spiritually clueless? To what or to whom can this "middle class" turn for ethical or metaphysical grounding when its sense of history is so vapid, its culture lacking critical perspective, and its economic ideology derived from the unhesitating assurances of utopian unsustainability? These are not adequate frameworks for resistance.

And yet one can also see, paradoxically, that the stripping away of traditional cultural underpinning forces people, even unconsciously, to risk trusting the political moralisms and spiritual ethics previously kept in the pious realm of abstract ornament: love your neighbor as you love yourself; practice servanthood and stewardship; treat Earth with deep respect; one person, one vote; refuse to obey illegitimate authority; and so on. All such ideas were "nice"; but everyone knew they were "impractical," just as the "kingdom of God" was unattainable. Industrial, consumerist alienation, in this sense, may not be entirely negative. It may also work as solvent, freeing us from restrictive, ingrained consumerist habit and economic abstraction. End Times alienation might cause us to reconsider what we formerly thought impractical or unachievable due to original sin. The wrecking of traditional religious forms opens the possibility of a quantum leap to Green socialism with firm ethical underpinning.

While liberation from cultural convention can work in the direction of aimless distraction and clueless breakdown, it can also work (if Spirit is welcome in us and allowed to stay) toward astonishing and unexpected eutopian transformation. This is the either/or point we've begun to reach. Democracy can not only be salvaged, it can also be magnificently extended and wonderfully deepened. But this political deepening depends on spiritual deepening. If we've given up on "culture," perhaps it's only the spiritual or ethical we have left as trustworthy guides.

As far as I can tell, only libertarian democratic ecological socialism—Green socialism—offers a spiritually and ethically wholesome way out of our predicament. The question is not whether human beings are, in principle, capable of going down the path of Green socialism—we are absolutely capable—but whether the "false consciousness" of civilized utopian consumerism has so bewildered, distorted, and impounded the human mind that, by the time people begin to wake up to the magnitude of the predicament we face, it will be too late to overcome the new corporate aristocrats with their mercenary Blackwater and Bulletproof enforcers. (Or will they too—will we all—be transformed?)

We are swiftly approaching such a "revolutionary moment." Will this be yet another missed revolution? Or do we—even unconsciously—have the spiritual groundedness by which to grasp the moment and transform servanthood and stewardship from "impractical" spiritual abstraction into political, social, and cultural reality—transform utopia into eutopia?

3

This Totalitarian Temptation

Andrew Bacevich and Economic Restoration

In "Twilight of the Republic?," Andrew Bacevich says the hard-headed founders of the American Republic "did not set out to create a church." They did not intend to "save mankind." Never during the United States' rise to power did this republic ever "exert itself to liberate others" without an "overriding perception" of its own "security or economic interests."[1]

"If the young United States had a mission," writes Bacevich, "it was not to liberate but expand." Accordingly, expansion was achieved "by any means necessary," including "diplomacy, hard bargaining, bluster, chicanery, intimidation, or naked coercion." We stole land. We "harassed, filibustered, and, when the situation called for it, launched full-scale invasions." We practiced "ethnic cleansing." We "blithely jettisoned agreements that had outlived their usefulness."[2] Well, Bacevich means agreements no longer useful to *us*.

Although Bacevich says there was "one overriding aim" (the enhancing of "American influence, wealth, and power"), the "rationale offered to justify action" tended to vary with the circumstances. Rationales include our being God's Chosen People, with a number of intermediate concepts slipped in, including American Exceptionalism, the doctrine of our very special specialness, an article of faith in how exceedingly good our goodness really is.[3]

Out of expansion came abundance, and out of abundance came "substantive" freedom, a "symbiosis between affluence and liberty." Prosperity underwrote freedom. So says Andrew Bacevich.[4]

This analysis is unassailable—except for the assertion that freedom is derivative from abundance, which, in turn, is derivative from expansion. (If true, the assertion of derivatives ultimately means that freedom depends on coercion; or, alternatively, freedom for some depends on coercion of others. Freedom is for those strong enough

---

1. Bacevich, "Twilight," 10.
2. Bacevich, "Twilight," 10-11.
3. Bacevich, "Twilight," 11.
4. Bacevich, "Twilight," 11-12.

to coerce others. Such a view, if true, means that the greatest spiritual teachers, including Jesus, were political idiots and intellectual fools. But we can come back to that.)

With the embrace of derivatives, Bacevich's analysis begins to edge off the rails. Once he gets to what he calls a "second narrative of expansion," his analysis becomes dangerously wobbly.[5]

Bacevich's tipping point historically is World War Two. Prior to that war, progress in the "privileges of citizenship" was "fitful." But, after the war, "access to freedom constituted the central theme of American politics." The energy behind this achievement—involving blacks, Jews, women, Asians, Hispanics, working stiffs, gays, the handicapped—lies squarely on the Left. "Had Martin Luther King in the 1950s and 1960s counted on William F. Buckley and *The National Review* to take up the fight against racial segregation, Jim Crow would still be alive and well."[6]

But, says Bacevich, reformers were in "tacit alliance" with postwar officials, oil executives, and defense contractors—although he neglects to show us how this linkage connects. This was "an ironic kinship."[7] Bacevich says the alliance was tacit, but he doesn't explain how it worked. Bacevich apparently is telling us that "liberals" can't promote "freedom" unless they also support and encourage "abundance," since it's "abundance" that produces—or at least allows for—the existence or presence of "freedom." And, since "abundance" needs "coercion," liberals are only conservatives with a guilty conscience: addicted to abundance, embarrassed by coercion.

Then he says the "nation's abiding cultural preoccupation" with "freedom" was "from the outset" a "collaborative one to which both Left and Right contributed, albeit in different ways." This alleged collaborative cultural preoccupation enables Bacevich to slide, first, into hammering "radicals, pinks, liberals, and bleeding-heart fellow-travelers" for "promoting a radical new ethic of human sexuality"—and then to say that this new ethic includes homosexuality, abortion, divorce, out-of-wedlock pregnancies, children raised in single-parent homes, pornography, pop culture, and popular music. So if you've got a "human sexuality" problem in your neighborhood, feel free to pin a tail of blame on the liberal pink donkey.[8]

After the pinko Left gets bonked on the head or pinned in the butt, the Right gets bonked, too, but for reasons of conspicuous consumption. Yet Bacevich manages to imply that conspicuous consumption somehow *derives* from this alleged new ethic of human sexuality. The Left may not have *made* the Right do it, exactly, but the Left opened the sexual door and beckoned alluringly. The Left is the serpent in the garden. Or maybe Eve (who took the serpent's offering) is a "liberal." Adam (who was deviously tricked into taking a bite) is a hoodwinked "conservative." Mommy Party. Daddy Party. Mommy is wickedly seductive while Daddy works late at moral reconstruction.

5. Bacevich, "Twilight," 12.
6. Bacevich, "Twilight," 12.
7. Bacevich, "Twilight," 12.
8. Bacevich, "Twilight," 12, 14.

However, along with this two-pronged "radical change in American culture," Bacevich points to a more or less simultaneous shift from an "Empire of Production" to an "Empire of Consumption." This shift, too, has the Second World War as its tipping point, although it was in the 1960s before the whole thing really began to topple. So now, he says, the "books don't balance," we "refuse to live within our means." We don't save. We won't trim entitlements. We ignore our addiction to oil. We are acquiring a mountain of debt. And the "unspoken assumption is that our credit line is endless and that the bills won't ever come due."[9]

We had "autonomy" from 1776 through the 1950s, Bacevich says, and in that period Americans would have dismissed our current blithe assumptions as twaddle. We need, he says, to "restore our economic house to order."[10]

Restore? What, so far, has Professor Bacevich offered that's worthy or deserving of *restoration*? If abundance comes from expansion and expansion depends on coercion—?

Now, right smack in the middle of his essay, Bacevich drops a remark from one of his favorite political seers. Here's the quoted passage, from Edmund Burke: "Men are qualified for civil liberty in exact proportion to their disposition to put moral chains upon their appetites."[11]

Well, isn't that swell! Bacevich opens his essay by insisting that freedom is derivative from abundance, and abundance is derivative from expansion, with all manner of chicanery thrown in, as needed, to expedite the coercive process. But now the party pooper tells us we need *chains* on our appetites in order to qualify for civil liberty!

I beg your pardon! Which point of view does Professor Bacevich want us to believe? He tells us ("as if explaining the self-evident to the obtuse") that Theodore Roosevelt declared in 1899, "Of course our whole national history has been one of expansion." And Bacevich says Roosevelt "spoke truthfully. The Founders viewed stasis as tantamount to suicide. From the outset, Americans evinced a compulsion to acquire territory and to extend their commercial reach abroad."[12]

So after this barging Bull Moose confession from Mr. Roosevelt, Professor Bacevich tries to give us a moral spin with Mr. Burke's appetite chains. As he slides toward his conclusion, Professor Bacevich says "these narcissistic and fallacious claims . . . have polluted our discussion of foreign policy" and our "self-induced confusion about freedom, reflected in our debased culture and disordered economy, increases our susceptibility to this totalitarian temptation even as it deadens our awareness of the danger it poses."[13]

9. Bacevich, "Twilight," 14.
10. Bacevich, "Twilight," 14.
11. Bacevich, "Twilight," 12.
12. Bacevich, "Twilight," 10.
13. Bacevich, "Twilight," 16.

I have to say that this seems to be acute perception in a state of ideological confusion bordering on blindness, evasive but sophisticated whining.

Perhaps Professor Bacevich has to decide whether it's Teddy Roosevelt he admires or Edmund Burke. If he believes Teddy Roosevelt, he should be happy to ride the prospect for a new American century to its inevitable conclusion and disastrous consequence. It would be, after all, heroic to do so. The captain is *supposed* to go down with the ship. But if he believes Edmund Burke, he can't very well tell us that freedom is derivative from abundance or that abundance is (benignly?) derivative from expansion. Something has to give.

To put it differently, if freedom is not the froth of expanding Empire, what is it? Where does freedom come from? Who has the moral and spiritual clarity by which to teach us anything of its formation or foundation? Could it be key persons in the founding of the world's religions? Could it be people like Henry David Thoreau, Leo Tolstoy, Mohandas Gandhi, Dorothy Day, Dietrich Bonhoeffer, Martin Luther King, or Kathy Kelly?

If so, our current mess—which promises to get much, much messier—is not a *detour* from our origin or an *aberration* of our founding but, rather, *the culmination and logical conclusion of willful economic aggression.*[14] If freedom, in a deeply ethical sense, can be characterized as the sustained practice of servanthood and stewardship—and this takes us back to foundational spirituality—then its ethical political expression would be—has to be—libertarian, democratic, ecological socialism. We have to repudiate aggression and empire and embrace humility and limitation if we want to know what freedom means. Steady-state ecological economics. Learning what "sustainable" actually looks like as we quit rationalizing greed and aggression.

---

14. In the February 8, 2016, issue of *The Nation*, pages 22 through 25, Bacevich takes on the military-industrial complex ("Who Runs the Pentagon?"). He calls the current Secretary of Defense—Ashton Carter—a technocrat who "flies around the world visiting the troops and consulting with field commanders. He presides at ceremonies, hosts visiting dignitaries, testifies before Congress, makes speeches, holds press conferences, and appears on TV. He manages—or pretends to manage—a sprawling bureaucracy. He makes decisions, sometimes dressed up for the occasion as 'historic,' but typically representing an incremental departure from past practice—lifting the ban on women serving in combat, for example. And by no means least of all, he facilitates the expenditure of money in staggeringly large quantities.

"What Carter has not done is pose first-order questions related to national-security policy and practice. Instead, he has deferred to and thereby protected existing routines and arrangements. This shouldn't come as a surprise. Averting change while pretending to foster it represents the defense secretary's foremost, even if unacknowledged, function."

Bacevich says of the Pentagon that there's "no one really in charge and therefore no one accountable." So instead of a "coherent approach to the world, aimless forward momentum prevails." (Well—a marvelous phrase—aimless forward momentum describes America in many aspects besides the Pentagon.) But when Bacevich asks "What *should* command the defense secretary's attention?", he drifts off to hammer "the national security establishment." This is not exactly a bad thing to do; but it enables him to evade looking down the gun barrel of America's global imperialism. That is, Bacevich remains a growly "conservative" whose perception is sharp and acute but very narrowly focused.

This doesn't signify *chaining*, however, for chaining never works, or at least it never lasts. It's even a bit sadistic. What's needed is less the chaining of our appetites than a transformation of our hearts. Humility and a "steady-state" economy may be more about loosening our repressions than tightening our chains, for repression of our true desires ramifies as false needs "satisfied" through aggressive expansion and commercial coercion. Internal chaining is an interior component of the same tightly channeled energy which, directed outward, ramifies as aggressive conquest. What's needed is dissolution of that energy field. The name for this is spiritual repentance, which is, in fact, the breaking of the chains. Such a breaking or dissolution puts us in the realm of spiritual and cultural transformation. Its economic ramification would be Green socialism.

Our need for such transformation has never been greater; and unless we are blessed with an unprecedented shift in orientation and behavior, we will descend into an absolutely ruthless restoration of vicious aristocracy—unless we blow the world to hell, first.

So I accuse Professor Bacevich of evasive dabbling, of not getting down to core dynamics, of allowing "conservative" morality to obstruct and obscure spiritual ethics. He's a bull buffalo in a china shop. Well, he's in the right china shop. Give credit where credit is due. But his snorting and grunting and knocking things over is not very edifying.

Things are far too serious for mere dabbling, grunting, and snorting. If Andrew Bacevich is too timid, or too "conservative," to grab the American expansionist beast by the horns, let him step aside and clean the buffalo chips off his shoes. (The irony of bluff and gruff "conservatism" is that it's largely based on fear of intimacy and anxiety about vulnerability.) Personally, I think Andrew Bacevich has the gumption and the marbles to do a lot better. He's no dumbhead. Only he's got to massage some rigid male buffalo musculature, if "musculature" is how to name where his confusion or illusion is lodged. If expansion was the guiding "mission" of the United States since its founding (not to speak of England's prior purpose), and if "freedom" depends on the abundance "expansion" provides, and if coercion is the means of expansion, then we've got ourselves a far bigger problem, a problem requiring a solution far more trenchant, profound, revolutionary, and transformative than the moral *chaining* Bacevich drags in from Burke. I especially recommend Lewis Mumford for a refreshing and fleet-footed change of posture, and Norman O. Brown for a brilliant examination of the chains.

4

Structures of Deception

Why Civilized Christian Fascism
Is Unfolding In America

It is no easy task to gain some understanding of human affairs. In some respects, the task is harder than in the natural sciences. Mother Nature doesn't
provide the answers on a silver platter, but at least she does not go out of her
way to set up barriers to understanding. In human affairs, such barriers are
the norm. It is necessary to dismantle the structures of deception erected by
doctrinal systems, which adopt a range of devices that flow very naturally
from the ways in which power is concentrated.

Noam Chomsky, *Failed States*, page 103

NEARLY FORTY YEARS AGO, perhaps in the winter of 1977, a sequence of thoughts
came to me that felt more potent than mere insight. I felt it then, and still feel it today,
as revelation. Of course, revelation may be a suspect or even wacky word—it may even
have an affiliation with the apocalyptic—so it's caveat emptor, which is Latin for "Keep
your hand on your wallet."

This revelation—excuse me if I call it that, even if the term causes eyes to roll
or laughs to bulge up sleeves—this revelation was such, it hit with such force, that it
essentially posited a growing and intensifying conflict between True Believers in all
three Abrahamic religions (Judaism, Christianity, and Islam), a conflict of such ferocity and magnitude that it could (or will) bring down the current world order. There
also was—and is—an alternative to this horrific conflict, although that alternative depends on spiritual humility and mythological repentance; but, since neither of those
conditions—humility and repentance—has as yet been embraced or carried through
with an adequate degree of commitment or achievement, the forecast for disaster still
stands. Therefore the dystopian program seems, with its "structures of deception," to
be unfolding slowly but steadily, in irregular fits and starts.

II

The burr under the saddle of this revelation was an innocent and seemingly unrelated question that kept bugging me: Why are small farms dying? In my twenties, living in a big city, missing the countryside of my farm boy upbringing, I realized small farms were biting the dust. I wanted to know why.

A number of historians (most notably Lewis Mumford) helped me understand that what we call civilization arose from the armed expropriation of agrarian village abundance, some five or six thousand years ago, an expropriation that quickly became normative. If neolithic gatherers were (or became) the first gardeners and farmers, the complex agrarian dynamic they initiated was eventually strong-armed by nomadic raiders who forced relatively prosperous farmers, both women and men, who former-ly got to keep or freely share what they grew or raised, into relatively destitute peas-ants, villagers whose "surplus" was systematically stolen by an "aristocratic" elite. So began the classic civilized dynamic of a dominant minority (a mafia-like aristocracy) permanently repressing and expropriating a nondominant majority (the "protected" peasantry).

This pattern continued more or less in its classical mode until the industrial revolution brought about its termination or, perhaps, its radical mutation. That is, the food-producing peasant base of society, as much as ninety percent of the total popula-tion, began, with the industrial revolution, to be forcibly evicted from the commons and countryside until—in some countries like the United States—it (or its small-farm descendent) was squeezed into a demographic of, at most, one or two percent.

So we might say the original "farm crisis" featured the rise of an expropriating aristocracy and the emergence of civilization, with a corresponding impoundment of the agrarian village and blockage of its cultural evolution—its "surplus" stolen and its life evolution violently constrained. The second "farm crisis" has been the squeez-ing of food production out of its noncivilized, peasant, folk, or small-farm base and into agribusiness forms of explicitly civilized rationality, essentially exterminating the agrarian village altogether. This latter scientific squeeze has occurred, obviously, with accelerating industrialization and burgeoning urbanization, and it has become a global phenomenon. Terminator servitude. Genetically modified culture.

So, with all things new about the modern period, we might point out two things specifically, with inverse relationship, that are stunningly new: the virtual extinction of folk-based, noncommercial food production that was otherwise, in its various forma-tions, as old as human life on Earth; and, its evil master and undoer, the globalization of civilized presumption, complete now with ecocidal weaponry and climate-chang-ing economic "externalities." This is our historic moment. Civilization has overcome eutopian "backwardness"; dystopia is its consequence. Yet we are so deeply civilized in our everyday mentalities, we can't seem to understand what's happening. Or, if we realize *something* is happening, we can't seem to get a handle on *why*.

III

Ecocidal weaponry and climate-changing economic presumption, if nothing else, might lead one to conclude that the globalization of civilization is not only unsustainable but is the very agency of accelerating disaster, since both lethal weaponry and economic aggression are in no way extraneous to civilization's historic mode of conduct but at the core of its way of being in the world. Civilization came into being with violent expropriation that quickly ramified as rigid class structure, and civility has never shed that diseased way of doing things, those traumatic institutions, even as it claims to have become "democratized." The task, then, is not to "protect" civilization from undeserved badgering and battering, but to recognize civilization itself as the primary force behind and within global destruction—both the destruction already operative (just to mention climate change) and the destruction lying in ecocidal wait (just to mention atomic weaponry).

IV

The secular worship of civilization is a difficult nut to crack. Its most exposed and vulnerable "weakness" is intellectual openness to rational thinking (i.e., truth disclosed by evidence) and to the conclusions and potential consequences that critical thinking, especially in its scientific forms, might lead one to seriously consider and act upon. Among the secular intellectual elite there is, it seems, uneasiness regarding ecocidal weaponry and climate-changing economic behavior, even as such concerns are typically couched in the language of "saving" or "protecting" civilization from disruption or disaster. The seculars, as it were, recognize the problem or, rather, they recognize the *symptoms* of the disease, even as they decline to trace symptoms to root causes and draw obvious conclusions. And, because they refuse to draw obvious conclusions, they persist in the narcissistic role of system managers, little gods in control of Spaceship Earth. Experts in technofix. Building a better planet.

An even bigger nut to crack, in some ways, lies in those human minds where the exultation of civilization, especially in its exceptional American mode, is wrapped and packaged in religious imagery, ideology, and mythology—the Christian Right in particular. If the secular worshipers of civilization can, as a broad generality, be construed as "liberal," a significant characteristic of which is the supposed willingness to take seriously the discoveries and conclusions of science, these latter religious folks are generally sheltered under the awning of "conservative," although there is practically nothing that bears any resemblance to "conserve" or "conservation" in their political suitcase. Science for them is a mere wardrobe option, something to put on or take off insofar as it does not distract from or diminish a fashion desire for mythological clothing, including the mythology of unlimited material progress. God's bounty is inexhaustible. Drill, baby, drill.

There is in this mythological worldview an awesome energy of conviction, a manic fanaticism fully buttressed by its connectedness (or its desire for connectedness) to overwhelming power, both in government (certainly in the military) and in the corporate economy. The George W. Bush administration was loaded with such "conservatives." Had it not been for the shocking and awesome stupidity, greed, and murderous incompetence of the debacle in Iraq, that administration's policies might well be in process of direct perpetuation elsewhere—in Iran, perhaps. Iraqi sand, as it were, chewed up some mythological gears and, with the attendant economic debacle generated both by the wars and by Wall Street (with its "derivatives" whoopee party), popular disgust was sufficient to achieve both the election and re-election of Barack Obama. Meanwhile "Iraq," we might say, has metastasized into Syria.

Obama represents that portion of the corporate world given to what I'm calling the secular worship of civilization—cognizant of the problems, wonkishly "brilliant" with techno-tweaking "solutions" to those problems, but politically and intellectually unwilling to look the monster in the face and call it by name. Some of this unwillingness is internal or endemic to the "liberal" worldview—its operational idealism does not contain an alternative to constant "progress" or a critical appraisal of civilization—and some of its unwillingness is, we might say, external or extrinsic. That is, potential willingness to follow rational thinking through to honest conclusions is obstructed by the saturating magnitude of civilized mythology in the general population (especially as goaded by elite rhetoric) and also by the awareness of political danger posed by "conservative" forces, including "conservative" control of much of the media by which any critical analysis of civilization would be mercilessly attacked as heresy, treason, and blasphemy. (Flag burning would be relatively trivial by comparison.) So the secular, "liberal" forces are captivated not only by their own mythology (rational evidence to the contrary notwithstanding), but also by fear of political consequences if skepticism were allowed to become as bold and truthful as human intelligence is capable of perceiving and articulating.

In other words, the endemic institutions and mythological mindsets of predatory civilization are at the root of our problem; but these are areas where critical consciousness refuses to go. Myth holds such thoughts at bay. Myth denies admission to such analysis. Or, if critical perception recognizes the roots, political consideration vetoes any meaningful public articulation of that recognition. Therefore the conquest project of civilization, despite fretful handwringing at the margins, despite impending disastrous consequences, continues unabashed.

V

In the winter of 1977, I'd been thinking about the neolithic origins of agriculture, followed by the marauders' impoundment of agrarian villages. I was also puzzling over the women's movement. Specifically, I was wondering, especially in light of the apparent social stability of the precivilized agrarian village, what it was about the modern period that had instigated the rise of feminism. And (this was the trigger) I was reading *Socialism* by the democratic socialist Michael Harrington; in that book, Harrington laid out what he considered the more significant antecedents of socialist thought. Featured rather prominently was a twelfth-century monk, Joachim of Floris.[1]

Joachim's contribution consisted of a schema he devised (perhaps it came to him as revelation), a schema constructed from the merging of two primary elements—the Old and New Testaments of the Bible and the Three Person configuration of the Christian Trinity. Putting those elements together, fusing them historically and mythologically, Joachim said the world is built of three ages. First, the Age of the Father, corresponding to Judaism, the Old Testament, monarchy, discipline, and law. Second, the Age of the Son, corresponding to Jesus, to Christianity, and to love institutionalized in the church. But, said Joachim, there is a third age yet to come, the Age of the Holy Spirit, an age of consecrated anarchy or holy freedom.

Now I had not been raised in a fundamentalist church. I had, in fact, attended the United Church of Christ, generally considered "mainstream" Protestant and "liberal." But Bible stories were taught in Sunday School as true and literal history—this was the crew-cut 1950s—and I eagerly absorbed these stories. They were the most significant articulation of what was true and real. George Washington and Abraham Lincoln were important, too; but, in the end, they couldn't compare to Adam and Eve, Noah, Moses, Joshua, or Jesus. Biblical history was what counted. It was the real history of divine purpose and human meaning. So I became a literal believer by educational default. Meanwhile, such history as I had learned in high school (I was only briefly in college and took no history classes there) was, as usual, all about King So-and-so and Duke What's-his-name, fighting it out at Such-and-such. Nothing deeply probing, controversial, or troublesome ruffled my teenage mind. History was a seemingly interminable list of facts (almost all of them involving terrible conflict between upper-class males, with a lot of peasant pike men murdering each other and occasional peasant revolts brutally suppressed), all of which was to be recalled for a test and then forgotten.

So when, in my twenties, I became a serious reader of history, looking to understand why small farms were dying, it came as a shock, primarily a spiritual shock, to learn about the roots of agriculture, its neolithic origins, and the extent to which women's horticultural productivity and feminine spirituality pervaded the early agrarian period. (In the nineteenth century, a Swiss archaeologist, Johann Bachofen, did extensive archaeological investigations in the broader Mediterranean area and wrote a book—*Mother Right*—whose formulation of a Mother's age prior to the rise of civilization hugely influenced Friedrich Engels and became a buried but important element in Marxist anthropology.)

---

1. See pages 146 through 167 in Paul Tillich's *Political Expectation* for a compacted summary of Joachim's enormous influence in European thought.

When all this congealed in my mind, the synthesis resulted in my own "revelation": it's not three ages; but *four*. Joachim, with his understanding of history as gleaned from the Bible and from the teaching of his day, operated under the same intellectual limitation I had as a child. That is, he believed the Genesis account of Creation to be real history. He had no inkling of the depth of evolutionary history, no way of knowing what Bachofen, seven centuries later, would call a Mother's age.

So, as Joachim's enlarged sequence became Mother, Father, Son and Holy Spirit, the significance of the women's movement did a fireworks display in my mind. The disguise of "Holy Spirit" became apparent, and the "ages" (to be consistent) became Mother, Father, Son, and *Daughter*. That was the revelation that washed over me in 1977. By recognizing in our dominant religious imagery a massive mythological projection of collective gender dynamics in a setting of civilizational power concentration, it became possible to discern an interior progression of development in cultural evolution, a depiction not only of where we've been but also where we're headed. Or at least possibly headed. I was discovering that religious myth can project images of cultural evolution on a mass scale.

VI

The next problem was one of transition. That is, if the shift from Mother to Father involved the "world historical defeat of the female sex," as Engels asserted—on page 22 in *The Creation of Patriarchy* Gerda Lerner quotes from Engels' *Origin of the Family, Private Property and the State*—and if the transition (even if partial and incomplete) from Father to Son was occasioned first by the crucifixion of Jesus and then the destruction of Israel in 70 A.D., what do we think it takes to ease ourselves into the holy freedom of the Daughter? Do we imagine this a case of instantaneous mass enlightenment, largely free of conflict or carnage, embraced with eager human will, at once acutely rational and spiritually wholesome? What if the bulk of human consciousness, especially that portion comfortably embedded in religious orthodoxy, political entitlement and consumerist privilege, will only come kicking and screaming into the Daughter's embrace? What if we realize that the three Abrahamic religions—Judaism, Christianity, and Islam—feed from a common reservoir of supernatural male superiority and gender presumption; and, although they may hate each other with demonic sibling rivalry (fully gilded as holy fidelity to God the Father Almighty), they represent the ultimate congealing of male religious prerogative in world history? All of a sudden, the fundamentalists' Armageddon is no laughing matter, no idle fantasy, but is instead a lurid projection of bloody fraternal conflict brought to lethal culmination in what Norman O. Brown, on page 19 of his *Love's Body*, has called an end to war, an end to brotherhood.

But where, exactly, is civilization in this mythological catastrophe?

VII

Well, here are a few pondering thoughts from Noam Chomsky. I am (in April 2009) reading Chomsky's *Failed States*. It is, as is usual for Chomsky, an array of lucid and stunning details embedded in an analysis resting on an explicit and admirable moral base, flavored with exasperation and occasional sarcasm. (Chomsky is sometimes beside himself with aggravated astonishment at the elite capacity for hypocrisy.) By the time Chomsky gets to his third paragraph in chapter 1, he's already laying out his moral ground:

> Among the most elementary of moral truisms is the principle of universality: we must apply to ourselves the same standards we do to others, if not more stringent ones. It is a remarkable comment on Western intellectual culture that this principle is so often ignored and, if occasionally mentioned, condemned as outrageous. This is particularly shameful on the part of those who flaunt their Christian piety, and therefore have presumably at least heard of the definition of the hypocrite in the Gospels.[2]

Chomsky goes on to say, sarcastically, that "Fortunately, Western commentators are saved from the unambiguous conclusion, thanks to our self-exemption from the most elementary of moral principles, the principle of universality."[3] That is, American Exceptionalism is really mythological *exemption* from the moral principles of universality.

Here are two more passages from Chomsky's view of how self-exemption from elementary moral principles plays out:

> The conventional task of doctrinal managers is to protect power and those who wield it from scrutiny and, most important, to deflect analysis from their rational planning in pursuit of the real interests they serve.[4]
>
> It is a rational calculation, on the assumption that human survival is not particularly significant in comparison with short-term power and wealth. And that is nothing new. These themes resonate through history. The difference today is only that the stakes are enormously higher.[5]

What particularly interests me here is the gap between Chomsky's obvious and sincere affinity for the most elementary of moral truisms (it is the ethical basis for his analytical brilliance) and his occasional use, usually with positive intent, of words like "civilized" and "civilization." Apparently he intends these terms to convey or embody the principle of universality he holds dear.[6]

2. Chomsky, *Failed*, 1.

3. Chomsky, *Failed*, 36.

4. Chomsky, *Failed*, 28.

5. Chomsky, *Failed*, 37.

6. Here's an example. On page 2 of his tribute to Howard Zinn in "Howard Zinn's Legacy of

It may come as no surprise that I consider such linkage between moral universality and civilization to be bogus. Or, rather, the protection of power and the shielding from scrutiny of those who wield it consist of core operating principles within civility. Admitting to and repenting of our civilizational crimes is intellectually and politically impermissible. Chomsky comes close to saying as much when he says the assumption of human survival is not particularly significant in comparison with the pursuit of short-term power and wealth, that the assumption is nothing new, that it resonates through history. I would assert—via the lens of agrarian analysis that sees the "farm crisis" originating with the violent impoundment and systemic expropriation of agrarian village agriculture—that short-term power grabs and long-term wealth anticipations are precisely the real universals of civilized conduct. The moral universality Chomsky invokes and cherishes can only be said to have been embraced by civilized elites whenever it suits their (self-serving) purposes—a fact that deeply aggravates Chomsky and inspires his (occasionally sarcastic) rebuke and denunciation.

I therefore consider Chomsky's positive use of "civilized" and "civilization" a semantic cataract causing serious intellectual and spiritual opaqueness as a consequence. We cannot invoke the disease as a cure for the disease, unless we revert to notions of inoculation or homeopathy; but I don't believe that's Chomsky's intent. The rapist may come dressed as our therapist, but it's a serious error of judgment to not see through the costume.

VIII

One sees this—what to call it?—bafflement or irresolution at work, although more openly and explicitly, in Lewis Mumford's *The Myth of the Machine*. In his final paragraph in section 5 of chapter Eight, Mumford says this:

> Apart from murder and rape, the most horrendous crimes punished by civilized authority stem back to the 'unpardonable sin' of kingship: disobedience to the sovereign. Murderous coercion was the royal formula for establishing authority, securing obedience, and collecting booty, tribute, and taxes. At bottom, every royal reign was a reign of terror.[7]

And then Mumford goes on, in section 6, to talk about Civilization and 'Civilization,' one usage with quotation marks and one without. Civilization without quotation marks

> . . . implies a cumulative effort to further the arts and sciences, and to improve the human condition by continued advances in both technology and

---

Words and Action" (in Davis D. Joyce's *Howard Zinn's Legacies*), Chomsky says Zinn's tireless activism made the country "far more civilized as a result." Chomsky, of all people, should know better than to utter such a deadly platitude.

7. Mumford, *Myth*, 185

responsible government. All these terms of admiration and praise, which seemed in the eighteenth century self-evident and self-justifying, except to an occasional dissident like Rousseau, have now become ironic: at best they represent a hope and a dream that have still to be fulfilled.[8]

And 'Civilization' with quotation marks denotes

> . . . the group of institutions that first took form under kingship. Its chief features, constant in varying proportions throughout history, are the centralization of political power, the separation of classes, the lifetime division of labor, the mechanization of production, the magnification of military power, the economic exploitation of the weak, and the universal introduction of slavery and forced labor for both industrial and military purposes.[9]

These latter institutions, Mumford goes on, would have certainly

> . . . discredited both the primal myth of divine kingship and the derivative myth of the machine had they not been accompanied by another set of collective traits that deservedly claim admiration: the invention and keeping of the written record, the growth of visual and musical arts, the effort to widen the circle of communication and economic intercourse far beyond the range of any local community: ultimately the purpose to make available to all men the discoveries and inventions and creations, the works of art and thought, the values and purposes that any single group has discovered.
>
> The negative institutions of 'civilization,' which have besmirched and bloodied every page of history, would never have endured so long but for the fact that its positive goods, even though they were arrogated to the use of a dominant minority, were ultimately of service to the whole human community, and tended to produce a universal society of far higher potentialities, by reason of its size and diversity. Even immediately their symbols perhaps attracted those who were only spectators of these achievements. This universal component was present from the beginning, because of the cosmic foundations of royal power: but the efforts to create a universal society were delayed, until our own day, by the lack of adequate technical instruments for rapid transportation and instantaneous communication.
>
> Yet the claim of universality itself, from Naram-Sin to Cyrus, from Alexander to Napoleon, was repeatedly made: one of the last of the 'all-powerful' monarchs, Genghis Kahn, proclaimed himself the sole ruler of the entire world. That boast was at once an aftermath of the myth of divine kingship and a prelude to the new myth of the machine.[10]

---

8. Mumford, *Myth*, 186.

9. Mumford, *Myth*, 186.

10. Mumford, *Myth*, 186-87.

So we have, on the positive Civilization side, the invention and keeping of the written record, the growth of the visual and musical arts, and the effort to widen the circle of communication and economic intercourse far beyond the range of any local community. And, on the negative 'Civilization' side, we have—I won't repeat Mumford's awful list—what he elsewhere summarizes as "traumatic institutions," with predatory violence and systemic theft at their core.

But see what Mumford is doing with his quoted and unquoted Civilization. He apparently wants us to believe (because, I presume, he either wants to believe it himself or he doesn't wish to face the opprobrium his articulated disbelief would invoke) that unquoted Civilization is the Real Thing even as his overall analysis suggests (I would say proves) exactly the opposite. Writing, the arts, a wider and friendly circle of communication—or, even, as he says earlier, an effort to improve the human condition by continued advances in both technology and responsible government—are (to borrow a term from economics) "externalities" to civilization, perhaps even subversive and treasonous externalities punishable by prison, banishment, or death. (Shall we mention the names Daniel Ellsberg and Edward Snowden here?) That is, these positive features do not lie at the heart of the civilizational project; or, to use Noam Chomsky's words, they are not particularly significant in comparison with short-term power and wealth.

So, taking James Carroll's epigram to heart—"The study of history always implies a study of its alternative"[11]—we can easily conclude that the characteristics of Mumford's positive Civilization are, largely if not totally, traceable to the richly complex agrarian village culture the bandit aristocracy overpowered, plucked, and squeezed. Those humanitarian characteristics are contracivilized. (This becomes obvious, for instance, in the elementary moral truisms contained within the Beatitudes, as with the kingdom of God proclamation in the first three Christian gospels.) Civilization's actual "universality" is, as Mumford explicitly says, a claim to sole rulership of the entire world. (In Barbara Tuchman's The Proud Tower, her display of the Euro-American world leading to World War One, "civilization" is the semantic rope claimed by both prowar imperialists and antiwar citizens. Needless to say, the imperialists won the tug of war. Civilization is, after all, their rope. They own it. And what a prize they won.)

But Mumford's other claim—that the universal component of positive Civilization was present from the beginning, only delayed in being realized because of the lack of rapid transport and instantaneous communication—reduces ethical unfolding to technical contrivance or mechanical convenience and, as such, is pathetically laughable. (Are we to believe that the ethical emerges from the technological?) Nor should we blithely ignore the fact that the "positive goods" of 'Civilization,' although once strictly arrogated to the use of a dominant minority, have now, because of industrialization, been made commercially available, perhaps in vulgar form and disposable quality, to the larger consuming public, and that this democratization of "positive goods" has

11. Carroll, Constantine's, 17.

become an ecological disaster. That is to say, even the so-called "positive goods" of 'Civilization' must now be considered critically not only when looked at through an ethical or moral lens in regard to human culture, but also in regard to the toxic impact of such "goods" on Earth's evolutionary ecology. Yes, civilization has arrived at One World. But this Oneness has been achieved by aggression and violence. Aggression and violence remain at the core of this drive—just look at military budgets and the sale of weaponry—despite the widespread dissemination of spiritual ethics that prescribe otherwise. This contradiction is our circumstance. Its resolution is our task.

IX

But why this fussing over words? What's the big deal about "civilization"—with or without quotation marks?

There are a variety of ways to answer this question, but let's begin with a comparison, or a contrasting, that has at least partial merit—the word or concept "Empire."

There seems little doubt, first of all, that America is an Empire. (The dictionary defines empire as "supreme rule; absolute power or authority; dominion," and so on. Well, if America doesn't have absolute power or supreme rule, let's decapitalize Empire to empire.) There also seems little doubt that Republican administrations since Reconstruction often embraced empire more fully and with less hesitation than Democratic administrations. But we shouldn't forget that the long disaster involving Vietnam goes back at least as far as the Truman administration (Margaret MacMillan, in her *Paris 1919*, says the Paris kitchen worker Ho Chi Minh's petition was too obscure to be considered in Versailles) or that it was under the greatly ambitious "liberal" Lyndon Johnson that the toxic assault on Vietnam was hugely escalated. (Richard Nixon, of course, with his alter ego Henry Kissinger, did his "conservative" part to make a terrible situation even worse.)

There is vague talk of "hard power" versus "soft power," and there may be correlation between "hard" and "conservative" as between "soft" and "liberal." But Barack Obama has not asked forgiveness from the Iraqis; he's not offered restitution or reparations for the colossal damage done by two Gulf Wars, with a decade of crippling sanctions pressed between; he's not proposed the indictment of George W. Bush, Dick Cheney, Donald Rumsfeld or any of their associates for war crimes. (And the war, of course, has since spread into Syria and generated a massive refugee crisis.) I see, in other words, no retraction of empire forthcoming. (Redaction, to be sure; but not retraction.) There may be a bit more Civilization (without the quotation marks) under Democratic administrations than under Republican—Kennedy's "Camelot" will do as an example—but one has to be fully padded with wishful thinking to believe that Democratic administrations (including Obama's) have been any less committed to 'Civilization.' Breaking or dissolving entitlement to empire may be the single most difficult task humanity has ever faced.

X

We are led back to the problem of transition. The key to this problem is the extent to which the construct of civilization (often in opaque conjunction with the extent to which biblical creationism has formed a psychological and intellectual black hole in our grasp of history) is of such magnitude that we are unable or unwilling to see behind, around, below, or beyond it. Real life stops at, or fails to go beyond, the boundaries of civilization. Our thinking occurs and functions only within this construct. All that lies outside is repulsively primitive, psychotic, or simply evil. Civilization, in other words, represents our metaphysical encapsulation within goodness, stability, and all things ethically wholesome. It is the geopolitical boundary we live within and don't wish to do without. We want to remain *inside* civility's protective enclosure. What's *outside* is barbarous, primitive, backward, pagan, and evil.

If the study of history implies a study of its alternative, and if that idea is difficult to grasp, how much more difficult is it to think contracivilizationally, to begin to realize that cultural creativity and spiritual profundity neither died with the emergence of bandit aristocracy, nor did civilization eliminate them. To be sure, we all were taught, often with visual aids, to celebrate the cultural monuments of civilization, especially its imperial architecture, amazingly inventive weaponry, and magnificent body armor; but seldom, if ever, were we told that elemental creativity was not something needing civilization as a stimulus but, rather, that it's intrinsic to the human soul, even as elemental creativity was bent, channeled, and constrained by predatory imperial intention and directed by imperial will.

The termination of civilization, unless it's an end achieved by civilizational ecocide, in no way spells the terminus of human creativity. On the contrary, the end of civilization will restore a brutally interrupted cultural evolution and liberate numbed cultural creativity from its multimillennial impoundment, a creativity—given all the hard lessons we've learned regarding the hubris of civility—that, once again, holds deep reverence for the natural world and yearns, in very practical ways, for a far more deeply achieved integration with nature.

Here, then, with Mother Earth, Mother Nature, Gaia, and the blossoming of feminine sensibility generally, is the import of the Daughter's age, signaling a wholly new body of spiritual comprehension, a truly postcivilized world. To get to this place requires either confession and repentance or such horrific death and destruction that the world will hover on the edge of an abyss, an abyss whose depths we can already intuit.

Civilization and male-intoxicated religion are not precisely the same thing, it's true. But when religion operates as a mythological (or suprapsychological) repository for male superiority, hubris at the civilizational level simply becomes normative. Insofar as civilization is built on a base of armed violence and systemic theft, such violence and theft are overwhelmingly male phenomena. God the Father, King of kings, justifies the divine right of kings and the supremacy of civilization. The "great religions" of the world (without question the Western ones) were formed in a period in which civilized values predominated—though it absolutely has to be said that the core *spiritual* understandings of these religions are deeply and vividly contracivilized. (In fact, many of the stresses within Christianity at present—say John Dominic Crossan versus Pat Robertson—are based on an exhilarating ethical grasp of gospel proclamation versus an immobilizing literalistic biblical mythology that celebrates religious evil as among the holy works of God.) Mythological theology depicts a wrathful God of supernatural angry Maleness; demythologized spirituality reveals a humble Spirit of Gandhian "self-suffering" and boundless compassion. There are more and more people who have left the former, or are in process of leaving, so it's not as if "repentance" is without social traction. It is, in fact, a growing phenomenon.

But, it hardly needs saying, what's overwhelmingly dominant—what's *orthodox*—is still very much the mythology of civilized male certitude, the hegemony of civilizational prerogative. Civilization is rapidly making things much worse (End Times weaponry and climate-changing economic behavior are obvious examples); but religions become the refuge for insecure or battered souls, and "fundamentalism" (like AM talk radio) stirs aggravation, resentment, and fear into holy outrage. Insofar as American policy has repeatedly thwarted democratic evolution in Islamic countries (we might take the CIA-sponsored coup in Iran in 1953 as a template of sorts), popular resistance gravitated to the mosque, while American empire continues to be most fervently promoted by the Christian Right, and Israeli Zionism continues to overpower hapless Palestinians by brute force, obscene separation walls, and invasive settlements. God the Father continues to flex His muscles, and His Abrahamic sons flex theirs accordingly.

XI

Several Green intellectuals have scolded me for my analysis of and prognosis concerning Civilization. Their stance seems parallel to that of "liberal" Democrats who caution against public denunciation of empire. Such denunciation is supposedly too divisive, too polarizing, only serving to obstruct or discredit the sincere efforts of political insiders and policy operatives who are working furiously to ameliorate the situation (say on global warming) without calling undo attention either to themselves or to the nature of their task. Better to let sleeping dogs lie while the kennel fence is being reconfigured.

Of course, one immediately has to ask: Who or what is being appeased? If it's good to let sleeping dogs lie, what dog is this? Whose dog is it? Is the dog really sleeping? Does timid and circumspect silence restrain the beast or does it empower and embolden its self-regard?

I am waiting for a persuasive answer, particularly in light of the aphoristic moral truism that it's truth that sets us free. Or, if truth is too much for us to handle, what does this say about our collective possibility of coming out of this predicament alive and well?

5

The Enchanting Spell of Resentment

THIS LITTLE ESSAY GOT nudged into a bare-bones beginning in the fall of 2010 when my friend Dennis Boyer sent me a copy of *The New York Times Book Review*, dated October 24. Browsing through the articles, I paused to read "Criminal Mind" by Elyssa East, a review of *The Killer of Little Shepherds* by Douglas Starr. The book's primary subject, a man named Joseph Vacher, was a wandering murderer in late nineteenth-century France who stabbed and stomped one woman to death and killed other people in ways too gruesome to describe. A secondary subject is Alexandre Lacassagne, a criminologist who studied Vacher. East quotes Lacassagne as saying, "Societies have the criminals they deserve."[1] Is that true? What consolation does that offer to victims? Are victims random sacrifices for the criminality society deserves? And what, exactly, does society deserve? What's the offense for which society is to be punished?

The two cover stories, however, the ones Dennis thought might interest me, are archly bridged by a common title, "The Ideological Divide." That the title both announces the divide while bridging it may be a sly and amusing irony, a clever joke, or it may be a revealing symbol: the "divide" may be less a chasm between sharply opposing ideological camps than a common coin whose faces appear to look in opposite directions, even as they share a hidden occipital bone. Anyway, the articles are by Jonathan Alter ("liberal") and Christopher Caldwell ("conservative"), and they are, of course, laid out accordingly left and right. Reading the two pieces, one could conclude that societies also have the politics, politicians, and political analysts they deserve. But that's something of a brutal sneer, not a thought necessarily helpful in constructive understanding. It's still compassion—if we can't quite muster love—that maximizes our ethical ophthalmology. That doesn't mean critical thinking evaporates, only that rage is abrasive salve for festering evolutionary wounds.

A good part of the difficulty in trying to make sense of the "ideological divide" is that, first, "conservative" and "liberal" are largely useless and even obfuscating terms, "conservative" even more than "liberal." "Conservative" automatically suggests certain root or related words—conserve, conservation, conservancy—words with etymological integrity—but whatever linkage there may once have been between "conservative" and conservation is no longer evident. "Conservatives" are not conservative. Second,

1. East, "Criminal," 21.

the so-called divide between the talking heads may be less about occipital ideology than about donkey-or-elephant mascot emotionality carefully groomed by the two major parties, Mommy and Daddy. It certainly seems, at the upper levels of policy formation in both parties, there is precious little difference between "liberal" and "conservative"—one party with two heads or one system with two mascot emblems—a hardheaded elephant and an (occasionally) soft-hearted donkey, a Big Daddy E with a huge swinging trunk, and a somewhat shaggy Mommy D with long, furry ears.

Jonathan Alter opens the "liberal" side of the argument like this:

> It's a sign of how poorly liberals market themselves and their ideas that the word "liberal" is still in disrepute despite the election of the most genuinely liberal president that the political culture of this country will probably allow. "Progressive" is now the self-description of choice for liberals, though it's musty and evasive. The basic equation remains: virtually all Republican politicians call themselves conservative; few Democratic politicians call themselves liberal. Even retired Classic Coke liberals like Walter F. Mondale are skittish about their creed. "I never signed up for any ideology," he writes in his memoirs.[2]

Unpacking that remark about Barack Obama as "the most genuinely liberal president that the political culture of this country will probably allow" is where Jonathan Alter needs to go in order to arrive at deeper understanding. But don't hold your breath while waiting for him to sort through the contents of that crate. (Does he mean by "this country" the electorate generally or the corporate vetting system specifically?) Alter then goes on to say (while we're waiting for something resembling a definition of "liberalism") that:

> Liberals are also at a disadvantage because politics, at its essence, is about self-interest, an idea that at first glance seems more closely aligned with conservatism. To make their more complex case, liberals must convince a nation of individualists that enlightened self-interest requires mutual interest, and that the liberal project is better constructed for the demands of an increasingly interdependent world.
>
> That challenge is made even harder because of a tactical split within liberalism itself. Think of it as a distinction between "action liberals" and "movement liberals." Action liberals are policy-oriented pragmatists who use their heads to get something important done, even if their arid deal-making and Big Money connections often turn off the base. Movement liberals can sometimes specialize in logical arguments (e.g., Garry Wills), but they are more often dreamy idealists whose hearts and moral imagination can power the deepest social change (notably the women's movement and the civil rights movement). They frequently overindulge in fine whines, appear naïve about

2. Alter, "Ideological," 1, 14.

political realities and prefer emotionally satisfying gestures to incremental but significant change. Many Democrats are an uneasy combination of realpolitik and "gesture politics."[3]

So, after consorting with dreamy "liberal" idealists who overindulge in fine whines, let's trek over to Christopher Caldwell's side of the Great Divide, where he waits until his final paragraphs to tell us what "conservatives" are about and what they want. He says conservatism largely boils down to "enhanced self-rule" and a "citizenry sufficiently able to govern itself to be left alone by Washington," even though:

> Americans are not in the position to roll back their politics to before the time when Franklin D. Roosevelt or Woodrow Wilson or whoever-you-like ran roughshod over the Yankee yeomanry. Town, county and state governments no longer have much independent political identity. They are mere "conduits for federal mandates," as [Angelo] Codevilla puts it. He notes that the 132 million Americans who inhabited the country in 1940 could vote in 117,000 school boards, while today a nation of 310 million votes in only 15,000 school districts. Self-rule depends on constitutional prerogatives that have long been revoked, institutions that have long been abandoned and habits of mind that were unlearned long ago.[4]

Self-rule prerogatives require certain economic and social contexts in which to thrive; radically change those contexts (i.e., radically industrialize, consolidate, and centralize the economy) and the prerogatives are not so much "revoked" as they simply wilt and decay—as with the massive loss of 102,000 school districts over a period of seventy years. The "habits of mind" also need cultural context; but this requires an exploration far deeper than mere handwringing over the (rather abstract) "revocation" of constitutional prerogatives. (Who or what, exactly, was responsible for the revocation?)

How *did* things get so big, standardized, and centralized? Why are there now only 15,000 school districts when, in 1940, there were 117,000? Is this the fault of "federal mandates"? A very strong argument can be made that the two biggest magnifiers of bigness in American history—catalysts, perhaps—were the Civil War and the Second World War, both of which served to hugely concentrate the power and accelerate the growth of what Dwight Eisenhower would eventually call the military-industrial complex. That is, war, just as it sucks wealth and vitality out of the countryside, serves as a mighty spur in behalf of standardized mass production; and the huge corporations profiting from government contracts have a strong incentive to financially assist in the election of people (with the appropriate ideology) who will help "keep the country safe," and "safety" requires permanent armed vigilance or a permanent war economy. Yet war, despite its intensification of the standardizing,

3. Alter, "Ideological," 14.
4. Caldwell, "Ideological," 18.

centralizing and commercializing process, was only part of the hubristic tendency that obsessively asserted its right—even its obligation—to crush and displace all forms of cultural "backwardness." And, of course, part of what got crushed since World War Two was the bulk of the 117,000 school boards Caldwell alludes to, and many of these schools were one-room and rural, whose shuttering directly reflected the demise of small-scale farming and the extinction of rural culture—that is, the end of the American "yeomanry." *The extinction of small-scale farming meant the extinction of rural culture and, with those extinctions, so went the small rural schools.* Once again *civis* lifting *pagus* out of its backwardness.

Before we proceed any farther here, we might take note that Amaury de Riencourt, in *The Coming Caesars,* chapter V, "The Fateful Decisions," pages 70 through 83, shows how the decentralized period immediately after the American Revolutionary War, organized around the Articles of Confederation, was championed by *liberals* and its termination achieved by *conservatives* who used the Constitutional Convention of 1787 to centralize the federal government:

> This new Constitution was devised by basically conservative men who saw in the virtual independence of the states the sure road to catastrophe. They were security-holders, manufacturers, ship owners, planters—all those who had a "stake in society"—and they designed a strong central government powerful enough to check the demagogy of state legislatures dominated by insolvent debtors.[5]

De Riencourt doesn't say much, if anything, about Shays Rebellion, although his slap at "state legislatures dominated by insolvent debtors" is probably aimed, if only indirectly, at that uprising. That slap might also be directed at the late nineteenth-century Populists, for the Populist movement, especially in its political form as People's Party, was a reincarnation of sorts of Shays Rebellion in Massachusetts. It too elected "insolvent debtors" to state legislatures and to congress. That is, both uprisings congealed around the issue of rural impoverishment and agricultural destitution at the level of the small farm and rural community, an impoverishment and destitution in large part due to governmental policy decisions giving free rein to commercial interests pursuing profit and power. (But, of course, "conservatives" go after "regulators" not corporations. So much for their righteous protection of the "yeomanry.")

For a larger analysis of the constitutional process, however, let's go to chapter 5, "A Kind of Revolution," in Howard Zinn's *A People's History of the United States.* We'll start with Zinn referencing the historian Charles Beard:

> Thus, Beard found that most of the makers of the Constitution had some direct economic interest in establishing a strong federal government: the manufacturers needed protective tariffs; the moneylenders wanted to stop the use of paper money to pay off debts; the land speculators wanted protection as

---

5. de Riencourt, *Coming,* 72-73.

they invaded Indian lands; slaveowners needed federal security against slave revolts and runaways; bondholders wanted a government able to raise money by nationwide taxation, to pay off those bonds.

Four groups, Beard noted, were not represented in the Constitutional Convention: slaves, indentured servants, women, men without property [de Riencourt says "property qualifications restricted suffrage to 15 per cent of the adult males"[6]]. And so the Constitution did not reflect the interests of those groups. . . .

By 1787 there was not only a positive need for strong central government to protect the large economic interests, but also immediate fear of rebellion by discontented farmers. The chief event causing this fear was an uprising in the summer of 1786 in western Massachusetts, known as Shays Rebellion.[7]

Zinn then goes on—pages 90 through 95 of *A People's History*—to describe in detail this "rebellion" of debt-ridden farmers, many of whom had fought in the Revolutionary War, and whose protests against their economic condition were put down by state violence. There were, however, enough people sufficiently well-off to provide a political moat around the wealthy and protect them from "discontented farmers." Zinn continues:

The Constitution, then, illustrates the complexity of the American system: that it serves the interests of a wealthy elite, but also does enough for small property owners, for middle-income mechanics and farmers, to build a broad base of support. The slightly prosperous people who make up this base of support are buffers against the blacks, the Indians, the very poor whites. They enable the elite to keep control with a minimum of coercion, a maximum of law—all made palatable by the fanfare of patriotism and unity.[8]

Perhaps in later editions of his *People's History*, Zinn altered his thoughts about the American system doing enough for middle-income people to sustain a broad base of support. If so, that support may be in process of eroding. (My edition of Zinn's book is dated 1980, published long before the onslaught resulting in the Wall Street meltdown of 2008, the Tea Party as a kind of shock troop directed by corporate wealth, and—now in Wisconsin with the Scott Walker administration—an open assault on both public-sector and private-sector unions.) The enormous political reshuffling that we might say began in 1968, more or less, with racial, sexual, and countercultural energies causing, if only as a catalyst, a huge shift of white resentment (including white working-class resentment) turning toward and into the Republican Party—this reshuffling merged into permanently sustained wedge politics under Ronald Reagan. That is, the temperature of white resentment began to be almost scientifically attended

6. de Riencourt, *Coming*, 73.

7. Zinn, *People's*, 90.

8. Zinn, *People's*, 98-99.

to (God, Gays, and Guns), in order to facilitate the offshoring of manufacturing, the assault on unions, the deregulation of financial institutions, an escalation in military budgets and international interventions (both overt and covert), the systematic block-age of alternative energy and conservation programs, and new "free trade" agreements, like NAFTA, resulting in a hammer blow to Latino farmers, thus generating a huge wave of immigration to the U.S., which wave, in turn, was used as yet another wedge issue ("illegal aliens") in order to inflame the requisite resentment.

It is this carefully honed wedge of resentment—with Republicans at the federal level, for example, who cunningly postured as the opposition to the Wall Street bail-out—that's the caddy in which the Tea Party has been steeped: with financial support from such people as Charles and David Koch. Of course, the current wedge-faced incarnation personified by Wisconsin's Republican governor, Scott Walker, with his dismantling of collective bargaining for unions, reducing the state's budget for social programs, and prohibiting local units of government from raising revenues to plug the budgetary holes, is teetering, quite possibly, on the edge of a new 1968. That is, either the small property owners, mechanics, and farmers will realize—too late!—that they've been duped (with the new Ronald Reagan looking more and more like Benito Mussolini) or—dare one hope this?—the spell of enchanting resentment will be bro-ken and the American Rasputins unmasked.

Writing immediately after the 2010 elections, Bob Herbert, in *The New York Times*, said:

> The Democrats are in disarray because it's a party that lacks a spine. The Re-publicans, conversely, fight like wild people whether they're in the majority or not. What neither party is doing is offering a bold, coherent plan to get the nation's economy in good shape and create jobs, to bring our young men and women home from the wars in Afghanistan and Iraq, to rebuild the education system in a way that will prepare the next generation for the great challenges of the 21st century, and to reinvigorate the can-do spirit of America in a way that makes people believe that they are working together toward grand and constructive goals.[9]

But—despite its obvious truth on the one hand and, on the other, its canned boiler plate of "great challenges" and "can-do spirit"—all this contains no hint of ecological tolerances or resource limitations. It begs the question of why Democrats lack spine and why Republicans fight like wild people or why Mommy's supine while Daddy's strutting with his Bible and his missiles. It's a variation, really, of the same question (or comment) Jonathan Alter makes about Barack Obama as the most "liberal" president American political culture will allow.

Probing into this conundrum, I can't find a more solid explanation than God and king. That is, Republicans fight like wild people because, for all the apparent

9. Herbert, "Tone-Deaf," 1-2.

ambiguities, they feel themselves firmly in a tradition of religious conviction and civilizational superiority saturated with assertive and aggressive male energy, a tradition they feel under threat. No one I know lays this out more clearly than Lewis Mumford. Here he is from chapter Eight, "Kings as Prime Movers," in The *Myth of the Machine*:

> Out of the early neolithic complex a different kind of social organization arose: no longer dispersed in small units, but unified in a large one: no longer 'democratic,' that is, based on neighborly intimacy, customary usage, and consent, but authoritarian, centrally directed, under the control of a dominant minority: no longer confined to a limited territory, but deliberately 'going out of bounds' to seize raw materials and enslave helpless men, to exercise control, to exact tribute. This new culture was dedicated, not just to the enhancement of life, but to the expansion of collective power. By perfecting new instruments of coercion, the rulers of this society had, by the Third Millennium B.C., organized industrial and military power on a scale that was never to be surpassed until our own time.[10]

Of course the contemporary Right—because we are a "democracy"—has to dress in the ill-fitting clothing of antigovernmental peasants and unappreciated (white) workers in order to beat down all horizontal functions of government that impede the flow of vertical wealth and the concentration of power in corporate/aristocratic control. (Contemporary Republicans are an amazing illustration of the power of deliberate hypocrisy hiding in a cloak of traditional mythology.) Mumford goes on to say:

> The increase in the food supply and the population that marked the dawn of civilization may well be characterized as an explosion if not a revolution; and together they set off a train of minor explosions in many directions, which have continued at intervals over the entire course of history. But this outburst of energy was subjected to a set of institutional controls and physical compulsions that had never existed before, and these controls rested upon an ideology and a myth which perhaps had their faint beginnings in the magical ceremonies in paleolithic caves. At the center of this whole development lay the new institution of kingship. The myth of the machine and the cult of divine kingship rose together.[11]

We might say—though saying it is fraught with ambiguities and contradictions—that "liberal" Democrats have an emotional linkage, something unconscious and subterranean, not only back to the "early neolithic complex," but to the fiercely leveling "kingdom of God" proclamation repeated scores of times in the first three canonical gospels, while "conservative" Republicans, with their far more orthodox (and otherworldly) religious adherence, reflect not only the "authoritarian, centrally directed . . . control of a dominant minority" but also the Constantinian accommodation by

10. Mumford, *Myth*, 164.

11. Mumford, *Myth*, 168.

which Augustine of Hippo justified empire in behalf of God's will. Democrats, at their best, sometimes begin to reflect the ethics of the "kingdom of God," ethics requiring social servanthood and ecological stewardship in an economic context of modest sufficiency. But this is far less a civilizational *tradition* than it is a sporadic *upsurge* of ethical revelation, bursting forth here and there in history with amazingly pure energy; yet never, until recent scholarship began to carefully explore the roots of civilization (e.g., Lewis Mumford, Arnold Toynbee) as well as the nature of the "kingdom of God" proclamation (e.g., Walter Rauschenbusch, John Yoder, Ched Myers, Marcus Borg, John Dominic Crossan) has there been a coherent alternative analysis, a firm and unified ethical stance, capable of putting the "justified" Constantinian tradition of God and civilization in proper perspective—that is, a perspective capable of peeling away the gilding and mythology from Christian civilization in order to reveal the underlying elitist and predatory content, a content very much still with us, armed and deadly.

The disparity between mythologically empowered Republicans and (to some extent) demythologized Democrats, between "traditional" "conservative" and "progressive" "liberal," causes the latter to look weak in their often inarticulate ("bleeding-heart") compassion, while the former nearly glow with the self-assured strength of an assertive ("tough-minded") righteousness. There is a passage from William Blake's *A Vision of the Last Judgment* worth quoting here. This is Blake's comment on Dante's vindictiveness in the *Divine Comedy*:

> In Hell all is Self Righteousness; there is no such thing there as Forgiveness of Sin; he who does Forgive Sin is Crucified as an Abetter of Criminals, & he who performs Works of mercy in Any shape whatever is punished, if possible, destroy'd, not thro' envy or Hatred or Malice, but thro' Self Righteousness that thinks it does God service, which God is Satan.[12]

In our context, this struggle is only in part, perhaps only remotely in part, about God and Satan. In terms of present political psychology, the issue is Compassion and Sufficiency versus Self-Righteousness and Affluence. Democrats, if they wish to be true to Compassion and Sufficiency, must follow Mohandas Gandhi and Martin Luther King into the liberation achievable only by spiritual nonviolence, the renunciation of economic excess and undeserved advantage, while putting into political practice forgiveness and mercy, even as it is "Self Righteousness that thinks it does God service, which God is Satan."

Well, a day or so after the arrival of Dennis's gift of *The New York Times Book Review*, the November 8, 2010, issue of *The Nation* appeared in the mailbox. With my penchant for reviews, I went right to Rick Perlstein's survey of fifteen (!) books on the general subject of the 1970s. Perlstein quotes a 1967 remark from George Ball (whom he calls a "Democratic mandarin"): "national boundaries only 'impede the fulfillment of the world corporation's full potential as the best means yet devised for using world

---

12. Blake, *Complete*, 616.

resources.'"[13] Now that is one exceptionally packed and powerful utterance, the myth of the machine on steroids. To put that in some sort of larger American context or perspective (for such global assertions certainly don't come out of thin air), let's go first to Ched Myers' *Binding the Strong Man* and then back to Amaury de Riencourt's *The Coming Caesars*. Here's Myers:

> The managerial rationalism of realpolitik is only a secular restatement of the old myth of divine right, which in the American empire is articulated by the national theology of manifest destiny and cold war. Whether it is the scholarly articles of foreign policy journals, the commentaries of network news, or the high metaphors of campaign rhetoric, the aim of mainstream political discourse is the same: to justify geopolitical domination abroad and insular privilege at home.[14]

It may be that "Manifest Destiny" is just the concept we're looking for, in order to flesh out the metaphysical fulfillment of world corporations' full potential; and it so happens that there are two Index references to it—to Manifest Destiny—in *The Coming Caesars*. Here's the first: "In 1845, a Democratic editor coined the apt expression 'manifest destiny'—manifest destiny to increase American power and territory, bolstered by the firm conviction that American institutions and way of life were the best to be had in the world."[15] And the second reference, after preliminary remarks by de Riencourt regarding the "rise of undisputed American supremacy in the Western Hemisphere, prelude to a greater supremacy to come across the oceans"[16]:

> The first conscious formulation of America's global imperialism began to arise at the end of the nineteenth century. Idealism and religious proselytism often assumed an expansionist tinge, as expressed by the famous missionary Josiah Strong of Ohio, for instance: "It is manifest that the Anglo-Saxon holds in his hands the destinies of mankind, and it is evident that the United States is to become the home of this race, the principle seat of its power, the great center of its influence." . . . Other Americans, more secular-minded, expressed their faith in their racial superiority—a notion that was basically alien to the Classical world and is a distinctive characteristic of the northern Europeans and North Americans. John Fiske expressed his Darwinian racialism in his celebrated article "Manifest Destiny" and joined many others in expressing their belief in the racial superiority of northern people, a conviction that led a generation later to closing the gates of immigration not only to Asians but to southern and eastern Europeans. Senator Beveridge of Indiana linked racialism and expansionism in an 1898 speech eulogizing Ulysses Grant: "He never forgot that we are a conquering race and that we must obey our blood and

13. Perlstein, "Seventies," 32.

14. Myers, *Binding*, 452.

15. de Riencourt, *Coming*, 132.

16. de Riencourt, *Coming*, 194.

occupy new markets and, if necessary, new lands. He had the prophet's seer-like sight which beheld, as part of the Almighty's plan, the disappearance of debased civilizations and decaying races before the higher civilization of the nobler and more virile types of men."[17]

There we have it, perhaps even the Righteousness that thinks it does God service, for it is, after all, part of the Almighty's plan. And if we go back to the second page of de Riencourt's chapter V, we find:

It was George Washington who perceived the tight connection between centralization and territorial expansion, and saw the inevitability of the twin trend at the same time. His journeys to the West convinced him that the Mississippi Valley was destined to be rapidly colonized and that, under existing conditions, the new country would fall under Spanish domination since the mouth and the west bank of the great river belonged to Spanish Louisiana. Without trade outlet to the sea, the westerners would vote themselves into the Spanish Empire or, at any rate, secede from a loose confederation which could not protect them. The very safety of the original states would be endangered by the rise of another republic across the Appalachians. The safeguard of the United States therefore required the protection and incorporation of the West—and this could only be guaranteed by a strong central government.

Thus, even in those early days, the Americans were inevitably committed to expansion and centralization out of sheer self-protection; and thus started the fateful, unintentional, and unplanned expansionism which, in less than two centuries, was to establish the frontiers of American security well into the hearts of the European and Asiatic continents, all the way across the globe's two greatest oceans.[18]

Allowances for de Riencourt's mawkish and sanctimonious the-devil-made-me-do-it rationalizations for empire—"sheer self-protection," "fateful," "unintentional," "unplanned"—especially in light of the remarks by Josiah Strong, John Fiske, and Senator Beveridge (who openly celebrate the racial superiority of northern people and who not only had no moral qualms about the expansion of American empire but were convinced that such expansion was God's will), we have in these passages the full-throated, dual streams of "idealism and religious proselytism" converging in the fully intentional doctrine of "Manifest Destiny" and, in due time, in the breathtaking corporate utopianism of George Ball.[19] But isn't it interesting how an earlier, aggres-

17. de Riencourt, *Coming*, 195.

18. de Riencourt, *Coming*, 71.

19. On pages 221 through 223 of his *Endgame*, Derrick Jensen quotes lengthy extracts from a 1900 congressional speech by Senator Beveridge in behalf of the American conquest of the Philippines, a speech oozing with racial, religious, and civilizational superiority. It is a stunning piece of oratory. More of Albert Beveridge can be found in Barbara Tuchman's *The Proud Tower*, pages 153-54 and 164 ("We will not renounce our part in the mission of our race, trustees under God, of the civilization of the world"), as well as in James Bradley's *The Imperial Cruise*, which is about American imperialism

sive generation openly and boldly asserted its racial superiority and intended world supremacy, while a later one, apparently troubled ethically by the flagrant arrogance (but still stubbornly loyal to the ideology of civilizational uplift), puts spread fingers over its eyes and says, with a false smile, "unintentional"?

Now George Ball was a fixture in Lyndon Johnson's Great Society administration, so we can assume that Ball was "liberal." But what does that tell us about "The Ideological Divide"?

At one point, Christopher Caldwell says that "broadly speaking, the Democratic Party is the party to which elites *belong*."[20] The implication is bogus that the Republican Party is therefore made up of homespun nonelites, plain people, honest but resentful peasants who can hear the Democratic aristocrats frolicking happily in a fine mansion on the far side of the forbidding gates. Which is not to say that Perlstein's citation of George Ball is not only apt, but it puts one of the key issues—call it globalization or call it empire—front and center. I would call it the globalizing of civilization's diseases and traumatic institutions by means of commercial lust, religious obsession, intellectual hypocrisy, and military brutality.[21] I think George Ball's blithe arrogance reveals the absence of any real "ideological divide" between the major parties, at least at the upper levels where commercial, military, and foreign policy is constructed. Both parties are party to imperialism and full of arrogant righteousness, without which imperialism would wither.

As long as we're at this review mongering, let's lift a paragraph from Amitabh Pal's review, in the November 2010 issue of *The Progressive*, of Andrew Bacevich's new book, *Washington Rules: America's Path to Permanent War*. We might remember, as we read this, that Bacevich is a retired Army colonel and a self-described Catholic conservative:

> In his new book, Bacevich presents a convincing and readable case: that the American self-image as the indispensable nation committed to bringing liberty and justice to all has resulted in the overreaching and hubris that is the central, bipartisan foundation of U.S. foreign policy. This comprises, Bacevich says, a global military presence, global power projection, and global interventionism. These are the Washington rules (a nice double play on words) that Bacevich uses as the leitmotif of the book.[22]

---

and how, under President McKinley, the motives of America (page 99) were expressed as "efforts of great compassion and sacrifice" in which Americans "had a Christian duty to help."

20. Caldwell, "Ideological," 17.

21. Here is an exact list of at least some of the "chief features" of the "group of institutions that first took form under kingship," at the dawn of civilization. This is Lewis Mumford's itemizing, on page 86, in *The Myth of the Machine*: ". . . the centralization of political power, the separation of classes, the lifetime division of labor, the mechanization of production, the magnification of military power, the economic exploitation of the weak, and the universal introduction of slavery and forced labor for both industrial and military purposes."

22. Pal, "Toll," 43.

This is good and honest stuff. Pal goes on to quote a sardonic remark of Bacevich's—
"The United States is either the victim or an innocent bystander, Washington's own
past actions possessing no relevance to the matter at hand"[23]—but Pal also says that
"For redemption, Bacevich looks back to George Washington and John Quincy Adams. He proposes a radical retrenchment from offence abroad to defense at home."[24]
But Amaury de Riencourt (also a conservative, but of a more aristocratic strain) has
already told us that it was, in fact, George Washington who "perceived the tight connection between centralization and territorial expansion," just as Mumford shows us
that centralization and territorial expansion lie at the heart of the civilizational project. I therefore don't believe it's possible to find an intellectual safe haven of "radical
retrenchment" in George Washington's warning against foreign entanglements or, for
that matter, in Dwight Eisenhower's alarm in regard to the military-industrial complex. Both utterances were undoubtedly sincere in their own way, as far as they went;
but they were sheepish bleats of late-blooming lambs in process of shedding old lion
uniforms—mere backward glances, second thoughts, concerned reflections—but way
too little and much too late.

Interestingly, neither the "liberal" Alter nor the "conservative" Caldwell says
much about American empire, American militarism, or the size of the military budget: fifty-seven percent of the total U.S. budget, according to the American Friends
Service Committee. But this oblivion (like "unintentional") is the norm within American political discourse, among both "liberals" and "conservatives." We may be the
indispensable nation, the greatest country in the world, or even the greatest country
in the history of the world (no point in hiding behind false modesty), but if we have
a big, tough military it's only because the rest of the stupid, backward world hates our
freedoms and envies our affluence, so we are obliged to stomp out the devilish little
fires before they merge in a smoking-gun conflagration that could engulf us. "Sheer
self-protection," says Amaury de Riencourt, with an apparent straight face; "either the
victim or an innocent bystander," as Andrew Bacevich puts it sarcastically.

The truth is that we not only have a largely useless cacophony of talking-head
chatter about "liberal" and "conservative," we also have almost no serious discussion
about what an ecologically and spiritually healthy culture, economy, and political
order would consist of or look like. Our minds are so contaminated—I think "contaminated" an apt word, although it may be too restrained—by a "manifest destiny"
combination of globalized civilization and otherworldly Christianity, a combination
so powerful and engulfing that we simply cannot imagine what an ecological economy
would look like or socialist political democracy would do for us.[25]

23. Pal, "Toll," 43.

24. Pal, "Toll," 43-44.

25. By socialist economy I mean an arrangement much like that proposed by late nineteenth-century Populists (see Lawrence Goodwyn's *The Populist Moment*), made even clearer by R. H. Tawney,
in 1920, with the publication of *The Acquisitive Society*, and further refined by ecological wisdom. In

The very thing we need—grounded, compassionate, ethical earthiness—is what we are both blind to and repulsed by. Why? Because utopian religion in collusion with civilizational utopianism has served to demolish and demean the neolithic *pagus*: the primitive, the peasant, the pagan, the country place, and, in the end, nature in its ecological and evolutionary coherence. Because of Original Sin even nature is fallen and corrupt. We now live in the utopian City of God—Senator Beveridge's Almighty God—thanks also to that obsessed Platonist, Saint Augustine of Hippo, although the good bishop was only a small (but very important) cog in the giant wheel of civilizational perfection—the Moses, perhaps, of Christendom.

"Conservative" and "liberal" are little more than brand-name commercial products in a race for achieving the global dystopia of ecological collapse. The only sane politics is the Green "kingdom of God"; but its early advocate got nailed to a post as a sadistic and mocking example for all would-be tree huggers to witness and draw a lesson from. When Andrew Harvey says "the earth has AIDS," and that "AIDS is a kind of training ground for the apocalypse,"[26] we have to realize not only the aptness of the metaphor but that the infecting virus is a politically engineered blend of civilizational chromosomes with otherworldly religious chromosomes, producing Caesar with the mask of Christ—a true mutant alien.

The usual sobriquet for this disaster—Anti-Christ—is so tarnished with scapegoat ambience that it has essentially lost its spiritual impact and eschatological meaning. So let's just call it antineolithic and anti-Jesus, and let it go at that. For if the Constantinian/civilizational project locks in a final utopian victory, the "kingdom of God" will undergo a crucifixion from which there may be no resurrection whatsoever. Righteousness will have won, and Compassion will be consigned, without exit, to vindictive eternity in Dante's Inferno.

---

broad outline, we need an ecologically sustainable economy in which vital large-scale entities are in the public domain (thus preventing the recurrence of aristocratic wealth concentration) and in which small-scale initiatives are privately, cooperatively, or communally owned—thus securing liberty at the level of functional democracy.

26. Harvey, "Rebirth," 57.

6

Two Peas in a Pod

Wendell Berry's Commonwealth

THE SUBTITLE OF WENDELL Berry's *What Matters?* is "Economics for a Renewed Commonwealth." His subjects are the decrepitude and demoralization of rural culture, what wholesome land use would entail in the realm of cultural revitalization, and how the industrial economy keeps sucking the life out of the countryside, both its people and its landscape.

Berry—if I might use this ridiculous figure of speech—is, for the most part, right on the money as regards the economics of the local and small-scale. He understands the close linkage between wholesome local economics and the coherence of local culture, and he is adept at conveying that understanding in readable, witty and, at times, elegant prose. He even activates my envy as a writer.

Our geographical regions and the particulars of our rural lives are rather different. Berry, who has farmed with draft horses, is from Kentucky. I'm from northern Wisconsin. He's at least ten years older than I am—which, in the contexts of our respective childhoods and youth, represent significantly different manifestations of rural culture aptitudes: by which I mean ten years was quite a bit of time in the rapidly changing nature of rural culture in the first half of the twentieth century, namely the shift from nonelectrical self-provisioning and four-legged horse power to electrical commercialization and steel horsepower. But we share a sustained sympathy for and tendency toward rural culture. We've each written books on the subject—pretty good ones, too, in my completely objective opinion—although I am an obscure unknown compared to Berry, who has produced many volumes of poetry, fiction, and book-length collections of essays (like *What Matters?*) and, of course, his frequent lectures and speeches around the country. It could be said of Wendell Berry that he's been the most sought after advocate of and spokesman for the culture of small-scale farming in this country for the last thirty to forty years. He's earned his reputation.

Now I've not read everything Berry has written, not by a long shot. But I've read enough of his works, over the last thirty-something years, to recognize his strengths and weaknesses. His strength is on full display in *What Matters?* His weakness is only implicit, between the lines, showing itself in occasional fleeting glimpses. But, being who I am (and, perhaps, not to discount writer's envy), I wish to explore what may be hidden between the lines of Berry's horsewriting skills.

In Berry's opening essay, "Money Versus Goods," nearly thirty pages long, there's a detailed list of sixteen points in behalf of what he calls "a new, long-term agricultural policy." Here is the economic bedrock of Berry's strength. In my estimation, his list is exactly right; it shows deep groundedness in ways linking agricultural economics to rural culture. Here's the list, from pages 27 through 30, condensed and abridged:

1. No price supports or subsidies without production controls.

2. 100 percent parity between agriculture and industry.

3. Enforcement of anti-trust and anti-monopoly laws.

4. Help young farmers to own farms.

5. Phase out toxic chemicals.

6. Phase out biofuels.

7. Phase in perennial plants for pasture, winter forage, and grain crops.

8. Set and enforce high water quality standards.

9. Eliminate animal factories ("those abominations").

10. Return animal production to pasture and to scale.

11. Encourage local food economies.

12. Encourage local adaptation of domestic species and varieties of plants and animals.

13. Encourage local, small-scale forestry.

14. Study and teach sustainable forestry.

15. Promote good use and care of farm woodlands.

16. Encourage development of local forest economies.

This list, of course, is not all there is to be said for or on behalf of rural culture, including its economics, but it is the base of our food supply and a large portion of the base (at least potentially) of our need for logs, lumber, and stone.

Berry's weakness lies in omission. And although it could be said that what I'm calling omission lies outside his subject matter and is not omission at all, but only my private peeve, I don't think that's true.

The first clue lies in the subtitle of *What Matters?* It's the word "commonwealth." The word (in my fat, old *Webster's*) means public welfare, the common good or public well-being, and it seems to involve, or at least imply, some sort of governing structure created for and operating in behalf of the common good. (It should be understood— yes?—that common good requires a fair degree of common wealth.) In regard to the rural portion of that political equation, Berry is vocal, searing, and eloquent. And, in his list, a good many of his particulars require public governance on various levels.

While he repeatedly excoriates the industrialization of primary production, and how policies of industrialization have ruined rural culture, he never comes close to addressing what a proper realm of *industrial* commonwealth would look like, consist of, or how we might get there. If agriculture and industry are yin and yang, Berry is all yin and no yang. That is, to propose correctives for agricultural policy—which Berry does, and in the main they are detailed and substantial—without corresponding corrective policies for industry (even if they would be less comprehensive, due to a general absence of concrete experience), is to ask a one-legged man to dance.

I don't have a rounded explanation for why Wendell Berry is all yin and no yang. But, in my inquisitive estimation, the circumstance is serious enough to venture an analysis, which is mostly speculative. Perhaps the heart of this speculation is the extent to which the word "socialism" is a spook house relic, a poisonous term half-buried in ragged spider webs, dusty, dirty, occasionally moving without apparent reason or cause, emanating a venomous, dull glow, something truly creepy, but fascinating in a way not to be discussed in public. That is, the only honest and democratic way to control the limitlessness of industrialization is to bring it into the public realm, under the umbrella of *commonwealth* analysis and *democratic* governance. Some of this, in principle, may involve breaking into smaller hunks "too big to fail" corporate entities, which supposedly would then be free to fail. (See point three in the abridged form of Berry's list above.) But what we've seen repeatedly in the last century is that smaller hunks of dismembered monopolies have a magical propensity to re-member, to reunite, get glued back together, for experts in gluing to operate in a revolving door between industry and government, with occasional sabbaticals and rests from their magical gluing exertions at prestigious universities or well-funded "think tanks." (Perhaps these are glue-fume detox centers, akin to laundry facilities for dirty money.)

The only other options, in principle, to cutting corporate entities down to size, are to let them alone and see what happens as a consequence (I think the jury is in on that one), or to socialize them in the manner and spirit of R. H. Tawney's prescription in *The Acquisitive Society*.

I don't believe the first option—cutting corporations down to size—is practical or realistic in the long-term. That is, corporations *almost* too big to fail will, via clever lawyers or detox impresarios, soon find the requisite legal glue with which to attach severed parts. Letting corporations freely rule, as they now largely do, without meaningful democratic oversight or social direction, is to perpetuate, prolong, and intensify their accelerating destructiveness. We're already well-advanced in a Global Crisis largely of their collective making. (Plus we've all seen how feeble, inadequate, and sluggardly have been the regulatory reforms considered by the once-overwhelmingly Democratic congress—the supposed "liberal" watchdogs of the public domain—under the supposed "liberal" presidency of Barack Obama. And these were supposedly the "people-friendly" good guys as compared to the Republican business puppets.)

Tawney, in the book referenced above, not only advocates for the socialization of absentee shareholder corporations, he also insists that socialization would correspondingly make possible the "restoration of the small master in agriculture or in industry, who cannot easily hold his own in a world dominated by great estates or capitalist finance." Such socialization, Tawney goes on, would facilitate the "restoration of the small property-owner in those kinds of industries for which small ownership is adapted." He even goes so far as to insist that a "socialistic policy" toward corporations is a *precondition* for the increase and protection of small-scale property ownership and use.[1]

Well, to be fair, systemic economic collapse or dysfunction—the Great Depression of the 1930s will do as an illustration—can also serve as a spur to small-farm increase. But that's a by-product of tough, unanticipated circumstance, not a viable policy in and of itself. Of course, insofar as prior forms of socialism swallowed the mirage of Total Industrialization—say so-called "communism" at its Stalinist worst or the Wal-Mart supplier China seems to have become as a subsidiary of Uncle Sam's Club—socialism deserves its seclusion in a cobwebbed cellar. (But, then, it should have capitalism for a gaunt, pale cell mate, equally hollow-eyed and skeletal.)[2]

Socialism, despite its obvious and accepted benefits (public libraries, public roads, public parks and protected wilderness areas, public lighting of streets, municipal water and sewage systems, fire and police protection, public schools, public health departments, public boat landings and beaches, the post office, Social Security insurance, Medicare, and any number of other useful things), and its exceedingly moral, passionate, and democratic advocates (from Walter Rauschenbusch to Eugene Debs to Norman Thomas to Ralph Nader to Bernie Sanders), continues to be a Tea Party caricature of tar and feathers, fire and brimstone, a basement burlesque, a scapegoating exercise partly calculated, partly a product of accrued stupidity, whose function is to hold the *solution* of our difficulties (or, at least, a fairly substantial portion of

---

1. Tawney, *Acquisitive*, 86-87.

2. Paul Tillich, on pages 49 and 50 in *The Protestant Era*, adds an important spiritual dimension to this discussion. He says that "socialism, in spite of all its criticism of the bourgeois epoch, has been unable to keep itself free from its negative element, namely, its attempt to exclude the unconditional from the spheres of thought and action and, accordingly, to create the new epoch merely through technology and strategy. Socialism . . . in this fashion . . . was prolonging the old epoch. . . . When it fought against 'bourgeois' science, it did not see how it itself shared the basic presupposition of this science, the purely objectifying relationship to the world, to spirit, and to history; . . . it did not see how . . . it was fettered within the bonds of that attitude. . . . If it made the highest possible increase of economic welfare into the all-determining and foremost aim, it did not see that it became thereby a mere competitor of capitalism. . . . If socialism intended to deprive the spiritual and religious life of its intrinsic value, considering it as a mere ideology, it did not sense that it thereby strengthened the attitude toward economics and life in general that is characteristic of materialistic capitalism." Green socialism must recognize and correct this flaw.

the solution) up to public ridicule and contempt precisely so the solution won't be taken seriously and treated accordingly. Socialism, in this sense, is (like rural culture) a conceptual Christ figure, perpetually crucified with a crown of Wal-Mart thorns and a trickle of Monsanto GMO commie blood slipping down each gaunt cheek. This means, in terms of public advocacy, that only a fool would stand in behalf of either socialism or rural culture. The din of hoots, jeers, catcalls, and whistles—not to speak of a lynch rope, if things got serious enough—seems a guaranteed public response.

And that raises a question: To what extent is Wendell Berry, a truly wise and thoughtful man, not so much protecting himself from ridicule and scorn (I suspect he's had lots of exposure to scorn and ridicule over the years for his small-farm advocacy) as he is protecting the small, tough, but vulnerable community of small-farm advocates from a seemingly inevitable landfill of additional abuse and contempt— protecting those folks, that is, from laughingstock irrelevance by refraining from associating the renewal of rural culture with hard-nosed policies of democratic socialism, a socialism that, in our American context, is a direct descendant of the late nineteenth-century Farmers Alliance and People's Party or "Populists"? And if it is to be asserted that Tawney's socialism is pie in the electoral working-class sky, then so is Berry's rural culture a complementary pie in the demographic peasant sky. But in the sky or on the table, these are twin pies, and neither will be giving off its succulent odors without the other on the menu.

I don't think Wendell Berry can be accused of cowardice. I'm not making that accusation. Calculated prudence, maybe, not cowardice. But calculated prudence is an hourglass steadily running out of sand. Waiting for the Right Moment to advocate for libertarian ecological democratic socialism is, probably, like waiting for rapture: excellent for the practice of patience; not much else can be said in its behalf.

Then again, I might be wrong. That is, Berry comfortably and competently quotes Dante, Marlowe, and Goethe; he obviously has great respect for Hardy and Wordsworth. But his sense of history, other than moral gleanings from literary classics and the Bible, seems to center on the industrial revolution. He appears to believe that our modern troubles need not be traced back to any further origin or cause. As he says explicitly on page 19, "At the root of our problem, we now need to suppose, is industrialism and the Industrial Revolution itself." He may drop terms like "domestic colonialism" (page 59), "expert servitude to the corporations" (page 32), "financial nobility" (page 25), and "decadent ruling classes" (page 10), or say that we are "free" to become "as conspicuously greedy and wasteful as the most corrupt of kings and queens" (page 42), but there is no historical hint of Zinn or Mumford or Toynbee in his probing, no suggestion that our dominant economic tendencies are derivative from an aristocratic worldview and predatory ethos whose roots lie in the origin and rise of civilization itself, in the *first* farm crisis. In medical terms, Wendell Berry is diagnosing a nasty skin condition rather than recognizing bone cancer. Perhaps Mr. Berry, for all his familiarity with the classics and his polished prose (sometimes reminiscent of Yeats), really is a committed provincial who can't see beyond or behind the eighteenth century, at least when it comes to economics.

Well, nineteenth-century Populists were committed provincials, too; but that didn't prevent them (I'm referencing Lawrence Goodwyn's *The Populist Moment*) from recognizing that racism was a political wedge used to divide white and black farmers or that "socialism," as a tar-and-feather effigy of the Devil, was employed by moneyed powers to scare voters away from a Populist ballot. If R. H. Tawney is right, and I obviously believe he is, then a limit on private wealth and a curb on aristocratic forms of private ownership is the requisite capstone in a political yin-and-yang arch comprising the healthy rural culture of Wendell Berry and the vibrant democratic socialism of Eugene Debs—only pruned (both agriculture and industry) to waste- and toxin-free dimensions by razor-sharp ecological considerations.

But this "vision" will go up in smoke unless there's a broad-scale public recognition of the value and importance of rural culture and a corresponding political energy by which that value and importance can achieve policy implementation. We the people have to want it. The ecological crisis—ecocidal weaponry and climate change above all—is forcing this issue. Not that rural culture needs an ecological crisis to be metaphysically justified. Rural culture is justified without any such crisis. It has, we might say, evolutionary validity on its very own merits. Its justification disappears in the mists of our creaturely past.

But the Global Crisis created by the globalization of civilization proves a number of things simultaneously: utopian civility is a deeply flawed spirituality; rural culture needs a wholesome life; industrialization must be carefully controlled by a thoughtful democratic process both ecological and socialist—in a manner, perhaps, akin to how the Amish evaluate and regulate economic innovation and cultural novelty within their communities.

We know what's needed—land as community to which we belong, as Aldo Leopold so succinctly put it in *A Sand County Almanac*. That means democratic socialism for everything too important to remain in private control ("too big to fail"), and it means the resurrection of the sort of wholesome rural culture Wendell Berry has spent his life advocating for and describing. These two—vital rural culture and energetic democratic socialism—are two peas in a pod, two pies on the table, two energies in a circuit. Neither will come into being by itself. We won't achieve one without achieving the other. It's time these energies started collaborating—*pagus* and *civis* intellectuals earnestly shaping a political and cultural transformation.

7

An Unfurled Narrative of Utopian Fulfillment

If a narrative is so important, readers may ask, why don't you unfurl one? As
I see it, the much-needed narrative must arise out of dialogue. . . . Indeed, as I
see it, to present a narrative not based on dialogue is to invite rejection.

Amitai Etzioni, "Needed: A Progressive Story,"
in *The Nation*, May 21, 2010, page 22

ALLOW ME TO UNFURL a narrative, at least a partial one. This narrative arises from
two main sources. First, my own experience. Second, an attempt to make sense of
that experience by absorbing and utilizing the thoughtful, scholarly analysis of people
whose work resonates with my experience.

But I have to confess that dialogue with persons alive and present, in regard to a
progressive story, has been difficult to engage and thin in outcome. Perhaps this thin-
ness is due, on my part, to insufficient clarity or inadequate persuasiveness. Perhaps
I've been overbearing. Perhaps the narrative I've developed is so contrary to received
conventions, both historical and religious, so unsettling, that it is (or I am) held at
arm's length like a smelly rag unceremoniously escorted to a trash can.

Amitai Etzioni says "Successful movements have a narrative that usually takes a
historical form. The narrative provides an account of the forces that got us into our
predicament and the rising forces that will save us, and an image of the more perfect
union we are going to reach once we put our shoulders to the wheel."[1] That description of narrative process seems reasonable. But it fails to anticipate the magnitude of
resistance to a new narrative and the extent to which the old narrative continues, in
profoundly subtle ways, to hold us in its grip. Etzioni's implicit presumption seems to
be one of effortless transition from old to new. He appears to believe that, on hear-
ing the new narrative, our response will be "Of course! Why didn't we think of that
before?" But a new narrative providing "an account of the forces that got us into our
predicament" is far more unsettling and morally challenging than we are willing to
acknowledge or admit. The old narrative is more deeply embedded—*protectively* embedded—in our consciousness than we realize. We are less ready to relinquish the old

---

1. Etzioni, "Needed," 22.

narrative than we imagine, even if, as Will Durant says in one of the epigraphs that open this book, an advance in narrative carries with it remnants of the narrative displaced. (He also reminds us that revolution is illegal. We might take this revolutionary illegality in both a secular and a religious sense.) This resistance goes for "liberals" as well as for "conservatives." ("Liberals" just orbit convention at a higher altitude than "conservatives.") Our problem is that a new narrative tips our mental world upside down, or at least sideways, and almost nobody seems to welcome the transformational vertigo. We want change, of course; but not anything too upsetting, please.

II

Born just after the Second World War, I was raised in northern Wisconsin on a small, homestead farm, a farm with less than twenty cows. Two one-room schools in the township, neither with running water. Twelve miles to the nearest city—a "city" of less than ten thousand people. High school by yellow bus, three hours of bumpy riding on back roads each day. And then a summer's factory work, a couple years of college, a brief stint as a Montana cowboy (where I got to make hay for a thousand head of cattle rather than a dozen or so)—before the voracious military, heroically holding up leaning dominoes in southeast Asia, caught up with me and tried to train me in institutional murder and organized mayhem. (My draft situation, like that of a million other young men, is captured in its essence in a chapter called "On the Rainy River," especially pages 54 through 61, in Tim O'Brien's *The Things They Carried*.)

It's largely irrelevant, or at least a distraction, to say—beyond the word "alienation"—how I ended up in St. Louis. Nearly ten years in the inner city. The antipoverty program. Land surveying. A janitor at an alternative school. In some ways I was lost and didn't know how to be found. The basic necessities of life goaded me to work for a living—a wife and two children— but I didn't identify with the world I reluctantly labored in. While blue-collar work felt more honest than white (the higher the altitude of income and class the greater the betrayal felt), blue was also imbued with comprehensive alienation and saturated with diffuse resentment.

But an alienated betrayal of *what*? What's an account of the forces that got us into our alienated predicament? What would our world be like without systemic alienation, resentment, and betrayal?

Meanwhile, I was discovering in myself a deep longing for a certain sort of rural life. This longing was real. It was grounded in the northern Wisconsin countryside of my youth, even as it was given intellectual support—"validated," I suppose—by an influential writer like Paul Goodman, with his frank advocacy for rural reconstruction.

Now nostalgia is a fairly simple word—it basically means "homesickness"—but as a concept, symbol, or state of being it is akin to the "kingdom of God," a yearning for something powerful and elusive. That is, there is deep longing in such spiritual "nostalgia."

My path out of feeling lost started with a simple step: I began to ask older men (they were all men, as I recall) to explain to me why small farms were dying. I no longer remember what they said. I knew immediately they didn't have a clue. Economistic clichés, maybe. Some "progressive" platitudes. Nothing of substance. Nothing that rang true or felt solid. Nothing worth remembering.

But now I had a second burr in my underpants. The first was "Why are small farms dying"? The second was: Why is an answer to this simple question about small-farm disappearance so elusive, so apparently hard to grasp? I didn't yet realize that I had discovered, or was about to discover, the civilized institutionalization of betrayal and alienation. I had stumbled across a retrogressive pathway out of my lostness. I was about to discover that the mission of *civis* was to harness, exploit, and, if possible, exterminate *pagus*, and that *pagus* was our ancient, evolutionary home from which we were incrementally evicted by civilization and its Christian accomplice. I was on the verge of discovering that the ancient enemy of agriculture, especially and particularly small-scale agriculture, was—civilization.

III

A word of caution. Essentially all of us are dealing with a fairly pervasive sense of unease, dis-ease, and estrangement. It is, we might say, the world condition, a condition whose virulence gives every indication of intensifying. That this condition has been intensified and compounded by the industrial/financial/electronic transformation of human society has been pretty well documented. This implies that the previous social and cultural conditions, though difficult and harsh, were, for all their roughness, in some ways less estranging, and that preindustrial society, at least in the mainstream Western sense, was largely agrarian and small-scale and, in a cultural sense, more grounded and more livable. Shorter lifespan? Yes. More life? Also yes. The conclusions I eventually came to, especially after reading and thinking about the revelations of Lewis Mumford and Norman O. Brown, have to do with the modern intensifications of alienation, estrangement, and betrayal.

As human beings, we are in a difficult and paradoxical situation. If I ask myself—What do I *really* know?—the answer is astonishingly meager and tentative. Even my name is an exterior, social construct. I therefore generalize to the broader human condition by saying that we all are quite limited and dumb. Perhaps that's why Amitai Etziona says we need dialogue—so that narrative can be something more than mere opinion or private hallucination. (Of course, *public* hallucination—e.g., "the forces that got us into our predicament"—can be even more dangerous and deadly, even as they are utterly normal.)

We now realize that human technology (like nuclear weapons) and the "externalities" associated with technology (like the massive oil gush in the Gulf of Mexico, the Japanese nuclear disaster at Fukushima, the steadily accruing greenhouse gasses in the atmosphere) have brought Earth to a Global Crisis, a possible consequence of which could be mammalian extinction. So we are caught between profound limitations of personal, temporal consciousness and the cumulative, catastrophic consequences of what seems to be a largely male and elite technical process—may we call it a narrative of utopian civilization?—built with brilliant insight, shameless greed, ruthless violence, disguised but extremely powerful fear, and a kind and quality of spiritual sanctification that has served to justify the very forces that have gotten us into our predicament. We might call it stupidity versus hubris, although hubris and stupidity are not mutually exclusive, watertight compartments. Hubris infects everyday stupidity; and stupidity, no matter how intensive the security checks, cannot be excluded from the Top Secret precincts of hubris. Stupidity may even guard the door and be its own Secret Service. Stupidity at that level is how fear rationalizes "security."

So I'm putting my finger on civilization as our most concentrated and unselfcritical repository of hubris—unselfcritical to a stunning degree precisely because "civilization" as metacultural narrative is essentially devoid of anything negative—it always exonerates itself—although I'd like it understood that this fingering of civilization does not exclude or exempt precivilized cultures, especially the violence within them, from containing roots of what became civilized hubris. We may have a strong impulse to idealize the precivilized or noncivilized past (allow me to reposition the word "nostalgia" here to include such idealization); but idealization of this sort can also be a kind of wishful cultural Manichaeism, a splitting of good and evil into separate camps, a splitting that only muddies the water and muddles the mind. It's true that civilization globalized has created the planetary crisis we're now in; but civilization is also a human creation, a human construct. It wasn't, so far as I know, shipped in from outer space. We're all implicated in the civilized narrative. Civilization clearly mutated the warrior impulse from raid and rape into magnified, institutionalized militarism and systemic agrarian slavery; but civilization did not invent the empathy-deficient warrior. The warrior predates civilization and may be a poorly weaned male in an ancient cultural context of tense sexual arrangements and human malaise. But we'll chat about that later.

IV

So here's what I learned, directly or indirectly, from Mumford and Brown. First, until ten or fifteen thousand years ago, all our ancestors lived by gathering and hunting and, before that, in the far distant past, they lived by grubbing and scavenging. Everyone of us has such ancestry. We wouldn't be here if we didn't. Whatever may have been the impetus (Kirkpatrick Sale itemizes his thoughts in *After Eden*), our gathering foremothers, after the last Ice Age, moved in the direction of gardening and horticulture. Over time—lots of generations—this movement from gathering to planting both concentrated and increased specific aspects of the food supply to such a degree that villages became stable in location as human population enlarged, and the young of select wild critters were domesticated for village life. Eventually, an ox or burro was hitched to a digging stick, the plow "invented," and men integrated into this new thing we call agriculture. Mumford especially sings the praises of the early, precivilized agrarian village, its egalitarianism within the context of a largely feminine spirituality, and its relative nonviolence.

It seems that the rise of the city changed all that, violently and brutally. With the city came kingship, an aristocracy, institutionalized violence and institutionalized servitude. Or that may be stating it backwards: with kingship, with an invading warrior "aristocracy" that stayed to permanently expropriate rather than merely raid, rape, pillage and leave, the city grew out of the fortified compound in which the expropriating "aristocracy" lived. The city is the home of thieves and a king. The king's home was built by slave labor. With that came the enforced reduction of villagers into expropriated, coerced and destitute peasants, taxed both of their wealth and their vitality. If the precivilized agrarian village can be seen as a new wrinkle in the evolution of folk culture, moving in a cultural direction never before explored, a direction without a ruling class, civilization (i.e., the urban utopia) blocked, thwarted, and capped that evolution. We can, in fact, say that the systemic impoundment of agriculture, this brutal "domestication" of the agrarian village, lasted right up to the industrial revolution. At that point, because of machines, chemicals and fossil fuels, the peasantry was no longer needed by the urban utopia. Peasants were therefore liquidated by eviction. Or just plain liquidated. Folk culture (as constrained as it may have been) died as the self-sustaining peasant village, with its traditional commons, was crushed. With the death of the last peasant, the neolithic comes to an end. Or, to give it Christian coloration, with the death of the peasantry, the agrarian village undergoes a final crucifixion. The shepherd, the husbandman, the sower of seeds—all these become culturally anachronistic. Civilization has done its best to kill them all. We might even say that "terminator seeds," as a metaphor, conveys the civilized agenda extremely well. *Civis* now owns—has patent rights on—the seeds of *pagus* and no longer needs the children of *pagus* to till the soil or harvest the crops.

V

So what about the death of small-scale farming, the question I asked smart men over forty years ago? Europeans and those of European descent invested a huge amount of energy in the creation of small farms in this country, on this continent. (That's not to say there weren't Native American farmers already here, or black farmers after the Civil War, or Hispanic farmers in the southwest.) Small-scale farming was encouraged until and somewhat beyond the Euro-American conquest of what's now the continental United States. If the electoral defeat of the People's Party in 1896 marked the overt political undoing of the Jeffersonian vision, and if the Great Depression of the 1930s granted small-scale farming a temporary demographic reprieve and even a small window of recovery, post-World War Two military-industrial affluence, with its triumphant commercial utopianism, began squeezing the life out of the countryside in a final way. (Dare we call it a Final Solution?) Small-scale farming was tagged an economic anachronism, a drag on industrial-financial prosperity, a cultural atavism. *That* was the answer to the question I had asked smart men in 1970 or thereabouts.

Small-scale farming was culturally "obsolete." It was almost as dead as the autonomous Indian village. Civilization had uttered its decree. The village had to be destroyed in order that it might become civilized.

This means, of course, that "globalization" is the world hegemony of utopian civility. What used to be spotty, regional, strutting its stuff here and there, has now taken control of the entire world. Building a better planet. We might even date utopian civility's globalization, somewhat whimsically, from 1492. The force that suppressed folk evolution five thousand years ago, by impounding the agrarian village and reducing its inhabitants to extorted and impoverished peasants, has now asserted its extractive, suppressive, dominating hubris over the entire Earth. Utopian civility prided itself— and continues to pride itself—on the progressive achievement of ever greater levels of refinement both culturally and spiritually, surpassing and discarding backwardness in all its many forms. (It probably should be said, however, that "progressive achievement" now seems to consist of cobbled props for tottering institutions, celebrating the latest smart phone or remotely controlled predator weapon, while consolidating the rule of the World Trade Organization and other such entities.) The small farm was as contemptibly disposable as the Indian village. Neither had a place in the New World Order. The only good farm is a dead farm. Utopia had a global vision. *Pagus* was an obstruction in the achievement of that vision. The only good pagan is a dead pagan. The only good seed is a patented seed, preferably bioengineered.

VI

Perhaps it would be useful to clarify and elaborate upon the word "utopia," a term I've used here rather freely. My College Edition *Webster's* defines utopia as "not a place," as "an imaginary island" with "a perfect political and social system," also "any place, state, or situation of ideal perfection" or "any visionary scheme or system for an ideally perfect social order," and, of course, the "subject and title of a book written by Sir Thomas More in 1516."

I didn't know until thirty-some years ago, and then via my Michigan friend Maynard Kaufman, that Lewis Mumford, in 1922, had revived Sir Thomas More's dialectical and far more grounded term "eutopia," meaning the good place or the good garden. (See Mumford's *The Story of Utopias* or my *Green Politics Is Eutopian* for deeper ramifications of the eutopian concept.) For our purposes here, however, the really relevant text is Mumford's "Utopia, the City, and the Machine," chapter 23 in his

Interpretations and Forecasts. In that essay, Mumford explicitly links utopia with the city: "the first utopia was the city itself."[2] And he goes on to link utopia and the city to the machine because the early "machine" of the city was compulsory human labor in the form of slavery: human labor organized to perform tasks now consigned explicitly to machines. The first machine was the agrarian village enslaved.

With coercive organization coupled to the myth of divine kingship, the city not only surpassed the "earthbound" village, hamlet, and country town by untold degrees of achievement, it was itself "primarily a religious phenomenon: it was the home of a god, and even the city wall points to this super-human origin. . . ." The city was "something 'out of this world,' . . . an ideal form—a glimpse of eternal order, a visible heaven on earth, a seat of life abundant—in short, utopia."[3] This home of the gods, this heaven on Earth, was built by slave labor.

To call the city a "religious phenomenon" is not a mere literary tag or historical conceit. Marcus Borg in *The God We Never Knew*, especially in pages 63 through 69 and then again in pages 134 through 136, patiently and methodically explains what impact the "monarchical model" of God had on social structure (namely a "domination system legitimated by God"), as he unfolds how "preindustrial agrarian society" was governed by a system "intrinsically hierarchical, economically exploitative, and politically oppressive."[4] (I quote Borg at length in chapter 4 of *Green Politics Is Eutopian.*)

It's not that difficult to understand how the aristocratic "heaven on earth" was built on a kind of living hell for peasants. Industrialize this "ideal form," this "glimpse of eternal order," extinguish the peasantry in favor of mechanized, chemicalized and bioengineered agribusiness, pile on the technological novelties and multiply the deadly "externalities," and we arrive at our historical moment, what Mumford calls "a negative utopia, a dystopia or kakotopia."[5] However, we are hiding from the naked truth if we imagine that dystopia or kakotopia is utopia gone wrong. Dystopia is not utopia gone wrong. Dystopia is *the logical outcome* of utopia—even, we might say, its ultimate fulfillment. It is the globalization of Class and War, the world victory of *civis* enslaving *pagus* or, at minimum, the redesign of *pagus* in a *civis* mode.

On page 186 of "The Total Economy," the final essay in *What Matters?*, Wendell Berry says a corporation "goes about its business as if it were immortal." Earlier in that paragraph, he discusses corporations as legal "persons."[6] But he doesn't put the two together. That is, he doesn't say that corporations are therefore *immortal persons*. That

2. Mumford, *Interpretations*, 241.

3. Mumford, *Interpretations*, 249-50.

4. Borg, *God*, 69, 136.

5. Mumford, *Interpretations*, 251.

6. Berry, *What*, 185.

is, *corporations are gods*. Corporations—*civis* entities—are the "legal person" utopian gods of civilization.[7]

We might say the most immediate and apt model for such a construction is the church—a supposedly divine, supernatural, and permanent (immortal) institution. And while that linkage may be useful, it doesn't recognize that the church picked up its immortal baggage not from Jesus but from the church's fourth-century fusion with the Roman Empire, a marriage consecrated by Augustine and passed down as normative to subsequent Western history. Not only was the Roman Empire itself the overwhelmingly dominant form of utopian immortality in the first-century Mediterranean world, it later coaxed or coerced an increasingly urbanized and compliant Christianity into a marriage of convenience, having previously conspired in the murder of the "husband" of the "bride of Christ." It was Constantine who made the church a legal utopian person. And, since the church's god was Almighty God, the marriage was duly blessed and consecrated as *Holy* Roman Empire.

The "immortality" of corporate "persons," while mockingly imitative of the church or of transcendent theology, really has a more venerable and patrimonial linkage to the "ideal form" and "eternal order" of foundational urban utopia, just as the oldest model of American agribusiness is not the small farm of New England Puritanism but the commercial slave plantations of the London Company's Jamestown.

VII

There are two major constructs into which to delve more deeply. One is religion, Christianity in particular. The other is democracy. Let's start with the latter.

Whatever the roots of democracy in classical Western history, such as may be argued from examples in ancient Greece or Republican Rome, there are two eutopian roots not much appreciated or discussed. One lies too far back in time for most people to take seriously—plus its time frame is morally repugnant to Christian fundamentalism—and the other has been so etherealized by Christian orthodoxy that to grasp it as a reservoir of democratic unfolding is to risk the odor of false understanding or heresy.

The far-back-in-time root is, of course, the precivilized agrarian village. That is, insofar as the precivilized agrarian village's social arrangement can be construed as horizontal (as contrasted to the imposed vertical control structure of utopian civilization), we can, I think, legitimately infer something of a democratic polity, even if we don't know its self-governing techniques or cooperative procedures. (The cultural evolution of folk communities may not conform to our contemporary understanding of democracy, but such evolution involved the entire community and not just a self-selected elite.) The other root, the etherealized one, lies buried in plain view in the first

---

7. See *The Powers That Be* by Walter Wink for a useful, if also limited, analysis of institutions as Powers and Principalities.

three Christian gospels; it is the alternative organizing principle repeatedly articulated by Jesus—the "kingdom of God"—built on the twin ethical blocks of radical servanthood and radical stewardship.

Jesus' alternative social and political vision—consciously or unconsciously—harkens to the precivilized agrarian village, a social construct preceding the appearance of civilization and, even more importantly, a construct fully capable of sustained, ethical self-governance, a kind of governance based on the cooperative horizontal rather than the controlling vertical. This horizontal self-governance, however, unconditionally depends on a deeply embedded conviction of systemic sharing and vigilant ecological reverence: that is, the deepening of servanthood and stewardship from something strictly spiritual to something that's also functionally economic and political, with no strict line of demarcation between them. The Global Crisis is teaching us that utopian verticality, even if superficially "democratized" at the level of a commercially complicit middle class, is unsustainable.

Global Crisis is the supremacy of utopian verticality triumphant over the eutopian horizontal: civilization's impounding and suppressing of folk culture; *civis* exterminating *pagus*. Pollution, climate change, overpopulation, the extinction of species, and the Damocles Sword of Nuclear Annihilation are some of the "externalized" consequences of this multimillennial vertical thrust. When the American officer in Vietnam said "We had to destroy the village in order to save it," he was articulating, in a localized and particular way, the cultural and religious conviction of the vertical in relation to the horizontal. This conviction—or its universal ramification—now applies to the entire Earth. The world-destroying expectations of Christian fundamentalists represent the most perfect illustration of this impulse, even though it is utopian civility that actually builds the instruments creating the End Times prospect. Otherworldly utopian religion may be the most obvious mythic expression of insane verticality; but utopian civility is the planning department, experimental workshop, and production facility. This is how corporations get to be "immortal persons." They are otherworldly, utopian agents engaged in the manufacture of dystopian raptures.

VIII

Let's keep going with spirituality and democracy.

Given the sheer ecological and cultural impossibility of maintaining a vertical thrust in either a democratic or consumerist mode, we are faced, it seems, with three major options: various magnitudes of planetary devastation; restoration on a global scale of explicit aristocratic control and elite governance; or resurrection of folk culture evolution with a keenly sharpened ethical realization and political conviction: servanthood and stewardship as structural beams in a global Green economy.

With the emergence of kingship, the city and aristocracy, governance of, by, and within civilization was explicitly vertical. It should therefore come as no surprise that the three Abrahamic religions—Judaism, Christianity, and Islam—all of which arose in a political atmosphere dominated by pre-existing institutions of utopian civility, should have developed explicit theologies based not only on a Male God but on a Male God outside of and beyond nature, a God of strict patriarchal morality and over-powering violent wrath, a God who is King of kings, above, beyond, and utterly tran-scendent—in other words, a God of awesome verticality, what Marcus Borg calls the "monarchical model." God is outside of and beyond nature just as a king is outside of and beyond the peasant village. This image of the divine has been the Western norm. It was—and it remains—the dominating icon of our relationship to or with authority.

But, as everybody knows, Christianity is in the throes of major internal conflicts and theological reformulations, represented on one side by fierce orthodox adherence to "conservative" and transcendent verticality and, on the other, by an often sluggardly and reluctant "liberal" groping for the immanent and horizontal. This struggle is both framed by and entangled in the metaphysical verticality of received religious indoc-trination and political disposition. That is, "democracy"—and here we especially need to bear in mind the major "founding" revolutions of the last 240 years or so—was not created so much for the liberation of the suppressed and oppressed horizontal (i.e., the agrarian village in particular), as it was oriented toward the "liberation" of a new ideological verticality promising rapidly accelerating economic velocity for all. Or, at least, for all those willing to get up to speed. (See R. H. Tawney's *Religion and the Rise of Capitalism* for an extremely well-written survey.) This speedy economic verticality had and continues to have a trajectory of ersatz aristocratic taste and utopian aspira-tion. Every man a king, every home a castle. Its core metaphysical energy was and remains civilizational. This proves true in unexpected places.

The Foreword to Wendell Berry's *What Matters?* is by the distinguished "steady-state" economist Herman E. Daly. On the second page of his Foreword, Daly goes for "definitional correction" in the language of economics. He immediately invokes Aristotle, informing us that:

> Aristotle distinguished "oikonomia" from "chrematistics." Oikonomia is the science or art of efficiently producing, distributing, and maintaining concrete use values for the household and community over the long run. Chrematistics is the art of maximizing the accumulation by individuals of abstract exchange value in the form of money in the short run. Although our word "economics" is derived from oikonomia, its present meaning is much closer to chrematis-tics. The word chrematistics is currently relegated to unabridged dictionaries, but the reality to which it refers is everywhere present and is frequently and incorrectly called economics. Wendell Berry is, I believe, urging us to correct our definition of economics by restoring to it the meaning of oikonomia and freeing it from confusion with, and excessive devotion to, chrematistics. In replacing chrematistics by oikonomia we not only refocus on a different reality

but also embrace the purposes served within that different reality—community, frugality, efficiency, and long-term stewardship of particular places.[8]

Well, it's true. My unabridged and somewhat battered 1910 *Webster's* has an entry for "chrematistics" (the "study of wealth as measured in money"), although my 1936 *Encyclopaedia Britannica* does not. So I dug out *Aristotle: On Man in the Universe* (1943) and, in the "Politics" section, Book I, pages 246 through 272, I found the chapters on economics. I presume this is the material Daly references, although there's no Englishified Greek in my text—no oikonomia or chrematistics.

There are thirteen chapters in Book I of Aristotle's "Politics." The explicit economic stuff begins with chapter 8 and proceeds, more or less, through chapter 13. It consists primarily of an elaboration, in Aristotle's lofty style, of oikonomia versus chrematistics—household management versus commerce. And Aristotle says pretty much what Herman Daly says he says.

So I agree with Wendell Berry, Herman Daly, and Aristotle (or Harry Stottle). That is, an economy of ethical sufficiency and natural limit is exactly what the Global Crisis is demanding of us. Aristotle is about to be proven correct in this important but partial way.

However, I say "important but partial" because chapters 2 through 7 in Aristotle's "Politics" set the stage for chapters 8 through 13. And what we find there (in chapters 2 through 7) are unhesitating assertions about rule, supremacy of the male and master, the *naturalness* of the state and of slavery. (In chapter 8 we also find that "the art of war is a natural art of acquisition," especially when directed "against men who, though intended by nature to be governed, will not submit."[9] Perhaps like the American Indians? The Mexicans? The Cubans? The Filipinos? The Koreans, Vietnamese, Iraqis, or Afghanis? How about the Iranians?)

No doubt it's possible to say, viewed anthropologically in the long-term, that oikonomia is a natural cultural expression of ancient human subsistence behavior, and that chrematistics is an aberration, a mutant impulse, that found its opportunity for aberrant growth and mutant expansion precisely as the so-called "natural" state (i.e., civilizational expropriation) pushed its utopian control rationalizations, by means of the "natural art of acquisition," toward *oikos* containment and pillage: somewhat humble and pious oikonomia at home, brutal chrematistics imposed on those who stupidly won't submit.

But if we say, as Aristotle does, that "the state is a creation of nature,"[10] then we are reduced, sooner or later, to affirm everything as natural, everything as a creation of nature. And, if everything is a creation of nature—perhaps like the entire Bible in all its particulars is God's authentic Word—then why isn't chrematistics a creation

---

8. Daly, "Foreword," x.

9. Aristotle, "Politics," 261.

10. Aristotle, "Politics," 252.

of nature, too, even if it's something of a latecomer, even if it's now everywhere present, much like God, NSA surveillance, the droning U.S. military, or our very own immortal-person corporations?

Everything in this oikonomia-versus-chrematistics argument, at least as it derives from or pertains to Aristotle, hinges on whether the state, war, slavery, and male domination are creations of nature. If you say yes to Aristotle, that the state, et al., *is* a creation of nature, something purely natural, then quit griping about chrematistics because you've just entangled yourself in a hopeless coil of contradiction. If war is the natural art of acquisition, and if chrematistics is the art of maximizing accumulation, there's no essential difference between the art of acquisition and the art of maximum accumulation, except that the former is directed outward toward the "enemy" (and is explicitly violent) while the latter (predatory in cunning but completely legal ways) may be outward or inward or both simultaneously. The only way to affirm oikonomia as true and right is to recognize civilization as an *un*natural imposition of the very things Aristotle insists are completely natural—male domination, violence, slavery, and war. Given Aristotle's core assertions regarding "natural" domination (slavery and war), his advocacy of oikonomia (use values for the home and community), even if subjectively sincere, is sophistry. (Where is Noam Chomsky's universality of moral values?) The irony, of course, is not that Aristotle's *oikos* advocacy is, finally, sophistical, but that his larger, grand assertiveness about male superiority, slavery, and war is complete and utter pandering to civilizational supremacy. His recognition of *oikos*, while true, is actually *an aberration* in his ideological architecture; and that makes citing Aristotle as a Grand Cultural Authority a bit of a problem. The Golden Rule—let's do onto others as we would have them do onto us—reveals the hypocritical core of chrematistics. If chrematistics is "natural," then it takes transformative spirituality—a spiritual biology—to create a new and more wholesome "natural"—which is only another way of talking about our core spiritual and evolutionary dilemma: how to minimize chrematistics and maximize oikonomia.

IX

All this is to say that our crisis is horizontal versus vertical in multiple ways. Insofar as we can say that the overall Global Crisis is the product or by-product of a successfully imposed vertical hubris of planetary dimension—war as natural, male domination as natural, slavery as natural, even (despite Aristotle's apparent distaste) chrematistics as natural—we can also say that the resolution to this crisis is the implementation of the transformative horizontal in every possible way. We can accurately say we have entered a transformative period, even if the accrued (and still accruing) momentum of the destructive vertical continues on its utopian blundering pathway of stupendous stupidity. All in all, our addiction to utopia is so embedded in us—consider the gigantic oil blowout in the Gulf of Mexico or the fracking in Oklahoma that causes earthquakes or the toxic tar sands extraction in Alberta—that we will continue to rationalize these toxic disasters as the unfortunate but necessary consequence of risks we are obliged to take in order to maintain our civilized style of life and consumerist standard of living. Our ethical and ecological horizon is that constricted by the narrative of civilized progress; and progress implies (whatever other baggage it may carry) an essentially aristocratic standard of living, a standard never to be abandoned or reduced, if at all possible.

So-called "conservatives" (i.e., those who conserve nothing except utopian conviction) may be the most densely packed repository of the vertical principle, while "liberals" (some of whom are becoming anxiously conservative in an etymological and ecological sense) remain largely addicted to a guilt-ridden affluence they realize is unsustainable, an affluence created and "sustained" by utopian verticality, but also an affluence with which they are too comfortable to seriously challenge, modify, or abandon. (The decrepitude of the Green Party is a mirror image of middle-class comfort.) Plus, what is or could be horizontally achievable in fairly short order—Medicare for all, low-speed mass transit in a public mode, massive demilitarization, solar panels on all municipal and most private buildings, real policies to promote and encourage the growth of small-scale farming and CSA gardening—is blocked, resisted, thwarted, or avoided not only because politicians remain on financial life-support feeding tubes connected to immortal corporate money, but also because the transformative horizontal has not only been crushed historically and surpassed culturally, it has also been demonized as metaphysically backward at best, and possibly even evil. If small-scale farming is "inefficient" and "backward," Medicare for all or public mass transit is, like socialism, a kind of political evil that links to communism and atheism. The urban vertical not only conquered the rural horizontal, it also poisoned the cultural and metaphysical wells of the cooperative impulse. *Civis* poisoned the ethical and intellectual wells of *pagus* and now sells bottled soda pop to bewildered rustics as their backyards get fracked and their faucets belch toxic chemicals. The victorious vertical has force fed its subjects the spiritual and cultural equivalents of genetically modified terminator seeds. Utopian kool-aid with "natural" flavors.

X

To repeat the three basic options: devastation; aristocratic restoration; eutopian resurrection. From my vantage point in the woods of northern Wisconsin, each of these may have its kick at the can. The weapons are in place to do us in. Wealth is sufficiently concentrated (with its requisite security guards and mercenary forces) to assume aristocratic control. But something is happening in the human soul that, for all our hesitations, contradictions and denials, is steadily congealing toward political, metaphysical, and spiritual transformation in a eutopian mode. If utopian civilization has undergone exponential growth in the last five hundred years, can we also say that eutopian folk consciousness has been engaged in its own hidden-in-plain-view exponential growth in a corresponding, spiritually transformative way?

Joachim of Fiore, a twelfth-century Italian monk, expounded the Three Ages of history, meshing Trinity with Old and New Testaments, pulling divinity down to Earth: the Age of the Father, based on monarchy, discipline, and law; the Age of the Son, love institutionalized in the church; an Age of the Holy Spirit, an age yet to come, an age based on consecrated anarchy or holy freedom.

Joachim didn't know about the precivilized agrarian village with its overarching divinity of the Mother. But now we do know. We can therefore expand Joachim's Three Ages to Four. Mother is restored to first position. However, to be psychologically and mythologically consistent, we are obliged to recompose the ages as Mother, Father, Son, and Daughter. We are entering the Daughter's Age. We are on its turbulent, transformative cusp—the women's movement, for all its confusions and contradictions, is its incoming wave—unless the righteous sons of the Almighty Father blow us all to hell, first.

Here, perhaps, neither horizontal nor vertical holds our attention so much as *spiral*: neither vertical progress into limitless infinity nor horizontal eternal recurrence in an endless circular loop. We are in process of arriving at a home in which we never fully knew how to live. Our homesickness is about to end—or at least it's about to reach a place of substantial spiritual, cultural, and psychomythological amelioration. Eutopia is struggling to be born. We all need to be responsible midwives and help birth this unexpected baby.

8

A Review of Maynard's Sunflower

In early November of 2008, a beautiful book arrived in the mail. With its lovely sunflower cover, *Adapting to the End of Oil: Toward an Earth-Centered Spirituality* is the work of my friend Maynard Kaufman. In the accompanying letter, Maynard asked if we could trade reviews. That is, he was offering to review my *Green Politics Is Eutopian*, published late in the spring of 2008, if I'd review his sunflower. The thought tickled and pleased me.

I had an impulse to pump my review as full of golden, glowing praise as possible, as golden as the petals on Maynard's sunflower cover. But I won't do that. That's not because I think the book a superficial effort. It's not superficial. It's both deep and complex. Precisely because it's such a serious effort at articulating a way out of the global crisis growing around us, it would be intellectually insulting to swap Maynard's review of my book (which I hope will be tough and thorough) for a colorful balloon of celebratory hot air.

Maynard's old enough to be my father. But, without asking permission or bothering to take out legal papers, I adopted him as my older brother, somewhere around 1980. Maynard and his wife Sally were then farming and gardening, just outside Bangor, Michigan. They lived in an old brick farmhouse with a woodburning cookstove in the kitchen. The place was rich with home-grown food and jugs of wine on racks, slowly fermenting. The place *smelled* as self-provisioning households have smelled for millennia. Maynard, with his stocky build, blue denim jacket, crooked cap, and short, thick beard, was the quintessential Jeffersonian farmer. There were dairy and beef cows, pigs, different kinds of poultry, the inevitable barn cats, huge gardens, an orchard, and a smokehouse. The School of Homesteading he and Sally had started in the early 1970s was still functioning, though—apparently—always a little inclined toward countercultural mood enhancement rather than practical skill learning. Oh! Those university hippies! (Horticulture is a diverse and complex science that satisfies many needs.)

But Maynard was—and is—a solid peasant. He'd grown up Mennonite, on a farm in South Dakota, husking corn by hand as the wagon, pulled by horses, creaked slowly down the already-picked rows, leathery leaves scraping on the underside of the wagon, rigid stalks snapping at the eveners. As a child, Maynard was immersed in a physical rural culture and agrarian way of life. He was and is an earthy man.

There are ways our backgrounds are quite similar, although thirty years—between, say, 1930 and 1960—were enough to give us a significantly different grounding in self-provisioning experience and homesteading skills. Maynard's grounding was deeper, more comprehensive and thorough—older in rural culture aptitudes and time. Mine was vitiated by electricity, tractor power, television, and the oozing consumerism of the 1950s. It's hard to overemphasize the magnitude of change in the countryside in the thirty years between 1930 and 1960, how self-provisioning was shrinking as commercialization was expanding.

Maynard, I think, was, in contrast to me, bolder and more self-confident. From South Dakota Mennonite peasant, he went on to a Ph.D. from the University of Chicago, in the fields of religion and literature. He loved James Joyce and the wonderfully literate Out There Freudian explications of history and culture coming through the magical pen of Norman O. Brown. Maynard was and is a poetic peasant intellectual, a designation I've also used for myself when convenient or when simply grabbing the opportunity to be provocative. Therein is the root of our brotherhood. We are kindred agrarian souls. Peasant brothers.

However, my intellectual cupboard is stocked with stuff from the bookshelves of thrift stores and library discard sales. I never made it to an undergraduate degree. I've been a farm and ranch worker but never a farmer or a rancher. I am, in some ways, more meek and retiring than Maynard. So there are odd and somewhat paradoxical contrasts between us. He's a sturdy peasant boy from the age of draft horses and kerosene lamps who has an erudite Ph.D. from one of the more prestigious universities in the country, while I have been withdrawn almost to the point of antisocial pathology—no degree, no career, no accomplishment, bursting out in laughter when asked for a Curriculum Vitae. I know how to split kindling, dig a well, and build a rock wall. But such things are unfit for a resume in the modern world.

While Maynard thrusts forward his energy analysis—the "end of oil" will generate a huge increase in localized gardening and farming—I think it fair to say we both yearn for a reconstruction of rural culture, quite aside from the necessity imposed by climate change constrictions. We want a countryside so economically vital—in an ecological way—that it will be capable of creating and sustaining a rich and vibrant culture. The kind of rural culture I have in mind would have elements of money economy in it (small commercial farms, gardens, orchards, CSAs, etc), but it would be heavily shaped—even primarily shaped—by practices of self-provisioning, sufficiency, and barter. Rural culture's taproot—Aristotle's "oikonomia"—is sufficiency and self-provisioning at both the household and community levels. There's a place for the sale of "surplus," but "surplus" as economic ideology is culturally ruinous.

I suggest the agrarian population should be, at minimum, twenty percent. Such a thought is close to hilarious in the present period, for we've become accustomed to an almost total absence of indigenous culture in the countryside. Such an absence is simply normal at this point in time. Yet this normality is so ecologically and historically abnormal its uniqueness in evolutionary time would be too tiny to chart or graph. This lack of the indigenous, the absence of rural coherence and cultural vitality, is a historical anomaly the "end of oil" will certainly reverse, although even serious environmental thinkers seldom regard the revitalization of rural culture as an issue worthy of attention or a cultural construct crucial to any Green economy. Rural culture is considered a sort of historical, geographical, or psychological prison from which escape is to be cheered and celebrated. Of course the countryside as "wilderness" has metaphysical charm, the place for immersion into pure Nature with a capital N. (So long as the mosquitoes and deer ticks aren't too bad.) But the agrarian countryside, as Aldo Leopold quipped, is only the space between cities on which crops grow. Maynard's effort to articulate an "Earth-Centered Spirituality" must therefore be seen in the context of his largely preindustrial farm background and his desire for a far richer rural culture to live in, including what may develop as its spiritual convictions and religious rituals. For all his High Culture accomplishments and tastes, Maynard is a committed peasant, fully comfortable with his rural identity, a man of *pagus* who's found some useful *civis* particulars to bring into the emerging future of rural culture.

Yet I sense a major difference between Maynard's book and mine has to do with how we have or have not remained psychologically rooted in various aspects of our respective peasant upbringings. Maynard, being bolder, just broke certain constraints and went on to new discoveries and convictions with a tough-mindedness I lacked. I too broke constraints—by remaining a perpetual economic failure, by the pain and suffering of broken marriages, by a stubborn refusal to enter the middle class—but I don't think I abandoned some things from my religious upbringing in ways Maynard did.

I'm groping here, but maybe Maynard was bold enough, confident enough, to just say no to certain religious assertions. On the other hand, I don't think I said no so much as I said I don't know. I have tended to live with a lot of doubt and uncertainty, and I've found, over time, there are riches in that cloudy darkness. The Cloud of Unknowing is not all gloom and doom, not just cold dampness and dreary depression.

Over the past thirty years, we've each flirted with Green politics. (I once ran for the Wisconsin Assembly as a Green, getting the usual three percent of the vote. I was, in truth, a dreadful candidate, much too introverted for that sort of public exposure.) I told Maynard that Greens need to embrace and incorporate socialism into their policy platform. Maynard said socialism is freighted by so much bad baggage it would be better not to use the word at all. (Therefore I invoke R. H. Tawney's *The Acquisitive Society*, where Tawney begins to lay down guidelines for determining the boundary between small-scale private property and the magnitude and qualitative features of those economic entities necessarily belonging under public jurisdiction; he explains how these two formulations—small-scale private or cooperative ownership, large-scale public ownership—reinforce each other's health and integrity. This is a view I find compelling.) Although I'm not intending to delve very deeply into the socialism question—maybe we'll get to it later, anyway—I am intending to use "socialism" as a bogie word to introduce another bogie word that may connote even greater wickedness and evil. That other word is "pagan."

But first let's attend to Maynard's use of the word "demonic."

In *Adapting to the End of Oil*, there is a cluster of pages (42 through 46) where the subject of the demonic is raised and explored. This demonic cluster immediately follows a section on Christopher Marlowe's Faust, that is, Faust the literary character who sold his soul to the Devil in exchange for power over nature. Or, as Maynard says, "The Faust legend very explicitly introduces a demonic dimension into Western civilization; it diminishes the possibility of contentment or satisfaction."[1]

In the following pages, Maynard moves quickly to "Demonic Powers and Money," that is, to corporations. "Because they embody the denial of limits most completely and arrogate absolute power to themselves," he says, "I have come to think of these multi-national corporations as demonic structures."[2] Later he says, "Because such corporate greed is without limits it is inherently demonic and its evil effects are seen in its social irresponsibility."[3]

However, if we asked your average Jane or John to name the two most dreadful demons in American culture, I suspect the winners (perhaps I should say the losers) would be paganism and socialism—although terrorism would now give socialism and paganism a run for their money, and maybe even win the race. It's hard, however, to think of two words carrying more negative freight historically than those two, pagan even more than socialism. What's so interesting about the demonization of paganism and socialism is how they imply *curbs* on limitlessness, *curbs* on maximized individualism. So when Maynard (invoking Marlowe, Goethe, Paul Tillich, Norman O. Brown, and others) pins the demonic tail on *corporations*, we are bewildered, stunned, and giddy. How in the world can clean, muscular, extroverted, responsible, productive entities—so human as to be designated legal persons and given both free speech and unlimited campaign money rights by the U.S. Supreme Court—possibly be demonic? Aren't demons sneaky little bastards, afraid of the light, devious, cunning, weak and subversive, exuding exactly that sort of sickly pseudospirituality implied by "pagan" and the whining, bleeding-heart pseudopolitics projected by "socialist"? Or are these demonic legal "persons" in the process of putting on metaphysical weight and building ontological muscle? Will they come out of the political gym dressed in the Ayn Rand musculature of resurrected aristocracy?

Maynard lists several understandings or definitions of demonic power. First, there's the denial of limits. Second, these limit-denying structures could render Earth

---

1. Kaufman, *Adapting*, 41.

2. Kaufman, *Adapting*, 43.

3. Kaufman, *Adapting*, 44.

unfit for human habitation. Third, the demonic keeps us in a "demonic trance" so we won't object to the exercise of demonic power. "Many of us are 'demon-possessed' in this sense," says Maynard.[4] Such language seriously ups the ante as to the deeper meaning, for instance, of climate change denial and the degree to which denial is induced in the general public by means of "demonic" propaganda. (This may be what Amitai Etzioni meant by "an account of the forces that got us into our predicament.")

But this may be too weird for most people. First we are, to some extent, in cultural and psychological recovery from the demonization of paganism and socialism, and now we are to see *corporations* as demonic and *ourselves* as "demon-possessed"? But Maynard, with his wonderful scholarship, invokes a lot of hefty personages to back his assertions. Remember, please, that it's *limitlessness* that constitutes the demonic, the trading of soul (or intimacy or community or ecological integrity) for power over nature, money over love—chrematistics, we might say, over oikonomia, fracking over Freud.

But I get a little impatient with Maynard's fuzziness in locating this limitlessness in history. Well, he clearly sees (page 46 onward) the industrial revolution as a major magnification of limitlessness. He also says that empire "may have been embryonic in America from the outset."[5] If so, that empire embryo must have come from Europe. Did Europe invent it? Isn't "Europe" the progeny of Christendom and the Roman Empire? How far back in time and place shall we go in our pursuit of empire limitlessness? If we can only speculate about its evolutionary origination, we can clearly see its institutional consolidation in theft-and-war civilization. Maynard alludes to a "traditional view of Western Civilization which has promoted the conquest and domination of nature as a hostile power."[6] How about Egypt and Babylon? How about civilization altogether?

Global Crisis occurs right along with the globalization of industrial civilization. Global Crisis is globalization's shadow, its collective externality. What's being globalized—or has been, let's say, since the fifteenth century—is civilization itself, primarily its economically aggressive and predatory Western mode. Globalization explicitly has meant the breaking of limits: the civilizing of the world has been achieved by armed force, by conquest, and by economic aggressiveness. So, using Maynard's terminology, I'd say civilization's globalization is demonic. Civilization, after all, came into being with the violent and systematic expropriation of the precivilized agrarian village, roughly five thousand years ago, with institutionalized slavery and institutionalized militarism, with what Arnold Toynbee calls diseases of Class and War and Lewis Mumford calls traumatic institutions. *Civilization introduced and institutionalized limitlessness,* and it did so by means of organized violence and systemic coercion, which means that violence and coercion are the means and instruments of demonic limitlessness, even

4. Kaufman, *Adapting,* 46.

5. Kaufman, *Adapting,* 49.

6. Kaufman, *Adapting,* 50.

as we civilized people have been—and continue to be—beneficiaries of the forces that got us into our predicament. It's our comfort level, our satisfaction as beneficiaries, that constitutes our being "demon-possessed."

So the crisis we are in is the crisis of Civilization in demonic, planetary dimension. Here is where Maynard's use of "demon-possessed" has major, uncomfortable bite. It's one thing to say corporations are demonic—lots of conventional leftists (and even some serious Tea Party rightists) can more or less go with that, especially if the term is used figuratively. But what happens to our cultural equilibrium when it's asserted that *civilization* is demonic, when one of our two major identity constructs (the other is "God") begins to deconstruct both internally and externally? Maynard says "the way out of the grasp of Empire will not be easy."[7] But what if the grip we need to get out of is not merely empire (in the current American sense) but demonic civilization in its fuller historic magnitude, including our very own "demonic trance"? What sort of bubbly vertigo does *that* create in us? How fully caught in civilization's demonic trance are we who think ourselves so intellectually liberated? How capable or willing are we to imagine an ecological future—an ecological economy—free of civilization's traumas, diseases, and demons? Or is this where we drool in our shoes and pee in our pants? Are we "demon-possessed" in proportion to our lack of stewardship understanding and servanthood commitment? Is the doctrine of Original Sin one of the ways by which we are "demon-possessed"—that is, rendered limp and helpless in the face of catastrophes we are incapable of addressing, passive and dazed, in an ideological trance precisely because our most venerable teaching insists we are not only powerless to resist but indulging in willful sin if we even try to resist?

II

Maynard divides his *Adapting* into two parts. I wrote the first section of this review after reading the first half of his book. I've now read the second part—"Religion and Spirituality after Oil"—and it's time to finish the (hatchet?) job. (I split kindling with a hatchet; I try not to bash my fingers or my friends.)

Some of the energy facts Maynard marshals are simply stunning. Did we realize that "one gallon of gasoline produces work equivalent to 97 manpower hours, or one man working eight hours a day, five days a week for about 2.5 weeks"?[8] Or that, in the industrial mode of farming, "roughly 11 calories of energy are invested to produce 1 calorie of food"?[9] Or that the U.S., with five percent of the world's population, generates thirty-three percent of its carbon dioxide?[10] Or that "the top 1 percent

7. Kaufman, *Adapting*, 51.

8. Kaufman, *Adapting*, 58.

9. Kaufman, *Adapting*, 66.

10. Kaufman, *Adapting*, 45.

has twice the income as the bottom 100 million Americans"?[11] In other words, the industrial revolution, with its fossil fuel base, has removed us from basic labor and earthy nature, as well as from the ancient culture of folk self-provisioning; agriculture is absurdly industrialized and unsustainably overenergized; we are the world's greatest greenhouse gas polluter; and, in the context of our "democratic" braggadocio, the actual gap between the super-rich and merely affluent Empire proles has reached a divergence equal to, if not greater than, the wealth chasm between aristocrat and peasant in preindustrial times. What a litany of "democratic" successes!

Maynard, of course, opens his book by saying the "bonanza of cheap energy never happened before and will very likely never happen again."[12] I accept this as true, although none of us knows whether other energy forms might be (perhaps even ecologically) harnessed in the future. What we can see is that several things occurred more or less simultaneously in, say, the last 250 years: the increasingly complex exploitation of fossil fuels, starting with the burning of coal to power steam engines to lift unwanted water out of English mines; the industrial revolution itself as steam use rapidly expanded to power the new factories; the curtailment of monarchies with their explicit hereditary aristocracies; eruptions of revolution; the globalization of Western institutions, both economic and religious, in the wake of military excursions and commercial invasions; exploding world population (from 1 billion in 1800 to well over 7 billion at present); the undermining of cultures based on subsistence and self-provisioning; the "development" of Western economic entities virtually everywhere in the world, all made hugely more powerful and penetrating by technologies of electrical speed.

This list is far from complete or exhaustive. Maynard does a good job of putting the finger on Christianity as the suppressor of indigenous European religious traditions—the suppression of the European "pagan," in broad strokes—resulting in a cultural demographic of Christian imperialism, thus setting the stage for the unhesitating suppression of "pagan" cultures by the globalization of European imperialism from 1492 onward. What Maynard doesn't ask (or answer) is: Where did Christianity get such power? The answer, of course, is that the power came with Christianity's adoption by the Roman Empire, initially as that empire's state religion. This made "permanent" Christianity's alignment with the state. Nor should it pass unnoticed that the Roman Empire was primarily responsible for the legal murder of Jesus, in principle the "founder" of Christianity. Nor should it pass unnoticed that Rome was the current top civilizational power in the world, at least in the Western world, a power that had passed through several previous demonic empire incarnations, all the way back to the dawn or founding of civilization as an act of aristocratic armed robbery from an agrarian village community descended primarily from the gardening diligence and horticultural expertise of early women gatherers. *Civis* (city/civilization) versus *pagus*

11. Kaufman, *Adapting*, 48.

12. Kaufman, *Adapting*, 9.

(country district or country dweller) does *not* begin with the consolidation of Christian doctrine but with suppression of the village into a systematically expropriated peasantry at the dawn of civilization. If we're going to pin tails on donkeys, let's get the right critters in the barn.

To say, as Maynard does, that there is an antiecological predisposition in the Judeo-Christian tradition, requires us to recognize that the Judeo-Christian tradition emerged in a world dominated by harsh empire, by male-dominated aristocracy, and by a conception of the otherworldly divine as projected through monarchy—God as King of kings. But not only God the King. The imperial king was himself considered divine; peasants and slaves were to serve the king's glory. That Christianity took on the monarchical model is true; that official post-Constantinian Christianity suppressed paganism is also true. But the model on which monarchical suppression operates goes back to the rise of kingship, that is, to the bloody origins and metaphysical rationalizations within civilization. Kingship was by virtue of its very limitlessness the embodiment of the demonic.

So the big dog in this fight is not Christianity (which has coercive power only insofar as it uses, relies on, or hides behind Caesar's sword) but the civilizational structures predating all Abrahamic religions. Now one can say that the Abrahamic religions are corrupted as spiritual vessels by their male presumption, empire machinations, and transcendent male projections of God; they have been corrupted by demonic, civilizational, superego infections. (I do not, however, include Jesus in this accusation. He, after all, was brutally put to death by civilized Powers and Principalities.)

But I don't think Maynard adequately frames his overall argument in behalf of the pagan, paganism, or neopaganism. (The opposite of "pagan"—*pagus*—isn't "Christian" but—*civis*—"civilization.") Second, there is a great deal not said in Maynard's book about whether, or to what extent, Jesus is or is not responsible for Christian imperialism. What, for instance, did Jesus intend by his "kingdom of God" proclamation? That proclamation must have been sufficiently agitating and disturbing to get him into serious trouble, for the result was his hasty execution. Third, Maynard is aware of the problems associated with myth, but he doesn't really aid in solving those problems when he says, "A more serious charge [against *Adapting to the End of Oil*] could be that this earth religion represents a regression to mythical thinking. In earlier parts of this book we worried about the confusion of myth and science in partisans of the religious right, and now I am proposing a worldview that had been embodied in myth in the hope that it would help us adapt to the end of cheap oil."[13] But Maynard's enough of an Enlightenment modern (as I am) to take factual science seriously. Spirituality can no longer pretend to live in a world above and beyond rationality. Myth is not exempt from the discoveries of scholarship. But neither is "mythical thinking" necessarily a "regression." Myth is an indispensable aspect of human culture. We need a mythic story explicating our earthly need for servanthood and stewardship.

13. Kaufman, *Adapting*, 125.

I think it perfectly safe to say that factual science is what demolished the image of God with which we were raised, and that the notion of God clung to by the contemporary religious Right depends on the select ignoring if not the suppression of science. Well, maybe not so much its suppression (though that too may occur) as the denial of its truthfulness or relevance when its warnings, as with climate change, cause ideological comfort distress. As Maynard says on page 146, the vision of the religious Right is blinkered by denial; its theocratic, mythic vision is at odds with both science and democracy. Of course the Right's theocratic, mythic vision is a direct descendent of imagining the divine through the lens of civilizational empire: God as King. For that very reason, theocracy is demonic; it is party to limitlessness.

Metaphorically speaking, I think it legitimate to speak (as Maynard does) of the pagan as a "recessive gene": "All these aspects of earth religion are recessive genes in our cultural organism, and they had been repressed by the dominant genes, but we are now seeing the return of the repressed."[14] But if *pagus* is the recessive gene, *civis* is the dominant gene, even if it is, ultimately, a terminator gene. (I suppose that makes civilization the template for GMOs, demonic mutants.). Perhaps Maynard moves from metaphor to myth when he talks, on pages 130 through 132, about "the earth as a living being" or "Gaia as a personification of the earth" or "the earth as the body of the Goddess." If science has wrecked our image of God as King—a transcendent and infinite Being outside of nature, beyond Earth, the essence of limitlessness—what makes us so eager to embrace Gaia as Earth Goddess? Is this psychomythological relief from having been freed from coerced allegiance to an absent, harsh Almighty Father? So now we rush into Mama's warm embrace for some long overdue cosmic comfort? I admit to such tugs and inclinations myself. But something in me holds back from this gendered either/or.

There are at least two aspects to my hesitation. First, thirty-some years ago, meditating on Joachim of Fiore's Three Ages (Father, Son, and Holy Spirit)—Maynard references Joachim on page 117 of his sunflower—I realized not only that Joachim hadn't been aware of an earlier age, the horticultural/agrarian village age, but that this earlier age can and should be called the Age of the Mother. But by putting Mother in front of Father, it was semantically and psychologically necessary to put Daughter after Son. This represents something that's neither the linear history Maynard says we need to get away from nor the cyclical ("eternal recurrence") to which he is proposing a return. If the linear is scientistic myth, the cyclical may be spiritually retrogressive. (Maynard tells us that "This is the ultimate expression of a traditional society: a person becomes real by ceasing to be himself or herself and becomes real by repeating the gestures of another, preferably divine, being." Or, as he also says, "reality is achieved . . . by imitating or repeating a divine archetype."[15]) But Mother-Father-Son-Daughter is neither linear nor cyclic. The key understanding here, or the doorway to this understanding, is

14. Kaufman, *Adapting*, 15.
15. Kaufman, *Adapting*, 124.

to recognize Christian Trinity as unfinished mythic construction, incomplete mythic depiction. Trinity is neither factually true nor factually false. The construct is mythic, but incomplete and unfinished. Perhaps the enlarged construct—Mother, Father, Son, Daughter—resembles a spiral. As spiral, it offers something creative and new without succumbing either to the tyranny of limitless linear Progress or to the endless circular repetitiveness of Divine Archetype.

We are in process of going beyond a certain layer or level of mere mimetic behavior. We will become real, not by ceasing to be a self, nor by repeating another's gestures, but by deepening our interior lives. The next step is, in fact, a *deepening* of self, intellectual strength integrating with spiritual humility.[16] The Age of the Daughter necessitates transformation of human behavior and character in ways that create—not a weaker—but a stronger self. The Daughter's age requires a transformative deepening of our everyday lives in creation.

---

16. Paul Tillich (on pages 130-31 in *The Protestant Era*) says "Humanism has created the ideal of a personality in which, on the basis of a definite individuality, all potentialities of man's spiritual being are actualized as much as possible" and "this ideal controls modern ethics, culture, and education." But, he says, the ideal "has also developed dangerous consequences, not by accident but by its very nature. The humanistic ideal of personality tends to cut the individual off from his existential roots, from the social group, its traditions and symbols" resulting in a lack of "spiritual center." Tillich goes on with a critique that speaks to our present situation with astonishing relevance, almost as if he anticipated the emergence of political characters like Donald Trump:

"The most disintegrating consequence of the victory of the humanistic ideal of personality is the fact that the latter can be appropriated only by a social class that has the external prerequisites for such an abstract universalism. And even within the class that is able to receive and to mediate this humanistic education, only a small elite use it for a development of their personalities, while the majority adopts the ideal only as a condition for their belonging to the ruling class and not for the sake of giving form to their personalities. But even worse is the consequence of the humanistic 'ideal of personality' for the large masses of people. They participate in it only by receiving unconnected pieces of the humanistic culture through the all-powerful means of public communication and as a matter of detached interest or subjective thrill. Even this kind of adult indoctrination is not without some value. It liberates people from all kinds of narrow provincialism and opens world horizons. But, on the other hand, it tends to destroy the sources of concrete experiences and individual formations. It produces a general level of normality and mediocrity above which even more intelligent and creative people rise only with great difficulty. This situation is the opposite of what the humanistic ideal of personality intended. And out of this situation the contemporary reaction against not only the ideal but also the idea of personality has grown, namely, the passionate desire for a return to the primitive level. But now it appears in naturalistic terms as the Fascist ideal of a new tribal existence. The rise of the personality above the community is followed by a fall of the personality below the community."

I attempted to speak to this situation in my Introduction to the collected essays on the Wisconsin "uprising" (*A Whole Which Is Greater: Why the Wisconsin "Uprising" Failed*), edited by David Kast and myself. My reference then was to Arno Mayer's essay (in *Small Comforts for Hard Times: Humanists on Public Policy*) in which Mayer's subject was "The Lower Middle Class as Historical Problem," a penetrating but flawed exposition of the relationship between the lower middle class and the "upper establishment." That is, the current "Tea Party" represents both Mayer's lower middle class and Tillich's "large masses."

Resolution of this dangerous and even explosive problem lies in enlarging Trinity to Mandala, with a corresponding reformulation of politics and economics in a mode of Green socialism. It's this that will facilitate the deepening of everyone's interior life.

That's one aspect of my hesitation in regard to Maynard's "divine archetype." The other is the oppositional terms (myth versus truth) Gil Bailie sets up in his *Violence Unveiled*, a book built around the anthropological work on "sacred violence" of René Girard. Bailie says "The root of the Greek word for myth, *muthos*, is *mu*, which means 'to close' or 'keep secret.' *Muo* means to close one's eyes or mouth, to mute the voice, or to remain mute. Myth remembers discretely and selectively."[17] Bailie goes on to say: "In the New Testament, *mythos* is juxtaposed both to *Logos*—the revelation of that about which myth refuses to speak—and to *aletheia*—the Greek word for truth. *Aletheia* comes from the root *letho*, which is the verb 'to forget.' The prefix *a* is the negative. The literal meaning, then, of the Greek word for truth, *alethia*, is 'to stop forgetting.' It is etymologically the opposite of myth."[18] Bailie also says "The gospel *truth* gradually makes it impossible for us to keep forgetting what myth exists to help us forget. It thereby sets up a struggle between the impulse to sacralize, justify, or romanticize the violence that generates and regenerates conventional culture and the impulse to reveal that violence and strip away its mythic justifications. Fundamentally, human history is a struggle between myth and gospel."[19] (Here I would say that human history is not an either/or struggle between *mythos* and *logos* but an evolving dialectical wrestle between the two.) And if End Times is the anticipated outcome of Christian *mythos*, perhaps we will come to realize—as the mythological blindfold drops from our eyes—that *apokalypsis* means liberating revelation and not predestined doom. But we can get some distance from Bailie's religious convictions by talking about a struggle between *mythos* and *logos*, rather than myth and gospel—a distance that provides a little freedom from sectarian insinuation, even as we need to be careful not to approach myth (as Bailie seems to) with utter negativity.

In his Introduction to *Violence Unveiled*, Bailie says that René Girard "uncovered the role violence plays in archaic religion and the role these religious systems play in human culture"; that "Primitive religion is the institution that remembers the reviving violence mythologically and ritually reenacts its spellbinding climax"; that "cultures have forever commemorated some form of sacred violence at their origins and considered it a sacred duty to reenact it in times of crisis"; that "cultures rely on scapegoating violence"; that "this ancient recipe for generating social solidarity has ceased to have its once reliable effects"; and that sacred violence has been "gradually shorn of its religious mystifications, and, as a result, its ability to promote cultural order has waned."[20] I believe we need to take this critique very seriously, but in a way that includes the Abrahamic religions and civilization among the specimens under observation. We also need to be aware of how huge a role violence plays in this critique of myth; but not all myth is a cloak for hiding or glorifying violence.

17. Bailie, *Violence*, 33.
18. Bailie, *Violence*, 33.
19. Bailie, *Violence*, 34.
20. Bailie, *Violence*, 6-7.

Maynard doesn't advocate any role for violence in his explication of paganism or eternal recurrence. Well, I would be shocked if he did, given his pacifist or near-pacifist Mennonite upbringing. But Bailie's point is that "sacred violence" is integral to cultural identity: "Primitive religion grants one form of violence a moral monopoly, endowing it with enough power and prestige to preempt other forms of violence and restore order. The famous distinction between 'sacred' and 'profane' is born as the culture glorifies the decisive violence (sacred) that brought an episode of chaotic violence (profane) to an end and made warriors into worshipers."[21] It certainly is the case that violence stands at the root of civilization, and that civilization, in the form of state power, claims a moral monopoly on violence. It's at the heart of Arnold Toynbee's Class and War and Lewis Mumford's traumatic institutions. We can say that violence has been structurally crucial for both the founding and the maintenance of civilization. It's the energy it relies on. Violence or its threatened use is the force that sustains and perpetuates civilization with its structural inequalities and ecological brutalities. (Why else is there such extraordinary allocation of resources to the military?)

One can say the "end of oil" will constrict all this; the capacity of civilization to control and overwhelm will be radically reduced. But it's wishful thinking to imagine, short of spiritual and cultural transformation, there'll be no restoration of explicit aristocracy, for aristocracy has extensive experience and institutional expertise in living on expropriated labor and stolen production. Aristocracy has had thousands of years of such experience. Its expertise in domination cannot be denied. We are living in an alienating civility in which democracy (flexible folk self-governance) is just starting to wake up from its induced somnolence, its multimillennial impoundment by aristocratic expertise. Corporate capitalism is its present mode. Aristocracy's explicit reinstitution would also mean restoration of overt predemocratic class violence, even as the bulk of the population could revert to archaic rituals of eternal recurrence. And insofar as one believes in E. F. Schumacher's "small is beautiful" or Leopold Kohr's size-reducing prescriptions for the breaking down of nations (Lewis Mumford in *The Pentagon of Power* says "From the standpoint of human survival, to say nothing of further development, a flint arrowhead is preferable to a hydrogen bomb"[22]), smallness of scale could develop simultaneously with explicit aristocratic restoration. Smallness of scale and aristocratic rule are by no means mutually exclusive. They've known each other for thousands of years. The ecological advantage of such restoration, of course, would be that "democratic" hyperconsumption would be curtailed, providing nature room to recover some degree of ecological health, even if a high level of consumption persisted at the restricted level of aristocratic wealth and power. One could even make the case that "paganism," in its apparent contentment with eternal recurrence and frugal, earthy lifestyles, might serve as an enabler for aristocratic privilege, with peasants

21. Bailie, *Violence*, 6.
22. Mumford, *Pentagon*, 203.

afraid to be self-governing and more or less content with the grumbling resentments of ongoing victimhood.

Bailie says that at the heart of the Christian faith, buried as it may be beneath multiple layers of accrued obfuscation and blithe contradiction, is the stark and brutal murder of an ethically innocent man, killed because his charismatic vision for an ecologically sustainable and culturally wholesome society threatened the foundations of exclusive privilege. But Bailie also says that "By mystifying human violence and attributing it to the gods, archaic religion endowed a certain form of physical might—usually the most powerful form—with metaphysical significance. As long as the myths that mythologized certain human violence remained in effect, this sacralized violence was able to ward off other violence or crush it with religious conviction when it arose. As the myths that divinized the violence were weakened, the difference between order-destroying and order-restoring violence likewise began to break down."[23] And what is the chief enactor of this divinized violence if not civilization? Or, in more recent history, *Christian* civilization, Christendom in full global conquest.

In fact, it is the incapacity of what Bailie (on page 60) calls the "primitive sacred," its loss of mystifying power, that constitutes one dimension of our modern predicament. Violence no longer works as it once did. The Western world in particular is divided between those who cling to what we might call restorative violence, with End Times Christians one of the most influential blocs of such advocates, at least in this country, and those who, like the Network of Spiritual Progressives, advocate for global security based on systemic sharing and compassionate stewardship. End Times Christians, if they could achieve success, would usher in either total devastation or harsh theocracy. Spiritual progressives, if they were to have the ethical clarity and electoral strength to fully follow through on their vision, would usher in the end of civilization as we know it—the end of "sacred" or righteous violence, the end of violence-enforced inequality, the end of ecological plunder, and the dethronement of an Elsewhere God. ("Progressives" are trying to build the kingdom of God that "conservatives" say can't be built because of Original Sin. And it's certainly not incidental that "conservatives" are also the fiercest advocates for the rigorous use of "sacred" violence.) Mumford, in his *Pentagon*, talks about the significance for cultural wholesomeness by "locating the 'organizer' within the cosmic system from the 'beginning' and attributing design, not to any original plan, but to the increasing tendency of organized processes and structures to combine with the selective aid of organisms into more purposeful emergent wholes."[24] So we are talking here about two incompatible spiritualities: one that trusts and wants to trust indwelling Spirit; the other that fears indwelling Spirit, thinking it pagan and a lure of the Devil. That is, the "divinities" of these incompatible spiritualities are at political loggerheads.

23. Bailie, *Violence*, 7.
24. Mumford, *Pentagon*, 87.

A fuller and more complete democratization of our culture, a democratization embracing ecological limitation and "resource" frugality, not only implies a restored small-scale, both regional and local; it also requires democratic ownership and control of the large-scale (railroads, for instance), all infrastructure necessary to modern social life but too big to be left in private (i.e., nascent aristocratic) hands. Yet the concept of a restored "paganism," in my estimation, is not sufficiently comprehensive to encompass the necessary transformation. If that's the best we can do—well, from an ecological perspective, it might be a reprieve from complete global devastation. But "paganism's" failure to embrace and incorporate socialism reveals its intellectual shortcomings, a tendency toward spiritual quietism, and perhaps its unacknowledged attachment to two kingdom Manicheanism.[25] We need *comprehensive* transformation of the *entire* commonwealth, and that means integration of *pagus* and *civis*. If democracy is one of those tendencies of organized processes and structures combining into more purposeful wholes, then we can also say that democracy has assertive (but unfulfilled) spiritual energies at its core. These energies are globally inclusive. They are equalitarian. And what finer spiritual insight is there than recognizing servanthood and stewardship as the ethical and ecological engines within earthly democratic purpose? We evolutionary creatures simply must become ecologically self-governing. Aristocracy is itself an original sin, but the religious doctrine of Original Sin serves to protect aristocracy from democratic contamination.

Perhaps it's true that no society will ever be totally free from violence or coercion. Collective will—speaking democratically—almost always overrides smaller concentrations of political will. (Ethical police power will always be a reserve necessity.) But we are at an ethical threshold with Global Crisis. I yearn, as Maynard does, for a vigorous and vital rural culture of economic stability and ecological reverence. Democracy has not failed. Or, rather, it has failed to the extent that it has been embedded in and perverted by civilized mythology, with misconceptions of aristocratic prerogative and upper-class impulse as being normative for all. (Every man a king, every home a castle; every human a royal sovereign, every home an aristocratic palace. This is the divine right of kings "democratized.") We need to move from utopian "democracy" to *eutopian* democracy, from castle doctrine to village consensus. What democracy needs is a quantum leap into spiritual maturity, into radical servanthood and radical stewardship, into learning what "sustainability" actually means and looks like.

---

25. See Margot Adler's interview with Sharon Devlin in which (page 147) Devlin calls herself a "spiritual socialist" in contrast to most so-called "pagans" who apparently are stubbornly apolitical ("Interview with a Modern Witch," pages 136 through 152, in *Drawing Down the Moon*). Although Adler correctly describes the etymology of "pagan" on page 9 of her opening chapter, the "paganism" portrayed in *Drawing Down the Moon* seems to be largely seat-of-the-pants retrogression, the product of severe alienation. I don't—except for the delightfully sharp tongue of Sharon Devlin—find this sort of "paganism" my cup of tea. What's needed is integration of the best aspects of *pagus* and *civis* simultaneously with the enlargement of Trinity into Mandala. This would also resolve the "recessive gene" problem.

Technical Progress and Eternal Recurrence will find their places in the satisfactions and contentments of the Daughter's age. But all this is connected to and dependent on a more deeply realized self, a self—along with lots of other selves—who have gone through an *apokalypsis* of civilizational and religious transformation.

My main criticism of Maynard's analysis is that he attributes the suppression of *pagus* to Christianity rather than, more fundamentally, to *civis*. This analytical flaw causes deflection from deeper insight into civilization's traumatic institutions. Recognition that cultural transformation requires the comprehensive healing of *civilization's* diseases is therefore muted. Maynard can thereby deal lightly with democracy and be dismissive of socialism. But democracy is the political expression of evolutionary folk spirituality working its way to global realization. Ecological socialism is part of this "recessive gene" realization, the "return of the repressed" with a far fuller and more comprehensive understanding of history. Commonwealth is not just about the countryside. Commonwealth is how we regain our folk heritage of cultural evolution: society as self-regulating eutopian organism of spiritual selves fully alive on Earth, not a civilized organization of indoctrinated utopian personnel waiting for an elsewhere immortality.

III

Let's wrap up this sunflower pruning. The core teachings of Jesus and the core teachings of Gotama (the Buddha) are too profound and too painfully arrived at to be neglected in favor of either Perpetual Progress or Eternal Recurrence. If those teachings are among the most basic of human spiritual understandings, it's time they were brought into political, economic, and social reality; the ethics of the spiritual need to be integrated into "secular" realities. We can no longer tolerate the righteous amorality of civilizational self-justification, for its globalization could result in universal devastation or restoration of explicit aristocracy. Realization of the Age of the Daughter is exactly what's needed. Although the Daughter's age would see the lifting of the demonic foot of *civis* from the eternally recurring neck of *pagus*, I don't believe "eternal recurrence" is either the fullest or best summation of the Daughter's vitality. As long as Earth orbits the sun, the seasons of the year will continue to provide perpetual eternal recurrence, just as the daily spinning of Earth on its axis gives an endless succession of sunrises and sunsets. And, of course, there's the moon with its faithful bright face and dark butt providing monthly regularity. There's no danger of eternal recurrence disappearing any time soon. That's not an issue. Eternal recurrence has not gone away. In fact, eternal recurrence has strong linkages to the Mother's era, to the feminine horticultural village, to the seasons and rhythms of life on Earth. A lot of Mother ambience will reappear as Daughter draws our attention again to nature, as our thoughts, inclinations, and earthy behavior bring *pagus* back to life.

Jesus was a peasant. As a man from the countryside, he rose from the *pagus* and his sayings, anecdotes, and parables contain powerful *pagus* sensibility. But I believe Jesus was after something that was neither *civis* nor *pagus* in their archetypal distortions. The "kingdom of God" proclamation can be boiled down (no doubt a reductionism) to two ethical prescriptions: radical servanthood and radical stewardship. To give this conception modern political designation, it could be called libertarian ecological democratic socialism—a rich blend of the ecological resettlement of the countryside, with small, clean towns and cities, economic socialism in that manner clarified by Lawrence Goodwyn and R. H. Tawney, renewable energy, mass transit, both a floor under and a ceiling over personal wealth, universal health care, sailing ships, bicycles, horses and buggies. Jesus envisioned an ecological "kingdom of God" on Earth, and we are now in a situation where that realization, that possibility, is the only viable political path forward. The spiritual has become political. Its alternative is simply unlivable.

To some extent I have skirted the question of the divine. Is Earth a living being? If Gaia is *pagus*, does *civis* think itself god? Is Gaia Earth Goddess or Daughter? Is Spirit's relationship to Nature analogous to what our consciousness is to our bodies? Are our individual lives drops in Spirit's ocean? If we've moved beyond theism, are we now pantheists or panentheists? It seems we're all pretty limited when it comes to spiritual wisdom or spiritual discernment, and we shouldn't pretend otherwise.

Nevertheless, for all our rational incapacity to grasp or pin down the "divine," there *is* an ethical door available to us. It has matching, swinging sides. One side swings in for servanthood. The other swings out for stewardship. These doors lead to a complex path of self-emptying, forgiveness, humility, gentleness, nonviolence, and love. As we wander farther and deeper down these meandering, wonderfully ethical pathways, we will steadily grow in spiritual comprehension and evolutionary wisdom and maybe even, from time to time, with a kind of peripheral vision, catch a glimpse of the divine, about whom we may be unable to say much of anything—except, perhaps, for a far-seeing gaze, a radiant smile, or a tender kiss of peace.

Civis globalized leads to End Times demonic breakdown. We know it because we're there, it's called Global Crisis, and things are, with accrued momentum, on a trajectory to get much worse, possibly even terminal. But returning to the womb of *pagus* as an act of archetypal eternal recurrence is, in my estimation, spiritually regressive and politically evasive. If all we have to hang on to (on this rocky, narrow, scary ledge that leads to the Daughter's rich enfleshment of an Earth-centered spirituality) is an ethical prescription for radical servanthood and radical stewardship—well, then that's all we've got. I believe it's enough.

9

Repositories of Reflexive Deference

*(for Dorothy Peters, 1925–2015, and
Mary Mangold, 1942–2015)*

My wife Susanna and I have attended an odd, little group for about ten years. Some have called our gathering by the name Contemplation, others say Meditation. The group was started, I believe, by a Holy Cross sister. (The Holy Cross order is Swiss-based, with its American headquarters, now populated almost entirely by geriatrics, in my northern Wisconsin home town.) Our little group is presently down to two Catholics and five Protestants, the latter of various disaffiliated stripes. We meet, usually, once a month, listen to a tape or discuss a book, then enjoy a meal of homemade soup and bread. We are friends. We enjoy each other's company.

When Susanna and I first met with the meditative contemplationists, the speaker (on tape) was the Franciscan evangelist Richard Rohr. If there's a speaker who has popped up again and again over the years, it's Richard. The Catholics especially like him. A sister once brought a video of a Rohr talk for us to listen to and watch. In that video, Rohr introduced a speaker I'd never heard of, an independent Catholic intellectual by the name of Gil Bailie. I was so taken with Bailie's presentation I scanned the video a second time, scribbling notes, while everyone else wandered away to do other things. Later I obtained a copy of Bailie's book, *Violence Unveiled: Humanity at the Crossroads*, and I read it carefully.

What Bailie purports to be about, in the words of his mentor René Girard, who wrote the Foreword to *Violence Unveiled*, is the anthropology of religion. The core argument is this: Archaic religion is larded with the mythologizing of violence, "sacred" violence, violence requiring a scapegoat on whom is focused the requisite destruction and/or rejection by which the primary social order is created or maintained, a way of determining who's in and who's out. Sacred violence via scapegoating—the projection of evil or sin or, perhaps, simple undesirability onto a third party—is the backbone of cultural continuity. It defines who's acceptable and who's unacceptable, who's good and who's bad. What keeps this system functional and functioning is sacred violence dressed in a robe of sanctifying myth, for it's by violence that the undesirable is suppressed or ejected. Therefore the violence itself is sacred. It protects us from evil by overcoming evil. Good violence suppresses bad violence.

But, says Bailie, the functions of myth and gospel—*mythos* and *logos*—work in opposite directions. Myth disguises, hides, and obscures the truth. Myth builds a cocoon around self-justification. Myth piously protects "moral" righteousness while *logos* works to understand the truth, even if it hurts. *Logos* drills into every self-protective cocoon and insists on truthful fresh air. In other words, we humans are a volatile tension consisting of a strong desire to embrace and expose the truth and a reflexive impulse to resist and conceal the truth; this contradiction runs the spectrum from individual lives to public institutions, from private thoughts to corporate secrecy, political ideology, and religious mythology. The evil we would suppress in others is a reverse image of our personal self-regard. We couldn't possibly exercise such violence without that well-protected self-regard, even if it's built on pretense.

Bailie says Christian gospel introduced a radically new element into human culture, an element undermining the ingrown mythic stability of sacred violence. That new element is sustained empathy for victims, the capacity to look at victimization from the victim's point of view. Jesus is our finest mythic representation of breakthrough into spiritual empathy, and it's by no means incidental that this representation came from the countryside of exploited peasants. Or, as Bailie says at the end of his first chapter, "Today the victim occupies the moral high ground everywhere in the Western world. The cultural and historical force that caused this reversal is the gospel."[1] Jesus is, obviously, the prototype innocent victim of unjust, expedient condemnation and brutal execution, the most significant scapegoat victim in Western culture, the core image of victimized crucifixion. Here, in what became an emblem of cultural consciousness for most of twenty centuries in the West, is vulnerable *pagus* speaking truth to *civis* power protecting its mythic prerogatives, to the point where legal murder is used to suppress the truth. Jesus' death, says Bailie, set this undermining process in motion. That story—religious and state authority combining to legally murder a spiritually revolutionary peasant—became (although quickly shrouded in disguising myth) the principle religious story in the West, a story now spread around the world. The crucifixion makes us irreversibly aware of the unjust treatment of victims and, increasingly, of the function the scapegoat plays in this victimization. To become aware of the scapegoating phenomenon is to become aware—perhaps painfully aware—of the myth in which the scapegoating persists.

Bailie says sacred violence no longer works with the efficiency it once did, precisely because of the unjust crucifixion of Jesus. The crucifixion of Jesus, with its emblematic pervasiveness in Western culture, has wrecked the efficacy of scapegoating by throwing the scapegoat process upside down, by opening our eyes to victimization, even as it's taken centuries for us to get the message. Of course, the crucifixion of Jesus was quickly packaged in obscuring myth, with "the Jews" identified as his persecutors

1. Bailie, *Violence*, 29.

and the weak Roman governor of Judea caving in to the Jewish mob's bloodthirsty demands. This myth continues to portray Jesus as victim, only his killer is intentionally misidentified. By this means, *civis* remains mythically pure. But it now takes bigger and bigger doses of sacred violence to make a sacred dent in behalf of sacred order; the entire process (or, at least, its functional coherence) steadily undermined by empathy for victims (which is not identical with but is closely related to *logos* or truth, for truth relates to understanding while empathy relates to love; that is, the new realization is the spiritual integration of heart and head), and this in turn is connected to the infiltration of gospel ethics into the larger world, into patterns of private thought and public conscience, an infiltration that, over time, has rendered sacred violence increasingly suspect, erratic, irrational and ineffective, even to the point—via careful scholarship— where we discover how gospel has been distorted by civilized myth. Sacred violence certainly hasn't gone away—just listen to the evening news—but its efficacy has been undermined and functionally disabled by an increasingly clear-sighted *logos* that sees with greater and greater spiritual clarity how religion is the protective shroud around civilizational violence. We are, in fact, reaching an extremely dangerous tipping point where the world will either explode in compulsive violence, as the mythic impulse to exercise violence becomes more desperate and increasingly reckless, or violence will be renounced and humanity will organize itself on the basis of something other— something profoundly better—than rage, righteousness, fear, a desire for retribution, and violence. Therefore we're at a global and evolutionary threshold, inescapably so. Either the end of violence or it's the end of us.

That's a severe compaction of *Violence Unveiled*. And while I have alluded to or quoted from Bailie's book in other writings—gospel or *logos* as myth disabler *is* a novel and powerful thesis with lots of unexplored traction—there is in Bailie a presumption of cause and effect I find inadequate. Oddly mirroring Ivan Illich's assertion that the corruption of modern society is reflective of a perversion within Christianity, Bailie's view lays a similar degree of responsibility for the structural breakdown of society on the deconstructing capacities of gospel. That is, both men look to Christianity, the church, or the gospel as the agency responsible for the crisis in the modern world. For Illich, the modern mess is due to the church's perversion of gospel. For Bailie, gospel has been steadily disabling the functionality of sacred violence so that (we might say) the global mess reflects the ongoing deconstruction of social order built on myth.

Neither man, it seems to me, takes into adequate account the pre-existing force of expansive, imperial civilization, with its modern industrial incarnation reaching global dimensions. That is, what Karl Polanyi said of modern industrial economics—that it has practiced the "smashing up of social structures in order to extract the element of labor from them"[2]—does not necessarily need a perversion of gospel or a *logos*/*mythos* overlay to be comprehensible. Civilization from its inception engaged in systemic violence and economic expropriation. That's how it came into being. That's

---

2. Polanyi, *Great*, 164.

how it continued to exist all these millennia. If civilization (any kingdom or empire) could contain or overpower a subculture within its reach for purposes of exploitation and control, it simply did so. But when and where noncivilized cultures stood in the way of land acquisition, access to Earth resources or the reliable use of labor, "smashing" was not out of the question. Smashing was diplomacy by other means. This country was almost entirely obtained by smashing. Myth in this sense is not just about covering the naked loins of archaic religion seeking to disguise its violent propensities or its cultural self-righteousness retroactively; it's also about the gilding of civilization's rapacious appetite for anticipated expansion and control, an appetite protected, empowered, and justified by mythic doctrines of civilized superiority and religious supremacy. That is, the Girard/Bailie thesis works as well, and perhaps works even better, when applied to civilizational mythologies as it does to religious mythologies. The systematic wrecking of traditional cultural forms—say Native American cultures in their vast continental plurality—was achieved by brute civilized force, even if preachers in their pulpits, as part and parcel of the dominant Christian mentality, justified conquest in the name of Almighty God or Christianity or Christian civilization.

Two questions keep teasing from the edges of consciousness. First, how do we ascertain the veracity of Bailie's claim that gospel is the spiritual solvent in which myth is steadily dissolving? Second, if Bailie's analysis is in essence true, what would human culture look like if it were largely devoid of violence ("sacred" or otherwise) as the means for the maintenance of structural exploitation and the prop for institutionalized inequality?

I think one has to begin (at least I have to begin) by confessing an incapacity to prove or disprove Bailie's claim in anything resembling scientific terms. I can say that gospel-undermining-myth rings true to me, just as *logos* acts as a truth-discerning solvent in relation to evasive hypocrisy. (Hypocrisy likes hiding in myth.) But I can be accused of looking for arguments (posing as evidence) to buttress a spiritual predisposition. (The same charge might be leveled against me in regard to climate change. I believe climate change is real and that it's due primarily to fossil fuel emissions. But do I believe that because it reinforces my pre-existing convictions regarding utopian overdevelopment and excessive consumption? I certainly do not have the scholarly or scientific qualifications to prove my convictions. We humans always need to seriously consider such uncomfortable thoughts and weigh them to the best of our ability.)[3]

3. Burton L. Mack, in *The Lost Gospel: The Book of Q and Christian Origins*, says some interesting things about the inapplicability of our present myths. On page 210, he says that "When a social history introduces changes in the structure of a society and its patterns of activity, the function of a myth is challenged because it no longer depicts how the present state of affairs came to be. Such a challenge demands that both the myth and the new social configuration be rethought." On page 251, he elaborates: "Myths, mentalities, and cultures go together. Myths are celebrated publicly in story and song. Mentalities are nurtured just beneath the surface of social conventions by means of unexpressed agreements. Myths, mentalities, and cultural agreements function at a level of acceptance that might be called sanctioned and therefore restricted from critical thought. Myths are difficult to criticize because mentalities turn them into truths held to be self-evident, and the analysis of such cultural

There is spiritual energy operating in the worldwide Myth Clearance Program. The same sort of stubborn, independent, scientific impetus that gave us modern astronomy, geology, biology, and anthropology has also given us intensive, ongoing scholarly inquiry into the Bible, theology, and the core meaning of the spirituality operating within religious traditions, including our own. (Psychoanalysis has a shaggy dog in this fight, even if other participants think it an aggravating pup that chews on slippers and socks and drags stinky old bones onto the living room rug.)

What Daniel Williams calls "pre-scientific supernaturalism" and "the error of making an inflexible and infallible law out of the historically conditioned precepts in the Biblical record" continue to be operative in present-day fundamentalism.[4] Insofar as fundamentalism remains the main religious repository for mythic conviction, the tension between fundamentalism and what we might loosely call "liberal" Christianity carries forward the conflict between myth and gospel. Insofar as the traditional Christian story is built of mythic stories—Adam and Eve in the Garden of Eden, Noah and the Ark, the virgin birth, resurrection and ascension of Jesus—the solvent of gospel-as-relentless-truth has eaten away not merely the supporting posts of fundamentalism but the credibility of the orthodox Christian story itself. (Burton Mack's position is that the "lost" gospel of Q—Jesus sayings absorbed in the synoptic gospels—also helps eat away the supporting posts.) Fundamentalists may cling to "traditional" conviction, but liberals often seem not to know what they believe beyond a few (slightly embarrassed) pious clichés. For people unable to swallow Jonah's fundamentalist (i.e., mythic) whale, there's also an understandable refusal to nibble at anemic liberal minnows. Skeptics may go trolling elsewhere for spiritual nourishment, or they may quit fishing altogether.

Insofar as these tendencies can be read in bold and even brazen dimension in American politics, we could point to the disastrous eight years presided over by

---

assumptions is seldom heard as good news." On the same page he says that "Christian myth and western culture go together. This is true whether we imagine a long, continuous history of Christian influence on western forms of art, literature, thought, and politics, or whether we imagine a series of missions to expand the borders of western Christian empires. For example, one might call to mind the spread of early Christianity, the crusades, the age of discovery, colonial expansion during the eighteenth and nineteenth centuries, and the envelopment of the world in modern times by western armies, ideologies, and corporations. In every case, Christianity and empire have taken possession of the territory hand in hand. Christian missionaries have gone along to bless the conquests and spread the good news. Since we have never questioned where this sense of mission comes from, we have never been quite sure of the reasons for all of these expansions and who should get the credit for them, the kings and commanders, the spirit of western culture, or the church." On page 253, Mack goes on to say that "What we do not know or talk about is the mythic equation, how these factors are rooted in mythologies, how myths surface to inform new patterns of motivation and association, how they impinge upon the creation of new mythologies, and how a mythology works in return to inform and support a particular social configuration. We do not know how to talk about the mentalities that underlie a culture's system of meanings, values, and attitudes. Some cultural critics are saying that it is time we set to work at cracking that equation." Perhaps "cracking that equation" is exactly what these present essays are attempting to achieve.

4. Williams, *Reinhold*, 203.

George W. Bush—a vast stomping of the mythic dinosaur—and (although I write in mid-March 2009) the bold-sounding but largely timorous policies of empire- and capitalist-perpetuation of Barack Obama—the mere wiggling of liberal minnows as a tidal wave of catastrophic transformation closes in. That is, Republican versus Democratic politics provides a rough and crude comparison for "conservative" versus "liberal" religious conviction. (If "conservative" means fully icebound, "liberal" means the lake is no longer safe for ice fishing.) Just as the "fringes" of the Democratic and Republican parties sometimes find themselves in concurrence—say Democrat Dennis Kucinich and Republican Ron Paul in regard to the war on Iraq—so it may be that those who take gospel seriously, irrespective of where they start politically, will eventually find agreement on the gospel principles of radical servanthood and radical stewardship, although "conservatives," by clinging to Original Sin, are afraid of taking stewardship and servanthood as seriously as those constructs need and deserve.

In some ways it may obscure more than it reveals if Gil Bailie, Marcus Borg, John Dominic Crossan, and Burton Mack are identified as liberals. I would call them radicals (although I certainly don't mean that as an epithet) in a way similar to Kucinich and Paul. They are "fringe" in that they are beyond the slushy mainstream. In biblical terminology, their fringeness might be called prophetic.

II

Over the years I've become increasingly interested in whether, or to what extent, we might place Jesus' proclamation of the kingdom of God in a larger context of agrarian village culture historically oppressed by aristocratic civility. That is, is it possible to recognize a cultural connection between the domination-free order implied by the kingdom of God proclamation and the egalitarian social order exemplified by the agrarian village prior to its impoundment by civilized kingship? Would the kingdom of God (whatever else it might do) recapture the abundant subsistence equality of that early period in cultural evolution? How could Jesus' exhilarating vision—*pagus* dissolving (or transforming) predatory *civis* by means of servanthood and stewardship—have been other than rural? Marcus Borg, for instance, has a rather lengthy section in *The God We Never Knew* on the monarchical model of God, the king as "the number one figure in the domination system," how this monarchical system of oppression was based on the backs of peasants.[5] John Dominic Crossan in *God and Empire* says bluntly that empire is "the normalcy of civilization's violence."[6] Facing this "normalcy" with spiritual honesty, however, requires letting go our worship of civilization as the overarching concept of cultural goodness—or, if "worship" seems too strong a word, we can at least say "veneration." And, if this monarchical system of

5. Borg, *God*, 69.
6. Crossan, *God*, 30.

oppression were to be lifted off the backs of peasants, wouldn't we find ourselves with a Green socialism determined to help create and sustain vital rural culture?

But we have such a dim, anemic, distracted, disinterested, and even hostile disregard for rural culture, and such breathless admiration for civilization, that even attempting to think this way seems beyond our mental capacity. It flies in the face of our cultural and religious mythology. To see or even consider the kingdom of God proclamation as the proposed resurrection of precivilized agrarian culture is, for most people, a total nonstarter. Fundamentalists instantly have biblical objection (i.e., there was no such thing as the precivilized agrarian village, so how could there possibly be a "resurrection" of something that never existed?), while liberals and many conservatives are reflexively Augustinian in outlook. How can civilization be in any way at fault if God blessed civilization and bestowed upon it His protection against paganism? Didn't civilization grow naturally out of agricultural abundance? Isn't civilization the good cop who keeps Original Sin under control? The plight of agrarian culture is, like the story of the robbed and beaten Jew in the Good Samaritan story (Luke 10:29-37), a crumpled figure in a ditch it's best to ignore and pass by without comment. It's more comforting to learn what's natural from Harry Stottle or what's supernatural from Saint Augustine.

Jerry Mander, in his book *In the Absence of the Sacred*, would push our consciousness farther back in time. Mander wants us to recognize, honor, and embrace the ecological and spiritual consciousness of indigenous people; only there, he says, do we find sufficient groundedness (never, until now, forced out of intimate daily life with the natural world) by which to properly assess and adequately resist the technological juggernaut. The indigenous remain a viable template for a certain magnitude of self-provisioning subsistence as well as a character structure and a spiritual perception never shaped by civilizational authoritarianism.

Of course we are immediately confronted with the religious Keep Out/No Trespassing sign warning us that indigenous "primitivity" is dangerous Pagan Land. Enter at your own risk. Fundamentalists can prove by chapter and verse that such an embrace is not only unbiblical but a steep, slippery slope leading into a swamp of evil. Both liberals and economic conservatives feel their solar plexus tingle with distress as the God of Constantinian civility is depicted in unflattering terms. All manner of negativities spring forth when ideas or proposals suggest a positive view of "backward," "primitive" or "uncivilized," or when anyone suggests the early Christian use of "pagan" was a cowardly scapegoating of rural people in order to avoid recognizing that the killer of Jesus was civilized imperialism. Biblical literalism blocks fundamentalists from accepting prebiblical social anthropology; an unexamined addiction to civilized mythology prevents liberals and economic conservatives from a similar effort, at least beyond intellectual museum slumming. Unpacking the past is an unacknowledged threat to the bland continuation of our mythically drugged—mythically *protected*—civility. Cracking the mythic equation comes with an enormous amount of resistance and denial, just as we persist in thinking *apokalypsis* means End Times disaster rather than (as it does etymologically) the *disclosing* of End Times dynamics.

Our intellectual concepts are rooted in an emotionality shaped by early childhood conditioning. To recognize what our cultural and religious institutions consider evil is to observe the collective, "public" projection of millions of "private" repositories of evil, largely internalized in childhood. These individualized, mass repositories may have their origin in the violent impositions of an aristocratic, landlord, bandit class hundreds of generations ago; and, although the forcible imposition—the trauma—may have lessened (for some of us) through the processes of democratization and consumerism, these institutionalized repositories of reflexive deference are sufficiently "normal" (and kept that way by the repetitive tamping of sacred doctrine) to be reliable defenders of the status quo, protectors of Constantinian civility. We are obliged to confess that "The only good Indian is a dead Indian" and "We had to destroy the village in order to save it" are assertions of cultural righteousness representing the internal disposition (or at least the conditioned acquiescence) of a broad social base. You can't kill Indians or burn Vietnamese villages without believing the lie or acquiescing to its righteous conviction. These doctrines of justification exonerate the crushing brutality and overpowering selfishness of civilized institutions operating with imperial presumption. They reflect the depth and extent of our conditioned expectations and collective acquiescence. The myth both justifies our actions and forgives any possible excess we might've enacted in a circumstance of extreme stress. (See Philip Caputo's *A Rumor of War* for a painful case study based in Vietnam.)

I've not forgotten that we're looking for answers to questions involving *logos* as spiritual solvent and descriptions of what our society or the larger world would look like were it, perhaps not devoid, but largely free of systemic economic exploitation and institutional violence. The Original Sin position seems to be that human intransigence is of such deeply rooted magnitude—even irreversibly biological—that gospel solvent is limited to being an enabler for otherworldly admission only. Original Sin is just too tough a nut for *logos* or gospel or even Spirit to fully crack. Salvation is limited to the Next World. There is no hope for anything resembling the kingdom of God on This World—at least no hope to bring, or even help bring, such a "kingdom" forward. Only God is capable of that forwardness, and His action will occur in His own good time. (But not in *this* life, not in *this* world.) Human beings may pray as they wait, but wait they must. This seems to be the "conservative" view. But it's also the traditional or orthodox view; and, as such, it's the primary eschatological inheritance of most if not all Christian denominations, whether "conservative" or "liberal." This eschatological inheritance allows ongoing exercise of the traumatic institutions of civility by doctrinal conviction in passivity. Civilization gets to impose its mandated order until the Second Coming. This is the will of God. Everyone is to stand quietly and wait.

To deconstruct the monarchical model is, in terms of gospel solvent, exceedingly exciting and promising. But fundamentalists immediately balk because the language of God as King is so thoroughly biblical. Plus fundamentalists will not abide an analysis that explores agrarian village evolution (or its impoundment) in a time frame that does not take the Garden of Eden literally. Liberals, meanwhile, are far too comfortable with "progress" (or, at least, uncomfortable with the prospect of being seriously critical of the etiology of "progress") to be willing to deconstruct the traumatic institutions, the structural exploitation and institutionalized violence, that are (as Crossan realizes) endemic to civility. We live within the structures of imperialist privilege; privilege has become our normative lifestyle. To willingly slide down the mountain of material affluence, because that mountain is largely constructed of stolen wealth, broken cultures, brutalized bodies and ravaged ecology, is against the grain of our economic expectation and cultural conditioning. We're quite comfortable with our standard of living. Perhaps if we believed the kingdom of God a subsidiary of Wal-Mart, or some other purveyor of commodities of better quality and higher class, we would be flocking to the concept.

So, is the world going to hell because gospel, as Bailie says, is undermining the capacity of sacred violence to sustain mythic order? Or is the world going to hell because the globalization of civilization, built on exploitation and violence, contemptuous of all lesser social forms and noncivilized cultures, has simply reached ecocidal capacity not only with its weaponry (which capacity is indisputable) but also with the economic externalities and ecological blowback of its heedless greed and hubristic righteousness? Is it a combination of the two? Christianity, needless to say, formally merged with the domination system in the fourth century and has remained married to it ever since. I have not noticed a divorce being considered. Enabling and codependency are long-term commitments not lightly abandoned. The Bride of Christ remains tax exempt, hereditary endowment maintained by contractual commitment to political passivity. (Just think of what Jesus might've been able to accomplish if he hadn't been so hamstrung by tax exemption!) So what *is* the relationship of Christian mythology to civilizational mythology? Are both based on the disguising and deflection of "sacred" violence? The answer is clearly yes. Civilization piously claims to have grown "naturally" out of freely given agricultural abundance; Christianity asserts that its merger with the Roman Empire "Christianized" the civilizational project—a natural development capped by divine blessing. Case closed.

Is it any wonder that theologians and preachers haven't known what to make of Jesus' kingdom of God proclamation—except to agree on its postponement to the Next Life? Are we, with all our hymns, creeds and confessions of faith, so convinced of our (rather abstract) original sin, so groveling in our (rather theoretical) conviction of evil (particularly as it pertains to the wickedness of others, especially those evil terrorists), that we will stand chained to our greedy appetites and conditioned fears, lacking the maturity or the will to saw off the locks? How bad do things have to get before we quit sitting on our clean, pious hands—because to actually use them is to risk getting them spiritually dirty? Or will global death find us in that stiff sitting position, proud of our uncalloused fingers and unused muscles, wonderfully convinced there was nothing to be done but wait for God to take us home to our heavenly *Altersheim*? Or kindergarten.

We know what happens when civilization brutalizes gospel. We see the consequences brutally brazen in the crucifixion of Jesus and corruptingly deadly in the Constantinian accommodation. We might even say the Constantinian accommodation was a second crucifixion. (If the first crucifixion nailed Jesus, the second drove spikes into the kingdom of God.) But do we know—do we even bother to think about—what happens when gospel "yeasts" civilization from the inside out? This is something we've never considered. If civilization devoured the gospel, if Constantine ate Jesus, if the Roman Empire unwittingly swallowed the kingdom of God, what happens to civilization when gospel yeast is sufficiently digested and its spiritual nutrients have infiltrated the body of civilized presumption and empire gluttony? Is civilization—in spite of itself—being transformed from the inside out? Did it eat something too spiritually irrepressible to fail?

III

To vividly describe what the world would look like if it were shaped by the economic wholesomeness and ethical liberties of the kingdom of God requires a consciousness sufficiently transformed by Spirit to undertake the description. I do not claim such a cleansed spirit or liberated consciousness. But I do claim the kingdom of God proclamation contains principles of radical servanthood and radical stewardship—"radical" in both cases because each principle is committed to deep honesty, with the former (servanthood) clearly deriving from the gospels and the latter (stewardship) perhaps only implicit in the gospels and more derivative from the Genesis creation story, where the human task is to tend the ecological garden. Just because we do not know what the kingdom of God would look like in its ultimate unfolding (or what "sustainable" really means, for that matter) does not prevent us from knowing (or advocating for) the necessary steps by which we might begin moving in the right direction. We'll learn by doing. Our spirits will be cleansed and our consciousness liberated as we embrace and enter the kingdom of God. Our captivity within the original sin construct will weaken as we rediscover original blessing.

We know—because it's clearly spelled out in the teachings of Jesus—that retribution and revenge are to be relinquished. (Every community may require something of a protective police presence—I am not suggesting the evaporation of all undesirable human behavior—but our orientation toward such behavior would tend toward restorative justice and compassionate rehabilitation, not punitive retribution. In international relations we have much forgiveness to ask and many reparations to make.) We are to renounce personal riches beyond basic need and share to the root and core of our possessions. We are not only to forgive our enemies but also love them.

We can, however, recognize a historical sequence by which this radically demanding simplicity was evaded and corrupted. First we can point to the intellectualized otherworldliness of the Apostle Paul who, whatever his theological brilliance and commitment to the Christ figure, nevertheless tamped down (or simply ignored) the kingdom of God construct in favor of earnest (perhaps even desperate) salvationism. The churches addressed in Paul's letters are urban. We no longer see—as we do in the gospel stories—a wandering through villages and small towns in an agrarian countryside, much as the earthy imagery of the gospels is lost or dispensed with in the letters. Parable and story, with roominess for unpressured consideration, exploration and interpretation, were replaced by exhortation and assertion, styles of delivery more in accord with random, chance encounters in an urban context, given to an assertiveness bordering on moral or theological interrogation: believe this or go to hell.

I don't know exactly when *pagus* (the country dweller) began to be a Christian epithet, but it surely was in place by the time the bishops allowed themselves to be strong-armed by Constantine. For Augustine it's the City of God that matters, the ideal image of governance with God as King, empire rationalized as God's mandate. While "pagan" has been negatively used countless times in Christian exhortation, I know of no instance where "civilized" has been employed in like manner. Given that it was a rationally calculating urban upper class that killed Jesus, rather than a peasant mob, this pejorative and even murderous use of "pagan" should at least incite in us a modest degree of curiosity.

If *scapegoating* is the name for pinning a filthy tail on a despised donkey, its opposite is *glorification*, whereby the murderer is seen as an innocent bystander or even celebrated as the rescuing hero. (In John's gospel—19:4–16—poor, overwhelmed Pilate acquiesces to the aggressive and bloodthirsty Jewish mob.) In this process, guided and protected by "sacred" language, "sacred" violence remains secured to the state, to the Powers that be, with the church's confirmation and blessing. This is how Christianity found a reliable way to keep the sword within arm's reach. By its pious otherworldliness, its incremental but steady urbanization, its contempt for and scapegoating of the pagan, its glorification of the civilized, and its merger with the very empire that murdered its founder, Christianity distanced itself from the ethically demanding kingdom of God proclamation and from the economic simplicity and communal sharing that proclamation implied and continues to imply. The Augustinian church has lived in its Platonic head, not its Jesus body.

With the sword justified in the hands of a supposedly Christianized Empire, class structure was rationalized in a manner commensurate with Marcus Borg's elucidation of how the monarchical image of God justifies a strictly hierarchical ordering of social class. This construct perfectly reflects the pathological reaches of the Constantinian accommodation and its historic consequences. Perhaps we also need to recognize that in the period after the death of Jesus (but before Constantine), the constituency of the church (although we probably should say churches) became primarily if not overwhelmingly urban and therefore more easily shaped by a theology of monarchical divinity and otherworldly salvation. Peasants no longer constituted the grounded social flour for whom and in whom Jesus yeast worked as revolutionary spiritual fermentation. When the Jesus movement left the countryside and became "Christian," it apparently left behind the kingdom of God. The kingdom of God never got to go to town.

Given the contemporary condition of the Christian church—splintered and fragmented, demoralized and directionless, given to hysterical literalism and droopy vagueness, massively eroded demographically by secular alternatives (even as there are pockets of brilliant insight and prophetic recognition)—it's impossible to see how the kingdom of God, as explicit Christian proclamation, can gain an inch or ounce of transformative traction by means of the church's semantically imprisoned traditional language. Christian proclamation may not be dead in the water, but it is a truly wounded whale; and it won't be through revivalism or any new Great Awakening that the kingdom of God will be recognized, embraced, or realized. The Christian church is dying in large part because it has been so spiritually hamstrung for over fifteen hundred years. For a great many people, the Christian church is already dead. It stinks of rotten compromises and devious sublimations.

So either the kingdom of God is a revolutionary lost cause that died with Jesus (or perhaps with the early Jesus people, as Burton Mack calls them), or it is an irrepressible virus, a yeast or fungus that by means of mysterious, elusive Spirit has, over time, infected and infiltrated all susceptible consciousness, slowly and patiently transforming human awareness from the belly up, as it were, digesting our impulsive fears and stubborn greediness, allowing us to more fully embrace stewardship and servanthood as the basis of human conduct, even as the larger church proceeds on its bizarre vacillation between rigid mythological reaction and vacuous foggy formlessness.

It's either the kingdom of God or we may well be doomed; either Spirit or disaster. Gil Bailie may say gospel has steadily undermined myth; but—while that seems true—unless gospel is some sort of unspecified magic, the deeper reality is that "gospel" is the subcultural articulation of Spirit. It's *Spirit* who is transforming the world. Gospel is a packet of transformative seeds, a glob of yeasty fungus whose job is to gentle and ethically strengthen the human animal. (I say "subcultural" rather than "supracultural" for the same reason I prefer immanent over transcendent when talking about divinity. This may be, in the end, an overcorrection; but we are so used to thinking of God, or of anything remotely godly, as coming to us from without, from beyond or above, from the capitol or head, that overcorrection is now a necessity for survival. We are so astonishingly ungrounded culturally, because of our obsessive orientation toward the utopian and the otherworldly, that regrounding ourselves on Earth, lest we go passively into the nuclear gas chamber, is the urgent task at hand.) The church, meanwhile, would be wise to remember that Spirit is not contained in or confined by the church's creeds, teachings, or rituals. Spirit is not in anybody's religious box. To worship in spirit and in truth requires an ethical embrace of the kingdom of God, of radical servanthood and radical stewardship, a leap from optional private charity to committed public policy. The only wholesome globalization is that which takes eutopian shape and this-worldly form from the insouciant and compassionate embrace of Spirit.

IV

It doesn't take a completely cleansed and transformed spirit to recognize the situation we're in or the direction toward which we must turn. If utopian overdevelopment, as an outgrowth and consequence of civilizational hubris, has brought us to a circumstance where ecocidal weapons are only waiting to be launched, where climate change is already occurring (and increasing in intensity) from the blind, reckless and heedless overuse of fossil fuels, then it should be obvious that we must move away from both utopian material expectations and devastating ideological confrontations as we disengage from an economic ideology based on limitless wealth accumulation and maximized commodity consumption, an ideology that's a civilizational luxury descendent of the aristocratic palace, upper-class appetite rationalized as "democratic" standard of living. "Democratic" utopia. Every man a king, every home a castle. It's certainly no coincidence that many of the wisest voices speaking to our predicament—from R. H. Tawney to Dorothy Day to E. F. Schumacher to Noam Chomsky to Wendell Berry— have been moved by spiritual ethics, for it's such ethics that confirm the foundation of Green socialism. Political ideology—including democratic ideology—is only as wholesome as the spirituality on which it is based.

Only a few generations ago, Christian socialist Norman Thomas (inspired by the social gospel of Walter Rauschenbusch) could run repeatedly for president and be a laughingstock of unelectability. Ralph Nader's repeated candidacy is a more contemporary comparison. (Is Bernie Sanders in process of joining this cloud of unelectable saints, or will this Bronx Jew end the electoral drought?) One has to conclude that such persons are either inherently "fringe," "weird," or "irrelevant" or else the Constantinian accommodation has so deeply perverted our understanding of gospel that, faced with lucid and deeply ethical prophetic voices, the great bulk of the electorate can only smile with sardonic amusement or sneer with "realistic" contempt. (Politically, we might say Jesus was an early example of a candidate—another weird Jewish socialist—courting "wasted votes," appealing only to a lunatic fringe.) Despite the oblivion toward conservation on the part of "conservatives," the situation is no longer theoretical, abstract, or even very funny. What previously could be dismissed as fringe, weird, irrelevant, and unrealistic as recently as sixty or seventy years ago—although even then Dresden, Auschwitz, Hiroshima, and Nagasaki had stunned the world—is now inescapably in our faces. The social gospel, deepened and clarified by what we might call an ecological gospel, is now, suddenly, the only viable path out of our global predicament. There simply is no realistic alternative.

If the Seven Deadly Sins—pride, covetousness, lust, anger, gluttony, envy, and sloth—were given permanent residence in the luxurious apartments of the Constantinian accommodation when empire was embraced and justified by Christian theologians, then contempt for spiritual simplicity has a long and venerable pedigree and is integrated into virtually all subsequent theological formulations and, consequently, into all secular ideologies that derive, with whatever measure or degree, from those theological formulations. The real force behind and within empire is the ruthless "sacred" violence of feral males, with their capacity to kill and eagerness to exploit, all gilded with holiness wrapped in pious mythology. To be riding on civilization's celebratory bandwagon has seemed infinitely safer and much more secure than to be thrust under its deadly chariot wheels. Better to get in on the flag-waving glorification than to be seen in the company of the lunatic fringe, whose future as possible scapegoats may not be very comfortable or bright.

But we have arrived at a totally new and novel circumstance. Violence and greed, fully gilded with the glorified righteousness of civility, have reached the cul-de-sacs of ecocidal externality and toxic blowback. Yet our minds, our thought, and our institutional rationale remain so packed with concepts of justifying superiority and cultural righteousness that we seem unable to believe our eyes. This simply cannot be happening. It can't be true. AM talk radio is there to buck us up and explain why it's either a liberal conspiracy or liberal stupidity that's the problem. Who would've foreseen that the Constantinian accommodation would be upheld by the likes of Rush Limbaugh or Donald Trump?

V

If Bailie is right, if myth obscures while gospel reveals, if *mythos* tries to keep *logos* in a closet, there's a paradox in this formulation. We can go back to the presidency of George W. Bush for an illustration.

It's apparently the case that a large majority of regular church attendees consistently vote for candidates of the Right. George W. Bush was a poster child, of sorts, for this phenomenon. His biggest constituency was the white Christian Right. Looking at the record of Bush's administration—its wars in Afghanistan and Iraq, its threatening of Iran, its unwavering support for invasive settlements and brutal suppression of Palestinians on the part of Israel, its relentless tax-cut policy for the wealthy and "free trade" promotion for corporations, its attempt to privatize Social Security, its lavish bailout of the same financial firms that imploded the world economy, etc—it is impossible to find any sustained ethical engagement with servanthood and stewardship, other than consistent efforts in behalf of the rich and powerful. This raises serious questions about spiritual discernment on the Christian Right or whether the Right's "discernment" is heavily filtered by mythological hypocrisy.

By "Left" and "Right" I don't mean to imply a strict correlation with "Left" and "liberal" or with "Right" and "conservative." While "Left" and "Right" hold a certain degree of semantic integrity, "liberal" and "conservative" are such fabrications that they are essentially worthless as meaningful ethical or even political markers. (If anything, "liberals" may be more hypocritical than "conservatives." The latter, while endlessly capable of sanctimonious pandering and deliberate obfuscation, are far more consistent in their domestic authoritarianism, reflexive obedience in behalf of the rich and powerful, deference to Augustinian empire justifications, and distrust of democracy. "Liberals," meanwhile, pretend to be against the war in Iraq, or for a two-state settlement to the Israeli-Palestinian conflict, or opposed to warrantless wiretapping, or shocked by torture, or dead set against the bailing out of the powerful men and institutions that disrupted the world economy and caused such distress at home, until, that is, it's time, before voting, to collect campaign contributions—at which point they buckle.)

To put it simply and concisely, the lure of civilizational opulence (or deferential awe in its presence) was both so strongly appealing and so powerfully threatening that it caused the early church to scapegoat "pagan" and align itself institutionally with the civilized entity that had murdered its inspirational founder. The historic consequences of this choice enabled civilized economic presumption to eradicate the "pagan" peasantry when the industrial revolution, in the firm and competent hands of a commercial middle class, made such eradication possible. We are now witnessing the global dystopian consequence of that deferential awe and adulation.

The Right sees no need to repent of the alliance between church and state. Its overarching mythology, fundamentalist or quasi-fundamentalist, with its explicit monarchical understanding of God in a corresponding hierarchical social order with the City of God as its template, leads easily to theocracy, to the merging (or at least to the reciprocal codependency) between religion and civilized governance. (Calvin's Geneva may be the Protestant template here. Calvin is Protestantism's Augustine.) The Left, meanwhile, is slowly awakening to the cataclysmic horror of that alliance global-ized and universalized. The Left may lack a clear and sharp image of the divine—a fact that's bound to be troublesome in the human quest for certainty and clarity—but we need to remember that even Judeo-Christian scripture warns against precise defini-tion of divinity.

In the political feedlot, "conservatives" and "liberals" mill and bawl between elec-tions endlessly perpetuating the status quo. But the political feedlot is a subsidiary construction site, a no-bid project of the Constantinian accommodation; only those who get beyond the metaphysical confines of the monarchical image of God are able to freely pasture in the lush meadows of servanthood and stewardship. The troubling paradox is that the clarity of "conservative" religious imagery, its undisputed tradi-tional lineage, provides enormous certainty in the linkage to civilized governance, while the pervasive opaque nature of Left theology—its cloudy imagery of or for the divine—necessitates a deep delving into gospel ethics in order to find spiritual traction and discern political direction. This requires both a distancing from the sharp mythic imagery offered so unhesitatingly by the Right, and a corresponding spiritual/psychological strength by which the ethical exploration of servanthood and stewardship can be seriously undertaken and diligently pursued. If the Right has an anachronistic mythology with a rigid morality to match, the Left is slowly realizing that the ethical articulation of stewardship and servanthood constitutes the legs it needs to stand up on and walk.

If myth obscures, its religious imagery can nevertheless be as precise as a Michelangelo sculpture. And if gospel reveals, its liberating truth will be found in the murky atmosphere of ethical groping—which can be difficult and even painful. The tight eye of this needle, through which we all must crawl, will scrape off accrued mythological encrustations, crack the mythic equation, even as it permits free entry into the cleansed heart of servanthood and stewardship. The kingdom of God is an ethically clean Green meadow in which Spirit's sheep may safely graze.

10

Leopold Kohr and *The Breakdown of Nations*

Does One Size-Theory Fit All?

We're building a world where everyone shares and no one is ostracized. . . .
And when eventually we have a world of peace and justice, the songs and
those who sing them will be some of the millions of reasons why. Is such a
world an impossibility? The alternative is no world at all.

Pete Seeger, Introduction to *Rise Up Singing*, page iii

So contrary to man's purpose are the concepts of union and unity that attempts at establishing one-world systems seem almost blasphemous.

Leopold Kohr, *The Breakdown of Nations*, page 113

LEOPOLD KOHR, IF ONE were to judge from the energy in *The Breakdown of Nations*, was
something of a bon vivant, a man of pubs, coffee shops and cafes—or, as Kirkpatrick
Sale calls him in his Foreword to the 1978 E. P. Dutton edition of Kohr's book, "a most
engaging raconteur."[1] Kohr's chapters bristle with the gleaming, well-honed business
ends of rapier debate, lightweight, deft, and deadly. His sentences sparkle with insouciant wit—or, perhaps, an insouciant wit occasionally glittering with moral outrage
paradoxically tempered by a seemingly deep acceptance of the human condition, both
its stunning creative accomplishments and its revolting destructive inclinations.

Kohr was an Austrian Jew, born 1909 in the little village of Oberndorf, close to
Salzburg. His father was a doctor. By amazing good fortune, Kohr managed to slip out
of the Nazi net in 1938 and find a home in North America. He wrote *The Breakdown
of Nations* after the war, while teaching economics at Rutgers University. It took him
four years to find a publisher; and, when he did, in 1957, it was a tiny anarchist shop
in London—Routledge & Kegan Paul. (Kirkpatrick Sale, in his delightful Foreword to

---

1. Sale, "Foreword," xvi.

the Dutton edition, tells how, in rather quirky circumstances, he heard about the book and what a difficult time he had finding a copy.)

The thesis of *Breakdown* is disarmingly simple: Human beings, given by nature to aggression and violence, will never change their behavior; but the magnitude of brutality and the degree of disaster are directly proportionate to social size. Big political entities generate big brutalities. Little political entities are, correspondingly, limited to little disasters. Therefore, to ratchet Kohr's formula up a notch, global powers with ecocidal weapons only represent extinction in abeyance.

The only remedy for preventing this disaster—though few grasp, believe, or want it—is radical reduction in political scale, shrinking aggression and reducing violence to local proportion, thus rendering disaster fairly inconsequential. Or, to use E. F. Schumacher's later compaction of Kohr's essential message: small is beautiful. But we are so addicted (psychologically? spiritually?) to the big and universal, we cling to it even as it promises to kill us. Kohr says it *will* kill us, unless the massive thing falls apart internally first.

Kohr is not sanguine about progress or what he prefers to call "advance." He says the "hallmark of *advance* is not love of peace but the discernment of truth, which, as it may be beautiful, may also be ugly, and as it may be good, may also be wicked."[2] I take that to be as close as Kohr gets to a frank avowal of anything resembling religious or spiritual conviction, aside from conventional literary pieties, mostly of a deistic nature. We may be permanently stuck in outbursts of deadly violence, but we can acknowledge our situation honestly and appraise it without platitudinous cant.

Although I find no scapegoating in *The Breakdown of Nations* (as one can find it, stunningly if also a touch obliquely, in Viktor Frankl's "Experiences in a Concentration Camp," where Frankl is told by an Auschwitz inmate that a Moslem is a "man who looks miserable, down and out, sick and emaciated, and who cannot manage hard physical labor any longer. . . . That is a 'Moslem'"[3]), there is in Kohr a reservoir of stereotypic convention worth looking into. (Is stereotype a way station on the journey toward the scapegoat?)

Chapter One of *Breakdown* is called "The Philosophies of Misery." It's a survey of misery's causes, real or alleged. In a subsection entitled "Biology of Aggression," Kohr quotes Cicero in behalf of the idea that all men are alike, all of us made of "biologically conditioned attitudes."[4] In regard to aggressiveness, irrespective of nationality, we have "only rarely expressed a genuinely felt aversion to it."[5] Here's the remainder of that paragraph:

---

2. Kohr, *Breakdown*, 8.

3. Frankl, *Man's*, 32.

4. Kohr, *Breakdown*, 16.

5. Kohr, *Breakdown*, 16.

On the contrary, collectively as well as individually, most of us are usually full of praise for it. What we actually reject as slightly contemptible is not aggressiveness but peace-loving gentleness. No business man has ever been known to have advertised an opening for a peace-loving, humble, unassuming salesman or executive. The prime qualifying virtue for these jobs is considered to be aggressiveness, and most of us say so quite bluntly. No true woman, even in war-hating societies, has ever been known to have expressed a desire for a peace-loving slipper addict as a husband who might surround her in a cloud of gentleness and verses. What she most likely wants of him is force and aggressiveness, and if he clicks his heels in addition, all the better. And the masses of people, being for ever feminine, will for ever admire the same things. "When they treat of their love affairs," writes the French philosopher Julien Benda, "the most civilized people speak of conquest, assault, siege and of defence, defeat, capitulation, thus clearly tracing the idea of love to that of war."[6]

Kohr goes on to talk about monuments to generals and victors, beasts of prey as representative of "our heraldic animals."[7] He says "there is nothing peculiar about these choices, for though the national theorists may be troubled by this, nothing seems to be more natural to man than aggressiveness and his delight in it."[8]

But as for the masses of people being forever feminine, tracing the idea of love to that of war, even if posing as peace-loving slipper addicts, we must turn to the supramasculinist theologian C. S. Lewis to find equally grandiloquent language. As Lewis's hero Dr. Ransom says in *That Hideous Strength*: "What is above and beyond all things is so masculine that we are all feminine in relation to it."[9] The passive female adores the aggressive male, and the male smashes stuff and breaks heads in order to obtain the adoration of his beloved . . . conquest? God, apparently, is the Ultimate Male who's warned us that the bulk of humanity is predestined for the eternal furnace, and there are men who want to act just like Daddy. It doesn't matter if you're Moslem, Christian, or Jew. God has no time for slipper addicts. God has divine testosterone and is on a mission to purify Earth of pagan trailer trash.

Now I am inclined to accept as probably true the assertion that femaleness is more biologically central or basic than maleness. Norman Mailer, in a quirky little book called *The Prisoner of Sex*, puts it this way:

> So do men look to destroy every quality in a woman which will give her the powers of a male, for she is in their eyes already armed with the power that she brought them forth, and that is power beyond measure—the earliest etchings of memory go back to that woman between whose legs they were conceived, nurtured, and nearly strangled in the hours of birth. And if women were also

6. Kohr, *Breakdown*, 16-17.

7. Kohr, *Breakdown*, 17.

8. Kohr, *Breakdown*, 18.

9. Lewis, *Hideous*, 316.

born of woman, that could only compound the awe, for out of that process by which they had come in, so would something of the same come out of them; they were installed in the boxes-within-boxes of the universe, and the man was only a box, all detached.[10]

A man, says Mailer, is "alienated from the nature which brought him forth, he is not like woman in possession of an inner space which gives her link to the future, so he must drive to possess it, he must if necessary come close to blowing his head off that he may possess it."[11]

Is this how we might trace the idea of love to that of war? We men must blow off somebody's head (possibly our own, preferably someone else's) in order to possess the feminine inner space?

In *Knowing Woman*, Irene Claremont de Castillejo says the "struggle for consciousness is the perennial struggle of the son to break free from the Great Mother."[12] In *The Creation of Patriarchy*, Gerda Lerner says that much of the "striving for autonomy" and "recognition of selfhood" arise from the "infant's struggle against the overwhelming presence of the mother." Or as Lerner goes on to say: "In order to find their identity, boys develop themselves as other-than-the-mother; they identify with the father and turn away from emotional expression toward action in the world."[13]

But lest we psychologize too much—even as Kohr says "what Bernard Shaw said of a woman's morality, that it is merely her lack of opportunity, applies to all our virtues"[14]—Kohr insists that "the source of aggressiveness lies nevertheless not in the psychological but in the physical realm."[15] Or, as he also says, "the dreaded result of a society's behaviour is the consequence not of evil schemes or evil disposition but of the power that is generated by excessive social size. For whenever a nation becomes large enough to accumulate the critical mass of power, it will in the end accumulate it. And when it has acquired it, it will become an aggressor, its previous record and intentions to the contrary notwithstanding."[16]

There's a powerful implication here. Well, first we should recognize that Kohr does not explore the origins of civilization. He simply doesn't go there. So his critique of the civilized big pertains, oddly enough, only to the modern nation-state or to its offshoots and derivatives. He seems to evince no desire to explore the thwarted agrarian village cultural unfolding at the dawn of civilization, but only in looking at the status quo ante of classical civility, a world voluntarily locked into the comic-opera city-state, too small to be seriously dangerous.

10. Mailer, *Prisoner*, 116-17.

11. Mailer, *Prisoner*, 111.

12. de Castillejo, *Knowing*, 47.

13. Lerner, *Creation*, 44-45.

14. Kohr, *Breakdown*, 41.

15. Kohr, *Breakdown*, 37.

16. Kohr, *Breakdown*, 35.

One can assume Kohr felt no need to explore civilized origins because his size theory of social misery already postulates (if only implicitly) an explanation for the rise of civilization. That explanation would go something like this: The agrarian village (or clusters of agrarian villages) unwittingly reached a critical mass of excessive social size, and critical mass spontaneously generated aggression, reflected both in external conquest and internal control. That aggressive leadership took the form of aristocracy and kingship seems, in Kohr's size-theory universe, essentially irrelevant. One way or another, once critical mass was reached, an explosion of aggression was inevitable. Leadership simply gave aggression a particular form and political direction.

It doesn't seem exactly irrelevant that Kohr's theory is oriented far more outward toward aggression than inward toward control. Slavery doesn't seem of particular interest to Kohr. Women, for instance, according to Kohr, have simply lacked the opportunity to achieve critical-mass power—he doesn't say why—but when and if they do find such opportunity, it'll just be déjà vu all over again. The gospels, likewise, may be ethically comforting to the intellectually weak and psychologically immature, but "if we want to discourage the development of crime-condoning attitudes and philosophies, we shall get nowhere by spreading the gospel. We must destroy those overgrown social units which, by their very nature, are governed not by the gospel but the number-conditioned law of averages."[17]

So there are two explicit building blocks to Kohr's conclusion about misery's causes. First, all men are essentially alike. (This supposedly includes all women.) The aggressive male (though perhaps we should say the aggressive masculine) is symbolized in our beast-of-prey political taxidermy—the tiger, the lion, the hawk, the bald eagle, etc.[18] Heraldic trophies reflect our "biologically conditioned attitudes." Second, these biologically conditioned attitudes, when concentrated demographically in critical mass, spontaneously produce collective aggression. Our only hope, given the ecocidal toxicity of present weaponry, is that "Like the ageing colossi of the stellar universe, it will gradually collapse internally, leaving as its principal contribution to posterity its fragments, the little states—until the consolidation process of big-power development starts all over again."[19] (One thinks here of Isaac Asimov and his seven-volume science fiction series on the two "foundations," of which the fifth volume—*Foundation and Earth*—is the most interesting.)

In the meantime, what are we to do? "If there is no chance of the restoration of a small-state world because of the unwillingness of the great powers to apply the principle of division to themselves, what then?"[20] Kohr has an answer for that question, too:

17. Kohr, *Breakdown*, 35.

18. See Barbara Ehrenreich's *Blood Rites: Origins and History of the Passions of War* for a fuller explication of heraldic animals in the form of predator beasts, perhaps especially pages 202 and 203.

19. Kohr, *Breakdown*, 216.

20. Kohr, *Breakdown*, 199.

> I cannot see why we should continue to resist a destiny which is ours even though we did not want it, and to reject the implications of an empire engulfing us on all sides simply because, as one of my students put it with the most desolately sour face I have seen, "empire is such an ugly word." This may be so but, unless we take a more outspoken and positive attitude towards it, we shall either become a nation of hypocrites or of neurotics, and still not gain the approval for which we seem so pathetically to crave. Many peoples have had empire and, instead of flagellating themselves, enjoyed it thoroughly. Why should not we?[21]

There is a certain whistling in the graveyard in that remark, gallows humor, perhaps even brutal glibness. Plus there's the question of who "we" are. Are "we" the several million Iraqis killed, maimed, orphaned, widowed, dislocated and made destitute by the empire we are currently enjoying? Or the current massive wave of immigrants—mostly Syrian—pouring into Europe? Or the several million Vietnamese previously graced by our empire attentions? Or perhaps the multiple thousands of Nicaraguans, El Salvadorans, or Panamanians caught directly or indirectly in our cat-and-mouse games with the former Soviet Union? Or the Native Americans whose land "we" stole in the creation of this happy empire? Are "we" having fun yet? Is a good Indian dead or just a trifle dispossessed?

Sometimes beneath the wit, insouciance, and verbal sparkle one senses a grim and dreadful pessimism. And although Kohr says pessimism is not despair, the cheerfulness he encourages seems the pugnacious grin of the convict who cracks jokes on the gallows.

I'd like to find Leopold Kohr really wrong about two things in particular. First, that it's not true that women are only a kind of men lacking testosterone opportunity for critical-mass violence. (Given the availability of hand guns and the low murder-related incarceration rate for women suggests that women either haven't discovered they have such opportunity—what slow thinkers!—or they are so far disinclined to exercise it. Or are women just poor shots?) Second, I'd like to discover it's untrue that gospel is irrelevant because (though Kohr doesn't explicitly say this) there's really no indwelling Spirit to empower us toward the blossoming of a more deeply pleasing human sweetness, with or without the slippers. This is not the same, exactly, as saying Kohr is a blithe sexist or cynical deist—but almost.

The paradox (if it is paradox) is that I generally find deists and atheists rather refreshing after excessive soaking in the pious bathwater of conventional theism. I suppose I have come to expect theists to lather lavishly in the soapy hypothetical idealism of religious mythology; but, when it comes to atheists or deists who celebrate the hard-nosed discernment of truth, I invariably find myself disappointed to discover at the bottom of their pot a mere retort of elemental chemicals or a grocery list of the laws of physics. Having followed *advance* from its humble beginnings in the love of

21. Kohr, *Breakdown*, 210.

peace to the lofty discernment of truth, we seem only to have made a leap from the ceiling of the Sistine Chapel to the basement of the chemistry building, from sublime idealism to stinkpot materialism. Is this really the epitome of truth discernment? Are those our only choices? God help us.

Kohr's force, his critical mass in the physical realm, is less about life than it is about geology. Its metaphor is not biology but earthquake, glacier, volcano, tidal wave, meteors smashing into tundra, or, as he suggests (in a footnote on page 75), atomic chain reaction. Kohr's critical mass is more like Hari Seldon's statistical "psychohistory," the "reactions of human conglomerates to fixed social and economic stimuli,"[22] as described in Isaac Asimov's initial *Foundation* trilogy, than it is like the deeply probing psychoanalytical investigations of Norman O. Brown in *Life Against Death*.

If *The Breakdown of Nations* has an enemy target, it's probably the idealism of materialism, the notion that Progress (though perhaps I should say Unification) is firmly in competent human hands, a competence not only culminating in civilization on a global scale, but a globalization convinced of its capacity to achieve its utopian blueprints.

Kohr, we might say, is a eutopian of city-state materialism or perhaps a comic-opera utopian. But his analysis doesn't exactly give him a leg to stand on. What's needed is something deeper. Let's call it eutopia of global soul.

II

Kirkpatrick Sale, in his Foreword, says the British reception of Kohr's book, in 1957, was "mixed." It seemed to have set reviewers "on edge." The *Economist* referred to it as "a maddening little book." Although Sale ironically attributes this latter view to Kohr's "bad form" of questioning empire, I doubt whether that interpretation is sufficient.[23] There is something of the street fighter in Kohr, something that suggests disciples are welcome within the circle of gleaming knives but disbelievers had better be alert for the stiletto. There's a mood that suggests if you're going to dispute or disagree, you'd better be prepared for a brawl, maybe a bloody one, followed—if it's been a good brawl—by a few bottles of wine and some instant replay.

Maybe it would be helpful to distinguish between what seems true in Kohr, what's questionable, and what's on really shaky ground. I am, it's true, in the small-is-beautiful tent, so I come positively predisposed to the issue of small versus big. There is, to me, no question as to the general virtue of the small. It's by far our deepest evolutionary heritage. The globalized huge is a real latecomer, and an awfully arrogant one at that. (It seems to think it owns the planet, with plans for a thorough redesign.) But I am disinclined to join Kohr's virile band of jolly fencers in the wholesale condemnation of the universal and the comprehensive.

22. Asimov, *Foundation*, 17.
23. Sale, "Foreword," xv.

I've been, for instance, in villages, towns, and small cities in Switzerland, Germany, Liechtenstein, Austria and Italy, and I was largely enchanted.[24] This is not the same as praise for Kohr's city-state ideal, but those villages, towns, and small cities (even granting their relative disfigurement by automobiles, advertising, electrical lines, and so forth) are simply gorgeous when compared to the commercial slapdash entities we call towns and cities in the United States. They—the European villages and towns—represent a slow, organic growth of great attentiveness, sensitivity and competence, while our hasty, careless, sprawling conurbations reveal shallowness, an inability to concentrate or follow through, and willful hyperactivity: attention deficit disorder on a mass scale. That the globalizing of this mass ADD is leading to and already causing global disaster is obviously true. Kohr, in that sense, was and is right on, although to attribute the comprehensive beauty of the small to the exercise of an endemic *individualism* is suspect. He says, for instance, that "Culture is the product not of peoples but of individuals."[25] But why would such an alleged individualism be represented in specific Swiss villages by a distinctive style of housing, costume, menu, or dialect? What's charming about a remote Swiss village is individualistic only in the sense that much of what can still be seen and enjoyed is the result of an extremely competent *common* folk handicraft of *inherited form* passed down for generations. It is in no way individualistic in any modern sense. It is precisely what Kohr says it's not—the product of peoples. It's a kind of collective cultural intelligence, even if—of course—it's individuals who carry the culture forward.

Kohr says the problem is bigness, that our obsession with unification is a kind of sickness. Smallness, he says, "is the design of God."[26] But we should recognize immediately that the God of smallness Kohr invokes is the Big Bang Prime Mover, who supposedly jumpstarted the whole shebang several billion years ago, but now is on well-deserved sabbatical. The small-scale has no need for an *active* God, says Kohr, although the large-scale needs constant management.

Only small bodies have flexible vitality. "Giant size does not fit the pattern of creation. Whenever it develops, it destroys itself in violence and disaster."[27] There is, says Kohr, *stable balance* in the stagnant and huge. But there is *mobile balance* among the living. *Mobile balance* needs no master, but *stable balance* demands "the ever-conscious will of God Himself."[28] In other words, as human governing systems reach giant proportions, they require a dictator. This, according to Kohr, is where the lust for unity and unification leads, toward the "fixity of death."[29] "Only the totalitarian delights in oneness and unity rather than in the harmony produced by balanced di-

24. See my travel journal *In Switzerland the Moon Is Always Male*, available on Amazon.
25. Kohr, *Breakdown*, 129.
26. Kohr, *Breakdown*, 80.
27. Kohr, *Breakdown*, 83.
28. Kohr, *Breakdown*, 86.
29. Kohr, *Breakdown*, 87.

versity," and so we come to require "the special effort of a stabilizer, a genius, a dictator who must consciously hold together what previously arranged itself automatically."[30] Or, as Kohr goes on to say, "what the despised small-state world could do so effortlessly, the glorified big-power world cannot do at all: govern itself. It requires an external controlling agent."[31]

But the controlling violence of the dictator is not simply external; it's also (and perhaps more importantly) internal. The rise of kingship and aristocracy is not spontaneous crowd contagion or mob eruption. Civilization is not critical-mass spontaneous aggression—village erupting unexpectedly as city, *pagus* exploding paradoxically into *civis*—as it is *the calculated and conscious expropriation of nonviolent villagers by a band of male bandits who systematically enlarge and consolidate their field of conquest.* The expropriation may also be oriented externally, stealing land or bodies or various kinds of natural wealth from beyond initial boundaries or established borders; but the expropriation is also *internally* systematic, with the theft of agricultural production and the enslavement of farmers. Civilizations have been built on a mix of internal slavery and external conquest. Peasants were the primary expropriated entity *within* preindustrial civilization. (More generally we can say that agriculture continues in the role of the expropriated victim; only food production has now been so completely rationalized, its condition so thoroughly "explained" by "scientific" chrematistics, that institutionalized expropriation is hidden behind chemical and bioengineering veils—the technological mythology—of civilized agribusiness. Utopian predation has become scientifically normative. Or, to put it differently, "science" now explains predation in a manner analogous to how Christianity made the "pagan" Roman Empire "holy" and "Christian.") Say it often enough and it will be true.

Kohr so desperately loves the small-scale he doesn't care—or, at least, he says he doesn't care—what political structure the small-scale may produce. He's a traveling salesman of small-scale political remedy. You can buy whatever colorful bottle of curative patent medicine you like—anarchism, a republic, hereditary aristocracy, a clerical state, a constitutional monarchy, an oligarchy, a president, socialism, communism—but none "has any inherent superiority over others."[32] All that matters is that each remains small, localized, and relatively harmless. Aggressive human nature will still be aggressive human nature, but nothing more than small-scale disturbance will ever come of it. What an appealing simplification!

Kohr beautifully distracts us with delightful descriptions of the small-scale—the Swiss cantons, for instance. But the problem is not so much *why* human governance didn't stop at the boundary of the canton or city-state, but *how* the overgrown huge came into being in the first place. If kingship and urban empire—Babylonia, Egypt, ancient China, etc—rose out of the concentrated abundance of agrarian villages, and

30. Kohr, *Breakdown*, 88.
31. Kohr, *Breakdown*, 89.
32. Kohr, *Breakdown*, 109.

if kingly empire emerged via the critical-mass dynamics Kohr proposes, than the only solution is not the status quo ante of city-states but the Earth First! status quo ante of the preagrarian hunter-gatherer band. If materialistic critical mass is an accurate and comprehensive description of causal dynamics, then only a return to stone arrowheads and digging sticks is an adequate retrogression. A *governor* becomes increasingly integral to economic life already with horticulture and agriculture, even with a garden (someone has to plant and weed and try to keep the rabbits, gophers, and woodchucks out); so in strictly economic terms, Kohr's prescription of retrogression throws us far back beyond any city-state idealism, even back beyond gardening and horticulture. His ideal really takes us to the outwash of the last Ice Age.

However, if Kohr's social-science physics of critical-mass is correct, there is no going back to anything unless the Global Unification Project breaks down and breaks apart in such ways (short of extermination or ecocide) that an unavoidable and wholesale retrogression is forced upon survivors. That, given Kohr's analysis, seems the only possible reprieve. Critical-mass theory combined with biologically conditioned attitudes combined with the total absence of indwelling Spirit (whose yeasty compassion could transform our consciousness and behavior) makes any sort of *mobile-balance* retrogression an improbable statistical fluke in a larger equation of unification catastrophe.

If Kohr's analysis is true, what's there to celebrate but bleak oblivion? No wonder a reviewer of *The Breakdown of Nations* found it a maddening little book; for if it's true, Auschwitz and Hiroshima are mere symbols, tiny templates, for what lies in wait for us all. Since when is such pessimism not tantamount to despair? To some difficult-to-interpret degree, Kohr flinches from gazing into the abyss of his own analysis. He diverts and distracts us with entertaining but—given his core dynamics—irrelevant sideshows of historical nostalgia. It doesn't take a genius to figure out why Kohr flinches. Not even a prophet of doom can stand to gaze into that molten crystal ball without going crazy. It's like staring into the depths of hell.

III

Well, okay, if Kohr's intellectual foundation is so weak, why has his argument in behalf of the small-scale had such influence on people like E. F. Schumacher, Kirkpatrick Sale, and Ivan Illich? (One could argue that the germ of Illich's *The History of Needs* can be found on page 137 of *The Breakdown of Nations*—luxuries "have become a necessity to satisfy our basic needs"—and the germ of *Shadow Work* lies on Kohr's page 143: "Instead of turning every maid into a housewife, progress has turned every housewife into a maid.") If Western philosophy constitutes a mere smattering of footnotes to Plato and Aristotle, then it might be said that a great deal of Green, bioregional, decentralist, and back-to-the-land writing is little more than an extended appendicle to Leopold Kohr's insights—like his chapter Seven in *Breakdown*, "The

Glory of the Small." But how can such countercultural success, such as it is, possibly rest on an unreliable base of argument?

The two major options here are a) all subsequent Kohrian writings are equally suspect, weak and unreliable or b) Kohr's *real* argument isn't dependent on the propositions he relies on—that is, his concoction of biologically conditioned attitudes, critical-mass social size, and the no-God-needed subtle dance of *mobile balance*. Well, yes and no. Kohr's "biologically conditioned attitudes" is more ideological construct than scientific truth. Even more would I say that in regard to critical-mass social size. Both concepts are scientistic reductionisms. But, perhaps paradoxically, the key to Kohr's easy fit within emerging Green consciousness lies in his no-God-needed *mobile balance*. This may be the wardrobe door into Kohr's Narnia. Let's see if we can squeeze through.

IV

If Terrence Rynne is correct in his *Gandhi and Jesus: The Saving Power of Nonviolence*, what's happening in contemporary theology is not merely the rejection of inherited notions and depictions of God (as is implicit in Rynne's critique of Anselm's soteriology, which depicts an angry and offended God who will be satisfied only with the voluntary sacrifice of a totally innocent person, a construct that—needless to say—glorifies the scapegoating process as a sanctifying religious act), but an exciting and liberating panentheistic realization of Spirit's indwelling, nonviolent, compassionate embeddedness within evolutionary unfolding. If we are in a massive shift in spiritual orientation, away from an otherworldly God who (as Prime Mover, First Cause, or God Almighty) stands outside the natural universe, and toward a Goddess who (whatever else She may be) is the Evolving Consciousness of living nature, then we are also in a corresponding shift in political orientation from monarchical obedience to democratic cooperation. That is, Jesus' death on the cross is no longer understood by invoking an angry God in need of sacrificial mollification but, rather, by the willingness of Spirit, for love of life, to endure the wrath of human Powers and Principalities whose assertive and violent righteousness is in fact sadistic and demonic. *Civis* crucifying *pagus*. The murder of Jesus becomes Spirit's unmasking of *civis* Powers and Principalities hiding within mythic robes of righteousness. In this light, Kohr's no-God-needed *mobile balance* fits perfectly the growing realization of Spirit's indwelling Green exuberance. Nature is alive. Nature, as Spirit, is Living Presence. Or, as Kohr himself says, it is a moving, breathing, dynamic universe, a *"mobile balance* of the living."[33]

It is in this sense, this vital "anarchism" of trustworthy self-regulation, that Kohr vehemently insists that giant size (or, as he also calls it, "gigantomania"[34]) requires a *dictator* who "must consciously hold together what previously arranged itself

33. Kohr, *Breakdown*, 86.
34. Kohr, *Breakdown*, 150.

automatically." By means of a story he tells on pages 95 and 96, Kohr comes close to identifying this dictatorial impulse ("organization is hell!") with Satan; as he goes on to say, "our mass-state citizen has invested this grunting low-grade organism with the attribute of divinity."[35] This grunting divinity of giant size, this low-grade dictator of glorified big-power, turns out not to be God but the Devil. (In psychoanalytical formulation, this means that civilization is demonic; and, if this grunting God is civilization's God, then civilization's God is also the Devil.)

In Kohr's thought, "Hugeness, as we have seen, needs conscious direction, supervision, control, obedience, conformity, efficiency, standardization, discipline, alikeness in habit and thought, unity, centralism—all concepts which in their sum constitute the essence and operating basis of socialism."[36] (Perhaps this is something of a non sequitur, but I continue to be amused by elderly friends who listen to right-wing talk radio, hate socialism, but love the library, public roads, fire protection, Medicare, and their monthly Social Security checks.) Kohr's political view is of a piece with his dusty deism, his biological determinism, and his atomic chain-reaction social theory. Kohr's deism, biological determinism, and critical-mass social theory not only are thin reeds as base hypotheses, they also limit and distort the conclusions he comes to. They bend his analysis in perverse ways.

E. F. Schumacher was not repulsed by socialism, as his chapter of that name shows in *Small is Beautiful*. R. H. Tawney, in *The Acquisitive Society*, was more explicit and helpful:

> [T]here is no inconsistency between encouraging simultaneously a multiplication of peasant farmers and small masters who own their own farms or shops, and the abolition of private ownership in these industries, unfortunately to-day the most conspicuous, in which the private owner is an absentee shareholder.
>
> Indeed, the second reform would help the first. In so far as the community tolerates functionless property it makes difficult, if not impossible, the restoration of the small master in agriculture or in industry, who cannot easily hold his own in a world dominated by great estates or capitalist finance. In so far as it abolishes those kinds of property which are merely parasitic, it facilitates the restoration of the small property-owner in those kinds of industry for which small ownership is adapted. A socialistic policy towards the former is not antagonistic to the "distributive state," but, in modern economic conditions, a necessary preliminary to it, and if by "Property" is meant the personal possessions which the word suggests to nine-tenths of the population, the object of socialists is not to undermine property but to protect and increase it.[37]

35. Kohr, *Breakdown*, 102.

36. Kohr, *Breakdown*, 214.

37. Tawney, *Acquisitive*, 86-87.

Tawney, unlike Kohr, does not despise socialism; instead, he puts socialism in its proper place. (Kohr, on page 168, acknowledges what he calls "natural monopolies," but he glides right over the political implications. Why? I suspect he'd already painted himself into a pretty small corner with his hatred of the big and therefore had no way to speak positively about public ownership of "*natural* monopolies" without making a fool of himself.) Kohr dreads the big, and is constantly beating its head with his comic-opera shovel, because he believes the big *always* is deadly and deadening. It requires a managerial devil to keep it operating. The only reasonable thing is to chop it down to proper harmless scale. Therefore his desperate pleading for the comic-opera city-state, his dearest political vessel—which means, instead of dissolving God, Kohr chops God into countless little gods, much as the divine right of kings gets slivered into countless fragments of individualistic sovereignty by means of civilized "democracy," the politics of the sorcerer's apprentice. Every man a king, every home a castle. But comic-opera city-state retrogression is sheer fantasy given Kohr's operating dynamics.

That means (in my estimation) there's only one thing left to trust—indwelling Spirit. And if we are capable of recognizing and achieving the *mobile balance* of the life-providing small-scale, then we might be capable of recognizing and achieving the *stable balance* of *natural* monopolies in a Tawneyesque socialism. Some things in the modern economy—railroads or the electrical grid, for two examples—are naturally or inevitably big. But Kohr does not trust the big because, it seems, his concept of the divine, of God, is stuck on a dusty shelf in a Prime Mover closet. God may have started the whole show with a Big Bang blowout way back when, but He's apparently nowhere to be found in the cosmic neighborhood these days. Therefore political ethics are devoid of spiritual dimension or spiritual wholeness; such ethics as there may be (if we can even employ the term) are rooted, as Kohr said, in "biologically conditioned attitudes." Therefore the destiny of the planet—or at least a huge proportion of evolutionary life forms on the planet—depends on the outcome of collective human judgment. And, of course, Kohr's book is precisely about his anticipation of what will be the result of the unrestrained collective. Collective human judgment is precisely what Kohr dreads.

Well, given the European (not merely German) attitude toward Jews, Kohr had ample reason not to expect much from collective human judgment as represented by Christian theology or the church. Hitler was never excommunicated. So is it surprising that Kohr cobbled together a pseudoscientific and deistic platform for his small-scale soapbox? He had a message—an urgent one—and, like any good academic, he had to give it legs. His message was better, richer, and far more compelling than the legs could support.

But he took his explanatory underpinnings much too seriously and was seriously limited by them. Those little legs pinched his perspective and deformed his message. To some extent, he nailed himself inside his own hobbyhorse. Now what?

V

A careful reading of chapters Ten and Twelve, however, suggest that Kohr, with a magician's finesse, built himself an escape tunnel. (Chapter Eleven doesn't count. It's entitled "But Will It Be Done?" and the text consists of a single word—"No!")

Well, maybe it does count. Maybe it's the disguised door to the tunnel. I'll try to explain.

Chapter Ten is called "The Elimination of Great Powers." In it Kohr says proportional representation regionally "would bring about the eventual dissolution" of any Great Power.[38] Why? Because it is a

> . . . characteristic feature of true federations that the principal share of public power is entrusted to the small member unit, while progressively diminishing amounts of power are reserved to the higher governmental levels. In this way power is given where it can do no harm, and withheld where it might assume dangerous proportions and invite abuse. With the highest organs in a federation possessing but few powers in their own right, no obstructive power complex can develop at the top. As a result, it would be relatively easy to transfer the last weak remaining national powers to a larger international authority. In this manner, division could be effected by the inoffensive device of the internal federalization of the great powers brought about through the offer of proportional rather than national representation.[39]

Although the political specimen under Kohr's microscope is France, the dynamic applies universally:

> The revolutionary change would be purely internal in character. It would be destruction by which nothing that counts is destroyed. It would be elimination without victims. There would be no foreign laws, no foreign occupation, no change in traffic or commerce or anything except in the fact that government and sovereignty would suddenly have come closer to the individual, endowing him within the smaller sphere of the new sovereign units with a dignity and importance not previously possessed. He would find this charming, not distasteful. His district would be infused with new vitality, his provincial capital would assume new glamour, and his prefect would be transformed from an appointed functionary into an elected head of state. A whole new range of intriguing activities would now take place close to his home instead of in distant Paris, new governments and parliaments would spring up and, instead of the ambitions of a few, the ambitions of many could be satisfied.[40]

---

38. Kohr, *Breakdown*, 191.

39. Kohr, *Breakdown*, 192-93.

40. Kohr, *Breakdown*, 193.

In chapter Nine, Kohr praises up and down the "two outstanding examples" of successful federation, Switzerland and the United States.[41] Well, well, well—here we have unanticipated praise for something big and (if we dare use that dreadful word) something *unifying*. What makes federated unity palatable (Kohr has no negative comments on the Swiss or the Americans) is the "possession of sufficient executive power to enforce its laws on all its members. In order to succeed, it must be slightly stronger than its strongest member state. This is not political theory but administrative arithmetic. In a small-cell organization, superiority of federal power over its strongest unit is easily accomplished because even the strongest unit is weak."[42]

The gist is that *unification*—that stinking, rotten, foul, repulsive word, that gagging blasphemy—suddenly becomes as sweet as a hedge of wild rose blossoms when it achieves the *federation* of regionally coherent entities, each entity (with proportional representation) jealous to preserve its political existence and determined to protect its regional identity. *Federation* thus guarantees the political vitality of the small while providing an overarching governing device by which the (collectively) small can achieve common ends and cooperative purpose.

Howsomeever, there's a fly in the ointment. In Kohr's last chapter, "The American Empire," the fly is the ghost of de Tocqueville, a world of two empires—the United States and Russia. Or, to be more exact, the United States *versus* Russia. One or the other is destined to prevail.

Let's presume, for the sake of argument, that the collapse of the Soviet Union was only a blip, a tweak, a fairly minor setback in the unfolding of de Tocqueville's prophecy. Or, to broaden out a bit, we might welcome into the Great Power fraternal fray such vigorous contenders as China, India, the European Union, and perhaps Brazil. Does this mean the world is headed for a repeat of World War One, that catastrophic confrontation of Great Powers bumping up against each other like rival street gangs, only this time armed with nuclear assault rifles? Perhaps. But here we need to keep an eye on Kohr's secret tunnel, his unifying federation of proportional representation.

Of course, Kohr's entire book is marbled with the excoriation of unity, unifiers, and unification, such as this passage from chapter Ten:

> There are, of course, people such as elementary-school teachers, national politicians, military men, collectivists, mankind maniacs, and others glorying in unitarian developments, who will oppose the concept of small democratic states with fanaticism and the outcry of reaction—as if the pattern of nature could ever be reactionary. But the bulk of the inhabitants of the regions in which these states would be restored have shown time and again that they think differently. They do not seem to want life in vast meaningless realms. They want to live in their provinces, in their mountains, in their valleys. They want to live at home. This is why they have clung so tenaciously to their local

41. Kohr, *Breakdown*, 172.
42. Kohr, *Breakdown*, 173-74.

colour and provincialism even when they were submerged in great empires. In the end, however, it was always the small state, not the empire, that survived. That is why small states do not have to be created artificially. They need only be freed.[43]

But Kohr ends chapter Ten with a plea as to how "an *effective* federal government" (Kohr's emphasis, not mine) would not only keep member states united but also apart:

> With the federal government having an easy margin of strength over the small individual states or even a combination of them, the danger of a successful regrouping of great powers would be a remote possibility.
>
> From all this we see that the technical obstacle to the division of great powers and the preservation of a small-scale pattern is anything but insurmountable. By using the device of proportional representation together with an appeal to the powerful particularist sentiments always present in human groups, the condition of a small-scale world, so essential a prerequisite of successful international union, could be established without force or violence. It would mean nothing but the abandonment of a few silly, though cherished, slogans of the turn-the-clock-back category, a bit of diplomacy, and a bit of technique.
>
> *It can be done!* And if unions are to survive, it *must* be done![44]

So here's the question Kohr never asks or answers: What's the size, exactly, what's the geopolitical scope of this (pardon me) *unifying* federal entity that so successfully keeps small member states both united and independent?

By Kohr's own analysis, more than one such federalizing entity would result (de Tocqueville's ghost) in critical-mass warfare. Therefore the only possible conclusion to "It can be done!" and it "must be done!" is *global* federation. Or, to put it in language that provides stimulus for apoplexy: One World Government. A federation of federations.

This secret-tunnel conclusion (or is it merely a buried contradiction?) is inescapable in Kohr. For all his historic posturing to the contrary notwithstanding, Kohr's love for the small leads crookedly but inevitably to this *unifying* conclusion—although he doesn't seem to want to admit it.

I will call this successful international unification by the name libertarian ecological democratic socialism. Perhaps someone has a better name. Just so it's not called Armageddon. But either federalism leads to centralization and disintegration ("If a federation has *several* great-power participants, it will break apart. It will end in disintegration. If it has only one, it will turn the smaller members into tools of the biggest. It will end in centralization") or it "is anything but insurmountable. By using the device of proportional representation together with an appeal to the powerful particularist

43. Kohr, *Breakdown*, 195-96.
44. Kohr, *Breakdown*, 196.

sentiments always present in human groups, the condition of a small-state world, so essential a prerequisite of successful international union, could be established without force or violence."[45]

All in all, we need Pete Seeger's world of peace and justice. Let's hope we rise up singing.

VI

Since I neglected to footnote "pessimism is not despair,"[46] Kohr's remark from his Preface to the 1986 paperback edition of *The Breakdown of Nations* (also published by Routledge & Kegan Paul), I have to add a section to accommodate the omission. Of course, footnoting the omission is only an excuse. But I'd like to share a little more fully what I'm seeing as underlying our present situation—the gritty, grounded, and relentless infiltration of eutopian theology steadily transforming utopian theology, stretching back centuries if not millennia.

Kohr's deism, meanwhile, and the atomic chain-reaction "social science" that goes with it, is a subset of utopian theology (that is, it's just a novel way of saying "original sin"), even as his passionate espousal of the small-scale, his *mobile balance* of the living, runs free of this utopian framework, escaping under, over, around, and through its walls. Those rigid utopian walls are in process of being dissolved, yeasted into something far more permeable and lovely, as eutopian theology discovers its spiritual life, exercises its creative vigor, and begins to stretch its wings.

In his section on the late Mennonite theologian John Howard Yoder, Terrence Rynne says Yoder "has had a profound influence on contemporary Christian theology":

> [Yoder's] contribution stems from the fact that he proposed afresh two fundamental questions: Do we find in the New Testament that Jesus taught a sociopolitical ethic? And, if Jesus did propose a distinctive sociopolitical ethic, what is its content and is it normative for his followers? Those two questions were asked and answered by Yoder especially in his books *The Politics of Jesus*, *The Original Revolution*, *He Came Preaching Peace*, and *Christian Attitudes towards War, Peace, and Revolution*. What was noteworthy and powerful about Yoder's approach was that he answered the questions using the latest tools of historical/critical biblical scholarship, bridging the gap between scripture studies on the one hand and moral and systematic theology on the other.
>
> Yoder studied under Karl Barth and Oscar Cullmann at the University of Basel on his way to completing his doctorate in theology. He was influenced by both of them in the way that he read the scriptures, but he was especially influenced by Cullmann's careful study of the political environment of first-century Palestine. During the 1950s and 1960s he used the scholarship of

45. Kohr, *Breakdown*, 179-80.
46. Kohr, *Breakdown*, 196.

many scripture scholars in addition to Cullmann as he developed his work on the politics of Jesus. Among them were C. H. Dodd, Hans Conzelmann, Rudolf Schnackenburg, John L. Mckenzie, SJ, Robert Morgenthaler, Robert North, SJ, Krister Stendhal, and Hans Dieter Betz. When he issued a second edition of *The Politics of Jesus* in 1994, he added epilogues to each of the chapters as well as the testimony of then-current respected scripture scholars: C. F. Moule, Marcus Borg, N. Thomas Wright, Dominic Crossan, Richard Horsley, Walter Brueggemann, A. E. Harvey, Gerard Lohfink, SJ, Adela Yarbro Collins, John P. Meier, Raymond Brown, and Walter Wink. The later scholarship for the most part confirmed and sharpened the earlier work, which described the political context of first-century Palestine and demonstrated the political implications of Jesus' actions and teaching.

In taking this approach of first and seriously attending to the scriptures to determine whether Jesus taught a political ethic and if it was presented as normative for his followers, Yoder challenged the typical ways that these fundamental questions had been addressed. In particular he directly challenged the "realism" school of Reinhold Niebuhr. . . .[47]

Niebuhr, says Rynne, "misunderstood the eschatology of the New Testament."[48] He goes on with Yoder's critique:

> As a historical theologian, Yoder looked back on the history of Christianity and regretted the loss of Christianity's commitment to nonresistance. That loss occurred when Constantine declared Christianity the religion of the empire, when the church in turn condoned the use of violence against the empire's enemies, when Augustine asked the emperor to use the sword to get the heretics, the Donatists, back in line. Before Constantinianism, the church had followed the example of Jesus and rejected the sword.
>
> For Yoder, once the power had been ceded to the state to punish and coerce with the sword those who were called God's enemies, Christianity lost its power to fight and minimize violence; the church became instead the legitimator of the state and could no longer be held guiltless for the subsequent history of violence.[49]

Yoder, says Rynne, "saw that in the Middle Ages the pacifist sentiment still lived as an undercurrent in the life of the church," but with the Reformation

> . . . that order was swept away. There were no more tangible islands of peace and holiness in the middle of a world at war. The princes assumed power over the local churches. The nation-state was the organ of the Reformation. The princes financed the churches and created their governing bodies and gave

47. Rynne, *Gandhi*, 96–97.

48. Rynne, *Gandhi*, 104.

49. Rynne, *Gandhi*, 105.

them legitimacy. That arrangement was confirmed in the Peace of Westphalia and the doctrine of *cuius regio, eius religio*.

The Reformation heightened the moral autonomy of the civil order. Luther underlined that fact with the doctrine of the two kingdoms, one for the word of God and one for the state, which is definitely not under the church. The prince was no longer under any criticism of the bishop. It was up to the state to keep order and straighten out wrongs, and thereby it was given an even stronger mandate for violence. . . .

In just about every book Yoder wrote he refers negatively to Reinhold Niebuhr's thought and on a number of occasions gives a detailed critique of Niebuhr's thought. He does so for two reasons. He recognized that Niebuhr's thought, or at least the sentiments behind Niebuhr's thought, had been embraced by most American Christians. Niebuhr had been a pacifist during the 1920s and 1930s, but with Hitler's arrival on the scene he disavowed the easy optimism of those years. He became convinced that those who thought the message of nonresistance could be translated into politics were not only naïve but irresponsible.[50]

John M. Swomley, in *American Empire: The Political Ethics of Twentieth-Century Conquest*, says Niebuhr "emphasized recognition of the sinful nature of man as the real root of his realism" and the "ultimate norm of Christian love is to the Christian realist always a contrasting standard of judgment, an impossible ideal rather than a redemptive force or living presence that alters political conduct."[51]

The key term here is "living presence," Living Presence capable of altering conduct both personal and political, Living Presence in contrast to "impossible ideal." In fact, I would say that everything pertaining to this discussion hinges precisely on the veracity of Living Presence, on whether Spirit is or is not transforming human consciousness in the direction and dimension of postcivilized eutopian culture—or whether we are in the closing days or End Times of an "impossible ideal," utopia ramifying as dystopia. The nature and destiny of sin does have political and ecological consequences. Our understanding of sin has been shaped by a *civis* theology that has pounded sinfulness into our bones.

Leopold Kohr, although I have no idea what he thought of Reinhold Niebuhr, had a view of "human nature" essentially identical to Niebuhr's. Niebuhr may have called his view "original sin," while Kohr preferred "biologically conditioned attitudes," but under the respective semantic hides are similar little beasts. Neither condition may be totally hopeless, but there's not much hope to be found there, either. Niebuhr's sinful man is incapable of reaching the kingdom of God on Earth—that's only an impossible ideal—while Kohr's perceptive man cringes in fear of unification because of biologically conditioned attitudes.

50. Rynne, *Gandhi*, 106-7.

51. Swomley, *American*, 12.

John C. Bennett, in an essay called "Reinhold Niebuhr's Social Ethics" (in *Reinhold Niebuhr: His Religious, Social, and Political Thought*), says that although Niebuhr had been greatly motivated by the "social gospel" propounded by Walter Rauschenbusch, he also "believed that Rauschenbusch shared the liberal illusions about the possibility of building a new society through education and moral persuasion."[52] Insofar as Rauschenbusch's vision was based on some sort of religious or moral Fabianism, itself derivative from the doctrine of Progress, I would agree with Bennett and Niebuhr. But I don't think Rauschenbusch can be stuffed into a "liberal illusion" box. In fact, Robert Ellsberg says flatly in his *All Saints* entry for Rauschenbusch that the latter was "the foremost theological exponent of the Social Gospel in North America," "believed the gospel today required the transformation of a social system that was responsible for so much poverty and injustice," but "never believed that the kingdom of God was to be identified with the march of social progress."[53] *Never* is a pretty strong word. Rauschenbusch's great discovery wasn't "progress," it was the "kingdom of God." Rauschenbusch may not have grasped the full meaning or energy or scope of the kingdom of God construct—who has?—but to dismiss Rauschenbusch as under the influence of "liberal illusions" is more than cruel. It smacks of intellectual condescension and spiritual contempt.

Bennett says Niebuhr carried on "a continual debate with both legalists and moral relativists,"[54] and "for him Luther was a stronger influence than was the case with most American Protestants."[55] It's worth noting that Norman O. Brown, especially in "The Protestant Era" section in his *Life Against Death*, shows that Luther deepened the Western perception of how fully evil rules the world, or what Brown calls "the tremendous extension of the Devil's empire in Protestantism." The sword now ruled the church. This, says Brown, is "tantamount to saying—and Luther says it—that the Christian remains under the dominion of the Devil" and that "God has retired into invisibility—Deus absconditus."[56] Well, as we have seen from Terrence Rynne, the doctrine of *cuius regio, eius religio* grew out of Luther's insistence on the God-ordained cleavage between the two kingdoms of church and state, with the state having the God-given authority to choose which church was to be allowed in the state's turf.[57]

---

52. Bennett, "Reinhold," 63.

53. Ellsberg, *All*, 317-18.

54. Bennett, "Reinhold," 56.

55. Bennett, "Reinhold," 62.

56. Brown, *Life*, 215.

57. Paul Tillich, in his "Author's Introduction," page xxi, in *The Protestant Era*, says "It is a shortcoming of Protestantism that it never has sufficiently described the place of love in the whole of Christianity. This is due to the genesis and history of Protestantism. . . . While Zwingli and Calvin, by their humanistic-biblicistic stress on the function of the law, were prevented from developing a doctrine of love, Luther's doctrine of love and wrath (of God and government) prevented him from connecting love with law and justice. The result was Puritanism without love in the Calvinist countries

Brown ties this constriction into Freud's construct of the death instinct: "Luther's devil is ultimately personified death."[58] Brown insists "the insight of Protestantism is its insight into the dominion of death in life, and its service to life and to love is its hope in another life which would be true life."[59] But Brown also says "If neo-orthodox Christianity cannot foresee the kingdom of Christ on earth, it consigns this earth to the eternal dominion of Satan."[60] And "since the Devil is lord of this world, we may say, in psychoanalytical terms, that Luther sees civilization as having an essentially anal-sadistic structure."[61] (This may be true; but Luther's training was as an Augustinian priest, and his theology was saturated with the Augustinian doctrine of two kingdoms. That is, Luther's acute peasant perception revealed the "essentially anal-sadistic structure of civilization," but for him the state's authority was nevertheless mandated by God because Paul the Apostle and Augustine said so.)

"In Luther's historical eschatology," Brown goes on, "the world was going to get worse before it got better."[62] And here we are, five hundred years later, with ecocidal weaponry and global climate change to corroborate the prediction. Yet Protestantism "represents a new stage in human history, a fuller return of the repressed." The world getting worse links to a "fuller return of the repressed" in that Luther (in Brown's view) recognized that Catholic theocracy disguised the dominion of the Devil or, as we might say, the traumatic institutions of civilization—that is, the Constantinian accommodation as rationalized by Augustine. To see the reality behind the robes is part of apocalyptic awakening. But since life "in this world is the life we actually live, the effect [of the world getting worse] is to surrender this life to the driving power of Eros' antagonist, the death instinct. Protestantism would therefore seem to mark an important stage in the psychic history of civilization: the death instinct becomes master of the house."[63] The death instinct, securely lodged in otherworldly superego and in our daily moral compass, is therefore civilization's hidden rudder.

Luther's failure was in limiting his critique to the papacy. That is, Luther recognized the opulence and attacked the corruption of the Vatican; but as an ideological Augustinian harkening to Romans 13:1-7, he accorded to the state a sacred godly

---

and romanticism without justice in the Lutheran countries. A fresh interpretation of love is needed in all sections of Protestantism, an interpretation that shows that love is basically not an emotion but an ontological power, that it is the essence of life itself, namely, the dynamic reunion of that which is separated. If love is understood in this way, it is the principle on which all Protestant social ethics is based, uniting an eternal and a dynamic element, uniting power with justice and creativity with form." Tillich may stop a fuzz short of explicit repudiation of the doctrine of two kingdoms—Luther's love and wrath—but *if love is the essence of life itself*, the two kingdom doctrine is a perverse constriction on the place of love in the whole of Christianity.

58. Brown, *Life*, 215.

59. Brown, *Life*, 216-17.

60. Brown, *Life*, 218.

61. Brown, *Life*, 225.

62. Brown, *Life*, 226.

63. Brown, *Life*, 232.

mandate and preached acquiescence to its authority. Lutheranism therefore has no overarching critique of civilization, except that of a pious scold. *Sola scriptura* (by scripture alone) and *cuius regio, eius religio* (the prince is to determine the religion of the region) reveal the mythic rigidity of religious conviction in a *civis* mode. Not only did Luther preach the schizophrenic doctrine of two kingdoms, his religious authority aided the death instinct in becoming "master of the house."

Brown concludes "The Protestant Era" by saying "psychoanalysis has no utopia"[64] and "neo-orthodox Protestantism has no eschatology."[65] I think I know what Brown means, but I would in part disagree. Psychoanalysis (except, perhaps, for its exuberant fling forty or fifty years ago with multiple therapeutic explorations) has so far failed to escape its own utopian imprisonment or find its way into eutopian liberation. (See, for instance, Brown's summary of psychoanalysis's project on pages 154 through 156, or again on page 185 of his *Life Against Death*.) Civilized utopianism and religious otherworldliness continue to have dominating grips on our collective consciousness, just as they have shaped the bulk of our institutions historically, culminating in the worldwide imposition of Christian Civilization. Meanwhile, neo-orthodox Protestantism has either surrendered the world to the Devil, to "anal-sadistic" civilization, or it has so aligned itself with nationalism and capitalist ideology that Luther's Devil has, in fact, become its God. At least it is extremely difficult to tell them apart. Or we might say the scholarship demonstrating the empathy-deficient theft and war origins of civilization has had no impact on Lutheran theology because—*sola scriptura*—the Bible tells us everything we need to know about the origins of the world and its human institutions.

So, as science and its associated critical scholarship have demolished what had been the literal historical ("fundamentalist") understanding of the Bible and, in the process, exposed the Constantinian accommodation for the spiritual betrayal that it was and still is, for the otherworldly *civis* consciousness it imposed on us, and as science and scholarship have provided complex understandings of both nature and human social evolution, then we who are presently alive are faced with a terrifically unsettled and unsettling world. The globalization of traumatic institutions ramifies as End Times, with the bulk of Christian institutions in passive acquiescence because God mandated those End Times institutions for control of original sin and restraint of the pagan. Weapons of ecocidal capacity, climate change, extinction of species, the corruption if not the extermination of noncivilized folk cultures, etc, etc—all this tells us something monstrous is afoot and that something has to give. Something has to radically change or we may be doomed to die at the hands of civilizational ideology linked to religious doctrine, both of which remain dressed in ancient robes of divine sanctity. Kohr's prescription of the small social and political unit, in the face of all

---

64. In terminology I've learned from Lewis Mumford, the correct word here is eutopia, not utopia. That is, psychoanalysis, like Christianity, remains stuck in utopian mentality.

65. Brown, *Life*, 233.

this, may be appealing, but his analysis prevents any exercise of hope. In fact, Kohr discourages such hope.

The only path open therefore (other than resignation before the righteous death instinct) is self-emptying ethical behavior—radical stewardship and radical servant-hood. But if there is no Spirit, no Living Presence by which or in which ethical behavior might grow, dance and reproduce, then the ethical path, too, will fail. That doesn't mean self-emptying is or ever was a false path—its essential wisdom is reflected in the greatest and most revered of our spiritual teachers—only that it may not be strong enough to digest the hubris and transform the evil that civilizational mythology, in league with religious mythology, continues to both perpetuate and hide from itself. Either eutopian theology is a sign of breakthrough into transformative Living Presence—which indicates arrival of the Daughter—or it's a last, desperate gasp of deferred spiritual wisdom—brilliantly expressed but insufficiently strong—before it gets obliterated by the political "realism" of all the deluded and demon-possessed worshippers of the civilized Devil/God.

If the world gets destroyed by our brilliant political "realists," as they "manage" the technologies of extermination and the geopolitics of extinction, they will have unequivocally proven correct the conventional, orthodox doctrine that says the kingdom of God is not attainable on Earth. But what an astonishingly perverse proof! Civilized Christian realism, with its fearsome tag team of fundamentalist stubbornness and Augustinian hubris, will have successfully played its part in the global victory of death, and Christianity will have fully morphed, righteously intact, into the all-conquering Anti-Christ, as Pontius Pilate once again washes his hands of any part in murder. Such is the disastrous eschatology of civilized, utopian Christianity. We have to destroy the world in order to save it: this is the managed outcome, the logical conclusion, to the paralyzing doctrine of Original Sin.

VII

Perhaps it's possible to wrap up a few loose ends or, at least, crumple a few pieces of newspaper around the loose ends in a pretense of wrapping up. Let's start with Kohr's remark about getting "nowhere by spreading the gospel" if our intent is "to discourage the development of crime-producing attitudes and philosophies," especially when the problem lies in "those overgrown social units which, by their very nature, are governed not by the gospel but the number-conditioned law of averages." Kohr never says, exactly, what he means by "gospel," but I think we can safely infer he doesn't mean what John Howard Yoder means. I believe Kohr intends by "gospel" a general reference to pious religious abstraction, a moralistic and otherworldly prescription bordering on the irrelevant. He obviously wants analysis and prescription with grit and traction; "gospel" as "nowhere" indicates an understandable impatience with vacuous religious abstraction. At least in principle, Walter Rauschenbusch and John Howard Yoder would agree with Leopold Kohr in regard to *that* sort of "gospel."

Second, overgrown social units require a dictator to keep them, to the extent possible, in *stable balance*. But the drive for unity and unification leads to the "fixity of death." (Shall we say Mutually Assured Destruction or Anthropocene Extinctions?) Unless we take "fixity of death" as mere colorful language, just part of the wit and sparkle that animates Kohr's prose—exuberant, you know, titillating, but not really serious—we can't help but be grabbed (or at least disturbed) by these remarks from Norman O. Brown:

> From the standpoint of the original Protestant theology, the deification of capitalism and of the calling is the deification of the Devil, or at least an utter confusion between God and the Devil. From the psychoanalytical point of view, if the Devil is Death, and if capitalism is the Devil, then modern Protestantism's alliance with capitalism means its complete surrender to the death instinct.
>
> It is therefore no accident that [Paul] Tillich, the theologian who has done most to recover the sense of the demonic, is also the theologian who has done most to disentangle Protestantism from its alliance with capitalism. Tillich speaks like Luther when he speaks of "a demonic possession in the grip of which modern society lives," and of capitalism as "the demonry of autonomous economics," which, together with the demonry of nationalism, surpasses all others in significance for our times. But again we wonder what the outcome of neo-orthodox theology is, as long as it fails to recover Luther's historical eschatology. Tillich's exponent James Luther Adams may say that "the way out of the present era can be found only if men can be released from the 'possession' of the demonic powers that now carry through or protect the bourgeois principle." But as long as (to quote Tillich) "the Protestant principle cannot admit any identification of grace with a visible reality," and cannot repeat with conviction the traditional Christian faith that the time will come when grace will be made visible, and that this goal is the meaning of history, it looks as if neo-orthodox theology will remain incapable of casting out demons, and therefore will be of limited service to the life instinct in its war against the death instinct. It diagnoses, but it does not cure.[66]

Well, it does not cure because its diagnosis is so limited and flawed.

Third, if we are willing to admit, even grudgingly, that Kohr's thinking tended—I suppose we might say "unconsciously"—in the direction Brown elucidates with such systematic rigor, then it may also be possible to say that "this grunting low-grade organism" which "our mass-state citizen has invested . . . with the attribute of divinity" is, in Luther's terms, the Devil or, in Brown's, the death instinct. If this seems weirdly outlandish, just think of what Weapons of Mass Destruction actually *means*

66. Brown, *Life*, 224-25.

or why there is such an astounding refusal to attend to the massive consequences of global warming and climate change. If this can't be called "death instinct," then what name shall we give it more accurately reflecting its willful blind insanity? How is it that members of our species, certainly a certain slice of the elite males of our species, have pushed Class and War, greed and aggression, entitlement and supremacy, to this threshold of planetary catastrophe? Are we incapable of cracking the equation of our "death instinct," or are we simply unwilling to try? Perhaps we are *civis* possessed.

There's no denying Kohr's love for the small-scale. It was his great passion. We should be grateful for that passion. But gratefulness doesn't require putting an image of Kohr in an alcove or a copy of *Breakdown* in a candle-lit temple full of pious hush. Let's face it: Kohr's explanation was crappy, cobbled out of discard materials, unable to support his passionate insight and even detrimental to it. It's time to liberate Kohr from his soapbox and his hobbyhorse. We might even call it resurrection. Norman O. Brown almost gets the last word:

> [W]hat is needed is not an organismic ideology, but to change the human body so that it can become for the first time an organism—the resurrection of the body.
>
> The resurrection of the body is a social project facing mankind as a whole, and it will become a practical political problem when the statesmen of the world are called upon to deliver happiness instead of power.[67]

Pete Seeger got it right, after all.

67. Brown, *Life*, 317.

11

Going for the Juggler

Thomas Berry and the New Universe Story

READING THOMAS BERRY IS like watching a juggler at work—or play—even to the point of not knowing how many balls are in the air at any given moment. Berry's writing, always returning to an ecological critique, covers a lot of territory. Although he calls himself a conservative Christian, even a "very conservative Christian,"[1] it's hard to know what Berry means by "conservative" or "Christian." *Apparently* he means adherence to the concept of "Cosmic Christ," based on the prologue to the gospel of John ("In the beginning was the Word: the Word was with God and the Word was God. He was with God in the beginning. Through him all things came to be, not one thing had its being but through him"), and verses 15-20 of the opening chapter of Paul's letter to the Colossians ("He is the image of the unseen God and the first-born of all creation, for in him were created all things"). All this is laid onto the "new universe story" of Pierre Teilhard de Chardin who, Berry says, "wrote the basic work of twentieth-century theology,"[2] "gave expression to the greatest transformation in Christian thought since the time of St. Paul,"[3] and is "the primary theologian who has been able to make this transposition, to move effectively from a spatially under-stood universe to a time-developmental universe and to envisage this developmental universe as an expression of the Christ story."[4]

In light of this new chronological model, Father, Son, and Holy Spirit—the or-thodox Christian Trinity—would no longer be understood as three extraterrestrial Beings, but would instead be described "in terms of a principle of differentiation: the Father; the principle of interior articulation, the inner principle of things: the Son; and the Holy Spirit, the bonding, the holding together of things, the spirit of love, the *spiritus*, the inner spirit of reality."[5] This etherealization of spiritual Persons or supernatural Beings into metaphysical abstractions—differentiation, interior articula-

---

1. Berry, *Befriending*, 79.

2. Berry, *Befriending*, 23.

3. Berry, *Befriending*, 6.

4. Berry, *Befriending*, 74.

5. Berry, *Befriending*, 16.

tion, and the bonding of things—pretty much does in the multiple Personhood of God as Father, Son, and Holy Spirit as traditionally understood. Berry is explicit about this: "Speculatively, we could talk about God as being prior to or outside creation or independent of creation, but in actual fact there is no such being as God without creation."[6]

So our traditional view of God as *outside* nature, *outside* creation, *outside* the universe—Creator as distinct from Creation—is repudiated by Thomas Berry. He wants religion to "perceive the natural world as the primary revelation of the divine, as primary scripture, as the primary mode of numinous presence. Christian religion would cease its antagonism toward the earth and discover its sacred quality."[7] For when we "destroy the living forms of this planet," we also "destroy modes of divine presence."[8]

There's a lot to explore here. The primary thing may be that Berry wants our spirituality based on actual experience—i.e., natural world as mode of numinous presence—not on philosophical assertion or metaphysical speculation. First wonder, then reflection, but a kind of wonder based in and of the natural world. But, perhaps befitting what I've called Berry's "juggler" propensity, he

> . . . was once with a group of people, and there was a woman philosopher there. I was talking about my Buddhist soul and my Hindu soul and my Chinese soul. I could see she was getting more and more tense. Pretty soon she pounded the table and said, "What do you believe?" And I said, "I believe everything. Tell me something, I'll believe it. I am a believer and I like to believe. Why should I limit my belief?" As St. Paul says, "Believe all things."[9]

This makes what purports to be revolutionary perception into playful whimsy, although Berry immediately says "The norm for my belief is really the earth community norm."[10] We'll have to see whether "modes of divine presence," in the context of an "earth community norm," fit well or poorly in Teilhard's "time-developmental universe." I have my doubts. Let's see how these thoughts play out.

II

Berry was a Passionist priest and author of the two books I'll be primarily referencing—*Befriending the Earth* and *The Dream of the Earth*.[11] Something of a North Carolina tough nut, Berry refers to himself, not as a theologian, but as a "geologian." He says it's time to listen to the Earth. *Befriending the Earth* is coauthored with Thomas

---

6. Berry, *Befriending*, 10.

7. Berry, *Befriending*, 23.

8. Berry, *Befriending*, 11.

9. Berry, *Befriending*, 18.

10. Berry, *Befriending*, 18.

11. Berry died on June 1, 2009.

Clarke, a Jesuit. Well, "coauthored" isn't exactly accurate. What Clarke does is provide a response to Berry at the conclusion of each of the five *Befriending* chapters. His function seems to be to assure the reader that Berry is sufficiently Christian, orthodox, and conservative to be taken seriously—or, if not taken with complete seriousness, at least not dismissed out of hand. Berry's "system," says Clarke, is "quite congruous with the Judaeo-Christian heritage"[12] and it serves to "extend what St. Paul has written about the involvement of the whole cosmos in the salvation process."[13] Thomas Berry, says Clarke, is a "conservative radical."[14]

Berry *is* a brilliant diagnostician of the world crisis, and he may even be a "conservative radical" in a manner similar to how Paul Goodman thought himself a radical conservative fifty years ago. But he—Berry—goes off the fifteen-billion-year deep end, in my estimation, while wearing an insufficiently tested Cosmic Christ scuba suit and oxygen tank with a mere two thousand years of experimental air inside. According to my very quick—and mathematically dilettantish—calculation, the odds of his story's survival are 7,500,000 to 1. (Fifteen billion divided by two thousand; that is, Big Bang divided by Christianity.) That *may* be enough to risk purchase of a cosmic lottery ticket, but not enough to seriously consider early retirement.

Christianity is in something of a desperate fix (its theology and core ecclesiastical structure remain stuck in civilizational male dominance and associated linguistic presumption), but Cosmic Christ is no golden parachute. Historically speaking, neither Christianity generally nor the Roman Catholic Church specifically is too big to fail. When religions brag about their eternal significance, we would do well to recognize that such "eternal" significance is actually on a sliding temporal scale.

There's no question, however, that the Catholic Church is a rich and complex institution or that it has nourished and trained an abundance of rich and complex intellects over the centuries. The bulk of freer-thinking religious people in my hometown in northern Wisconsin are, in fact, Catholic sisters, as ready to discuss medieval mystics, the spiritual significance of Vatican II, the spiritual evolution of Thomas Merton, the influence of Teilhard de Chardin, the importance of Mohandas Gandhi, Dorothy Day and Martin Luther King, the subversive impact ("subversive" vis-à-vis the male hierarchy) of liberated women religious, as they are ready to teach high school dropouts, care for the elderly, organize the local food pantry, help set up a free clinic for the poor, or "secretly" fund a clean-water project for a hospital in Iraq. Compared to the sisters, local Protestants are a dreadfully anemic lot, exceptions made for a few frustrated and aggravated individuals who feel like spiritual orphans at a picnic, wondering where the protest has gone, leaving only ants to carry off the crumbs.

Raised in the United Church of Christ, loosely affiliated for a number of years with disaffiliated Lutherans and with Catholic Worker-influenced women religious in

---

12. Clarke, *Befriending*, 29.

13. Clarke, *Befriending*, 56.

14. Clarke, *Befriending*, 82.

St. Louis, then for many years with no religious affiliation whatsoever, then for nearly a decade a (nonmember) Methodist, and now a (nonmember) Quaker, I sometimes tell people the next step down is the neighborhood bar—for the local Quaker group is composed almost entirely of dropouts from the religious mainstream, both Protestant and Catholic, most of us with severe allergic reactions to razor-honed doctrine and to silence-abhorring, obsessive-compulsive liturgy.

Given that our ragtag Quakers are left-of-center politically, at least in a generic "liberal" sense, there seems a fairly obvious correlation to our embrace of an ethical spirituality with—for some, at least—an awareness that meditative discipline enables a slow unfolding of insight at ever-deeper layers and levels of being—*if* we are able to settle deeply enough into silence and let the silence take us where we need to go. Are we theists or panentheists or pantheists or agnostics or atheists? Who knows, exactly, for as soon as the labels get peeled away, even a little, there is an abundance of underlying uncertainty and squirmy confusion. We are both awed by formulations of great complexity (like Cosmic Christ) and, when we dare again to breathe, inclined to guffaw at such presumption.

With Thomas Berry, I find myself locked in the horns of a dilemma. On the one hand, there's no doubt that Berry feels the ecological crisis in his gut. And there's no doubt that he brings all his power of mind—a very capacious mind—to bear on addressing that crisis in his own determined way and manner. That is, Berry's sincerity of feeling and depth of alarm are not to be challenged—not by me, anyway. On the other hand, Berry is something of a disciple of Teilhard de Chardin, who was full of grand, overarching concepts like "omega-point" and "noosphere." The terminology makes me wary.[15]

Lewis Mumford tears into Teilhard on pages 314-20 in *The Pentagon of Power*, calling Teilhard's noosphere a "film of 'mind'" and "an etherealized version of the megamachine." As Mumford says, "Perhaps nothing so well illustrates the fascination that the audacious pretensions of the power complex exert over the human mind than the fact that possibly the most attractive and animated version of its ultimate potentialities and its final character is put forward by this same Jesuit father, in the series of books that began with 'The Phenomenon of Man'—books whose slippery logical pavement is treacherously concealed by a fresh snowfall of gleaming metaphors."[16] Here, in a longer passage, Mumford builds his case against Teilhard:

15. *Webster's* says *nous* or *noos* comes from the Greek and simply means "mind" or "God regarded as World Reason." The dictionary (this is my old and battered unabridged edition, with a copyright preceding the First World War) goes on to drop the names Anaxagoras, Plato, and Aristotle before referencing Neoplationists and gnostics. So Teilhard's "noosphere" is World Mind or some such construct. Chris Hedges, on pages 62 and 63 in his *Death of the Liberal Class*, says "Greek philosophers did celebrate reason as *nous*, as a reflection of divine truth enacted in the human mind." The core problem seems to be making "the mental" equivalent to "spiritual," elevating mind to the status of Spirit, celebrating human intelligence as if it contained or enclosed the ethical or the sacred, rather than—much more humbly—recognizing consciousness as the gift of biological life.

16. Mumford, *Pentagon*, 314.

As a paleontologist, the co-discoverer of Peking Man, he spoke with authority in his chosen field; and he was quicker than many other scientists to come to the now almost inescapable conclusion, in the light of molecular physics, that the physical cosmos itself has experienced history, and that this historic process, beginning with the autonomous organization and specification of the atomic elements, has gone on without a break through more complex atoms and higher forms of organization, until immensely complex organic molecules became self-replicating forms of life. And with life came, at one of the latest stages of animal evolution, consciousness and purposeful organization. So far, well.

Teilhard de Chardin's further description of mind, however, is what must be subjected to searching analysis: for his interpretation of man's coming evolution rests on his embracing, without a critical revision, the notion that has been current since the seventeenth century: namely, that consciousness is measured by intelligence, and that the intelligence, in an increasingly abstract mathematical form, is the highest manifestation of mind. William Blake might have saved him from this error: for with his anxiety over the possible consequences of Newtonian physics, the poet had written: "God forbid that Truth should be Confined to Mathematical Demonstrations!" But if Teilhard de Chardin's premises were true, then this apotheosis of abstract intelligence, as embodied in the theorems of science and the magical practices of technics, would be the far-off divine event toward which all creation moves.

To avoid distrust and contention, let me quote his exact words in 'The Future of Man.' The proof of man's ultimate destiny, according to Chardin, is already visible; for "in fields embracing every aspect of physical matter, life and thought, the research-workers are to be numbered in hundreds of thousands. . . . Research, which until yesterday was a luxury pursuit, is in process of becoming a major, indeed the principal, function of humanity. As to the significance of this great event, I for my part can see only one way to account for it. It is the enormous surplus of free energy released by the in-folding of the Noosphere destined by a natural evolutionary process to flow into the construction and functioning of what I have called its 'Brain.' . . ."

Precisely. And in this narrowing of the processes of life to the pursuit and projection of organized intelligence alone, the infinite potentialities of living systems, as developed on our own planet, would be reduced to a trivial fraction: those which would further rational organization and centralized control. This whole transformation would be directed, on Teilhard de Chardin's terms, toward the point where the entire noosphere would function as a single world-brain, in which individual souls would lose their identity and forfeit their uniqueness as self-directing organisms in order to exalt and magnify the process of thought itself—thought thereby turning in upon itself and becoming the sole viable manifestation of life.[17]

17. Mumford, *Pentagon*, 315-16.

In the same section ("'Post-Historic' Culture") of chapter Eleven from which these passages are drawn, Mumford calls this narrowing toward mind the "hypertrophy of man's dominant trait: his intelligence," a development resulting in the "cutting off of pure intelligence from all its self-regulating, self-protecting organic sources, since the unique property that cannot be transferred to any kind of programmed automation is life itself."[18] While I plead a certain intellectual agnosticism (or straightforward ignorance) at this point—although I believe the "enormous surplus of free energy" Teilhard alludes to is, in actuality, the energy civilized institutions coerced into being "free" by the systemic destruction of folk culture combined with a quantum capacity to technologize Earth, what Karl Polanyi (in a more limited way) called the smashing up of social structures to extract their labor—I am inclined to stand by Mumford.[19] So Thomas Berry, meanwhile, recognizes that our old story—by which he seems to mean primarily the creation story of Genesis, with its depiction of God operating from *outside* creation—is not only inadequate in addressing our current crisis, but has been an ideological participant and mythological enabler in building that crisis; for if God is *outside* creation but free to intervene at will, then a similar freedom to act at will falls to us humans on Earth—we who are made in God's image, especially we males. Therefore we urgently need a new story, a story big enough and deep enough to reconnect us with nature, with the natural world, with our actual anthropological history, and even, perhaps, with the universe—whatever that may mean. (Orbiting our solar star is all the space travel most of us will ever do.) Via the prologue to the

18. Mumford, *Pentagon*, 312-13.

19. On page 87 in *Man's Place in Nature*, de Chardin provides something of a helpful definition: "By civilization I mean not a fully realized state of social organization but the actual process that generates the organization, and in that sense civilization is, ultimately, simply zoological 'specialisation' extended to an animal group (man) in which one particular influence (the psychic) that had hitherto been negligible from the point of view of taxonomy suddenly begins to assume a predominant part in the ramification of the phylum." I realize that "civilization" is a truly slippery word—I've been trying to get a grip on it for decades—but if by "civilization" we mean not simply its dictionary etymology of "city" but what historians like Mumford and Toynbee describe as a city-*system* founded on violence and expropriation, then it's not the benign "psychic" but murderous and thieving male will whose "specialisation" in violence and expropriation has resulted in ecocidal globalization: i.e., the "ramification of the phylum."

I don't think it irrelevant or unrelated to point out that "capital"—as in money, concentrated wealth, or capitalism—derives from *caput*, meaning head, and that civilization is the ruthlessly aggressive empiring of "the psychic" only in a very specific sense: willful male utopianism, armed with the keenest forms of technological violence and interrogatory surveillance. To celebrate the "psychic" *as if this were synonymous with the spiritual* is to make a grave and possibly even fatal error. It is precisely this "error" that lies at the heart of our current Global Crisis as caused by the globalization of civilization. Perhaps the National Security Agency (NSA), with its global dragnet surveillance, is how "noosphere" actually manifests itself.

Behind all this, as Ernst Cassirer says in *The Myth of the State* on pages 94 and 95, is the "pattern set up in the heavens" of Plato's Idea of the Good, followed later by Augustine, for whom "the Platonic ideas have become the thoughts of God." Teilhard's "civilisation," then, may well be the "psychic" extension and continuation of this Platonic/Augustinian idealization. But as far as I can discern, it is just this "error" that Mumford detects in Teilhard and to which he reacts so forcefully.

gospel of John and the hymn to the Cosmic Christ in the first chapter of Colossians, Berry links up with Teilhard for a new story of the Cosmic Christ, of divinity infused into and with creation—God *inside* the Big Bang rather than outside with match and fuse—all the while claiming to be a conservative Catholic.[20]

Well, let's acknowledge that there is more intellectual elasticity within Catholicism than there is within Protestantism. Catholicism has had so many theological formulations and has assimilated so many doctrinal assertions over the centuries that even its card catalogue has unreadable pages and missing sections, while its ancient warehouse of supernatural documents is crammed to the rafters with dusty artifacts "guarded" by creaky old geezers who sleep standing up. But where conventional Christianity has been surpassed—and by "conventional" I mean a pretty basic and flatfooted quasi-literalism: God the Father, God the Son, and God the Holy Spirit as eternal divine Persons—the surpassers frequently seem to be driving with a lot of anxious attention directed at the rearview mirror. (Sort of like the scene in the movie *Jurassic Park* where a dinosaur is chasing a speeding jeep, the scene filmed via the side mirror with its printed warning: *objects in mirror are closer than they appear*.) Orthodoxy may be closer than it appears. Or, if not orthodoxy, exactly, then an anxiety about wandering too far from orthodoxy's sacred bosom. (This is liberalism's not-so-secret neurotic insecurity.)

A lot of would-be Christian surpassers seem to have hooked a bungee cord to conventional Christian doctrine and, as they speed away from the theological dinosaur, eyes staring into the mirror, they're apparently hoping to see comforting doctrine stretching smoothly out behind, following along obediently as all good doctrine should. Well, "conservatives" love the dinosaur as is; "liberals" feel compelled to dress Dino up a little, with braces for those dreadful teeth and sheepskin slippers for the taloned toes. Perhaps even a little lipstick and nail polish as they consider changing His name to Dinah.

---

20. I'm somewhat puzzled here by what my good friend Maynard Kaufman says of Berry on page 110 in *Adapting to the End of Oil: Toward an Earth-Centered Spirituality*, namely that Berry "does not use, or seek to reinterpret, Christian language. Instead, he and his followers, especially the physicist, Brian Swimme, articulate a new cosmic creation story based on the evolution of the universe and of the humans within it. . . . As for Berry, a thinker who is rooted in Christianity, he is not just the next step in the tradition of Catholic natural theology, but a quantum leap beyond it." Well, Berry's theology may be a quantum leap, but his new creation story is only secondarily about an Earth-centered spirituality; it is primarily about a fifteen-billion-year *Cosmic Christ universe story*. And while it's true that Berry wants to get far beyond any Anselmian redemption formula—that Jesus died to appease an angry God—he does indeed use and seek to interpret Christian language. His entire association with the thought of Teilhard de Chardin is based exactly on an extension—a *cosmic* extension—of Christian language. The real question may be whether Thomas Berry wasn't so deeply conditioned by conventional Catholic thought that he was unable to break free of the underlying "psychic" idealism Teilhard channeled from Plato via Augustine.

III

When we leave the ancient warehouse of supernatural documents, it's a little ridiculous to try to pack the entire library into a temporal suitcase. Or, to switch metaphors in the middle of a stream of consciousness, one can't take a GPS device into a cloud of unknowing and expect it to function "normally." Perhaps it's time for a little Tao.

Writing of Lao Tzu and the *Tao Te Ching* in *The Religions of Man*, in a chapter called "Taoism," Huston Smith says:

> Man should avoid being strident and aggressive not only toward other men but also toward nature. How should man relate himself to nature? On the whole the modern Western attitude has been to regard nature as an antagonist, something to be squared off against, dominated, controlled, conquered. Taoism's attitude toward nature tends to be the precise opposite of this. There is a profound naturalism in Taoist thought, but it is the naturalism of Rousseau, Wordsworth, Thoreau rather than that of Galileo or Bacon.
>
> > Those who would take over the earth
> > And shape it to their will
> > Never, I notice, succeed.
> > The earth is like a vessel so sacred
> > That at the mere approach of the profane
> > It is marred
> > And when they reach out their fingers it is gone. (Ch. 29)
>
> Nature is to be befriended. . . . Taoist temples do not stand out from the landscape. They are nestled against the hills, back under the trees, blending in with the environment. At best man too blends in with nature. His highest achievement is to identify himself with the *Tao* and let it work through him.[21]

"Nature is to be befriended." Well, there's the title of one of Thomas Berry's books—*Befriending the Earth*—coauthored with Thomas Clarke. (The other book under inquisition here is *The Dream of the Earth*, published by a secular press—John Muir's very own Sierra Club Books, no less.)

I find Lao Tzu's Tao quite refreshing. Every breath partakes of Tao. But the Tao has no name. Those who claim to know its name only show they don't know the Tao. ("Those who know don't say. And those who say don't know."[22]) Maybe I've just had my fill of Christian proselytizing, for I grew up in an environment (I mean post-World War Two America) where Billy Graham and Fulton J. Sheen were almost inescapable. And God, how they *knew*! They knew and knew and knew until one practically pleaded for a fresh gasp or gulp of refreshing ignorance, a deep breath of unknowing. So I think it prudent—something of a precautionary principle—to put omega-point

---

21. Smith, *Religions*, 208.
22. Smith, *Religions*, 199.

and noosphere up on the To-Be-Examined-Someday shelf, perhaps taken down every few years, dusted off, and duly reconsidered over a bottle of beer or glass of wine. There's really no hurry. I doubt if planetary survival depends on mass acceptance of Teilhard's cosmic formulation.

However, I do believe some old stories are in process of killing us, so it's not as if the situation isn't serious. The Civilization story is one of those killers. The orthodox Christian story is another. These stories certainly have, in the West, interacted and supported one another since Constantine, but they are qualitatively different.[23]

Christianity at its core revolves (should revolve) around the Lord's Prayer: your kingdom come, your will be done, on Earth as it is in Heaven. That's the prayer Jesus apparently taught his followers to say, what they were to ask for, anticipate, look forward to, and struggle to achieve. It's a prayer oriented toward achieving the kingdom of God on Earth. But that's not the part of Christianity that's killing us. The kingdom of God as spiritual purpose has been mostly absent from the moment Jesus was murdered by the collusion of civilized powers.

---

23. On page 91 of my *Polemics and Provocations*, in a fairly long footnote, I quote theologian John Cobb, Jr. Cobb says he was raised with the view that *real* history only began with cities and civilization, uncivilized people were savages, and that women were not participants in real history. Well, Cobb also has a Preface in the 2009 book by Thomas Berry, *The Christian Future and the Fate of the Earth*. On page xi, Cobb says that Berry's "work in the history of religion led him to believe that the key to changing the way people see themselves and their world can be found in their creation stories," and that he "judged that today such a story must correspond with what is known scientifically."

Cobb's Preface is followed by an Introduction coauthored by Mary Evelyn Tucker and John Grim. On page xxv, Tucker and Grim say that in 1978 Berry "observed that in the West we were between stories—biblical and scientific." And, of course, the "scientific" story Berry went on to embrace was the new universe story.

There are various things to say about this. First, Christianity by the time of Constantine and Augustine had become a fully rationalized religion within a context of Roman civilizational power. The Jesus murdered by the "pagan" Roman Empire had become resuscitated as Savior Christ of the "Holy" Roman Empire. Second, the aggressive and violent spread (and eventual globalization) of Western civilization meant that the conquered peoples' creation stories were either overthrown or simply crushed. Third, it was a mix of sciences (including astronomy, geology, biology, and anthropology) that both undermined and exploded the traditional biblical story of creation and that now causes us to be "between stories." Fourth, *both* stories—the biblical and the scientific (at least the one Berry chooses as primary)—are *civilizational* stories: any resemblances to noncivilized creation stories would be incidental. Fifth, there is an unexplored exception here; that is, by recognizing anthropology as a science, and psychoanalytical thinking as an additional anthropological insight (see, for example, pages xi and xii in Norman O. Brown's Introduction to his *Life Against Death*), we who were otherwise raised with biblical stories are led into an awareness of ancient human life, with the vast bulk of that life in completely noncivilized contexts, including the multithousand-year period of horticultural/agricultural village culture prior to the "rise"—i.e., the violent imposition—of male warrior civilization, which "rise" also imposed an exclusively male God. Sixth, science also enables us to understand the divinity of the horticultural era primarily as feminine, an Age of the Mother.

In other words, there are scientific stories to tell besides the one Thomas Berry was drawn to, stories utilizing Christian symbols or Christian constructs in a different way than Berry's metaphysical, cosmic etherealizations. These other stories are not only earthy and Earth-based, they're also crucial for finding our way safely to a postcivilized, ecological culture.

Now John the Evangelist and Paul the Apostle may talk a lot *about* Jesus, and John (besides unfolding some exquisite short stories) puts Jesus on rather tall not-of-this-world soapboxes; but Jesus (if we go with the first three gospels) kept talking about the "kingdom of God." So, at the core of gospel Christianity is a Jesus-invoked yearning for the kingdom of God; and, whatever else it may contain, the kingdom of God certainly embraces radical servanthood and radical stewardship. That is, the "kingdom of God" is both profoundly *ethical* and profoundly *earthly* in its humble "Taoist" spirituality. It's not some grand cosmic vision of extraterrestrial salvation but, rather, a yearning for deep and unflinching ethical committedness *on Earth*—sharing a coat or a meal, being the least, laying down your life for your friends. It's about personal, social, cultural, and political *transformation*.[24]

Civilization, on the other hand, has no claim to ethical underpinning. It may have spun off an amazing variety of inventions, incredible technologies, and stimulating cultural minglings (some of which have absorbed ethical content) as a consequence of its will-to-dominance; but the positives are, we might say, externalities and incidentals. They weren't deliberate causes or direct intentions. Civilization's core drive was and is will-to-power within a controlled and controlling ruthlessness that sought and seeks to bring the entire world into "First World" subjection. (Constantine did not coerce the Christian church into becoming the state religion of the Roman Empire in order to build the kingdom of God on Earth. He did it in the interest of strengthening the Roman Empire. Meanwhile—an interesting coincidence—the Christian doctrine of original sin apparently dissolved any prospect of or hope for creating the kingdom of God on Earth.) Although we do not have Leopold Kohr's One World Government or Teilhard's infolded noosphere (unless the NSA is working it up as a Top Secret computer program), we *do* have civilized globalization, complete with penetrating and pervasive surveillance, a kind of psychic inquisition based above all on Christian Euro-American aggression, with its diseases and traumatic institutions increasingly "democratized." Most civilized people are detached spectators to the building of this electronic net, unwilling to identify with the plight of the indigenous, afraid to admit that "terrorists" have legitimate grievance, unable to empathize with the ecological agony of Earth. We are too busy living in our protected "civility" and self-absorbed "security." We have risen so far above the primitive and backward that empathy has thinned to the point of evaporation: if those folks who cling to backward primitivity want our sympathy, they'd better get their act together and behave as we do. Here is where Gil Bailie's empathy for victims runs up against—e.g., James Bradley's *The*

---

24. John Dominic Crossan, in *The Power of Parable*, page 134, says "Jesus is not just announcing to his audience that God's kingdom is now present. He is announcing that it is *only* present *if and when* it is accepted, entered into, and taken upon oneself. If discussion and debate, agreement and disagreement, argument and contradiction do not arise from and because of his challenges, then no change in consciousness can take place, no paradigm shift can occur, and no kingdom of God can be present." This view correlates tightly to the understanding represented in the epigraphs opening this collection of essays, especially the remark by Nicolas Berdyaev as quoted by Matthew Fox.

Imperial Cruise—the ethical detachment of the civilized mind, where gospel is called "unrealistic" by doctrine derived from myth.

And this brings us full circle back to Thomas Berry. Christianity after Constantine became a willing imperial weapon in the arsenal of civility. It provided—dead peasant on a stick—an emblem by which to attack, invade, conquer, and occupy both lands and minds. The pope's diocese was the entire world, and everything that fell (temporarily) outside the Christian sphere was subject to (eventual) Christian taking. God wanted the whole world to be Christian, forcibly if necessary. Those who resisted—perhaps even those who didn't—were destined to have their homelands taken from them. Christianity became both integrated into and transformed by imperialism: not the Taoist Christianity of the humble kingdom of God, but the civilized Christianity of the Cosmic or Universal Christ whose desire was to overpower paganism and take possession of the entire Earth. Humble Taoist kingdom of God ethics had already been largely abandoned in favor of orthodox theological supremacy. The sword proved to be so much more compelling than humility or empathy. The sword was infinitely more efficient at overcoming stubborn resistance and getting things accomplished.

So when Thomas Berry metaphorically offers the host of Cosmic Christ to take and eat, I'm keeping my hands in my pockets and my mouth shut. If and when he's willing to listen, I'll tell him I agree we need a new story; but that story needs to be humble, it needs to be (apologies to Galileo) Earth-centered and, by cracking open Joachim's twelfth-century Three Ages equation and computing a correction for Mom, we've already got that story—a new understanding for a fuller mode of divine presence on Earth. Perhaps noosphere will be helpful by and by. But, like Henry Thoreau once said, "One world at a time."[25] Plus there's some major religious reformulation, compensation, and restitution to be made on *this* world as we incorporate new understandings of divine presence. This is not about—yet again—inviting pagans to become cosmically civilized or pretending that Mother, having been chopped out of both civilizational and religious history, isn't where reformulation and restitution must begin.

IV

Something keeps nagging me about Thomas Berry. Maybe we've got to be a bit more detailed and ask: What's the old story Berry says is no longer adequate? Why isn't it adequate? What's his new story? What exactly makes that new story the right one?

Teilhard de Chardin, however, seems to be a burr under my saddle. Or, if he's not the primary burr, he's rubbing me a bit raw. Even Thomas Berry says he has

> . . . some criticisms of Teilhard. It is somewhat tragic that he is not fully "available" for contemporary ecologists because he was so intensely committed to

25. Thoreau, *Faith*, 17.

the technological world. For Teilhard, the evolutionary process was totally concentrated in the human. He could not understand the devastating aspect of the human. When Henry Fairfield Osborne in his 1947 book, *Our Plundered Planet*, proposed that, through human deeds, the world was undergoing grave ecological devastation, Teilhard refused to accept that this was happening. Others could see it, but Teilhard could not. He had an excessive optimism, based, I believe, on Jean de Caussade's *Abandonment to Divine Providence* (1861), a work of French spirituality. De Caussade encouraged abandonment to God's will. During World War I, Teilhard had a sense of excitement about being at the front. For him the worse things were, the better, because it meant that God had even more grand plans for things. Teilhard could not take seriously the destruction of the natural world. Once, when someone pointed out to him the destruction of the natural world, Teilhard said that science would discover other forms of life.[26]

I can't bring myself to believe that Teilhard's attitude should be characterized as "excessive optimism," unless it's the "optimism" Mumford found alarming: technological "intelligence" presuming to govern the entire world—genetically modified intelligence, perhaps. The word for this is not optimism—it's hubris. When Augustine wrote the defining justification aligning Christianity with Empire—because empires are not fortuitous but, rather, given by God—it follows that the playing out of empire is actually the playing out of God's will. (Doesn't this become philosophically explicit with Hegel?) Why else would Teilhard feel such "excitement about being at the front"? Wasn't he, as it were, on the cutting edge of God's "grand plans"? Isn't Teilhard simply extending Augustine's empire rationalizations to cosmic dimension? And, with the staggeringly blithe assertion that "science would discover other forms of life," aren't we getting a whiff of Augustine's Manichean formaldehyde—mind (the "psychic") over matter whenever there's a perceived conflict?[27]

I am inclined to follow Mumford when he says that although "Mind itself might almost be defined as the organism's mode of creating, utilizing, and transcending its own mechanisms,"[28] he also insists that "sexual reproduction is more essential to thought, biologically speaking, than thought to reproduction; for life not merely

26. Berry, *Befriending*, 25.

27. I readily confess that it's hard to pin down the elusive Teilhard. But pages 292-94 in *The Phenomenon of Man* have a rather concentrated section on God as "Centre of centers" and Christ as "principle of universal vitality" who "put himself in the position (maintained ever since) to subdue under himself, to purify, to direct and superanimate the general ascent of consciousness into which he asserted himself. By a perennial act of communion and sublimation, he aggregates to himself the total psychism of the earth." In this section, Teilhard invokes the "City of God"—an open Augustinian construction—as it tries to "englobe in its constructions and conquests the totality of the system that it managed to picture to itself." This does not exactly prove that Teilhard is a cosmic footnote to Augustine and Plato, but it surely raises eyebrows.

28. Mumford, *Pentagon*, 96.

encompasses but transcends thought."[29] That remark deserves to be repeated: *life not merely encompasses but transcends thought.* The "divine" is not simply the Biggest Brain on the Cosmic Block. Life is not the excrescence of mind; consciousness is the evolving rainbow blossoming of biological being.

This business in regard to "mind" also leads Mumford to critique Descartes and Newton in a way that brings us up to the "theological" question stated with modest circumspection by Lao Tzu and (in my opinion) with glaring Christian imperialism by Teilhard de Chardin. Here's Mumford:

> What Descartes did by equating organisms with machines was to make it possible to apply to organic behavior that quantitative method that was to serve so efficiently in describing 'physical' events. To know more about the behavior of a physical system one must isolate it, disorganize it, and separate out its measurable elements, down to the minutest particle—a necessary feat for understanding its operation. But to pass beyond the limits of a physical system into the realm of life, one must do just the opposite: assemble more and more parts into a pattern of organization that, as it approaches more closely to living phenomena reacting within a living environment, becomes so complex that it can only be reproduced and apprehended intuitively in the act of living, since, at least in man, it includes mind and the infra- and ultra-corporeal aspects of mind.
>
> Reductionism reverses this process: for it dares not even hint at such a primal thrust in the direction of organization as would account for the specific nature of atoms or the self-replication of crystals: aspects of matter that contradict the old views of a mindless universe of 'dead' atoms colliding at random. On any pure theory of causality or statistical probability, organization would be completely improbable without the external aid of a divine organizer.
>
> Newton in his 'Optics' did not hesitate to reach that conclusion, even with reference to the physical universe alone. But this inescapable condition can be stated, as Szent-Gyorgyi suggested, without resorting to any theological subterfuge: namely by locating the 'organizer' within the cosmic system from the 'beginning' and attributing design, not to any *original* plan but to the increasing tendency of organized processes and structures to combine with the selective aid of organisms into more purposeful emergent wholes.[30]

Now it could be argued that Lao Tzu, Lewis Mumford, Teilhard de Chardin, and Thomas Berry are all tooting the same horn, whistling the same tune, and perhaps in some ways they are. But I don't trust the relentless insinuations of Christian theological imperialism, even when excusing itself for modesty's sake to change costumes in the Men's Room and come out dressed in the sparkling garb of Cosmic Christ. (Well, this is not modesty but, rather, compulsive lust for narcissistic supremacy, even if it requires a new, glitzy wardrobe.) Plus the New Universe Story Berry wants us to grab

29. Mumford, *Pentagon*, 82.
30. Mumford, *Pentagon*, 86-87.

onto—fifteen billion years of cosmic evolution—is too immense a construct to fit as an everyday, down-home, Earth-grounded narrative for reverent ecological living. It's too big a head trip, way beyond modes of divine presence on Earth. For the foreseeable future, we humans will continue to live on Earth. Before we leap to astronomical spirituality, we'd do well to clear up—and clean up— some serious earthly deficiencies in our current depictions of divinity and how at least one of those depictions—God as King of kings—has served to justify civilizational predation and exploitation.

I suppose my proposed alternative—the Mother, Father, Son and Daughter modification of Joachim's twelfth-century construct—can be seen as a sneaky attempt at Christian restoration, for it too is based on explicit Christian formulation, at least an enlargement of such formulation. I will state flatly that, with my limited learning, I revere Jesus, Lao Tzu, and Buddha as my three greatest teachers, with Jesus (certainly in an ethical sense) the most dynamic of them all, carrying his cultural mission and ethical conviction into the terror of crucifixion. But I have something resembling disgust and contempt for the relentless arrogance and compulsive hubris of Christian imperialism—as if the "kingdom of God" morphed effortlessly and without fundamental contradiction into Christian imperialism, like the agrarian village supposedly morphed similarly into civilization. The Mother-Father-Son-Daughter construct bursts the imperialist pustule, drains it of cloying and corrupt righteousness, and enables a desperately needed humility in keeping with Jesus' ethical vision. With this modification of Joachim's construct, female and male achieve equal status in "divine" representation. Although sequenced as historical phases, with one gender or the other finding top billing for an extended period, recognizing Daughter as the phase we're now entering—while simultaneously restoring Mother to her rightful place in history—brings an urgently needed balance to the acute distortions of consciousness created by an excessive dose of patriarchal presumption, a presumption that has also glorified the "psychic" out of all proportion while simultaneously heaping condescension and contempt upon the "mere" reproductive body—which body, of course, is primarily the *female* body. The construct Mother-Father-Son-Daughter may be anthropomorphic, but we seem to be stuck being human and therefore stuck in the anthropological camp—and it's simply silly to pretend that we're not or shouldn't be.

Now Thomas Berry rightly says "The tragedy is that the dark, destructive aspect of Western patriarchal civilization has become virulent just at this time when the influence of the West has become so pervasive throughout the human community and when its technological capacity for plundering the earth has become so overwhelming that all the basic life systems of the planet are being closed down,"[31] that "It might not be too much to say that our spiritual traditions not only provided much of the context in which this assault became possible, but they also provided a positive, if often indirect, support for this process,"[32] and that "This cultural-spiritual phase was

31. Berry, *Dream*, 103.
32. Berry, *Dream*, 113.

so fully developed, so powerful in its coding, so effective in its communication of this coding to successive generations, that any significant change in the future would of necessity appear as destructive, immoral, heretical, anarchistic."[33] Well, that means we are, for the most part, incapacitated by cultural conditioning, from both a secular and a religious perspective, to act appropriately in the face of crisis. We might even say the world's actual Trinity is God the Almighty Father, civilizational empire, and male superego, or that noosphere is male fearfulness projected as global surveillance in imitation of the Almighty Father's suspicious and judgmental watchfulness. We are afflicted with a kind of "nuclear numbness"—really a *mythological* numbness—brought on by repeated injections of ideological and doctrinal Novocain. (But is Teilhard's cosmic vision an *antidote* to this numbness or only a new form of the old numbing drug providing illusory relief and provisional euphoria?)

While it seems that those who are left of center have a better grasp of crisis dynamics—the Left, in general, is more open than the Right to critical analysis, including critical analysis pertaining to religious myth—there remains a largely unrecognized bias among both "conservatives" and "liberals" against earthy living, a result of both civilizational conditioning and religious indoctrination. This bias manifests itself as negative attitudes against simple living, rural life, darkness, dirt, and the basic labor of self-provisioning subsistence. One sees this bias at a surprisingly high intellectual level on the Left, including the Left that is, or can be, cuttingly critical of civilized consumerism. Kirkpatrick Sale, for instance, quoting Jarad Diamond, essentially agrees that agriculture is "the worst mistake in the history of the human race."[34] Or, as Sale himself says, with agriculture we were "declaring war not just on a species but on a world."[35] And Richard Manning says, in an article entitled "Against the Grain" in *The American Scholar*—almost as if he were channeling the late Edward Abbey—that "Agriculture dehumanized us by satisfying the most dangerous of human impulses" (he means hunting for food and sex) and that he has "come to think of agriculture not as farming but as a dangerous and consuming beast of a social system."[36] (I don't believe the word "civilization" makes a single appearance in Manning's otherwise excellent essay in which he exposes, in clear, strong prose, the ruthless nature of industrial agribusiness in America, including the role of the monster corporation Archer Daniels Midland or ADM.) Gerda Lerner, in *The Creation of Patriarchy*, seems to point in the same direction: "In an ecologically constricted space, growing populations can be supplied only by increasing agricultural production or by expansion. The former leads to the development of elites, the latter to the development of militarism, first on a voluntary, then on a professional basis."[37] I find it interesting how agriculture

33. Berry, *Dream*, 117-18.

34. Sale, *After Eden*, 99.

35. Sale, *After Eden*, 96.

36. Manning, "Against," 35, 16.

37. Lerner, *Creation*, 56.

gets scapegoated for *causing* the cruelties of civilization, how the attentive gatherer/ horticulturalist is really the one responsible, in a developmental or structural sense, for the atomic bomb. This is beyond ridiculous.[38]

Mumford once again, with his depth analysis, even while freely acknowledging the limited horizon of the precivilized agrarian village, recognizes that "elites" and "militarism" were agents of the systemic theft and armed robbery of agriculture, the pivot point giving rise to civilization: "The thrifty habits needed to ensure survival had been artificially re-enforced, from the very beginning of civilization, by manufactured scarcity—the deliberate expropriation of the farmers' surplus for the benefit of the ruling minority."[39] In other words—in plain English—a "ruling minority" (i.e., a budding aristocracy) was building its elite infrastructure of wealth, glory, and power on the systemic *expropriation* of "the farmers' surplus," although "surplus" is a slippery word, a loaded concept, needing far more attention than it's getting here. ("Surplus" implies that farmers had too much stuff squirreled away, were stingy, that confiscating this "surplus" was actually a moral act, like disciplining a greedy child. But, of course, to turn this construct around—for there to be democratic taxation of upper-class wealth—is a brazen and shocking act of "class warfare.")

And if we ask the always-difficult question regarding the relationship between gender and the divine, we can easily say that the Age of the Mother is not just a neolithic, agrarian-village dynamic (although the practice of horticulture surely enhanced the Mother's prestige), but it—the Mother's Age—extends back into the mists of human history. We are mammals; and females, with their wonderful wombs and gorgeous breasts, are mammals of singular capacity—the mothers, feeders, carriers and nurturers of life. We males, as unborn babies, lived inside the mother and, once thrust out by birth and pushed away by weaning, found ourselves entangled in a retrogressive, reflexive impulse toward possessiveness and control, trying (unconsciously?) to recover the warm and cozy female den we once felt we owned. So if we are looking for the root of obsessive-compulsive dominance—or, if not its root, exactly, then its historical etiology of social control—we will find it in weaning, the incest taboo, male

---

38. Even Wes Jackson, founder and president of the Land Institute in Salina, Kansas, gets caught in this mimetic contagion. As he says in "Between Soil and Soil," in *The Progressive* for December 2010/ January 2011, page 35, "To take a swipe at Isaiah, the plow has destroyed more options for future generations than the sword. I suspect global warming began with agriculture, by getting at that carbon in the soil and in the forest." The only plausible explanation I can come up with for why Jackson, Lerner, Manning, et al., find agriculture such a consuming beast is that they remain mesmerized by the charming intellectual seductions of civility. Implicitly they are clinging to Leopold Kohr's ethically void assertion about social size; that is, it is *size*, pure and simple, that results in aggression and control. Therefore—presto!—since it's food abundance that allows for growth in human population, agriculture is to blame. And, since horticulture is the base of agriculture, and gatherers the original horticulturalists, it's *women* who are to blame—like Eve—for the worst mistake in the history of the human race. This is simply amazing. What this does, of course, is completely glide over and implicitly exonerate the male warrior extortion of the precivilized agrarian village, a systemic extortion (including slavery and militarism) that created what we now know as civilization.

39. Mumford, *Pentagon*, 321.

musculature and, by extension, in the "psychic" weapons of male will, as males have sought to conquer and control Mother Earth as compensation for gender estrangement and sexual alienation.

Thomas Berry says there are five phases of human transformation—"the Paleolithic, the Neolithic, the classical-traditional, the scientific-technological, and now the emerging ecological phase"[40]—but we can boil these five down to four. The Mother's Age encompasses both paleolithic and neolithic; the Father's is classical-traditional; the Son's is scientific-technological; and the Daughter's is the emerging ecological.

Whether we live ecologically in the world, what we do day to day in our lives on Earth, certainly depends on our reverence for Earth. Thomas Berry is right about that. He's right about a lot of things—and his sense of urgency is, I believe, completely justified. However, his (or Teilhard's) New Universe Story, even if empirically compelling, is too cerebral to be central to the transformational crisis we have entered and too out-of-this-world to address the pathological distortions hiding in plain sight within our religious mythology. Grasping the concept of a fifteen-billion-year-old universe does not provide any greater historical or ethical groundedness than did the astronomical discoveries of Copernicus and Galileo, with their sun-centered cosmology. And we have seen from Berry that Teilhard "would not take seriously the destruction of the natural world" and that "science would discover"—invent?—"other forms of life."

Joachim's modified Ages, on the other hand, even if based on Christian constructs, really do reflect historical progressions and cultural transformations on an earthly plane. They aren't time segments of equal length; but that's largely irrelevant. They represent psychospiritual transitions in human consciousness, transitions that correlate to real history, and the radical servanthood and radical stewardship of Jesus' "kingdom of God" proclamation will come to a far fuller fruition in the Age of the Daughter.[41]

I think Thomas Berry was ready and willing to enter the Daughter's Age. He just needed, to some degree, to get out of his overeducated head and (is this residual

---

40. Berry, *Dream*, 93.

41. Matthew Fox, on pages 266 through 268 of *The Reinvention of Work*, says *remembrance* is how we "tap into the collective memory of our ancestors, our shared morphic fields." He goes on to say that the "hypothesis of formative causation—the idea that self-organizing systems at all levels of complexity become organized by morphic fields—teaches us that rituals may be that personal and social experience by which communities organize themselves and individuals connect to larger memories of past and perhaps even future," and that "For our species to become authentic, we must link past and future." And although Fox says we do this linking "primarily and most playfully in ritual," we also have to recognize that ritual is derivative from overarching mythology. Where our governing mythology represents not the castration but the spaying of an entire epoch of cultural evolution—the way Mother has been brutally exorcised from Trinitarian formulation—we also must recognize that orthodox ritual perpetuates that exorcism. If we are to "redeem time and sanctify it," as Fox says we need to do, then we simply have to redeem (i.e., recover, set free, ransom, rescue, make amends for) the debasement of the Mother and the spiritual obliteration of her cultural epoch. And, finally, to actually do this vital, redemptive spiritual work of collective memory recovery is also to discover Daughter hidden in the ghostly disguise of Holy Spirit.

Protestant aggravation?) hang his overly tight priest's collar out to dry. More "king-dom of God" Taoism and less Teilhard "psychic" noosphere would have made him a prophet lucky to have escaped burning at the stake. But now, of course, we rarely kill prophets (exceptions for people like Martin Luther King, Malcomb X, and Mohandas Gandhi). We ignore them instead. With our cable-channel consciousness, alternative images are just part of virtual reality, entertaining for an hour or so. Without sufficient commercial backing, prophecy appears to have little traction in the futures market of consumer optimism, as unelectable as Ralph Nader.

V

Berry's chapter on patriarchy, in *The Dream of the Earth*, provides more grounds, at least implicitly, for declining his new universe narrative as the new, needed, and miss-ing story for the emerging ecological age. He tells us that although "this period of patriarchal dominance" has not totally obliterated "the heritage of the earlier matri-centric phase"[42]—the "divine Virgin can be considered as an effort to bring into the culture at least some remnant presence of the ancient Earth Mother"[43]—there are four "patriarchal establishments that have been in control of Western history over the centuries," establishments that "have become progressively virulent in their destruc-tive powers, until presently they are bringing about the closing down of all the basic life systems of the planet."[44] Berry names these four patriarchal establishments: "the classical empires, the ecclesiastical establishment, the nation-state, and the modern corporation. These four are exclusively male dominated and primarily for fulfillment in terms of the human as envisaged by men."[45] He goes on:

> None of the other revolutionary movements in Western civilization has pre-pared us for what we must now confront. Quite naturally this demand for change, as with all such moments of radical confrontation, brings with it a heightened level of psychic intensity. Everything is at stake. This is some-thing more than feminine resentment at personal neglect or oppression. It is possibly the most complete reversal of values that has taken place since the Neolithic.[46]

This is plain, strong speech. But two pages later, Berry diverts the analysis. He says that "One of the main characteristics of the emerging ecological period is the move from a human-centered norm of reality and value to a nature-centered norm. We cannot expect life, the earth, or the universe to fit into our rational human designs of

42. Berry, *Dream*, 145.

43. Berry, *Dream*, 150-51.

44. Berry, *Dream*, 145.

45. Berry, *Dream*, 145-46.

46. Berry, *Dream*, 150.

how life, the earth, or the universe should function. We must fit our thinking and our actions within the larger process."[47] Four more pages and he says "The most difficult transition to make is from an anthropocentric to a biocentric norm of progress."[48] But under the imperative of relinquishing an anthropocentric view in favor of the biocentric, the excluded feminine is abandoned. Well, perhaps not totally abandoned, for the emerging ecological phase is to somehow have a feminine ambience. But the real and deeper story is the New Universe Story. Goodbye to a human figure as spiritually representative. Forget the resurrection of Mother as an equal "Person" alongside Father, Son, and Holy Spirit. Forget Holy Spirit as Daughter.

I don't think so. Or, rather, while I concur with (and am even in awe of) much of Berry's compacted analysis, I don't believe that a) jettisoning the feminine at this crucial juncture is anything less than outrageous, or b) that human beings, by and large, can ever be expected to navigate life on Earth without something resembling an "anthropocentric" point of view. (Every member of every species represents its species' aptitudes and intents, and it is simply impossible, perhaps even ridiculous, to imagine humans as exceptions to this rule.) No matter how sensitive we may learn to be in the ecological age to come—and there is room for an enormous improvement in evolutionary consciousness and ecological behavior—we will continue to provide food, clothing, and shelter for ourselves at the expense of the surrounding ecology precisely because *we* intend to survive and even thrive, and not for any grand biocentric principle. I do not say this to thwart or discourage serious exploration into ecological living. (My wife Susanna and I live in a house built almost exclusively from scrounged logs and used materials. I have lived without electricity or running water for most of my adult life, with a woodburning cookstove, with firewood and gardens, and I love this way of life. So I'm not just blowing theoretical smoke here.)

The New Universe Story may well be built of good science, even science with shades and threads of Taoist humility in it; but the age we are entering is the *Daughter's*, and no last minute, taffy-pull Cosmic Christ, magically immanent or even pantheist at the last possible, desperate moment, will change that fact or alter our destiny. The magnitude and intensity of global devastation can, from here on out, be measured by the refusal of patriarchal consciousness to let go of itself (remember, please, Berry's four "patriarchal establishments") as we awaken to the embrace of the Daughter. Or, as Berry himself puts it in larger generality, "The sense of the sacred in any civilization is precisely that which cannot be questioned, for the sense of the sacred is the unquestionable answer to all questions. Thus the psychic shock in the reassessment that is presently being made."[49] Our *sense of the sacred*, overtly so in the dominant Abrahamic mythologies and covertly so in our ecclesiastical institutions and civilizational infrastructure, is in process of being hammered. We will either consent to a

47. Berry, *Dream*, 161.

48. Berry, *Dream*, 165.

49. Berry, *Dream*, 149.

thorough questioning of that which cannot be questioned, voluntarily enduring the psychic shocks of that reassessment, or we will be engulfed in catastrophe. And that goes as much for "liberals" as it does for "conservatives." That's the choice, insofar as it even is—or will be—a choice. We've been, as Western people, into a long "culture war" over unquestionable answers since at least the time of Galileo, even as the over-arching unquestionable mythologies kept chugging along. That process has reached a terminal stage, a culminating point, and a lot of the chugging mythologies—the three Abrahamic religions in particular—are in process of blowing each other's patriarchal establishment off the tracks of history. But it's the Daughter who's waiting for us, not the noosphere. Or, if it's the noosphere too, I hope it's a garment the Daughter can wear with unsurpassed gracefulness.

Of course it's necessary—given his capacity for promiscuous belief and his juggler's knack for keeping balls in the air—to (almost) let Thomas Berry have the last word:

> Meanwhile, in the obscure regions of the unconscious where the primordial archetypal symbols function as ultimate controlling factors in human thought, emotion, and in practical decision-making, a profound reorientation toward this integral human-Earth relationship is gradually taking place. . . .
>
> We might now recover our sense of the maternal aspect of the universe in the symbol of the Great Mother, especially in the Earth as that maternal principle out of which we are born and by which we are sustained. Once this symbol is recovered the dominion of the patriarchal principle that has brought such aggressive attitudes into our activities will be mitigated. If this is achieved then our relationship with the natural world would undergo one of its most radical readjustments since the origins of our civilization in classical antiquity.[50]

Well, maybe it's not necessary to choose between the new universe story and the maternal principle. Perhaps they complement one another in ways I'm too dense to discern. But there is enormous resistance to the advent of the Daughter's worldview. The "liberals" I know don't want to hear about it. Most of them self-identify as civilized Christians, and their assessment of Christian civilization is the opposite of mine. They say we're insufficiently civilized and inadequately Christian: if only we'd learn to be more of both. But I suspect "Cosmic Christ" is only another way to veer off from and postpone the radical readjustment. At some point, we men—but not only "we men," for most women, via the shaping power of the patriarchal establishments, are also enveloped in patriarchal consciousness, including the overwhelming patriarchal consciousness of the Christian church—we all will have to go, hat in hand, and tell Mama we're sorry. Plus we *really* will have to mean it. Telling Mama we're sorry is no sweetly pious condescension. Telling Mama we're sorry will transform our entire way

50. Berry, *Great*, 69-70.

of life. This will be one of the "most radical readjustments since the origins of our civilization in classical antiquity," and one of the "most complete reversal of values . . . since the Neolithic."

That means—what we seem too fearfully dull to realize—on the other side of sincere humility lies what Norman O. Brown (in the last chapter of his *Life Against Death*) calls "the resurrection of the body." If utopian civilization has built its megamachine on the transfer of repressed energy from denied body to arrogant mind, from peasant oppression to aristocratic hubris, the eutopian Age of the Daughter will, with "radical readjustments," restore the life of the body as we learn to live culturally rich, earthy lives. What Brown calls the "resurrection of the body" will entail resurrection of wholesome cultural evolution in a folk mode, even as this restoration involves richer spiritual comprehension and deeper erotic intimacy.

Or are we so habituated to the familiar channels and routine institutions of utopian compulsion that we would rather blow the world to hell—by drone remote control, of course, available for on-demand YouTube viewing—than make love in the eutopian garden? What does this say about our collective evolutionary wisdom? Or the arrogance of ultrabright aggressive boys who are so confidently programming a better planet?

VI

When your dearest intellectual friends are dead and gone, friends whose conversation you'd dearly love to sit in on, imaginative improvisation seems the only alternative to forlorn despair. What *would* these two have said to each other? How *would* conversation have transformed them by new comprehensions at a depth of crucial significance?

So, for my own edification (we'll see about the reader's), I'm slipping a Thomas Berry puppet on one hand and a Norman O. Brown puppet on the other to see if they'll have at it. I may succumb, here and there, to a little slapstick ventriloquism, but I will give it my best shot to not misrepresent either of these wise persons too much, men who have something fundamentally important for us to hear and, for all the pain and difficulty, something important for us to internalize. This will be not only about unprecedented ecological crisis but also about sex and gender: maybe it will be a lot about sex and gender.

We may on occasion say the two subjects sure to invite conversational trouble are politics and religion. True enough. We've all been there. But politics and religion are, in some respects, mere conversational toys compared with sex and gender. If religion is the bugbear of the superego and politics the poltergeist of the ego, sex is the pink gorilla locked in the offshore Guantánamo cellar of the id.

What if (I've put on the Brown puppet) the global catastrophe the human race has concocted has deep roots in the systemic repression of our sexuality, while the substitutes ("sublimations") institutionally locked into place over the millennia, especially the radically deepened magnitude of traumatic institutions brought about by civilizational consolidation, are cumulatively deadly as we try to suppress by psychological avoidance and conquer by physical force what we are afraid to embrace by vulnerable affection? What if the transformation needed, not merely to avert human and mammalian extinction, but to liberate us to live freer, happier, earthier lives—and both our puppet prophets are earnestly for such transformation—they're nodding their heads almost uncontrollably—what if the transformation is not composed just of deep moral resolution combined with global political reformation, but also contains (and must of necessity contain) a thorough cultural transformation in the idish area of sex and gender? Why, after all, have men expended such energy in the exclusion, controlling, belittling, repression, and glamorizing of women? Is this an accident of history? Is it a bad hobby that got out of control? What's the real story here?

The atmosphere around sex and gender can get pretty hot and sticky awfully fast. Call it global warming if you want too. Norman O. Brown would say it is the fetid confinement of the pink gorilla. And what would Thomas Berry say?[51]

Repression of the "polymorphously perverse body of infantile sexuality"[52] is the cell in the cellar Norman O. Brown keeps returning to, as he, with keen scholarly intent, follows the well-worn slipper tracks of Sigmund Freud up and down the basement stairs. Meanwhile, the would-be puppeteer of this psychoanalytical mummery discovers one of his puppets has an inexplicable case of stage fright or moral scruple. Thomas Berry has clammed up. Our celibate priest (I'm assuming Berry kept a vow of celibacy) says not one word about sex and only a tiny bit about gender. So we have, right off the bat, something of a problem. One of our puppets won't quit talking about sex, repression, sublimation, aggression, and the cumulative ever-deadlier institutional manifestation of our "progressive" predicament—"the essence of sublimation is the reification of the superfluous-sacred in monumental, enduring form"[53]—and the other, even if you threaten to take him to the woodshed, won't utter a word. Some conversation. Maybe the ventriloquist needs to take off his gloves.

Well, he's one stubborn fellow.[54] So, if Berry won't talk about sex, let's see what we can tease out of him in regard to gender. I suspect Berry and Brown are closer in

---

51. Richard Tarnas has dogs in this squabble. In the Epilogue to *The Passion of the Western Mind*, he first invokes (pages 419-21) Gregory Bateson's "double bind situation between a child and a 'schizophrenogenic' mother" in which the child is dependent on the mother, the child receives contradictory messages from the mother, the child is unable to resolve the contradictions, and the child cannot discontinue the relationship. Later (pages 425-33), Tarnas summarizes the "psychodynamic theory" of Stanislav Grof who (according to Tarnas) pushed beyond Freud and Jung to the reliving of one's own birth trauma, how the implications of Grof's work could help us understand how the "roots of male sexism" lie in the "unconscious fear of female birthing bodies," and even how psychopathological impulses toward war and totalitarianism arise from this trauma. In chapter 13 we'll see if Dorothy Dinnerstein can clarify this analysis and push it even deeper.

52. Brown, *Life*, 48.

53. Brown, *Life*, 283.

54. As if to support this grumpy opinion, here's what Berry says of himself on page 143 in the

understanding than we imagine. But before we extract Berry's gender from the woodshed, let's post a paragraph from Norman O. Brown as a template of sorts by which we can, if we wish, test the hypothesis of their underlying alleged similarity:

> The proper starting point for a Freudian anthropology is the pre-Oedipal mother. What is given by nature, in the family, is the dependence of the child on the mother. Male domination must be grasped as a secondary formation, the product of the child's revolt against the primal mother, bequeathed to adulthood and culture by the castration complex. Freudian anthropology must therefore turn from Freud's preoccupation with patriarchal monotheism; it must take out of the hands of Jungian *Schwarmerei* the exploitation of Bachofen's great discovery of the religion of the Great Mother, a substratum underlying the religion of the Father—the anthropological analogue to Freud's discovery of the Oedipal mother underlying the Oedipal father, and comparable, like Freud's, to the discovery of Minoan-Mycenaean civilization underlying Greek civilization.[55]

Well, think what you want about "castration complex"—it has yet to trip my trigger (unless it really means frustration, aggravation, and perpetual resentment—Gregory Bateson's "double bind situation"—because male weaning leads to emotional/physical/erotic exclusion from the female which, except for prostitution as a desperate ventiduct, seems both permanent and unendurable—"castration" as ongoing feral estrangement)—or the nasty swipe at the Jungian *Schwarmerei*—but let's attend closely to the gender dynamics Brown here presents. We start out dependent on the mother, with a sense of near totality. Male domination arises as a secondary formation, the child's "revolt," although "revolt" is really the estrangement of weaning turned inside out as frustration and resentment. Via Bachofen's archaeological work, we discover that the religion of the Almighty Father suppressed the religion of the Great Mother (i.e., *civis* violently dominating *pagus*), replicating to some degree in religious, political, and cultural structure—in actual human history—what we now know to be true psychologically. (Well, then there's the uncomfortable issue of kings and their harems—"harem" from the Arabic *harim*, anything forbidden or sacred, according to *Webster's*—and therefore suggesting that kings captured the women's temple of the Goddess, impounding it for reasons of pleasure and control, as they kept all lesser males, except eunuchs, at an enforced distance, so that "weaning" has a second level of exclusion caused by fear of superior male wrath. First Mama weans her boys, then Daddy forcibly obstructs the boys' access to Mama. Thus weaning, for nearly all males, has two levels of gender enforcement.) It's time to go back to Thomas Berry.

Appendix to *Befriending the Earth*: "I have always lived marginally. My mother told me once that I was so difficult as a child, that by the age of four, my mother and father had a conference one day about me, and my father said, 'We have been nice and sweet and kind to this boy. We have spanked him, we have punished him. Just nothing's going to work. I guess he will just have to raise himself.'"

55. Brown, *Life*, 126.

There are no index references for gender in *The Dream of the Earth* or in *Befriending the Earth*. There are, however, several such references in *The Great Work*. The ventriloquist believes these references do more to support his Four Ages modification of Joachim's Three Ages than they do to support Berry's embrace of Teilhard's New Universe Story. In fact, going back to Berry's praise of Teilhard as quoted in the opening paragraph of this essay, it could be argued that it was not Teilhard but *Joachim* who "gave expression to the greatest transformation in Christian thought since the time of St. Paul" and whose Three Ages configuration opened the way from the "spatially understood" meaning of Father-Son-Holy Spirit Trinity to a "time-developmental" understanding of a Mother-Father-Son-Daughter Mandala. Joachim took God (or Trinity) out of the sky, installed Three Persons as sequential historical epochs on Earth, thereby creating the conceptual framework by which we are obliged to restore Mother to the front—not of Trio—but of Quartet.

Berry's first index-reference use of "gender" occurs on page 63 in *The Great Work* and is part of a section on the use and misuse of language. He says, for instance, in regard to the word "progress," that

> . . . the ecologist is at a loss as to how to proceed; the language in which our values are expressed has been co-opted by the industrial establishment and is used with the most extravagant modes of commercial advertising to create the illusory world in which modern industrial peoples now live.
>
> One of the most essential roles of the ecologist is to create the language in which a true sense of reality, of value, and of progress can be communicated to our society.[56]

Well, yes to that. This essay—this entire set of essays—is precisely about that project. And here is the subsequent passage on gender:

> There are questions concerning "gender" that need consideration. The industrial establishment is the extreme expression of a patriarchal tradition with its all-pervasive sense of dominance, whether of rulers over people, of men over women, of humans over nature. Only with enormous psychic and social effort and revolutionary processes has this patriarchal control been mitigated as regards the rights of women. The rights of the natural world of living beings is still at the mercy of the modern industrial corporation as the ultimate expression of patriarchal dominance over the entire planetary process.[57]

The bulk of the remaining gender references—in fact, *all* the remaining gender references—are located in chapter 16, "The Fourfold Wisdom." (Berry's fourfold wisdom consists of—in the order presented—"the wisdom of indigenous peoples, the wisdom of women, the wisdom of the classical traditions, and the wisdom of

---

56. Berry, *Great*, 63.

57. Berry, *Great*, 63.

science."[58]) Since the "wisdom of women" constitutes the bulk of pages 180 through 185 in *The Great Work*, let's indulge in a fairly long, sequential quotation, extracted in bits and pieces:

> The wisdom of women is to join the knowing of the body to that of mind, to join soul to spirit, intuition to reasoning, feeling consciousness to intellectual analysis, intimacy to detachment, subjective presence to objective distance. When these functions become separated in carrying out the human project then the way into the future is to bring them together.
>
> The human project belongs to both women and men. . . . Each brings distinctive abilities to the single project.
>
> Because men in Western civilization have isolated women in the home and in a narrow band of service activities, and have appropriated for themselves both the reality and value of the adult human outside the home, the human project in its Western manifestation has become a patriarchal establishment in quest for unlimited dominance, a dominance unsettled in itself and a disturbance to the larger human community. In a corresponding way, because men have appropriated the reality and value of the Earth for their own purposes, the Earth is becoming dysfunctional. Again it is a quest for dominance.
>
> The only acceptable attitude of any mode of being is to recognize that existence is a mutual dependence of a diversity of components. The human is a single enterprise that brings together women and men, elders and children, the farmer and the merchant, the foreigner and the native. So too the Earth is a single enterprise, composed of land and sea, rain and wind, plants and animals and humans, and the whole magnificent universe. Nothing is itself without everything else. This centering of men on themselves, to the detriment of women, the home, and the family as well as the Earth and everything on the Earth, is identified as *androcentrism*.
>
> Among the greatest of terrors that women have encountered as a consequence of androcentrism is when they are considered the result of a genetic deficiency, are thought of as intellectually deficient, are seen as inherently seductive in their moral influence, are persecuted as malevolent spirits. In some societies women are required to undergo physical mutilation, are sold or forced into prostitution, or are traded off in arranged marriages. An endless list could be compiled of abuses and suppressions imposed upon women in the past and that continue even in the present, especially in the form of sexual exploitation. Women were thought to exist for the purposes of men.
>
> By asserting their place in every aspect of the social and cultural life of the human community, women are bringing their own resolution to this attitude of men. While women are thus fulfilling a duty they owe to themselves, they are also revealing to men the reality of the patriarchal dominance that men

---

58. Berry, *Great*, 176.

have been imposing on the human community. Women are also revealing Western civilization to itself. Without this newly assertive consciousness of women, Western civilization might have continued indefinitely on its destructive path without ever coming to a realization of just what has been happening in the exclusion of women from full participation in the human project.

This revelation of men to themselves and of Western civilization to itself might be considered the first most dramatic manifestation of the wisdom of women. The transformation of men and of Western civilization is a primary condition for every other change that is needed in shaping a future worthy of either men or women. Androcentrism and patriarchy bring down in ruins the finest aspirations of the religious and humanist traditions of Western civilization—and also, it seems, most other civilizations of the Eurasian world that have dominated the first several thousand years of the modern human project. It might even be indicated that the foundations of our cultural traditions have from the beginning tended in this direction. A truly realistic insight into the situation might reveal that the distortions we mention might be less a deviation than the fulfillment of certain aspects of the Western tradition. This new interpretation of Western history, as dominated by its patriarchal establishments, can be considered the most profound contribution to historical understanding made in recent centuries.

The first concern just now is for men to accept the transformation in Western civilization indicated by abandoning their androcentrism and their patriarchal dominance. This transformation is a historical task forced upon the society by women. Men can best assist by welcoming the transformation being effected and by recognizing their responsibility for the burden that women have endured through these past centuries, and by understanding what women are communicating to them.

One of the first steps for women now is assertion of their role within the larger realm of human affairs. Assertion of their personal dignity and their personal rights in the socioeconomic order is an elementary first step that needs to be taken. . . .

Out of their historical experience an immense store of wisdom is available to women for influencing the course of the future in its every aspect, from its social and cultural through its religious institutions, its educational establishments, and its economic functioning. Yet there is, it seems, a deeper background to the identity of woman, a background that reaches far back in time to the Neolithic Period, a background that is of special significance in relation to the task of moving the human project into a period when humans would be present to the Earth in a mutually enhancing manner.

The earliest and most profound human experience of woman in these former centuries of human development is found in identifying maternal nurturance as the primordial creating, sustaining, and fulfilling power of the universe. Mutual nurturance is presented as the primary bonding of each component of the universe with the other components. This experience of the universe as originating in and sustained by a primordial originating and nurturing principle imminent in the universe itself finds expression in the figure of the Goddess in the late Paleolithic Period and in the Neolithic Period in the Near East.

This Goddess figure presided over this period as a world of meaning, of security, of creativity in all its forms. This was not a matriarchy, nor was it a social program. It was a comprehensive cosmology of a creative and nurturing principle independent of any associated male figure. This is difficult for us to envisage, a world with a comprehensive cosmology of woman with a derivative sociology. It is a tribute to contemporary women that they are developing both a sociology and a cosmology of woman. . . .

From these archaeological studies of the Neolithic Period, also from historical references of the succeeding age, we can conclude that this period of the Goddess was a relatively peaceful time, of intimate human presence to the Earth and to the entire natural world. The first permanent villages were established. The first domestication of plants and animals took place in these settled communities. We are just beginning to appreciate how creative a time it was when the Goddess culture had a pervasive presence throughout human affairs. . . .

The male deities did not rise out of this context. These frequently warrior deities arose from without and became dominant throughout the Eurasian land mass as Zeus, Yahweh, Indra, and Thor. All of this was the beginning of the urban, literate, patriarchal civilizations, with the subordination of feminine deities in the Greek world and the denunciation of feminine deities in the biblical world. Once this dominant position of men as divine rulers or as rulers with divine sanction was established, a fixation developed that could not be successfully altered until the religious traditions of Western civilization and their associated deity came to be challenged in their basic meaning.[59]

Well, there we are. That's a fine summation of many of the understandings that have slowly but steadily unfolded for me, or congealed within me, over the last thirty-five to forty years: maternal nurturance as the primordial creating, sustaining, and fulfilling power; the subordination of feminine deities resulting in patriarchal fixation; and the pressing need for transformation of male consciousness (but not only male consciousness) as the basis for every other needed change: religious myth as the "divine" projection of gender dynamics. Not so much "demythologizing" as *remythologizing* gender dynamics to accommodate the buried past and to reveal a hidden future—merging, we might say, *mythos* and *logos* in a way that honors both.

Let's reposition Berry's "fourfold wisdom" just a bit. He begins with indigenous peoples and proceeds, in sequence, to women, classical traditions, and science. All we need do is move "women" from second to fourth place and we have a perfect

59. Berry, *Great*, 180-85.

correlation to a modified Joachimism: Mother = indigenous peoples (*pagus*), Father = classical traditions (*civis*), Son = science (*civis* on steroids), and Daughter = women (the Green reconciliation of *pagus* and *civis*).

Now I have no inclination (nor the competence even if I had an inclination) to dispute the science of the New Universe Story. But we should recognize the New Universe Story as the grand, cosmic vision of philosophical speculation, tweaked by specific New Testament assertions. That is, the New Universe Story represents the Western *science* story from Copernicus through Newton, with "Christ" blown to outer space and inhabiting an expanding universe. The New Universe Story is *not* the Daughter's story; it is the *Son's* story, and perhaps even its most audacious expression in a scientific/theological sense. It *is* a climax of sorts for what Thomas Berry calls "scientific-technological." But as Berry so eloquently points out, it's not just the human relationship with Earth that needs healing. Integral to the sustained, intensifying, and cumulative Earth abuse is the angry, resentful, fearful, and repressive behavior of men toward women—"androcentrism and their patriarchal dominance." The issues of ecology and feminism are joined at the hip of the agrarian village, as they will be again so joined in the Green future.

Why men feel and have felt fearful and resentful toward women is itself a huge and difficult subject. Norman O. Brown, in my estimation, is extremely helpful in exploring this situation, even though he's a man delving into psychoanalytical depths as articulated and revealed by yet another man (Freud) and presenting findings from a male point of view. (We therefore need a Norma A. Brown to explicate a correspondingly deep psychoanalysis from a feminine point of view.) Perhaps our core problem is male craving for fuller erotic access to the female as derived from nine months in Mama's womb, an extended period of nearly unlimited access to Mama's breasts and body, and then the pain and resentment of enforced weaning, the physical and emotional distancing that, in everyday behavior, is not correspondingly replicated in the unconscious.[60] "In the unconscious there is no time."[61] That is, we may never outgrow our sense of infantile need or entitlement. (But that, of course, raises the question of whether it's birth trauma or weaning trauma that's closer to the core of male aggression. Why, after all, wouldn't birth trauma also result in aggression in females?)

And if it's difficult to resolve or outgrow our "schizophrenogenic" frustration, then the Daughter's Age is not only about the liberation of women in a political sense, not only about a huge decrease in male domination in an economic and military sense, not only about energy conservation and ecological restoration, but also about a major erotic reconciliation whereby males can and will have erotic cravings more fully met and deeply satisfied by females whose desire for the male becomes freer and more openly expressive as male domination dissolves and lifts. Gentler men (I

60. See section II in "Their Fearful Energies" in my *Green Politics Is Eutopian*, especially pages 182 through 188.

61. Brown, *Life*, 274.

don't know about slipper addicts) will be hugely more attractive to freer women. The end of male domination will prove, perhaps paradoxically, to have a tight correlation with deepened erotic satisfaction and greater bodily fulfillment. (I realize this is terribly heterosexual, but that's my orientation.) Men will no longer "run the world," but erotic joy will begin to reach spiritual dimension. Harsh dominance and righteous possessiveness will, of necessity, be greatly mitigated and reduced, and we will learn to celebrate the fuller growth of the human self in more complex (but also more responsible) freedom.

The New Universe Story or the New Universe Story with Cosmic Christ embedded may be the scientific-technological culmination of the Son's Age, but it's not the core narrative of the Daughter's Age. The Daughter's Age requires humbling the vertical, pyramid Trinity into a horizontal, spiral Mandala. The Daughter's Age requires resurrection of the Mother's Age. A lot of Christian orthodoxy, with its supernatural doctrines and mythological creeds, will scrape off in the eye of this spiral. Much of the existing religious establishment may never stoop to enter. Doctrinal orthodoxy really is its God or, to put it differently, the religious establishment has "God" strapped tight in a doctrinal straightjacket. Only those men who voluntarily shed their patriarchal posture and masculine prerogative will freely come to Mandala: those who refuse will gather, ever more tightly, at the control center of those efforts—political, economic, military, religious, scientific—to prolong their repudiation of equalitarian reconciliation and perpetuate their reign of gender dominance, even as they may claim this domination as the will of God. This gathering effort is now more and more openly at the heart of reactionary global mayhem, and it represents—in both "liberal" and "conservative" modes (though much stronger in the latter)—a compulsive, obsessive resistance to transformation.

So-called "conservatives" conserve essentially nothing—their core repository of energy combines male aggression with reflexive invocation of a male God perfectly reflective of their encapsulated self-image—while "liberals" are brainy but wimpy compromisers, caught between adoration of the "conservative" male strut and fearful of it, reflexively protective of affluent advantage, given to technofix "solutions" in the face of crises requiring far deeper analysis and far more humble courses of corrective action. "Conservatives," we might say, express a raw and brutal warrior energy closer to the founding bandit core of the earliest civilizational kingdoms and empires, while "liberals"—softer, somewhat more intellectually ethical—are upper-level retainers who fear the loss of civilizational advantage but who will, if pushed, act with ruthless decisiveness when threatened by a transformational downsizing of their prerogatives and advantages. Hence we saw, in the first Obama administration, with both houses of Congress overwhelmingly in Democratic control, virtually no meaningful reform of the American energy/financial/corporate/military empire. Certainly, "conservatives" labored mightily to thwart even modest reform, but "liberals" obviously had no taste for fundamental economic change or ecological amelioration—even in the face of crises, especially in the area of climate change, whose magnitude of intensity is accelerating with every month and year. One wonders what degree of destructiveness or what magnitude of breakdown is necessary to reach a political tipping point. We certainly haven't reached it yet. And it's possible that "waiting for the right moment" or "waiting for the right conditions" only means the *democratic* moment might pass beyond recovery and our desperate descendants stuck with a grim aristocracy of global dimension and ruthless determination.

VII

Perhaps we need one more encounter with Thomas Berry. The issue is ethics, broadly speaking.

In my *Polemics and Provocations* I suggest (see especially chapter 10, "The Underlying Religion of Civilization") that the ethical content of Jesus' kingdom of God proclamation, namely its radical servanthood and radical stewardship, pulls us back to or aligns his vision with the precivilized agrarian village, and that alignment opens the door to the restoration of folk evolution at a more complex level. I don't think a close reading of the gospels, at any rate, can lead to a conclusion that Jesus was an advocate for empire or a booster of civilization. He was, after all, put to death by what Thomas Berry calls the "patriarchal establishment," which should tell us something about how that establishment perceived him. Jesus' parables and stories are folkish and (unlike the language in the remainder of the New Testament) his speech is full of vivid imagery pertaining to agriculture and fishing, the precise stuff of which peasant life consisted in his time and place. His "social gospel," if I might borrow Walter Rauschenbusch's beautiful term, if followed through by enough people with sufficient spiritual clarity and political determination, would result in the liberation of the peasant community, exactly on the basis of servanthood and stewardship—rolling away the massive civilized stone at the slave tomb of the agrarian village. If we dare see Jesus this way, and if we dare see him in light of the modified Joachimism I'm proposing *and* in light of the Goddess tendencies Thomas Berry suggests were operative in the precivilized, prepatriarchal agrarian village, then we might, with far greater historical *and* spiritual comprehension, say that Jesus was less the Son of God than he was the Son of the Goddess. That is, his agenda included the restoration of the atmosphere or "reign" of the feminine, with both his teaching in behalf of the peasantry and his brutal execution at the hands of the patriarchal establishment revealing the depth of his commitment to that restoration. If so, then the Age of the Daughter holds the promise of realizing the historical and ethical principles for which Jesus lived and died: the resurrection of the Mother's age at a much higher level of consciousness and a much fuller articulation of spiritual comprehension in the realm of ecological living.

I do not say this as a devious contrivance by which to snaggle people into a Christian fold. The Christian church is dying. Either it has to abandon its exclusive divinity of the male (with its side auras of "female" Wisdom or the veneration of Mary as "Mother of God," what Berry calls "at least some remnant presence of the ancient Earth Mother") and directly embrace the prepatriarchal Mother—and that requires recognizing the Holy Spirit as Daughter—which recognition enlarges Trinity into Mandala—or the church will be spiritually dead, only a religious relic in a cracked glass case. The new "theology," if we can call it that, will not be theist or deist but— take your pick—panentheist or pantheist. Spirit will be felt as Living Presence—or, as Lewis Mumford puts it in the passage quoted earlier, "within the cosmic system from the 'beginning' and attributing design, not to any *original* plan but to the increasing tendency of organized processes and structures to combine with the selective aid of organisms into more purposeful emergent wholes." The "cosmic system" with which we have the greatest familiarity and biological connection is the evolution of life on Earth. This is our home place, even if our bodily atoms are star dust. It seems Thomas Berry is saying basically the same thing as Lewis Mumford, as was Lao Tzu—nearly two and a half millennia ago—although "cosmic system" does tend to catapult us into outer space, back toward star dust, when what we desperately need is to realize our spirituality in the earthly context of evolutionary life. We are, after all, an evolved form of life on Earth, and our spirituality needs to reflect and embody that earthly reality. We need to love the Mother body out of which we've evolved.

So, I'm not trying to smuggle a transgender Jesus into a new religion as a sneaky way to rescue or prolong Christianity. Or, if I am, the "resurrection" I'm advocating is not a supernatural ascension out of this world into some star-dust outer space but the recognition of the astonishing brilliance, courage, and humane wholesomeness of a magnificently human and earthly Jesus, a combination of traits and capabilities so above average, so radiated with nonviolent but undeviating commitment, that de-spite all the ways he's been falsely "followed" and sanctimoniously "worshipped" for two thousand years, his life remains a reservoir of spiritual inspiration and ethical guidance—a man who invested his life in the prospect of the transformation of hu-man consciousness on Earth. You don't have to be a "Christian" to love this guy or recognize his extraordinary spiritual significance.

There are no index references to Jesus in either *The Dream of the Earth* or *The Great Work*. *Befriending the Earth* has a bunch of references—seventeen, in fact—but only six of these align with Thomas Berry. (Ten belong to Thomas Clarke, and one is in the Glossary.) All of Berry's Jesus references occur in chapter Three, "Christol-ogy." This is the chapter in which Berry says we are "overly concerned with salvation," where he suggests we should "give up the Bible for awhile, put it on the shelf for per-haps twenty years," and where he asserts that "Excessive concern with the historical Christ is presently just not that helpful."[62] There are no index references in *Befriending the Earth* to the kingdom of God, either. Perhaps Berry needed sustained exposure to

---

62. Berry, *Befriending*, 75.

scholars like John Dominic Crossan and Marcus Borg to show him why the historical Jesus is so crucial, what it means to recognize civilization as his murderer.

Anyway, in the larger context of these Jesus references, Berry starts by talking about the "basic belief structures of Christianity, particularly the Incarnation."[63] Then he goes quickly on to say:

> The issue is not whether or not Christianity is viable, or whether any other tradition is viable. The question is the viability of the human, or, more point-edly, the viability of the planet earth in its basic life systems as long as humans are around. This requires a rather extensive revision of our thinking about all human institutions, particularly about all religious traditions of the human. For ourselves, of course, as Christians, we must reconsider the dominant tra-dition that the Western world is heir to, our own Christian tradition. So it is necessary to reflect again on the Christ figure.
>
> Western Christianity, even Western civilization, is so intimately related to the Christ reality that they make little sense apart from the Christ reality. The art, the music, the thought, the social forms, the ideals—the moral ide-als particularly—are born out of the biblical story, especially the Christ story, the Christ reality. Civilizations generally are the product of some great story; often it is an heroic story, the story of a cultural hero. Christ undoubtedly is the central heroic personality who, at least until recently, was central to the cultural development of Western civilization.[64]

This is confusion. Jesus may well have become a cultural "hero," but he had to be stripped of his peasant vitality and his confrontational spirituality in order to be reshaped into otherworldly passivity, that he might enter Western civilization as its "hero" or "savior." He had to be packaged as the magic dead-and-gone Prince of Af-terlife Salvation—a Person not of this world—to be permitted into the imperial story. We can take the early church's vilification of "pagan" as something of a template by which to measure its distancing from Jesus the peasant revolutionary. That distancing is a crucial aspect of the Constantinian accommodation. To become Empire's *civis* re-ligion, Christianity had to hang its dead peasant up for display. Or, to put it differently, the cross didn't become a cherished Christian emblem until orthodoxy merged with the Roman Empire and became its state religion. (There is another layer here. That is, the revolutionary peasant Jesus was hidden in plain view in the gospels—a view that became more discernible to people with Gutenberg, increasing literacy, vernacular translations of the Bible, and the Anabaptist Reformation—all in a manner analogous to how Q was hidden in the synoptic gospels, waiting for dis-covery or *apokalypsis*. While Anabaptists rediscovered the kingdom of God, they did so from within ortho-dox theology. As Mandala replaces Trinity, the kingdom of God will take on greater

63. Berry, *Befriending*, 66.
64. Berry, *Befriending*, 67.

dimensions of earthly significance. Anabaptism will be liberated from its restrictive and restraining orthodoxy.)

Berry continues with a brief exposition of Thomas Aquinas and Duns Scotus as they wrestled with the "question of why the divine appears in human form."[65] The closest Berry comes to contending with the kingdom of God, however, may be in this paragraph:

> In the human order, the divine would have a very special modality and a community would be formed that would, in a certain sense, be an extension of this personality. The organic relation of the Christian community to Christ is expressed in considering the community as the Body of Christ in relationship to Christ, who is its head. Another metaphor is that of a divine kingdom emerging, since kingdoms were at one time the more brilliant examples of social order. But when we think of what is called redemption and incarnation, we must ask, "Where does the natural world fit into the picture?" It is easy enough to see how humans and the human community could share in this experience and enter into this story, but where the natural world fits into the picture is not entirely clear.[66]

Well, redemption and incarnation are awfully big ideas, especially when puffed up by centuries of abstract Christian theology. But incarnation and redemption are basic, everyday mysteries when understood in terms of our lives and the network of lives in which we live. How did I get to be me? What's the meaning of this consciousness, this bodily self-awareness? What exactly is the nature of my spiritual relationship to my parents or to my children? And if that's a slice of the narrow, personal part, what about the proliferation of all those life forms surrounding me, from trees to butterflies to porcupines? All those amazing lives, of all sorts, preceding my life by time out of mind and that, one presumes and hopes, will continue to birth and bloom into a future beyond reckoning? And if we ponder "redemption" in a more concrete and grounded way, how is it that some people seem to discover and be ethically cleansed by the inexplicable mystery of "incarnation" while others seem to take their personal existence as blasé entitlement and appear oblivious of life's awesome mystery? Which is the greater fidelity to mystery—to live a life of aggressive self-entitlement and smug self-absorption or a life of humble wonder? (Here we may be obliged to say that simple, grounded "mindfulness" in the Buddhist sense carries us farther in the direction of humble contemplation than anything in the Christian tradition, except for the contemplatives and mystics.)

We should, perhaps, take note of what Thomas Berry, in the passage above, describes as the Christian community's "relationship to Christ, who is its head." This is a formal theological assertion fully in accord with the orthodox canon. It implies

---

65. Berry, *Befriending*, 68.
66. Berry, *Befriending*, 69.

a narrow, restrictive, hierarchical understanding of the meaning of the "kingdom of God." But here's a clarifying paragraph from John Dominic Crossan's *Jesus: A Revolutionary Biography*. This occurs in a section called "How Not to Be a Patron":

> The equal sharing of spiritual and material gifts, of miracle and table, cannot be centered in one place because that very hierarchy of place, of here over there, of this place over other places, symbolically destroys the radical egalitarianism it announces. Radical egalitarianism denies the processes of patronage, brokerage, and clientage, and demands itinerancy as its programmatic symbolization. Neither Jesus nor his followers are supposed to settle down to stay in one place and establish there a brokered presence. And, as healers, we would expect them to stay in one place, to establish around them a group of followers, and to have people come to them. Instead, they go out to people and have, as it were, to start anew each morning. But, for Jesus, the Kingdom of God is a community of radical or unbrokered equality in which individuals are in direct contact with one another and with God, unmediated by any established brokers or fixed locations.[67]

"Unbrokered equality" is a very different kettle of fish than "Body of Christ" with Christ at its head. These are very different constructs reflecting very different understandings of who Jesus was and what he stood for. Berry's understanding was contained, in this regard, in a traditional and orthodox view both hierarchical and otherworldly: not that he, exactly, believed any longer in the traditional view, but that view colored his understanding of the construct and facilitated his rejection of it. Perhaps he failed to get beyond the hierarchical language of "kingdom" and, in his rejection, couldn't see the real meaning alive within the semantic box.

But let's go back to the last paragraph quoted from Thomas Berry's "Christology." I think we have here a fork in the road and an understandable but deflective flaw in Berry's thinking. It has to do with "divine kingdom emerging," with his wondering where the natural world fits into the picture. I am presuming "divine kingdom emerging" points toward the multiplicity of references to the "kingdom of God" in the first three gospels. Because Berry doesn't see where the natural world fits into this "kingdom" picture, he seems to have abandoned the kingdom of God as an important construct in favor of a "pervasive sense of the divine in the natural world."[68] He then goes on to say how

> . . . supremely important it is, from a Christian standpoint, to move now to a new sense of the sacred, namely the sacred dimension of an emergent, continually transforming universe. Unfortunately, we are having difficulties understanding the universe as a developmental process. We are at a complete loss as to how Christian thought can contribute to solving the problems we are

67. Crossan, *Jesus*, 101.
68. Berry, *Befriending*, 71.

confronting in any way other than extrinsically. We are seeing the earth's survival as simply another moral problem. In reality, this relationship of human with the natural world is not simply another moral problem; it is a profound, ontological problem. It is a profoundly *religious* problem. It is the basic issue facing humans. . . .[69]

Well, that's true—the human relationship with the natural world *is* a profound, ontological problem—but on the next page Berry says "If we are going to understand Christianity in the context of contemporary thought, we must understand developmental time, whereby the universe comes into being. We must understand developmental times as sacred time, as having a Christ dimension from the beginning."[70] Then he says that:

> The new story, however, the Christ story as we are proposing within this time-developmental context, is very different from what St. Paul and St. John were thinking about. Unless we move into this new sense of time, we will not be present to the world of reality as it exists and functions in our society. That is why Christians are alienated people in relationship to the present world. We cannot accept developmental time as sacred time. We cannot accept the story of an evolutionary universe as our sacred story.[71]

But note how Berry slides from wondering "where the natural world fits into the 'kingdom' picture" to a "new sense of time" within "an evolutionary universe." Earth shrinks from grounded, earthy context—from being our evolutionary *home*—to a mere dot in a universe beyond comprehension. We are alienated people, however, not so much because we lack a sense of cosmic time or a grasp of what "evolutionary universe" means, but because we have chopped the Mother's age—the so-called "prehistorical"—out of *our* historical and spiritual comprehension and rendered both historical and spiritual life totally male in overarching valuation. Our alienation is much closer to home than Berry locates it. It may seem paradoxical if not contradictory, but the new and growing understanding of the "kingdom of God" proclamation—despite its male vocabulary—actually moves us toward *remembering and restoring* the Mother's epoch with the historical and spiritual *meaning* that goes with it. This movement of recovery has been enormously aided by the sort of scholarship Terrence Rynne itemized in a previous essay.

Berry says he sometimes thinks "we worry too much about Jesus Christ." This worry has "focused out attention to such an extent that we have abandoned the most urgent projects of our times." Well, abandoned or simply declined to engage—it may be difficult to discern a difference. These urgent projects have to do with what he

---

69. Berry, *Befriending*, 72.

70. Berry, *Befriending*, 73.

71. Berry, *Befriending*, 74.

calls "the natural world and the Christ-universe equation."[72] However, I believe Berry's "Christ" is not the unbrokering Jesus of John Dominic Crossan's understanding but, rather, the "head" of conventional Christology, a "head" Berry wants radiated to cosmic dimension. Berry's affinity for the New Universe Story is related to his failure to understand the historical Jesus, the Earth-centered meaning of the kingdom of God proclamation, or that Trinity shuts Mother out of divine representation. Mother cannot assume Her rightful place without Trinity getting cracked. But once Trinity *is* cracked, Mother is restored, Father's hubris is painfully revealed, Son doesn't need a Cosmic Christ space suit, and Daughter can begin to heal ecological wounds—*and* the cultural and spiritual wounds of our alienation.

There is no question that Thomas Berry is addressing a huge gap, void, or flaw in Christianity, a psychospirituality that, reflecting the idea of and conviction about a Creator God *outside* the universe or, at least, totally distinct from it, has produced human personalities who have come to see themselves also as distinct from and outside the natural world, with disastrous consequences accelerated and magnified by the industrial revolution and the civilizational overthrow and suppression of essentially all noncivilized cultures. Berry sees the accrued consequences of that disaster closing in on us ecologically, over all the Earth; he is deeply concerned and greatly alarmed. So it's understandable, given the absolutely critical role kingdoms and empires have played in the jagged unfolding and violent spreading of the civilizational juggernaut, why he cannot bring himself to accept or embrace the imagery and language of "divine kingdom emerging" or why he thinks "Excessive concern with the historical Christ is presently just not that helpful."

Yet it's true that most of the exciting and liberating Christian scholarship of at least the last twenty-five years or thirty years, let's say, has come from people like John Dominic Crossan and Marcus Borg, scholars particularly interested in the historical Jesus *and* in the deeper, practical, and even political meaning of the kingdom of God proclamation. A lot of this scholarship shares critical features with Berry's work, including its focus on what Berry calls "patriarchal establishments." (See, for example, my use of Borg's exposition of the monarchical image of God in chapter 4, "The Perfectly Camouflaged Temple," especially pages 24 and 25, in *Green Politics Is Eutopian*.) A "kingdom of God" orientation may not be at cross-purposes with the "new universe story."

In fact, we see these stories overlap in the writing of the former (or do I say "resigned"?) Australian priest Michael Morwood in his book *Is Jesus God?* Morwood talks openly about the importance of the "New Story" (by which he means, among other things, "Contemporary scientific understanding of the universe and the development of life on earth"[73]), but he also embraces the significance of the kingdom of God—or, alternatively, the "reign" of God—as "the heart of the Gospel message":

72. Berry, *Befriending*, 75.

73. Morwood, *Is*, 36.

The urgency in Jesus' teaching is clear: this is what life is about. Be alert; seize the opportunity and the challenge. We are to "set our hearts on the kingdom first" and so build our "houses" on rock. If we do this we will be like people who have discovered a treasure in a field. Part of the treasure we discover will be an answer to the anxiety that has plagued many religions and many religious people: are we to fear God?[74]

Setting our hearts on the kingdom first, Morwood says, is the "salvation" that can set us "free from images, ideas, and practices that bind us into enslavement to a distant, overseer God."[75] Later, in a chapter bearing his book's title ("Is Jesus God?"), Morwood relates some of the trouble he got into with the archbishop of Melbourne, basically over questions of doctrine. I will quote several paragraphs here because I believe taking the kingdom of God seriously, even as obliquely informed by the "theology" of Lao Tzu, Joachim of Floris, Lewis Mumford and Thomas Berry, leads us, first, to an inclusion of the Mother in the theophany of historical unfolding and, second, to the recognition that the Age of the Holy Spirit is really the Age of the Daughter. This understanding, despite all the "fourfold wisdom" articulations in the world, can't be arrived at without taking, first, the kingdom of God proclamation more seriously than Berry takes it and, second, without recognizing that Joachim provided a "time-developmental" schema centuries before Teilhard's "complexity-centration." To repeat: the "new universe story" is an apex insight *of the Son's Age*; as awesome as it is, it's only a prelude to the inauguration of the Daughter's age. Here's Michael Morwood:

> The archbishop stressed I was expected to believe and make clear in a reediting of my book [*Tomorrow's Catholic*] that official church teaching on the Trinity refers to an actual reality.
>
> Here is a clear example of a faith explanation being used as a statement of fact.
>
> Church teaching on the Trinity is rightly recognized as an inspired attempt by human minds to explain the reality of God in the context of the religious perspective of the time. But to insist that this provides incontrovertible evidence that God is actually a Trinity of Persons is a huge shift and a rather audacious claim. It is also contrary to a basic Christian theological principle that any human language and images concerning God can at best only point toward an understanding. They can never be taken as actual description.
>
> Christian faith and understanding of God as a Trinity of Persons grew out of early Christianity's interpretation of Jesus' work of salvation. We recognize, however, that the worldview on which this was based no longer rings true to us today. The challenge for officialdom and theologians today is how to persuade people to believe that God is a Trinity when the contemporary worldview is so different from that which shaped the doctrinal definition.

74. Morwood, *Is*, 73-74.

75. Morwood, *Is*, 74.

If we disengage our understanding of Jesus from a dualistic worldview and a literal understanding of the Adam and Eve story, what happens to our understanding of God as a Trinity of Persons? If we think little or nothing happens, let us engage the issue and start talking about it, since there is nothing to lose and everything to gain by separating our faith from that dualism. If, on the other hand, something significant happens, let us engage the issue because intellectual integrity and genuine faith would demand we articulate what changes may flow from it.

Let us be clear. The issue here is *not* theological, spiritual, or devotional attempts to show how Trinitarian thinking can enrich the Christian understanding of sharing in God's life. There may be wonderful benefits in thinking about and relating with God as a Trinity of Persons. The issue here is Christian authority standing on a claim that its language and imagery about a Trinitarian God is factual, that this is actually who and what God is, and that Jesus of Nazareth is actually the incarnation of the Second Person of the Trinity.

Christianity is at a crossroads here. What seemed valid reasons for elevating some particular faith concepts into statements of fact in an earlier age are no longer valid reasons today. Christianity must take up the challenge to articulate its doctrinal beliefs with reasons that make sense today. Faith must build on reason. That has always been a strong principle of Christian theology. It is no help whatever to the modern mind to insist on belief solely because it is the tradition of the church. It is no help either to quote a catechism as if that now ends all discussion. The modern mind asks for reasons to believe and demands to be taken through a process that will command respect and encourage assent. This is adult faith at work.[76]

So, if God is no longer recognized as being *outside* nature or the universe (we are, remember, talking about human imagery, human metaphor, human imagination and human language which, as Michael Morwood prudently reminds us, is our attempt, with far from infallible certitude, not only to understand the mystery of our own lives and the mystery of the world but, insofar as our tiny and provisional conclusions can serve as something of a rudder, to actually help steer collective human behavior in an increasingly benign, peaceful, and ecological manner), then, God as Father or divine Male has had a multimillennial, deeply conflicted craving for the Female, a craving powerfully and resentfully channeled for the last five or six thousand years through harsh and narrow patriarchal establishments and civilized institutions, funneling male energy into an angry, unfulfilled, and unfulfilling control of female persons, combined with a massive effort to master and conquer Mother Earth. The Female, afraid, sometimes confused and often resentful, has not been in a position to satisfy or placate the angry Male, except through patterns of humiliating deference, sometimes to the point of bitter self-abnegation.

---

76. Morwood, *Is*, 97-99.

Civilization provided the organizational and technical means by which the Male could lord it over the Female in a way and to an extent beyond any precivilized culture's capacity; although it's also the case that male anxiety, with its conflicted energy of a powerful underlying pull toward the female versus an unremitting fraternal/patriarchal posture of male bonding and male exultation belittling the female, goes far back in time beyond the rise of cities, at least as far back as the paleolithic hunter. Transformation at this magnitude of frustration and conflict requires an immense therapeutic *reconciliation*, both individual and collective, and the time frame for this immense reconciliation is part of what we humans need to grapple with and understand to the best of our ability. Reconciliation is our most pressing cultural and spiritual task.

As much as I admire the tough insights and scrappy assertions of Thomas Berry—and I really do like the guy—his new universe story doesn't adequately address or come close to resolving the underlying sexual issues and gender tensions that web our inherited behavior with powerful forces operating, for the most part, below common consciousness. That inadequacy itself is reason to doubt the revolutionary efficacy of the new universe story as representative of any new age or phase. We don't need to go "higher" in our understanding as we need to go much, much "deeper," not out in cosmic space but back in evolutionary time. Add to this the realization that the new universe story is a culmination of scientific-technological analysis sprinkled with Cosmic Christ theology, and there's no doubt that the story is a crowning achievement of the Son's age. It may be a magnificent story but, at best, it only helps roll out the carpet for the Daughter's age. One of the Daughter's first tasks will be to secure recovery of the Mother. That in itself will burst the "patriarchal establishment" boundary of Trinity.

VIII

From a place outside orthodoxy, it's interesting to watch a scholarly feminist theologian—Elizabeth Johnson, in this instance, with her *SHE WHO IS: The Mystery of God in Feminist Theological Discourse*—displace the traditional Trinity of classical theology (with its male subordination and exclusion of all things female) with a radically new feminist Trinity: Holy Wisdom, the "unoriginate Mother of all things," Jesus-Sophia, "preaching the nearness of the reign of God," and Spirit-Sophia, who "blows where she wills, pervading the world with vitalizing and liberating power."[77] Although Johnson brushes up against a fourfold vision when she talks about the "notion that there are really four elements to be looked at in the study of God," she quickly explains that this means "one divine nature plus three divine persons."[78] As she says (pages 194 through 197, in a subsection called "Structure"), the "trinitarian relations in the classical model" generate a "practical inequality," with "neither Son nor Spirit attaining the authority of the Father. All originates from the first person, the apex of the divine

77. Johnson, *SHE*, 229.
78. Johnson, *SHE*, 224.

pyramid. Such a model is clearly coherent with the existence of patriarchal structures in church and society. . . ."[79] The "four elements" are really God as first element, then Father-Son-Holy Spirit as the remaining three, although "God" tends to equal "Father" in common consciousness, the "apex of the divine pyramid." Johnson also says the

> . . . symbol of the Trinity is not a blueprint of the inner workings of the godhead, not an offering of esoteric information about God. In no sense is it a literal description of God's being *in se*. As the outcome of theological reflection on the Christian experience of relationship to God, it is a symbol that indirectly points to God's relationality, at first with reference to the world and then with reference to God's own mystery. The Trinity is itself an analogy referring to divine livingness. Our speech about God as three and persons is a human construction that means to say that God is *like* a Trinity, *like* a threefoldness of relation.[80]

But if the Trinity is symbol, analogy and human construction, why should it be so difficult—and, though unacknowledged, so threatening—to enlarge Trinity into Mandala? Granting all of Elizabeth Johnson's arguments in behalf of inclusiveness vis-à-vis feminine divinity, why is it so crucial to repudiate total Male in favor of total Female? Is this just getting even? If an aspect of the ultimate quest is the loving *reconciliation* between female and male—fully granting accrued female aggravation and resentment as a consequence of the "patriarchal establishments"—what fuller reconciliation is possible than the enlarging and modifying of Joachim's Trinitarian construct into a fourfold inclusion of a complete divine "family"—Mother, Father, Son, and Daughter? (To bend Elizabeth Johnson's "four elements" into the modification I'm proposing, we'd have *five* elements: Mother, Father, Son, Daughter, and—underlying all four—"one divine nature," Spirit—which, if there is gender in this dimension, would contain both and be androgynous.)

This in-house theological mud fight, while vigorous, energizing, and sincere (within self-imposed limits), stays cautiously and obediently within the bounds of theological and ecclesiastical orthodoxy.[81] It may be therapeutic for a liberated female religious academic like Elizabeth Johnson, fully armed with brimming intelligence and exhaustive scholarly competence, to whack the patriarchal establishment across the face with a totally Female Trinity, and it may even be psychologically necessary to assert that *my* Female divinity is in process of pushing *your* Male divinity off his big, fat, smug pyramidical throne; but our collective need is bigger and much more urgent

79. Johnson, *SHE*, 197.

80. Johnson, *SHE*, 204-5.

81. One sees this spring-loaded energy in liberation theologian Leonardo Boff's *Cry of the Earth, Cry of the Poor*. Here is another brilliant mind, operating within the parameters of orthodoxy, inspired both by Teilhard and Berry, bouncing off the rubber walls of theological convention, *almost* breaking free in "The Spirit and the Female: Divinization of Woman," pages 169 through172. But the iron law of Trinity is apparently just too strong for Boff to break or bend.

than an in-house gender brawl, no matter how justified the pent-up rage. (We humans are simply wrecking a whole lot of evolutionary coherence. Polar bears, whales, and lions—I presume—could care less about our fights over theology.) Somebody needs to break the lock. Well, maybe no breaking is necessary beyond the "breaking" of the Trinitarian triangle. Joachim provided us with the key. It just turns out that the lock is a bit more complicated than Joachim realized, and so we are obliged to reconfigure the key accordingly in order to open Mama's cell door.

The problem for a great many "liberal" and even "radical" Christians is not that they're afraid of seeing beyond "conservative" rigidities, but that they're unwilling to recognize their own idolatrous dependence on Christian institutions, doctrines, and creeds. They're afraid, quite frankly, of spiritual freedom. They are confounding church institutions and sacramental traditions with historical truth and spiritual liberty. Since much of this institutional containment operates under the surveillance of established authority—including obligatory liturgical language—an overarching conventional obedience is perpetuated even as there is seething aggravation within. Hence the food fights. These fights *do* have a certain level of importance—they represent skirmishes in the battle to rattle patriarchal mindsets—but they are also diverting in-house conflicts (like whether women may be priests within the patriarchal establishment) even as the global earthquake that's steadily intensifying will bring the house to ruin. There'll be a woman pope—a woman "papa"!—when the Vatican is a heap of rubble.

It goes without saying that Daughter inherits one hell of a mess—make your own list of woes—and there's one big housecleaning job ahead. But it's not all dirt and grime. There's also a whole lot of house*making* to do, *home*steading to enjoy, and much of that will be liberating and exhilarating beyond our anticipations. A large portion of the joy will be—perhaps at times awkward—the discovery of reconciliation and intimacy between women and men, female and male; sometimes it may get a little messy, especially until new configurations of stable relationship are worked out and more supple boundaries achieved.

But sex and gender are integrally part of this dynamic. I don't consider myself a Freudian in a strict sense—there's much of Freud I don't get—but it's a kind of idiocy not to respect Freud's amazing exploration of the human unconscious. And, in turn, it's prudish stupidity not to see how hard and how brilliantly Norman O. Brown labored to explicate Freud and place him in the stream of Western depth understanding and even spiritual mysticism. Thomas Berry should be read in the context of both Norman O. Brown and the incredibly vast historical analysis of Lewis Mumford. (As usual, I recommend Mumford's *The Myth of the Machine* and *The Pentagon of Power*.) Set against Brown and Mumford, Berry's strengths and weaknesses become apparent, as do his contributions and omissions.

Meanwhile, Ilia Delio, in *The Emergent Christ*, tells us that:

The central message of Jesus, the reign of God, is a new, dynamic way of being in the world. The reign of God is a subtle and powerful reality, far more dynamic than any kind of realm we can conceive. Mark Hathaway and Leonardo Boff write that the actual word Jesus used in Aramaic to speak of God's reign—*malkuta*—is "much more similar to the concept of the Tao or to the Buddhist Dharma than to any kind of kingdom we might imagine." "The word's roots," they write, "elicit the image of a fruitful arm poised to create, or a coiled spring that is ready to unwind with all the verdant potential of the earth." *Malkuta* connotes an "empowering vision based on the divine presence in the cosmos, liberating and empowering a process toward communion, differentiation and interiority." What broke through in the person of Jesus was a new consciousness and relatedness to God that ushered in the world a new way of being God-centered, earth-centered, and in communion with one another.[82]

But what if we say that what broke through with Jesus and his "reign of God" proclamation was a "program" for the liberation of human life, liberation from the oppressive burdens of religious intimidation and economic exploitation, liberation of the self-provisioning and self-sustaining agrarian village from the violent, controlling, psychopathic dictates of sadistic civilization and its mascot male God? What if the "reign of God" is really a harkening to the village of the Goddess?

Neil Douglas-Klotz, an internationally known scholar of religious studies and psychology, former departmental head of comparative spirituality at Holy Name College in California, is the author of several books, including *The Hidden Gospel: Decoding the Spiritual Message of the Aramaic Jesus*. He opens chapter Six, "The Reign of Unity," like this:

In the four Gospels Jesus uses the word usually translated "kingdom" more than a hundred times, most of these in Matthew and Luke. No other word that Jesus used has been subject to so much speculation. Much of this has centered on whether the kingdom he had in mind was to be earthly or heavenly. Did he intend to set up a select group of devotees who would receive their reward later? Was he advocating a political revolution? Was he predicting the imminent end of the world? Did he change his mind about whether the kingdom was here and now, or later and somewhere else? Was the kingdom supposed to be "within" or "among"? Why did he use so many obscure parables to try to describe it to his students?

First, the word usually translated as "kingdom" is gendered feminine in both Aramaic (*malkuta*) and Hebrew (*mamlaka*). In fact, the word translated as "kingdom" in the Greek New Testament, *basileia*, is also a feminine-gendered noun. Quite apart from any consideration of political correctness, "queendom" would be a more accurate translation.[83]

82. Delio, *Emergent*, 62.

83. Douglas-Klotz, *Hidden*, 83–84.

Perhaps "queendom" provides the final clue: Jesus was *the Son of the Goddess*, and his "mission" was to resurrect the precivilized agrarian village—the *Mother's* village—by dissolving violent, predatory male civilization in the yeast of Spirit and recreate ecological, peaceful living on Earth at a finer level of reconciled servanthood and reverent stewardship. If the Father ruthlessly suppressed the Mother, then the Son's mission was to recall the Mother and restore Her rightful place in a new age of the Daughter.

Christian orthodoxy and the established church will not survive, except as relics, the transformation we are entering. Civilization as we've known it will not survive. The monarchical image of God is crumbling. We have already entered an immense spiritual and cultural transformation. But to take the "new universe story" as the core of this transformation is to mistake minor enablement for major outcome, detour for destination. The actual outcome and the real destination, unless the patriarchal establishment refuses to relinquish its pathological righteousness and simply blows us all to dystopian hell, will be revealed as the Age of the Daughter. I, for one, say the sooner the better.

12

Craving the Civility of God

Psychoanalysis, then, may well become operative in curing the historical process of some of its built-in impediments and in providing the conscious insights which are unconsciously sought in all manner of indirect self-revelations. I mean to say here that man by understanding the way he historicizes may yet overcome certain stereotyped ways in which history repeats itself—ways which man can no longer afford.

Erik H. Erikson, *Gandhi's Truth*, page 439

THE PROBLEM WITH "ID" and "superego" is that they are generally seen as useless abstractions, anachronisms from World War Two psychology textbooks. Yet when Marcus Borg, in *The God We Never Knew*, says the monarchical model of God "reinforces the superego" and "easily confuses God with the superego," we may be inclined to nod in agreement.[1] But, if asked to explain what our nodding signifies, we'd probably be hard-pressed to provide a clear or lucid answer. So, wading into my very own incompetence, I'd like to try to reel in these semantic kites (if I can) and provide them (if I can) a little coherent application.

I'd say the core problem with putting ontological flesh on these psychological abstractions is that, for whatever reason, we've refrained from acknowledging their social, cultural, economic, political, and historical embeddedness in our lives, embedded—perhaps—in our bones. It's not that "superego" is elusive; it's that it is so skeletal. Take what Borg calls the "monarchical model of God." The Holy Roman Empire, at its peak in the High Middle Ages, was a governing structure suffused with hierarchy (i.e., holy order) from top to bottom, from lofty emperor to lowly peasant, all of it under the dominion of the King of kings, Almighty God Himself, the entire construct as complete an articulation of the monarchical model as one could possibly imagine.

This God was several things simultaneously. He was Father. He was Male. He was not only Master of the Universe, He was the Universe's Creator. He was the single most powerful entity or force that ever was or could ever be. Furthermore, this God

---

1. Borg, *God*, 66.

was jealous. He wanted His human subjects to recognize His omnipotence and behave according to His rules. He also was a God of perfect judgment.

If any of us hopes to enter Heaven, we will first, in this monarchical way of looking at things, have to stand before the Throne of Heaven, before God the Judge, who will utter His yes or no, His verdict of Heaven or Hell. Fear of this God, who knows everything it's possible to know and has perfect judgment, and who may even have predestined most of us to everlasting Hell, can also suffuse the individual human mind, creating a similar hierarchy of psychic governance enthroning a judging temperament with watchful, transcendent vigilance. (Well, perhaps superego is neither flesh nor bone but the entire nervous system webbed out from the brain.) This internal judge is the personal superego, whose job is vigorous moral surveillance with corresponding moral judgment. (The irony, of course, due to cultural conditioning, is that an atheist can host an internal judge as fully as a pious religious believer.)

In social relations, we tend to reflexively defer to the moral authority of those holding superego position or radiating superego energy. In everyday traffic, it's the police. If we are children, our parents hold such position, energy, and authority. If we are students, teachers and administrators and the school system as a whole contain and exercise such authority. In the institutional church, it's the clergy and ecclesiastical hierarchy who peer over our shoulders. The process is hugely extended into the workplace with its nondemocratic authoritarianism, even when diluted and constrained by complex bureaucracy; workplace authoritarianism has become hegemonic as corporations have displaced and replaced small shops, stores and farms, as unions have lost ground, thus making employees vulnerable to the whims and vicissitudes of corporate impulse. The empathy-deficient objectivity of corporate superego mimics what we might call the moral objectivity of God. Since superego saturates religious institutions, particularly the more "conservative," we grow up with superego as normative. We might even say it's superego that makes corporations "persons," endowed with superhuman authority that, in some psychologically elusive way, derives from or imitates the authority of church or state, which in turn (the doctrine of two kingdoms) claims authority from God's will or mandate. Corporate persons mimic the Personhood of God. In such hierarchy, each step down the scale of authority reflects God's authority in an appropriately reduced way.

Now religion may crystallize or sanctify the superego in a manner similar to how the phosphorescent wall-plaque Jesus glowed in the dark; but the superego's most powerful secular embodiment occurs in governance, in all three branches. (Where else do we address people as "Mister President," "Ms. Speaker," or "Your Honor"?) The place where superego really gets to hone its practical hands-on skills in trauma, however, is in the military, with boot camp the locale for terrorizing and brutalizing the unassuming id (i.e., the simple life force) into instantaneous superego obedience, where recruits are nothing but f-ing maggots in process of transformation from bottom-feeding scum suckers to totally awesome narcissistic heroes. Superego may have no greater terrifying presence than a boot camp drill sergeant. And to become a gung-ho gunner for God makes violence justified—even itchingly desired as some soldiers can hardly wait to discharge their internalized intimidation and pent-up rage onto designated enemies.

Superego, in other words, instead of being an empty abstraction, something without meaning in our lives, actually saturates our social world, our various institutions, even as it pervades us individually in an interior and subjective sense. It is both external control framework and internal moral authority. It is, we might say, key to our political and psychic infrastructure. The centralized authority of God may have been disturbed by Copernicus and Luther, by astronomic science and Protestant Reformation, but God's image, even if dented and bent, has persisted quite well. The image is so strong, so deeply embedded in the Western mind, that its power radiation persists to this day. Its half-life is by no means exhausted.

If there is a place of ambiguity, it lies in the interplay between religion and "secular" governance. Is God a King? Is a king a civilized invention projected onto the divine? Could "God" even be a King before bandit aristocracy invented kingship roughly five thousand years ago? To what extent was the trauma of a murderous and thieving aristocracy transformed by peasant fear into an ongoing need to appease a dangerous and threatening Judge/King? A fear that, thanks to being spared from mayhem or maiming, reshaped itself into gratefulness and adulation. Thank you so much for not killing us. We love you more than we can say. What can we do to please you? That is, because superego is so deeply normal, we are blind to its shaping by centuries—even millennia—of authoritarian imposition. We bow our heads and hold hands over our hearts. We recite creed and pledge allegiance. We promise to be loyal and good.

Marcus Borg says that this linkage of God to superego is a "central dimension of the human predicament from which we need deliverance."[2] Well, that sounds intriguing, the sort of thing we'll nod along with. But what does it mean? What are its implications? What's the connection between God's superego and civilization as superego?

II

It's not that we've *refrained* from giving superego social application; its application simply saturates our lives, our culture, our religion, and our patterns of governance. Does a fish know it lives in water? We don't think about authority constructs as superego formations because they're so normal and normative. We have no idea how to live without them. They provide familiar structure and ongoing security. They're the framework of our everyday lives. Plus all real history is contained within the time capsule we call Civilization, which has a five-thousand-year momentum of governance by aristocratic superego. Everything outside Civilization is, for us, either unreal or

2. Borg, *God*, 67.

irrelevant. Superego protects us from id much as civilization protects us from savagery or terrorism, while political ego claims to be competently steering the U.S.S. Superego—otherwise known as American Exceptionalism.

But a force of considerable strength has been developing in this vast organism called human society. We might call it the return of the repressed, if we mean by the term an organic resurgence of folk evolution that, in its agrarian village formation, was smothered millennia ago by expropriating civilization. The word "democracy" is an indicator of resurgence, something like a huge, largely inarticulate psychospiritual fungus continuing to spread and deepen despite blockages, diversions, and setbacks. What drives and agitates this vast restlessness is Spirit, although some may prefer "collective unconscious." Spirit is attempting to break through to us, to lead or nudge us out of evolution-despising utopia and into evolution-reverent eutopia, from preoccupation with original sin to realization of original blessing.

But we have entered a huge crisis. Superego—like civilization—has become globally and unsustainably top-heavy. Not only is there a massive restoration of aristocratic wealth concentration (an economic fact veiled behind the "personhood" of corporations, with their "free trade" machinations), we are simultaneously facing reduced oil supply ("peak oil," even if temporarily postponed by poisonous fracking and toxic tar sands exploitation) and various other ecological catastrophes, most notably a rapidly accelerating climate change. Our social patterns as well as Earth's ecology are entering—have entered—turbulent transformation. There is no turning around this accrued and accruing transformative momentum. The entities "civilization" and "democracy" are engaged in a life and death struggle, a struggle which inherited superego is unlikely to survive intact.

III

It can be argued that the early agrarian village, prior to its impoundment by a self-selected "dominant minority," was slowly experimenting with or groping toward democracy, with a fairly dense but stable population, with increasingly complex occupations, with material abundance and collective wealth no ruling class controlled, coerced or manipulated, with a general absence of armed conflict and aggressive militarism, and with a rough, generalized sense of social equality and cooperative sharing. This sort of peaceful behavior apparently went on for generations. Its spirituality had feminine ambience. This was humanity's initial cultural departure from hunting and gathering, a departure led by women gatherers.

But feral males corked the fermenting agrarian village bottle with murderous, expropriating kings and arrogant aristocracy, and it has taken over five thousand years for democracy to re-emerge as a force to be reckoned with, a force spiritually fed and morally justified by the equalitarian ethics of all the great religions, a force increasingly (but still only dimly) aware of how deeply the trauma of civilized superego has penetrated human psychology and shaped human institutions: made us reflexively dependent on established utopian authority and hesitant to go down the democratic eutopian pathway. Democracy is the slow return of the repressed—in terms of both governance methodology and cultural psychotherapy—unconsciously committed, in a fundamentally idish sort of way, to the wholesome healing of gender, race and ecological wounds, capable of sensing God—Spirit really—not as righteous, wrathful Male Judge external to creation but as yearning, more-like-Female Caregiver internal to creation's slow and stumbling evolutionary unfolding. If Jesus achieved our redemption—take this religiously if you want to, or see "redemption" through the spiritual eyes of psychomythological understanding—then *life* is redeemed, *pagus* and peasant village are redeemed, and it's time we acted as if this were so.

So what would it mean to be delivered from captivity in the superego's utopian tower? Green politics tells us, with its ethical condensation of principles, that deliverance may be articulated as radical servanthood and radical stewardship. This eutopian Green vision is both possible and practical. It is eminently grounded in earthy and ethical reality. It is neither otherworldly nor utopian. But its realization depends on our willingness to go there. Transformation (unless imposed as catastrophe and collapse) is hinged to our spiritual maturation.

The real problem is not whether the Green vision is doable but that we are so addicted to its denial because of superego captivity. To deliberately move out of this captivity feels either like willful sin or the most ridiculous embrace of backwardness. We have been taught that original sin prevents Green deliverance, and this conviction dominates both theology and politics. We worship at the shrine of civilized fear and religious trembling. We take easy, vindictive recourse to overpowering violence in order to achieve our always-righteous political and religious agenda. We despise vulnerability and the humility required to embrace vulnerability. We persist in the induced evasion and denial of our mortal life cycle. The superego thinks it glows immortal, and it will kill you if you laugh. Therefore we all need to laugh.

IV

Instead of being hopelessly abstract and utterly devoid of social application, superego is the ramrod up the butt of our governing institutions. Nor—if Norman O. Brown is even remotely correct—is the vulgar image of ramrod-up-the-butt devoid of psychoanalytical significance. The vindictive anal sadism Brown writes about (see Part Five, "Studies in Anality," in his *Life Against Death: The Psychoanalytical Meaning of History*) shapes how society is structured and controlled by a still-dominant minority, a still-dominant minority we sustain and perpetuate primarily through our political institutions. (Congress apparently sees its job as empire maintenance abroad and upper-class wealth protection at home, and we keep electing these superego impersonators.) Liberals may believe that George W. Bush, Dick Cheney, and Donald Rumsfeld were anomalies, but that's not the view of intellectuals with deeper perspective—thinkers like Norman O. Brown, Lewis Mumford, Howard Zinn, or Noam Chomsky.[3] Writing in 1920, in *The Acquisitive Society*, economic historian R. H. Tawney said the "concentration of authority is too deeply rooted in the very essence of Capitalism for differences in the degree of the arbitrariness with which it is exercised to be other than trivial."[4] Of course it's not just capitalism; so-called communism catapulted superego to Stalinist dimension, in obvious imitation of the czar.

The problem with Marxism, however, is that its critical analysis never went deep enough. It seemed to assert that the problem is only as old as capitalism. If capitalism—as I believe—is only a limited "democratic" (i.e., mass commercial) mutation of what Mumford calls the "traumatic institutions" of civilization, of an aggressively commercial middle class grabbing a fairly large part of traditional superego from hereditary aristocracy (parallel to how Protestant sects wrested God from Catholicism), then our superego problem goes all the way back to the founding of the *original* traumatic institutions. A common core of expropriating or controlling violence runs through all such institutions. Communism as state capitalism only shifted the superego problem. It apparently believed that getting rid of corporate capitalism was setting the stage for human liberation, similar to how the Protestant Reformation was to usher in the priesthood of all believers. The Stalinist Soviet Union (like the Thirty Years War) is an object lesson regarding those convictions—though it has to be said that Yeltsin, Clinton, and the Harvard School of Business all did their part to help turn a softening dictatorship into a muscular oligarchy—an oligarchy with no apparent memory of or interest in the plight of the peasantry or working class, much as Luther repudiated the peasants and Anabaptists for offending God's order by insisting that equality of persons was a plain condition of the kingdom of God.

George Lakoff, in chapter 9 of his *Don't Think of an Elephant!*, says that "One of the problems is that the progressive religious community, particularly progressive Christianity, doesn't really know how to express its own theology in a way that makes its politics clear, whereas conservative Christians do know the direct link between their theology and their politics. Conservative Christianity is a strict father religion."[5] That is, people in the "progressive religious community" don't yet know how to understand "the divine" without reversion to the superego template. When Mumford, in chapter Six of *The Pentagon of Power*, says that in the face of the "quasi-religious cult of mechanization" the decentralized tradition he calls "polytechnics" was without a "cor-

---

3. See also "The Kissinger Effect" by Greg Grandin in the September 28/October 5, 2015, issue of *The Nation*. In the "Letters" section of *The Nation* for November 2, 2015, Grandin (on page 26) calls Henry Kissinger "the purest expression of American exceptionalism." And insofar as American exceptionalism constitutes American *exemption* from fundamental ethics, we need to realize that superego can be extremely moralistic, so assured of its righteousness that ethical exemption *for itself* is automatically assumed.

4. Tawney, *Acquisitive*, 129.

5. Lakoff, *Don't*, 102.

responding ideology to draw on,"[6] we should draw a parallel to Lakoff's observation regarding progressive Christianity. That is, the monarchical model of God and the "quasi-religious cult of mechanization" share a similar pattern of superego deference to the "strict father." (Lawrence Goodwyn, in *The Populist Moment*, says the twentieth century may well become known as "the century of sophisticated deference," that "it has proven difficult for people to think about democracy while employing hierarchical terminology."[7] This puts a finger on the problem even as a word like "terminology" fails to convey how deeply the hierarchical impulse has penetrated the human psyche.)

Deference to hierarchical authority is built into Christian scripture. In Romans 13:1-2, the Apostle Paul says "Let every person render obedience to the governing authorities; for there is no authority except from God, and those in authority are divinely constituted, so that the rebel against the authority is resisting God's appointment. Such resisters will incur judgment on themselves." And in Augustine's *The City of God*, we find (Book IV:33) "Therefore that God, the author and giver of felicity, because He alone is the true God, Himself gives earthly kingdoms both to good and bad. Neither does He do this rashly, and, as it were, fortuitously—because He is God, not fortune—but according to the order of things and times, which is hidden from us, but thoroughly known to Himself; which same order of times, however, He does not serve as subject to it, but Himself rules as lord and appoints as governor."[8] Augustine repeats much of this—"In a word, human kingdoms are established by divine providence"—in the opening sentences of Book V:1.[9] Therefore politics devoid of deference to God is anathema to civilized Christians.

If the superego, like capital, is lodged in the "spiritualized" head, then the superego, "sacred" money, capitalist economics, civilization as a process of eradicating indigenous, peasant and folk cultures, and God as author of earthly kingdoms (ruling as lord, appointing as governor) are all related constructs. As such, superego is so fully familiar that it's simply the air we breathe. As it says on our coins and bills, In God We Trust.

When Goodwyn says "The Populists have thus been, to date, the last American reformers with authentic cultural credentials to solicit mass support,"[10] we need to push that thought up against Mumford's assertion regarding the "scattered trades and crafts and vocations" whose "inner unity was largely an unconscious traditional heritage."[11] That is, the late nineteenth-century populist movement was an extension of this "unconscious traditional heritage." We might even call it the last Peasant Revolt in the predominantly white, English-speaking Western world. It's not so much that the

6. Mumford, *Pentagon*, 158.

7. Goodwyn, *Populist*, 318.

8. Augustine, *City*, 140.

9. Augustine, *City*, 142-43.

10. Goodwyn, *Populist*, 292.

11. Mumford, *Pentagon*, 158.

agrarian culture of nineteenth-century Populists, or the trades, crafts and vocations of medieval people, "had not yet been translated into a philosophy," as civilization, with its justifying and compliant otherworldly religions, has always asserted a kind of hegemonic power that brooked no rivals. The City of God will, if necessary, destroy the peasant village in order to save it. Since the folk heritage and its associated vocations had no written or legal "philosophy" to rely on, its practitioners and partisans (who were largely peasants of the *pagus*) were inarticulate in the face of power skilled in the facile justifications of "progress" and "God's will."

One can see with astonishment how this dynamic worked in the early development of Christianity, when Constantine took the church as his official state religion: not only did the church, in 313, align itself institutionally with the entity that had legally murdered its spiritually revolutionary genius, it also transformed the peasant Jesus into an aristocratic Christ while systematically bending the revolutionary, peasant "kingdom of God" into a civilized, superego doctrine fingering *pagus* as the enemy of the holy. The pagan had no place in the city of God. And if pagan links conceptually to id—a linkage that's obvious—then the suppression of the pagan (that which is rural) easily becomes the suppression of the id (that which constitutes the underlying energy of natural life). As Augustine's title so succinctly puts it, it is the *city* of God for which we are to yearn. We've been trained to crave God's civility and fear the Devil's *pagus*. And while superego craving may be more or less politically invisible in times of peace, any disruption—9/11, say, or the Paris killings in November of 2015—instantly activates the "sleeper cell" of our craving. The Patriot Act. Fear and retaliation as reflexive emotions. Rushing to the defense of civilization. Killing the terrorists. Exploring the roots of rage becomes tantamount to treason.

Civilization, with its "traumatic institutions," is a construct of totalitarian intent and authoritarian magnitude. Its righteousness is not to be questioned. It put up with noncivilized cultures, as well as with various peasantries, only so long as it had material need of them or as they were too difficult to overpower at the moment. Joined by and fused with imperial religious doctrine, civilization as a working concept defies critical self-examination. Precisely because the civilized self-concept contains no negatives—even its institutionalized "sacred" violence is understood as the containment of the original sin of others—it has no need for or patience with self-examination. It is justified—not merely justified, *established*—by God. Therefore to question the legitimacy of civility is, at least implicitly, to question the legitimacy of God, which is simply unthinkable. And this brings us to the idea and practice of globalization.

Globalization represents something absolutely new not only in human history but in the history of Earth's ecology. Never before has one species, we human beings, in a peculiar authoritarian system of superego compulsion, not only suppressed all other forms of human endeavor, all other patterns of cultural evolution, we are in process of inflicting grave, even irreversible injury onto evolution itself. Never before have the "externalities" of sacred violence and righteous inquisition resulted in such ecological and cultural catastrophe. Civilization (though it may have aspired to universality) was never truly global before the modern period. Therefore the modern crisis is a new kind of crisis—a planetary crisis—a crisis that (as far as I can see) might be resolved in one of three ways. The first way, the most catastrophic, would make Earth uninhabitable for at least all mammals. The second way would be regression to predemocratic aristocratic rule, vicious and cruel, a type of dominance reserving the civilized standard of living, as in previous historical circumstances, for the sole pleasure of a dominant minority. The third way would be transformational—the recovery of folk culture evolution from its civilized impoundment, radical servanthood and radical stewardship unfolding from the hugely neglected concept that lies at the base of the Christian gospels (the Green "kingdom of God"), and the practical enfleshment of folk culture aspiration into democratic ecological socialism built of a recovered cooperative small-scale and a newly constructed decentralized socialism for those economic entities too big or too important to be left in private or "aristocratic" hands. Everything "too big to fail" must be in the public domain, including Leopold Kohr's "natural monopolies." (The "kingdom of God" is not either/or, all or nothing; it comes in sliding scale proportion to the transformation of our hearts, minds, and political will.)

I suppose there's a possible fourth outcome: catastrophe short of extinction, disasters so brutally reductive and crushingly bleak that human culture would be set back thousands of years. Well, no, not "back." This darkness looms *ahead*, not back. It's our *fear* of "backwardness" that has the potential to make "backwardness" come true. Its name is dystopia. This "backwardness" is the logical culmination of utopian arrogance in its global "victory" over nature. "Arrogance" is an inadequate word here. Maynard Kaufman's "demonic possession" cuts closer to the bone.

If we want a healthy *recovery* of folk culture evolution, we will have to come to grips with the narcissistic superego totalitarianism built into civilization's traumatic institutions. Superego totalitarianism has cultivated, fed, and nourished this poisonous fear of backwardness, fueled by our collective refusal to confess our complicity with violence and theft. There's not a lot of time to diddle with this problem—and "solving" it certainly involves what Marcus Borg sees as the identification of God with superego—this "central dimension of the human predicament from which we need deliverance."

Meanwhile, most Republicans are manic for policies of superego sadism, while most Democrats seem to want it both ways: pandering and deferring to sadism while also trying to placate and "represent" an upsurge of transformational social energy rising sluggishly from below. (That this transformational energy *is* sluggish is closely related to the lack of "philosophy" for the folk vocations and heritage; and where there purports to be such a philosophy, it can be intellectually embarrassing, as in Leopold Kohr's cobbled constructs in *The Breakdown of Nations*. An adequate philosophy will emerge—is emerging—simultaneously with recognition of the dynamic inner meaning of the "kingdom of God" proclamation and with the realization of how Mother was brutally chopped out of human history and denied entry into Abrahamic divinity, including Christian Trinity.) Republican sadism (i.e., the strict, righteous Father principle) will work to control the political agenda until Democrats (or some other political formation) have achieved sufficient eutopian groundedness and "kingdom of God" conviction by which to express their theology in ways that make their politics humane, democratic, and ecologically coherent. But until such groundedness congeals—and this transformation involves the general population, not merely a few intellectuals or a handful of political activists—we're going to be on a roller coaster of intensifying catastrophe.

V

It's an image of limited versatility, but we are like fish milling in a pool—a pool whose changing dynamics are forcing us, or will shortly be forcing us, to alter our fishy behavior. But the situation is not sufficiently difficult to cause us to risk the upstream rapids—yet. We're still too comfortable and cool. Although we're becoming increasingly uneasy, our security has not yet shriveled to the stage of real concern. Mostly we whine and vent and growl without serious "lifestyle" change or political engagement. When things really start to hurt, we'll wake up to change and action—change and action, one dearly hopes, spiritually informed and intellectually empowered by a philosophy adequate to the crisis.

Then there's the really big question: In what way or ways are we to change? In what direction? Scary environmental documentaries like *An Inconvenient Truth* and *The Eleventh Hour* (Gore's movie especially) end with assurances that we'll sustain our lounging in the Standard of Living pool, comfortably so, if only we embrace new technologies with sufficient vigor and prompt conviction. Affluence will come clean with Green. In that perspective, the pool we're in only needs chartreuse technofix chlorination. Swim on, America! But perhaps a careful rereading of Jacques Ellul's *The Technological Society* would help us understand why technological solutions are the only kind of solution we seem willing to pay attention to. In what way or ways, exactly, are reflexive technological solutions connected to our superego addiction?

Our attitude toward the past, especially toward the rural or agrarian past, is so deeply negative, so powerfully colored by convictions of "backwardness," that ideas of change automatically move us in the direction of technological fixation. Technology will save us from cultural retrogression and social backwardness. Anything to keep us from sliding backward. There is in this attitude a barely suppressed panic, something emotionally akin to anticipation of major surgery one may not survive or a long-term prison sentence about to be imposed. It's hard to overstate our collective revulsion toward noncivilized life and rural culture—so deplorably backward and repulsive, so inexpressibly primitive and undesirable.

Having been herded over time into the modern pool or technological pen of progress, in which we directly gather or produce almost nothing whatsoever from the natural world, we live through the mediation of otherworldly expectations, corporate-owned "news," bureaucratic structure, and commercial commodities. We live *inside* the security machine called civilization. The outdoor self-provisioning and self-sustaining cultural life of indigenous, peasant, or small-farm communities—thousands of years in their changing, collective history—is a thing of the past—romantic if presented with sufficient artfulness as rustic entertainment, otherwise ignored or despised.

This situation cries out for explication and analysis, especially since the vast bulk of human beings for virtually the entirety of human existence have lived by self-provisioning in cultures of self-sustaining capacity. We are *so* unlike our ancestors, *so* estranged from self-provisioning aptitudes, that the *only* people with whom to compare ourselves historically are the aristocrats of predemocratic times—or, a notch down, the middle-class urban retainers of classical civility. And that means that "democracy," in the sense of Standard of Living behavior, derives from or aspires to images of (trickle-down) aristocratic affluence. It was, after all, the aggressively commercial middle class who captured superego from Catholic aristocracy and packaged it as Puritan morality and capitalist economics. Therefore we can say that "democratic" civilization is the (trickle-down) "democratization" of an aristocratic standard of consumption, which goes a long way in explaining popular acceptance of capitalism, colonialism, imperialism, and the global ecological crisis—and also why Democrats are, mostly, Republican Lite—fiercely committed to American affluence, to the civilized Standard of Living. Both Republicans and Democrats are political retainers of civilizational superego in a way empirically represented by their dependence on the financial backing of rich people who own and control the corporate "persons." Such politicians impersonate their superego funders; and their policies—particularly as folk sensibility deteriorates—move us steadily in the direction of aristocratic restoration.

Allow me to summarize both the conclusion I've come to and the process that led to these conclusions. First the process.

VI

My father was the third child, the oldest boy, in a family of thirteen children. The bulk of his childhood was lived in northern Wisconsin, his entire family packed into an abandoned logging-camp bunkhouse with no electricity or running water, but with a huge garden, a couple of cows, an old horse, and a great deal of illegal fishing and hunting. All heating and cooking was done with wood. With an eighth-grade education, robust and strong, my father was a lumberjack by age seventeen. He pulled a crosscut saw in the woods and worked on a logging-train loading crew with a steam jammer. He helped cut the last of the Old Growth forest in this area. At age nineteen, he bought a cut-over "brush forty" about two miles from the family bunkhouse. He built a little log house out of wind-damaged tamarack trees and began to clear land with axe, grub hoe, an old horse and stoneboat. His father helped him build a small log barn. This was in the early 1930s.[12]

By the time I was born—1946—the log barn had been replaced by a lumber barn (my father had cut the logs from which the barn lumber was sawn at a local mill); but the tamarack log house, added onto, was still in use—though by 1950 a new frame house was up, and the old log house sawed into firewood.

The year 1950 was also when my father drove a little Farmall tractor into the farm yard, a tractor purchased at a farm auction. Until then it had been strictly work horses. My mother gardened and did a great deal of canning. Potatoes were stored in a special room in the cellar. Sauerkraut foamed in huge crocks. Almost all our meat came from the woods, the chicken house, or the barn. My mother baked bread, cake, cookies, and pies. We drank raw milk from the cows. The house was heated with wood.

In other words, I grew up in the closing days of a self-sufficient agrarian/rural/woods culture: a culture, if it needs to be underscored, that was unselfconsciously subsistent. This was not the "new" subsistence of Helen and Scott Nearing, of alienated but hearty intellectuals returning to the land, but an old subsistence with an unbroken self-provisioning pattern connected historically to the neolithic and, behind that, to our ancestors in cultural evolution. This was still a *pagus* that knew how to feed and shelter itself; it had the aptitudes, skills, and cultural capacity.

In the 1950s, commercialism crept increasingly into our lives, into the neighborhood, into rural culture. Virtually all little farms got tractors, abandoned work horses, and bought equipment to match tractor power—which size rapidly escalated. The little farmers discovered their farms weren't big enough to support new machinery or the lifestyle presented so alluringly in magazines and on TV. Many of these little farmers got jobs in town or eked it out until retirement, then sold or rented their fields to the one or two farmers who got bigger and more mechanized. As the farms died, so did the gardening and the canning. Self-provisioning was ignored or derided. Commercialization was promoted and praised. "Homemade" became a term of humiliation and condescension.

This process of rural culture atrophy went on rapidly through the 1960s and 1970s. By 2000, there was one farmer left in the township; he quit after a bout with cancer, followed by a battering incident with a bull. All kids have been bussed out of the township for over fifty years. The last one-room school closed a year after I graduated from the eighth grade.

We have one bar, no stores, no parks, no boat landing (although the Wisconsin River forms our eastern township boundary), no church, no cemetery, and no common life. A huge portion of the northern part of the township is owned and controlled as

---

12. My father's stories and life history have been published in two volumes (*Get Poor Now, Avoid the Rush* and *A Windfall Homestead*), coauthored by C. D. (Seedy) Buckberry, both books available from Wipf and Stock.

county forest; big pulp trucks, loaded and snorting, are a regular feature on the county road. Our forest becomes toilet paper, literally so, "harvested" for optimal short-term financial advantage. (Lumber now comes from Canada and the Pacific northwest.) Virtually all houses have big screen TVs; many have satellite dishes mounted on house wall, roof, or yard pole. There are a handful of serious gardeners, mostly older women who grew up on farms, but only a couple of woodburning cookstoves. Life here is less suburban—because we mostly lack subdivisions—than working-class exurban, but it's still a "culture" of microwaves and satellite dishes, with regular trips to Wal-Mart.

Now elsewhere in the world, where indigenous and peasant life has not been fully eradicated, subsistence and self-provisioning continue, even if under the dual pressure of economic extortion and commercial lure. Yet the idea that "democratization" involves liberation from subsistence is not so much the dominant conviction as it is the only one that matters. Our reflexive notion of "democracy" is so infected with aristocratic and "civilized" viruses that we are incapable of processing the idea that democracy involves a liberating spiritual fermentation from the bottom up, rather than lifestyle conversion from the top down. The "democratization" of civilization has not meant the political, economic, and cultural liberation of the peasant village or a loving and respectful integration with the indigenous but, instead, their extinction or extermination. Democracies must be civilized and commercial or we reject them out of hand. We don't do democracy with pagans. "Democracy," then, allowing popular voting for candidates largely vetted by corporate money and screened by capitalist ideology, is about achieving and maintaining an ersatz aristocratic lifestyle, promoting policies perpetuating mass consumerism, which (given our technology, class and racial divisions, and nationalism) has brought us catastrophic wars, weapons of mass destruction, pollution of such magnitude that it enlarges deserts, wrecks coral reefs and melts glaciers, locking us into mental fixation of "civilized values" that will not budge from its religious illusions and aristocratic delusions unless and until it is forced by structural crumbling—although political manipulation from the hyperwealthy Right is employing "hatred of government" rhetoric in order to enflame the lower middle class so that enormous concentrations of wealth and power can be "democratically" protected from taxation and thoughtful legislative distribution into public projects—a Tea Party moat around the brothers Koch.

It's structural crumbling the American economic and political system is now facing, and it's obviously the intent of those with some degree of control to treat crumbling as a challenge to be overcome, as challenges in the past were overcome—always resolving them in the direction of greater Progress, Civilized Values, and Prosperity (even if, in this instance, prosperity will be reserved for the very few). But what if, as Lewis Mumford says in *The Myth of the Machine*, "scientific determinism not less than mechanical regimentation had their inception in the institution of divine kingship," inceptions carried forward by all subsequent civilizations?[13] What if civilization's "traumatic

13. Mumford, *Myth*, 174.

institutions" (Lewis Mumford) or "diseases of Class and War" (Arnold J. Toynbee) have, with globalization, begun to reach a terminal stage? What if civilization, globalized, is the disease that's ecocidal? What if, as Norman O. Brown says in the last chapter of *Life Against Death*, that "there is unlikely to be any smooth transition from the 'mechanistic' point of view to the 'organismic' point of view," and that it is "unlikely that problems generated in the mechanistic system will lead to organismic solutions"?[14]

These are precisely the sort of questions we need to be asking.

VII

I have no name with which to replace "civilization," unless it is "Green culture"— which is what I take Brown to imply with "the 'organismic' point of view." (And the tiny traction Green politics has achieved in the American political system certainly underscores Brown's doubt about any "smooth transition.") And then again, as some might ask, why is it important or necessary to replace "civilization" as a concept embodying our social, economic, cultural, and religious ideals? Why don't we just glom onto the positive aspects of civilization—its universality, its insistence on the rule of law, its rising above local custom and mores—and get on with it? What's the big deal with "civilization"?

Well, that puts us back in the civilized box from which all negatives are deleted. This is precisely the intellectual and spiritual process by which the traumatic, diseased institutions of civilization have been screened from recognition and externalized to oblivion, a process exactly parallel to the ecocidal "externalities" of the civilized economic system. Out of sight, out of mind. Sort of. Until things come back to bite us. In conventional religious terminology, there is no forgiveness without repentance. Or, to express it differently, there's no moral or ethical incentive to change until we recognize the evil that's hiding (in plain view) in our righteousness. "Civilization" is one of the primary containers of that evil righteousness. *Until we repent of our civility*—that is, be willing to recognize the criminality at the core of civilization from its inception—we'll also be unwilling to embrace Green culture. But this recognition requires the unthinkable: daring a spiritual psychoanalysis of civilization's superego.

The problems are now so deep, pervasive, and systemic—and the urgency of redress increasing with every passing month and year—that evading the issue of the historic criminality of civilization's superego is a delusion (or, at best, a felony postponement) we can't afford to perpetuate. This is far less a semantic fight over a word (or an intellectual brawl with books hurled across the reading room from behind upturned tables) than an attempt to stop the Titanic or restrain Ahab, even if "Titanic" and "Ahab" are mere piddly symbols for the planetary disasters that civilization, with

---

14. Brown, *Life*, 317.

its clean, clear-eyed, righteously obsessive mythological self-absorption, is bringing to terminal culmination.

At one level, I couldn't care less about a word brawl. Such a brawl would only prove we are, yet again, evading the issue. And it is precisely our evasion, our mythological blindness—*our willful mythological blindness*—that is the nut to crack. The nut may be named superego. (At least that's one of its names.) Either we crack that nut via tough personal change and determined political decisions or ecological disasters, economic meltdown, and structural crumbling will crack it for us in ways that make corrective action far more difficult and probably less effective. The longer we evade, avoid and postpone, the greater the inevitable disaster, meltdown and crumble. We can "crack the equation" on our own, in a brave and wholesome manner, or we can wait for events to crack it for us, as we weep and whine and gnash our teeth in suffering and regret.

Granted: it takes personal, collective, cultural, intellectual, and spiritual suffering to arrive at the place of liberation Green culture offers and points toward. It's not without difficulty that we let go of our civilized addictions, material attachments, mythological convictions, and righteous superego conditioning. Letting go, however, is the only rational choice in the direction of ecological and evolutionary health, perhaps even of mammalian survival. The spiritual word for this is repentance. The option is structural crumbling over which we will have less and less influence or effective control.

That this is a choice so hard to make, a choice (or set of choices) from which we are so easily distracted and willingly diverted, a choice we imagine can be indefinitely postponed, indicates the extent to which civilization has taken control of our intelligence. When civilized self-concept looks in the mirror, all it sees is pleasing narcissism: nothing there that a bigger paycheck or some new technology wouldn't enhance. But this smug innocence has become morally threadbare and ethically repulsive.

Paul Tillich might have called it demonic possession. Norman O. Brown *did* call it "the demonic character of capitalism."[15] Or, as the Devil told Jesus in the famous temptation scene in Luke 4:5-7, when he led Jesus up a high mountain to show him "in an instant" all the world's kingdoms: "All this authority and the splendor of them will I give to you, *for it has been handed over to me and I bestow it on whomever I please*; so if you will worship me, it shall all be yours."

The *Devil* as bestower of kingdoms—*sola scriptura* with a little *cuius regio, eius religio* tossed in for reasons of political stability—is an interesting construct from which to contemplate "civilized values"—or, as Brown identifies it, the "death instinct becomes master of the house."[16] Perhaps Augustine should have taken Luke's temptation story a bit more seriously than he did. Perhaps the good bishop had capitulated to the worship of civilizational superego long before he took to calling it Almighty God.

15. Brown, *Life*, 220.
16. Brown, *Life*, 232.

13

Norma A. Brown, God, and the Insolent Powers of Monstrous Divinities

As a person who lives in a log house in the woods, without electricity or running water, I've come to realize over the years how nearly everything in life has its time or season. This lesson should be apparent to a man in his late sixties. Last summer, however, I finally "discovered" Thomas Berry—this after reading Wendell Berry's *What Matters?*—and so a patch of time intended for physical work (tearing down an old barn and beginning to build a new shed with the used lumber) was instead devoted to wrestling with one Berry after another.

Several months of fall busyness have passed (the barn is down, the shed is not up). December's snow is knee-high and the thermometer has bottomed out (I hope) at thirty below zero. It's time to put another log on the fire and resume the intellectual wrestle that seems an abiding preoccupation—or, at least, one abiding preoccupation.

II

In front of me, on the table, are five books. There are treasures buried inside of each. I've already read two cover to cover—Elaine Pagels' *Adam, Eve, and the Serpent* and Garry Wills' *Papal Sin*. I'm nearly done with two more—*The Mermaid and the Minotaur* by Dorothy Dinnerstein and *Binding the Strong Man* by Ched Myers. But, with a fair amount of Index referencing and general page snooping, I've only dipped in and out of Michael Lerner's *The Left Hand of God*.

For my purposes here, it's Dorothy Dinnerstein's *Mermaid and Minotaur* that'll be the hub of my mental wheel, the axle of this wobbly essay, although there may be those who'd say this mental wheel and intellectual axle are spinning vigorously, effortlessly, and also uselessly in space. We are all, as it were, in orbit, spinning endlessly on a planetary axis. But what's good for this topsy-turvy planet should be good enough for me.

III

This ongoing wrestle with intellectual preoccupations is neither random nor predictable, although it seems to have a certain interior logic. I am not as intellectually pure as Plato, nor as spiritually "Manichean" as Augustine. Perhaps, like Thoreau, I will bow briefly in the direction of these ancient worthies as I delight in stacking the admittedly temporal but wonderfully physical firewood that will cook the garden produce my wife Susanna has raised and that we'll eventually be eating. Perhaps I am too much in love with the material world (do I feel Augustine glaring down at me, with fire in his eyes?); but I suspect our venerable mental worthies (both Augustine and Plato) had a problem getting out of their ideological heads. (Perhaps they need their names evolved—like Harry Stottle—to Auggie Tim and Play To Go.)

We have, as it were, a kind of dreadful proof of their intellectual error—or, perhaps, I should say their mental self-containment—for the utopia of ideal and perfect order they helped rationalize has now globalized as accelerating ecological and cultural disaster. The utopian Ideal turns out to be somewhat less than ideal. The City of God has turned into a gated, toxic slum, a spiritual ghetto of the deluded elect. It's time our *civis* gods got their polished veneration scuffed and nicknamed up a little. It's time to rein in our worship of utopian otherworldliness.

Eutopia, as ethically grounded earthiness, is the only way out of the consequences of utopia's sterile idealism—an idealism that has, perhaps paradoxically, ramified as toxic materialism. Utopian perfection is proving to be a house of illusions. Or we might say that idealism and materialism are opposite sides of the same toxic coin, with Plato's mug on one side and Aristotle's on the other. Play To Go with Harry Stottle. This point of view cannot help but place me in the camp of skepticism. And although skeptics are often accused of cosmic impiety or of betraying the natural order, skepticism is Taoist acknowledgment of our inevitable ignorance, an acknowledgment that refuses to pretend to believe in utopian pieties or in the natural order that Aristotle, for example, found so conveniently self-evident—the "natural" practices of slavery and war in particular. To start where we are—in doubt, uncertainty, and with a full load of honest ignorance—without flipping out into idealized, doctrinal orbit, may be hard, but it can be very rewarding. It is the eutopian path, stubbornly grounded on Earth, bravely exploring the Cloud of Unknowing.

The hulks of scholarly wrestling I keep going back to for additional eutopian training in earthly groundedness are Lewis Mumford and Norman O. Brown. In "Going for the Juggler," last summer's account of my wrestle with Thomas Berry, I not only put Brown in the wrestling ring with Berry, I lamented the absence of a "Norma A. Brown" who might, with psychoanalytical chiropractic, adjust the male posture of Norman O. Well, stupid me, not only did I already know of Norma A., I even (for the last twenty-five years!) had her wonderful book on my disorganized library shelf. More than that, I'd given her a flaming two-sentence cameo in the essay "Eutopian

Postscript," in my *Green Politics Is Eutopian*, an essay originally written in the late 1980s. That I had inexplicably "forgotten" Norma all these years may have to do with *my* male posture as well as the nature of the warning posted definitively in her Preface:

> To the extent that it succeeds in communicating its point at all, this book will necessarily enrage the reader. What it says is emotionally threatening. (Part of why it has taken me so long to finish it is that I am threatened by it myself.) And what the reader must be warned against, therefore, is a temptation: Since my argument is not armored with the wall of scholarly references and comprehensively acknowledged counter-considerations that a writer of different talents and temperament might have marshaled, it will be possible to fasten upon the gaps in my exposition—to welcome the presence of omissions and oversimplifications—as a means of avoiding the acute discomfort that must be faced if the main point I am making is valid.[1]

That might be taken as an epigraph for this essay, as well. Perhaps for the entire book.

"Norma" is, of course, Dorothy Dinnerstein (1923-1992), and her book (1976) is *The Mermaid and the Minotaur: Sexual Arrangements and Human Malaise*. This essay (so, at least, I am intending) will be an exploration into buried meanings in stories so paradoxically common and tediously foundational that we hardly give them a second thought. Dorothy Dinnerstein will lead us into this common, foundational darkness, into the acute discomfort we all may find enraging and emotionally threatening.

IV

Dinnerstein's book is central to this essay for a number of reasons. Most immediately, she identifies a serious flaw in the analysis of Norman O. Brown—and, behind Brown, Freud—and she proposes a deep and serious corrective. Regarding Brown specifically, she says he sees that

> . . . the prevailing structure of the human family both underlies societal despotism and constricts sexuality, and that these two effects interpenetrate. He is wonderfully eloquent, moreover, about "the androgynous or hermaphroditic ideal of the unconscious" and about the necessity to fuse maleness and femaleness within each self. But one feels—and I must count on the reader to go to Brown's text to confirm this feeling; it is too subtle and pervasive to be documented here—that this ideal emotionally androgynous humanity he prescribes is still, physically and literally, *male* humanity. In the world he evokes, one does not sense the presence of ideally androgynous but physically *female* humans. On the contrary, one senses mothers and their offspring still somehow tucked away together in nurseries while men roam about enjoying the polymorphous eroticism that is their birthright. Surely one cannot

---

1. Dinnerstein, *Mermaid*, ix.

imagine Brown's emotionally hermaphroditic men burping and diapering babies. I would be glad if this impression of mine were, after all, wrong. But what is clear is this: he nowhere indicates that the early parental figure whose importance he so heavily emphasizes can or should be an androgynous figure. Neither does he indicate that the femininity of this figure under present conditions has anything at all to do with the main problem he discusses: that is, with the present dominion of death in life.[2]

Let's just note, for the moment, the "prevailing structure of the human family [that] both underlies societal despotism and constricts sexuality." Perhaps—we'll see—if it's this that's so enraging and emotionally threatening.

Second, Dinnerstein's corrective, implicit in her critique just quoted, especially when juxtaposed with Merlin Stone's account of the origins of gender in the divine (in *When God Was a Woman*, which we'll get to fairly soon) provides a more complete template by which or through which we might hold Judeo-Christian theophany up to the psychomythological light—which holding lends even more weight, in my estimation, to the Four Ages construct of Mother, Father, Son, and Daughter. (That is, such an analysis also signals the end, the historical terminus, of the Abrahamic religions—or at minimum the erosion of their hegemony as major religious entities in the world—as civilization enters more deeply into its intensifying transformational crisis.) Third, Dinnerstein's analysis, while forcing us to look long and hard at the world-shaping consequences of male/female arrangements, specifically the massive impact of what she calls "our prevailing female-dominated child-rearing arrangement,"[3] includes a disarmingly simple but culturally transformative corrective—"shared early parenthood"[4]—even as she talks about "the related project of sexual liberty"[5] without providing much of a map for what that related project might entail beyond shared early parenthood. The "sexual liberty" aspect is, to say the least, inadequately explored in *The Mermaid and the Minotaur*. That it is (in my estimation) inadequately explored may be due to the possibility that Dinnerstein herself found such liberty emotionally threatening and acutely uncomfortable. She does, after all, suggest as much in her Preface. Nor does her *Mermaid* describe what "shared early parenthood" would look like. Is it mommy/daddy in equalitarian child-rearing balance? Or is it—possibly—a more communal householding constellation with a complex array of moms and dads, sisters and brothers? And how would "sexual liberty" manifest itself in either of those two constructs?

2. Dinnerstein, *Mermaid*, 184.

3. Dinnerstein, *Mermaid*, x.

4. Dinnerstein, *Mermaid*, xiii.

5. Dinnerstein, *Mermaid*, 245.

V

Is Dorothy Dinnerstein's analysis the correct one? Is it true that the prevailing structure of the human family underlies societal despotism while it constricts sexuality or that constriction and despotism reciprocally shape each other? Is it by the holding-in-place power of conventional sexual morality that we stay within the utopian energy field? No one can claim finality, and Dinnerstein certainly does not do so. But some analyses point us in the direction of deeper comprehension, as I believe *The Mermaid and the Minotaur* does. In addition, Dinnerstein says repeatedly in her book, in one way or another, exactly what she says in the first passage quoted above: namely, the changes needed in relation to the "deathly overall direction that human affairs are taking"[6] contradict our common sense and our embedded patterns of behavior and belief to such an extent that we are, in fact, powerfully opposed (or at least reflexively resistant) to the very changes that would not only divert us from the deathly overall direction but would also result in a magnificent growth of human freedom. We are in love with—or perhaps just in thrall to—our cultural and mythological chains. We are drunk on old wine and our collective hangover feels normal. Our desire for liberation is tethered to an ancient ballast of convention and normality. The transformation we need to achieve is so, well, transformational that our prevailing morality senses the impending liberation as spiritually sinful, a reckless leap into a dangerously risky unknown.

This implies, of course, that deeper understanding is necessary but not sufficient. That is, understanding by itself does not create the courage to act. Courage requires action, and action involves risk, and risk is inevitable because we cannot know with absolute certainty that (in this instance) Dinnerstein's analysis and prescription are sufficiently accurate. Ignorance always gets a place at the table. It sits, in fact, on every chair. So the understanding Dinnerstein asks us to consider will also make us acutely uncomfortable; working through that discomfort requires spiritual courage and a boldness strongly tempered by humility.

But let's bask in the golden glow of Dorothy Dinnerstein's loving light as we venture happily (or as happily as possible) into the arena of our acute discomfort.

VI

Now I need to confess—if it needs to be said, as if the fact is not glaringly apparent—that I am untrained in and academically unqualified for this exploration into our acute discomfort. I'm not only a college dropout, I've no intellectual credentials to strut or flash. Caveat emptor. How thin the ice may be depends on the weight of the reader's skepticism.

6. Dinnerstein, *Mermaid*, viii.

But what propels me onward (beyond, perhaps, a certain indigenous streak of stupidity and megalomania) is an autodidactic stubbornness and a deeply alarmed conviction regarding civilizational autism. That is, what the dictionary, in its omniscient definition of autism, calls a state of mind characterized by a disregard of external reality, is the shocking truth I stumbled upon decades ago when I went looking for an answer to the question: "Why are small farms dying?" That is, I discovered that it's *civilization*, or our worship of its mythological and pathological radiance, that constitutes the operative core of our collective megalomania—literally a mental disorder characterized by delusions of grandeur, wealth, and power; a passion for big things; a tendency not merely to exaggerate but to conflate male aggression with the will of God Almighty. Let's say Manifest Destiny, as an example.

This tendency to exaggerate and conflate produces a tendency to "unconsciously" misrepresent supremacy as revealed truth. This is the territory of myth. That is, myth protects supremacy from critical examination. While the human impulse to misrepresent group or clan or tribal superiority is a human trait older than civilization, far older than the United States of America, it nevertheless *is* civilization that has congealed and concentrated a body of misrepresentation into what's now an increasingly lethal Global Crisis. Or, as Dorothy Dinnerstein puts it in her own "prevailing male-female arrangements" context: "It is a massive communal self-deception, designed to allay immediate discomfort and in the long run—a run whose end we are now approaching—suicidal."[7]

This self-deceiving misrepresentation is also designated by the idolatrous depiction of the divine, of God, as strictly and utterly Male, nowhere more concentrated and unbendingly prideful than in the three Abrahamic religions; so The One True God not only has to juggle Himself as Three Persons in Trinitarian psychodynamics, He also has to straddle three historically hostile camps of devotees—Jew, Christian, Moslem—each of which wishes the other two diminished, constrained, or dead. This is the famous Brotherhood of Man in consort with the Almighty Father who remains something of a hapless mascot, obedient cheerleader, and compliant codependent for each Abrahamic sibling.

VII

I suppose this means we have to start with God. By "God" I mean the image or notion of Supreme Being that's explicitly part of the cultural evolution of those of us raised in the direct trajectory of the Judeo-Christian tradition. (Seyyed Hossein Nasr, however, says "it must first be remembered that, if one chooses not to speak of Judaism and Christianity but of the Judeo-Christian tradition, one should speak of the Judeo-Christian-Islamic tradition, which would thus include the three members of

---

7. Dinnerstein, *Mermaid*, 8-9.

the Abrahamic family of religions."[8] This is of course true. But the Islamic part of that construction has traditionally had a far smaller impact on those of us in the mainstream West—except as the wicked Other the Christian Crusades were to deter or vanquish. Yet the Islamic impact has in recent decades grown immensely larger as it also has, for the most part, grown exceedingly negative in Western public opinion.)

This primary Christian or Judeo-Christian trajectory, already well intellectualized before the Constantinian absorption (or creation) of orthodox Christianity in the fourth century C.E., before that trajectory received Roman Empire mutation and subsequent historical radiation and burst out of Europe in the late fifteenth century, has by now powerfully influenced, in one way or another, the entire world.[9] This exuberant global discovery and predatory economic colonialism was largely achieved under the justifying flag of God. God was the absolute high ground. Whoever grabbed hold of God won the ultimate prize. God's word was not only the first word, it was also the last word. When God speaks, all human arguments are over. Those who act in God's behalf act with moral impunity, certainly with a right of Christian discovery.

Of course, the question immediately is: What's God saying? Since those who claim to hear God's voice may be provided with suitable medication or their own broadcast outlet, let's acknowledge there's a big fight over God, over what God is saying, what God has said, what God might say, and what God would like to see happen on Earth. We in the mainstream West are obliged to recognize that God, like a giant snowball, may have originated (in our cultural mind) in the Bible, in the ancient Middle East, but He picked up all manner of other godly flavorings and cultural complexions from His long roll through Western history. It's also possible to suggest that Eastern spiritual blowback is, in part, causing God to enter a major identity crisis, bordering on divine meltdown.

If the Taoist tradition, according to Steven C. Rockefeller, views the cosmos "as a self-generating organic whole which is an open process of becoming," we shouldn't be too surprised to learn that "extensive environmental degradation in the East has to a large extent followed upon 'the intellectual colonization of the East by the West,' that is, the spread of the Cartesian and Newtonian worldview."[10] It is therefore ridiculous to assert that the West has simply won, for all time, the Olympic torch of total globalization. We've already entered the inevitable breakdown of that totality.

I am starting from the position that the world is in big trouble and that the Christian West has been and is, at minimum, the catalyst of that trouble. We're in

---

8. Nasr, "Islam," 96.

9. Here's how Riane Eisler puts it on page 131 of *The Chalice and the Blade*: "Already by 200 C.E., in this classic case of spirituality stood on its head, Christianity was well on its way to becoming precisely the kind of hierarchical and violence-based system Jesus had rebelled against. And after Emperor Constantine's conversion, it became an official arm, that is, the servant, of the state. As [Elaine] Pagels writes, when 'Christianity became an officially approved religion in the fourth century, Christian bishops, previously victimized by the police, now commanded them.'"

10. Rockefeller, "Faith," 157-58.

a very serious pickle, and the identity of God—our collective or dominant image of the sacred or divine—is part of our dilemma. Here's how Slavoj Zizek puts it in the Introduction to his *Living in the End Times*:

> The underlying premise of the present hook is a simple one: the global capitalist system is approaching an apocalyptic zero-point. Its "four riders of the apocalypse" are comprised by the ecological crisis, the consequences of the biogenetic revolution, imbalances within the system itself . . . and the explosive growth of social divisions and exclusions.[11]

Of course that's my view, too—except I say "globalized civilizational system," inclusive of the religions founded within the civilized context, rather than merely the "global capitalist system." The problem with so many bright social critics (such as Zizek) is the extent to which their analyses are jammed in the more or less modern period: they simply don't go back far enough in time in search of origins. They seem indifferent to the long-term energy of the civilizational trajectory, and (at least implicitly) they appear rejecting of that trajectory's historical significance in the creation and maintenance of core political and economic institutions, as well as the mentalities that go with those institutions. That's why thinkers like Mumford, Brown, and Dinnerstein are so crucial, for they carry us far back beyond the breathless present or recent past, and they enable us to examine the ancient roots (not just the top twigs and outer branches) of the crises culminating in our age and time. But Zizek goes on to say his book is

> . . . thus a book of struggle, following Paul's surprisingly relevant definition: "For our struggle is not against flesh and blood, but against leaders, against authorities, against the world rulers [*kosmokratoras*] of this darkness, against the spiritual wickedness in the heavens" (Ephesians 6:12). Or, translated into today's language: "Our struggle is not against actual corrupt individuals, but against those in power in general, against their authority, against the global order and the ideological mystification which sustains it."[12]

Well, our predicament *is* simultaneously historical and mythological. We can also say it's spiritual if we mean by "spiritual" not only foundational ethics but also the troublesome opaque nature of Spirit. It may well be that Spirit will always be mysterious, deep, and more elusive than the rational mind can grasp or define. But mystery need not be mystification. Not knowing doesn't have to capitulate to mystification. Humble scholarship is obligated to tunnel right through creedal assertion into the liberating light of honest investigation. We need not only a psychoanalysis of history but also a psychoanalysis of religious mythology, even a psychoanalysis of civilization's

---

11. Zizek, *Living*, x.

12. Zizek, *Living*, xv.

superego. These are the tracks this stumbling amateur is following onto the thin ice of the emotionally threatening.

VIII

Perhaps Ched Myers' *Binding the Strong Man* will provide a fruitful next step in our snooping into the precincts of God. If nothing else, Myers' title provides an ironic turn of phrase in regard to God. "Binding the Strong Man" refers us to Mark 3:27 or, rather, to a longer story in Mark 3 in which Jesus is accused by "teachers of the law" of being possessed by Beelzebub, the god of insects and the prince of demons. This story—verses 22 through 30 in Mark 3—is blocked in at both ends by accounts of Jesus' family, his mother and brothers explicitly, who think he's out of his mind, who want to take Jesus away from the public brawl he seems determined to provoke.

In the intervening parable, Jesus asks how a divided house or kingdom can stand, how Satan can drive out Satan. "If Satan opposes himself and is divided, he cannot stand; his end has come." And "In fact, no one can enter a strong man's house and carry off his possessions unless he first ties up the strong man. Then he can rob his house." In this essay, however, I am far less interested in robbing God's house than in examining the property deeds and legal abstracts by which ownership is claimed. We're making an effort to see if God is who He claims to be. To "tie up" the strong man is to subdue our fear of his threatening power, real or imagined, and to explore the historical and mythological psychodynamics of threat and fear.

Well, let's slide in with a passage from Myers' book:

> Ours is not a hospitable world for visionaries—and not without good reason, for charlatans abound. Gospel radicalism is still dismissed in the metropolises of the West by the dominant ideologies of Christian realism. Yet many are reconsidering, for "realism" has demonstrably failed us. In its name the four apocalyptic horsemen of empire, militarism, economic exploitation, and environmental revolt (Rv 6:2-8) ride freely over the earth.[13]

Please note that this inhospitable world is dominated by ideologies of Christian *realism*. Also note that the "Gospel radicalism" *dismissed* in the metropolises of the West has a history twenty centuries old. That is, the horrific fights between orthodoxy and gnosticism in the second and third centuries were, for instance, overwhelmingly about theological abstractions and metaphysical assertions. The far more elemental project of cultural and spiritual transformation that Jesus initiated (i.e., the "kingdom of God" proclamation)—this is Ched Myers' close reading of Mark's gospel—was largely lost in the swirling dust of righteous combat over conflicting views of abstruse doctrine. If orthodoxy is closely aligned with realism, then "realism" has an ancient pedigree in

---

13. Myers, *Binding*, 450.

Christian mythology and metaphysics. We might even say that Augustine remains the most authoritative architect of empire "realism," the Moses of Christendom.

Myers says that "The managerial rationalism of realpolitik is only a secular restatement of the old myth of divine right, which in the American empire is articulated by the national theology of manifest destiny and cold war."[14] In a section dealing with the "strong man" story, Myers says the "carefully chosen images" of Satan "bear remarkable correspondences to the ideological foundations of scribal Judaism," as well as to the "centralized politics of the Davidic state" and to "its symbolic center, the temple."[15] Yet Myers invariably rescues God from any demonic contamination; and I find it interesting to see how, in the general run of scholarship, both God and civilization always get to walk from every disaster unhurt, undisturbed, and without a smudge of dirt or splash of blood on their white and spotless gowns. No matter what happens, civilization and God emerge clean and bright.

Yet, as a broad generality, I share Myers' political convictions. (We both would fall within Michael Lerner's political category of the Left Hand of God.) I admire Myers for his powerful grounding of Jesus, who is not a dreamy, hippie-dippy, cloud-hugging, fat and pouty portal of everlasting heavenly bliss but, rather, a gritty flesh and blood man of such powerful will, keen understanding, and deep conviction that he scared the crap out of his closest associates. (How would *we* feel to be closely associated with a person whose opposition to both the political and religious status quo was so constant, intense, and unrelenting that we felt arrest, conviction, beatings, and—probably—torture and execution always hanging over *us*?) *This* Jesus is engaged in a project (under the general rubric "kingdom of God" or *malkuta*) fully intending to overcome not only the prevailing ruling powers of his day, but the "spirit and practice of domination ultimately embedded in the human personality and corporately in human history as a whole."[16]

Now that's one hell of a project. But before we laugh loudly in public or more quietly up our sleeves, let's face the fact that not only Jesus but also Lao Tzu and the Buddha—and who knows who else?—were engaged in world-changing projects. They and their efforts were recognized, at least by an alert few, for their unique and powerful coherence, for their amazing courage, dedication, insight, and wisdom. (Why else do we remember and revere them? Why do we consider them the best of human spirituality?) Precisely because they were so clear and brave, so unflinching in their understanding, so focused in their determination, their followers felt inadequate and insecure. Some were able to cope with the realization of inadequacy while living out, to the best of their ability, the core ethical insights. Others—perhaps the majority—moved to build a religious cult, elevating their "savior" beyond human reach, thus easing existential insecurity by means of liturgy and worship. In so doing, they

14. Myers, *Binding*, 452.

15. Myers, *Binding*, 166.

16. Myers, *Binding*, 103.

anesthetized the transformative ethical core and flipped the spiritual effort from concentrated earthly engagement to etherealized heavenly escape. They developed hardening of the spiritual arteries, ascended into cerebral creed and intellectualized dogma (channeled into repetitive liturgy), and then idolized the entire package into fantasies of overpowering divinity that—here we go full circle—form the "divine" that congeals yet again as the spirit and practice of domination, before which we are to grovel. This is how intense ethical spirituality gets "domesticated" as pious, otherworldly mythology.

In other words, the project of liberation, if it is to be successful, has to break the wheel that turns liberation back into domination. And, since we are now into the global actualization of the "four apocalyptic horsemen"—Myers' horsemen are considerably less fuzzy than Zizek's—this project of liberation has got its feet to the fire. Breaking the cycle of domination is the project we simply have to achieve. It's no longer optional or "unrealistic." And, since the two biggest self-promoting advocates for liberation (from earthly sin and indigenous backwardness, respectively) are God and Civilization, let's invite these two venerable Beings to a costume-free bonfire—no asbestos suits, please—to see if they can stroll sweat-free through the fires of transformation, or whether exposure will generate the biggest meltdown of civilized idolatry in human history.

IX

The problem is that we speak of God in the singular—the only God, the Almighty God of overpowering monotheism, the only One of His kind—but, in fact, there seem to be two monotheistic Gods—a big one and a little one, a God of vengeance and retribution and a God of love and forgiveness. Civilization owns the big, muscular God; religion rents the little one, tax exempt, on Friday (if Moslem), on Saturday (if Jewish), and on Sunday (if Christian)—a three-day weekend of work for Allah, Yahweh, or God—the same divinity in different mythological costumes. Michael Lerner references the Left Hand of God (the little one) and the Right Hand of God (the big one). The Left Hand relates to that aspect of the sacred "built upon the loving, kind, and generous energy in the universe," while the Right Hand "sees the universe as a fundamentally scary place filled with evil forces." In the first approach, we are encouraged "to be like this loving God," while in the latter, "God is the avenger, the big man in heaven who can be invoked to use violence to overcome those evil forces, either right now or in some future ultimate reckoning."[17]

Well, maybe there's One God with a split personality, a schizophrenic God. Lewis Mumford, in *The Myth of the Machine*, explores (or at least exposes) a parallel schizophrenia in our understanding of civilization—an entity always and invariably good, kind, creative, and loving except when it needs to be destructive, extractive, brutal

17. Lerner, *Left*, 2.

and cruel, which is frequent if not constant. In most branches of Christianity, there is a sharp cleavage between the two kingdoms, both ordained by God: a state realm of secular governance, and a realm under the purview or at least the guidance of the church, a realm to be reached only after death in a distant place called heaven. The former grips the sword and scans, with empathy-deficient eyes, the wicked rabble to be controlled; the latter, with compassion for the elect and pity for the damned, checks exit tickets at the gate. In general, all this implies that the soft-hearted may, if they wish, pursue do-good projects to their hearts' content, while "realists" know exactly where and how the rubber hits the road.

X

Well, let's expand on this civilization versus "civilization" dynamic a bit, for it's connected to the Left and Right Hands of God via what both Marcus Borg and Sallie McFague have called the "monarchical model." McFague, in her essay ("A Square in the Quilt") in *Spirit and Nature: Why the Environment is a Religious Issue*, says:

> Western culture was and still is profoundly formed by the Hebrew and Christian religions and their stories, images, and concepts regarding the place of human beings, history, and nature in the scheme of things. Moreover, I believe it is the major images or metaphors of a tradition that influence behavior more powerfully than its central concepts or ideas. For instance, it is the image of God as king and lord rather than the idea of God as transcendent that has entered most deeply into Western consciousness.[18]

Images are stronger than concepts; metaphors have more influence than ideas. If concepts and ideas are largely in the realm of intellectuals, therefore vulnerable to debate and alteration, images and metaphors sink more deeply into the general population and, as such, are more resistant to change. *Mythos* is suspicious of *logos*. God may be "king and lord," but this king and lord is *apart* from the material universe—certainly not resident on Earth. "King and lord" are as close as transcendent gets to being immanent in orthodox Christian theology. The image of God as distant and inaccessible permeates common consciousness, even as the invisible God is also a focused God of moral surveillance. But McFague's point is well-taken. Not only does she say the Christian tradition has been both androcentric and anthropocentric, its "dominant imagery has been monarchical. God is imagined as king, lord, and patriarch of a kingdom which he rules, a kingdom hierarchically ordered."[19] Expanding on this "dominant imagery," McFague says

> . . . its main tenets have seeped into the Western worldview to the extent that most Westerners, quite unselfconsciously, believe in the sacredness of

18. McFague, "Square," 47-48.
19. McFague, "Square," 48.

every individual human being (while scarcely protesting the extinction of all the members of other species); believe males to be "naturally" superior to females; find human fulfillment (however one defines it) more important than the well-being of the planet; and picture God (whether or not one is a believer) as a distant, almighty superperson. This dualistic, hierarchical picture supports another form of dangerous behavior: the superiority of one's own nation over others and hence the validation of a nationalistic, militaristic, xenophobic horizon.[20]

All this confirms Michael Lerner's Right-Handed God, who uses violence to overcome evil. Meanwhile, Mumford's explicit Left and Right Hands of Civilization are held up for inspection in *The Myth of the Machine*, in the final section of chapter Eight, "Kings as Prime Movers." Mumford's entire chapter is about the "profound change" that came into being when "a new set of institutions" he calls "civilization" sprang up "in a few great river valleys." This new set of institutions constituted "a new kind of social organization." This new social organization was erected on top of a "basic village culture" whose "three foundation-stones—communion, communication, and cooperation"[21] were seized by an authoritarian, centrally directed, dominant minority dedicated to the "expansion of collective power," who, by the third millennium B.C., had "organized industrial and military power on a scale that was never surpassed until our own time."[22]

Mumford says this new entity—a city ruled by a king—was also "the home of a god: indeed a replica of Heaven."[23] He says this "outburst of energy" created a "set of institutional controls and physical compulsions that had never existed before." At the "center of this whole development lay the new institution of kingship. The myth of the machine and the cult of divine kingship rose together."[24] But Mumford's not done:

> The agency that effected this change, the institution of divine kingship, was the product of a coalition between tribute-exacting hunting chieftain and the keepers of an important religious shrine. Without that combination, without that sanction, without that luminous elevation, the claims that the new rulers made to unconditional obedience to their king's superior will, could not have been established: *it took extra, supernatural authority, derived from a god or a group of gods, to make kingship prevail throughout a large society.* Arms and armed men, specialists in homicide, were essential; but force alone was not enough. . . . (Emphasis added)
>
> Under the protective symbol of his god, housed in a massive temple, the king, who likewise served as high priest, exercised powers that no hunting

20. McFague, "Square," 48.

21. Mumford, *Myth*, 163.

22. Mumford, *Myth*, 164.

23. Mumford, *Myth*, 167-68.

24. Mumford, *Myth*, 168.

chief would have dared to claim merely as the leader of his band. By assimilation, the town, once a mere enlargement of the village, became a sacred place, a divine 'transformer,' so to say, where the deadly high-tension currents of godhead were stepped down for human use.

This fusion of sacred and temporal power released an immense explosion of latent energy, as in a nuclear reaction. At the same time it created a new institutional form, for which there is no evidence in the simple neolithic village or paleolithic cave: an enclave of power, dominated by an elite who were supported in grandiose style by tribute and taxes forcibly drawn from the whole community.

The efficacy of kingship, all through history, rests precisely on this alliance between the hunter's predatory prowess and gift of command, on one hand, and priestly access to astronomical lore and divine guidance.[25]

Well, it's possible to keep extracting more of these astonishing insights and observations: "kingship everywhere partook of divinity," "gods are in fact kings of the unconscious," "kings in turn became incarnate dream gods."[26] But note that "submission" and "abject self-humiliation" *never* "had a counterpart among the humble members of any village community" until civilized institutions "filtered down from above. But this drill had the effect of turning human beings into 'things,' who could be galvanized into a regimented kind of cooperation by royal command"[27]:

> To ensure that the heavenly sanctions of kingship were sufficiently respected, kingship in the end must be ready to fall back on force: not merely naked force, but force in ferocious, sadistic forms, repeatedly magnified into nightmarish extravagances of cruelty, as dehumanized as those we have witnessed in the last generation in the ingenious horrors perpetuated by 'civilized' governments in Warsaw, Auschwitz, Tokyo, and Vietnam.[28]

That takes us up to Mumford's last section in chapter Eight. Here he tells us that civilization (without quotation marks, therefore the real thing) "implies a cumulative effort to further the arts and sciences, and to improve the human condition by continued advances in both technology and responsible government," while

> . . . 'civilization' in quotation marks [is used] in a much narrower sense: to denote the group of institutions that first took form under kingship. Its chief features, constant in varying proportions throughout history, are the centralization of political power, the separation of classes, the lifetime division of labor, the mechanization of production, the magnification of military power,

---

25. Mumford, *Myth*, 170-71.

26. Mumford, *Myth*, 176-77.

27. Mumford, *Myth*, 183.

28. Mumford, *Myth*, 183-84.

the economic exploitation of the weak, and the universal introduction of slavery and forced labor for both industrial and military purposes.[29]

It doesn't take a genius to recognize that the attributes Mumford ascribes to civilization-without-quotation-marks—the furthering of arts and sciences, improving the human condition by advances in technology and responsible government—mesh perfectly with the attributes—communion, communication, and cooperation—he says are the three foundation-stones of basic *village* culture, while the truly "new set of institutions" that "first took form under kingship" are primly and deftly swept into a dirty dustpan called, with pursed lips and wrinkled nose, "civilization."

We are brought here not to paradox, exactly, but to outright confoundedness, a contradiction, a double take that is kissing cousin to double talk, something double-faced and double-tongued, but not by any means your ordinary and familiar sort of everyday deceit. This is double talk that wanders in and out of a magical spell, in and out of the charmed charnel atmospherics of incarnate dream gods, a magical spell of dream gods with ferocious and sadistic wills, capable of nightmarish extravagances of cruelty and ingenious horrors, capable, in short, of obliterating the person or persons who dare to call a spade a spade.

One sees this same evasive impulse at work in the Introduction by Wade Davis to the National Geographic's *Book of Peoples of the World*, where great alarm is expressed over the enforced disappearance of flora and fauna, languages and cultures—e.g., "There is a fire burning over the Earth, taking with it plants and animals, human languages, ancient skills, and visionary wisdom"—but "Culture, in other words, matters. It provides the vital constraints of tradition and comfort that allow true civilization to exist."[30] And that is as deep as the diagnosis gets to go. If that's as deep as we can go, or as deep as we're willing to allow ourselves to go, then we are only fiddling with clichés while Earth burns, as we piously wait for dream gods to come with their virtual fire trucks to rescue "true civilization" from the conflagration that ("false"?) civilization has ignited.

The problem with Wade Davis's "true" civilization and Lewis Mumford's negative "civilization" is that they represent wishful but ahistorical idealism (in the case of Davis) and outright historical denial (in Mumford's usage). From Mumford's own analysis, *it is logically impossible to honestly arrive at the conclusion he offers*—i.e., "civilization" as semantically inauthentic civilization—just as Wade Davis's burning fire bears only inconsequential relationship to "true" civilization. The only sensible conclusion is that civilization/"civilization," rather like God, is supernaturally ambidextrous (Mumford says as much), and that the Powers and Principalities we are warned about in Ephesians 6 consist precisely of the conflicted ambitendency of God and Civilization. Supply quotation marks around either word as you feel the need, as

---

29. Mumford, *Myth*, 186.

30. Davis, "Introduction," 11.

you wish, as your understanding impels you: but pay close attention to your feelings, thoughts, and motives as you do so. If my studies over the past forty years have led me to a conclusion—and I realize only too well what a sweeping conclusion this is for a mere mortal to make—civilization fused with God really *is* the "fire burning over the Earth" *and* that the intensity of this global conflagration is fed and sustained by the psychoconductivity of our adherence to this supracultural, metaphysical meshing. Shall we say Mumford was merely indulging in colorful language when he said this "fusion of sacred and temporal power released an immense explosion of latent energy, as in a nuclear reaction"? I enjoy colorful language and have been known to indulge in it, but I believe Mumford was grasping for a metaphor adequate to his perception rather than simply blowing rhetorical smoke. "Globalization" means exactly what it says: this mythological fusion is a fire burning over the *entire* Earth.

How much longer do we intend to keep playing this cowardly mind game of "true" versus "false" civilization or of "civilization" versus civilization? Guessing which of God's hands is the real one? The longer we play with such evasions, the more this fire will consume. Do we need to say—again—that there are religious ideologies not only *expecting* global conflagration but doing whatever seems possible to *accelerate* its combustion? Do we need a more clinical description of what it means—Mark 3—to be "possessed"?

Maynard Kaufman was right, after all. If civilized corporations are "demonic," then so is the overarching civility endowing them with demonic "personhood."

XI

Although Ched Myers says early on in his book that he is "not anxious to enter into 'metasymbolic' debates" about God, and has therefore "tended to avoid talk about God," he nevertheless asserts the "traditional Hebrew 'Yahweh' in place of the Hellenistic 'God' or 'Lord' whenever possible."[31] God (or Yahweh) is a constant background presence in *Binding the Strong Man*—or, we might say, always present and never present—much as

> . . . Mark keeps postponing the fulfillment of the expectations he generates. Just when it seems the new order will be unveiled, something anticlimactic takes place, and the scene changes.
>
> Finally, in [Mark] 1:15, Jesus announces the awaited moment of God's intervention: the "time is fulfilled" (peplerotai ho kairos). The kingdom's arrival is "close at hand," an expression unique in the New Testament, connoting profound imminence, even liminality. Yet in 1:16, we are once again frustrated. Instead of a kingdom epiphany, the second act opens with Jesus wandering by the sea, bidding some common laborers to accompany him on a mission. The world appears still very much intact! Mark is obviously aware of the risk

31. Myers, *Binding*, 37.

involved in his appeal to prophetic and apocalyptic traditions, for they also were being used to bolster the triumphalistic eschatological expectations of Jewish nationalism. For this reason, Mark pursues a narrative strategy that consistently frustrates the equation between epiphany and victorious holy war.[32]

A few pages later, Myers says "By keeping the reader off balance, Mark subverts traditional notions about how Yahweh intervenes in the world."[33] Fifty pages further in, having noted the "remarkable affinity" between Mark's narrative of Jesus' "sociopolitical strategy and Gandhi's satyagraha," Myers says that "Mark's narrative, like satyagraha, legitimizes militant, direct action, yet at the same time severs any absolute relationship between such action and historical efficacy. It is up to the disciple/reader to sow the seed of the kingdom through nonviolent witness—but it is up to God to bring that seed to fruition."[34] Later yet, Myers says the "disciples express amazement at Jesus' insistence that the dominant order of economic stratification is not ordained by God (10:23-27)."[35] In addition:

> Jesus now has the task of convincing his disciples not only that the temple-based social order *can* be overturned, but that they should reconstruct their collective symbolic life apart from it. It is a most appropriate place to deliver a mini sermon on faith. "Believe in God!" is not the hortatory platitude it may at first glance seem (11:23). The modern reader must remember that in the social world of the first-century Middle East, a temple was closely identified with a deity's existence. This was supremely true for the Jew; one could not simply repudiate the temple without provoking the most fundamental crisis regarding Yahweh's presence in the world. Jesus directly challenges this identification, arguing that to abandon faith in the temple is not to abandon faith in God.[36]

And, finally, Jesus "appeals, as he does throughout the Gospel, to the sovereignty of Yahweh, who is true 'lord of the house' (13:35) despite the counterclaims of Caesar."[37]

It seems that what divides "conservative" from "liberal" Christians—or, at least, one of the deciding things—is belief in the physical resurrection of Jesus. (This is one of the "fundamentals" of Christian fundamentalists.) By resurrection I don't so much mean ascension into heavenly thin air, or some other nonterrestrial imagery, but that Jesus literally and physically became alive again after having been put to death by crucifixion. (Of course, if Jesus rose bodily from the dead but did *not* ascend into thin air, then we are left with the logical implication that he may still be alive on Earth.

32. Myers, *Binding*, 131.

33. Myers, *Binding*, 135.

34. Myers, *Binding*, 184.

35. Myers, *Binding*, 287.

36. Myers, *Binding*, 304-5.

37. Myers, *Binding*, 427.

This, if true, would constitute a serious ecclesiastical problem, for which theologically contentious church could properly lay claim or would wish to welcome into its congregation this illustrious vagabond? No wonder ascension is such a vital feature within orthodox Christianity. Jesus simply has to be gone in order for otherworldliness to be plausible. The kingdom of God apparently dissipated like a jet's vapor trail as Jesus soared heavenward.)

Many "conservatives" who believe or at least say they believe that Jesus became alive again after death are also so-called "realists"; that is, they tend to be advocates of a two-kingdom Christian metaphysics—one "kingdom" for state governance on Earth, another "kingdom" of church facilitation toward eternal life in Heaven. (They may say yes to the "kingdom of God," but only after death—only in the Next Life.) But Ched Myers seems to straddle this divide: "Was Jesus raised from the dead? I happen to agree with those who contend that nothing else can explain the genesis of the Christian movement."[38] This conviction and assertion (it would be interesting to know what Myers does or doesn't believe about ascension, whether Jesus may still be bumming about on Earth) goes a long way toward explaining why Myers' book is so angsty. Its "call to discipleship," while not hostile to spiritual or political fellow travelers who don't share his religious convictions, is limited to a small inner circle of believers who "take up the cross." There is in *Binding the Strong Man*, for all its grounding of a very Earth-committed Jesus, a strong mood of Sisyphean labor, a steep, uphill struggle without end, a wrestling not only with Caesar broadly speaking (i.e., Powers and Principalities) but, more painful and disheartening, with all the deeply compromised two-kingdom "realists" who have abandoned the core Jesus struggle (i.e., the Earth-based dynamics of the "kingdom of God") or who belong to denominations which have institutionalized abandonment in elaborate doctrine and elegant creed.

There is, I think, a continuum here with Michael Lerner's Left and Right Hands of God, which Hands seem confusingly crossed across God's Chest. (From explicit language of "extermination" of enemies in Exodus 23, and certainly up through the genocidal taking of Jericho in the Book of Joshua, Yahweh is a fierce, bloody-minded tribal god of the Hebrews. If Yahweh, as Lord of the house, even has a Left Hand, it is a congenitally withered Left Hand, kept in a protective sling and out of sight.) Jesus, of course, is the central figure, the main actor, in *Binding the Strong Man*; but Myers almost seems to say that Jesus is only acting in behalf of the main figure, which is God or Yahweh. (Incidentally, there are only two Index references to Holy Spirit in *Binding the Strong Man*, and in neither reference is there anything more than name usage. Myers may or may not be an orthodox Trinitarian, but God is clearly Yahweh, the Almighty Father, while Jesus is a very human "son of God." In Myers' book, the Holy Spirit is without role or substance. God is invisible but huge. Jesus is visible but only of human size. The Holy Spirit occupies no space whatsoever and apparently has no function.)

38. Myers, *Binding*, 447.

As a Bible-based Christian, Myers seems to accept Yahweh as cosmic God. For Myers, apparently, Yahweh *is* God. And while there is much scholarly referencing in *Binding the Strong Man* to historical studies of first-century Palestine, we are never given so much as a glimpse into possible origins of Middle Eastern god concepts or, for that matter, the origins of civilization itself in the larger Middle East, much less any hint of the agrarian village culture predating civilization or the gatherer/horticultural process resulting in agriculture. The God we get to "see" in *Binding the Strong Man* is no evolved or evolving cultural construct but, instead, an Eternal Divine Being, unbelievably powerful yet inexplicably invisible.

Can Jack Miles, a former Jesuit, help us get a glimpse of the elusive Yahweh? We'll soon see. But first a brief summation of proportionality from Kenneth Scott Latourette's *A History of Christianity: Beginnings to 1500*:

> Christianity is relatively young. Compared with the course of mankind on the earth, it began only a few moments ago. No one knows how old man is. That is because we cannot tell precisely when a creature which can safely be described as human first appeared. One estimate places the earliest presence of what may be called man about 1,200,000 years in the past. A being with a brain about the size of modern man may have lived approximately 500,000 years ago. In contrast with these vast reaches of time the less than two thousand years which Christianity has thus far had are very brief. If one accepts the perspective set forth in the New Testament that in Christ is the secret of God's plan for the entire creation, and that God proposes to "gather together in one all things in Christ, both which are in heaven and which are on earth," Christianity becomes relatively even more recent, for the few centuries since the coming of Christ are only an infinitesimal fraction of the time which has elapsed since the earth, not to speak of the vast universe, came into being.
>
> When placed in the setting of human civilization Christianity is still youthful. Civilization is now regarded as having begun from ten to twelve thousand years ago, during the last retreat of the continental ice sheets. This means that Christianity has been present during only a fifth or a sixth of the brief span of civilized mankind.[39]

XII

If it's not obvious, I confess to acute uneasiness in regard to religious assertions about God or Eternal Truths that are metaphysically self-contained and devoid of historical context or evolutionary perspective. It seems to me that an awareness of history, even if that awareness is quite pedestrian and limited, should produce or at least facilitate metaphysical modesty. Reading of the extended fight between orthodox and gnostic Christians in the period before the Constantinian accommodation (as described, for

39. Latourette, *History*, 3.

instance, in Elaine Pagels' *The Gnostic Gospels*), it's possible to weary of exuberant gnostic assertions regarding the nature of God or the divine. But—the stock in trade of the orthodox—abstract metaphysics derived from myth-understood-as-history (for example, Augustine's doctrine of "original sin" as biologically transmitted via the generational inheritance of Adam's semen[40]) creates a peculiar kind of human "knowing": it claims, with fierce certainty, to be historically and even biologically factual even as its actual foundation is a mishmash of myth and metaphysics—not so much an anachronism as a hallucination; that is, not something truly misplaced in time but a shimmering mirage of mythological magnitude taken as fact. Modern-day fundamentalism (and, with it, a large slice of the Christian Right) is not only caught up in this peculiar orthodox mentality, a mentality asserting myth as fact, its politics—think here of what Michael Lerner means by the Right Hand of God—provides a huge reservoir for militant "democratic" energy fueling (or at least upholding) empire in both militarist and consumerist modes.

Looking at Christian assertiveness through the context provided by Kenneth Scott Latourette—a human presence on Earth in the million-year range, folks with our type and size of brain for the last 500,000 years or so, human civilization only ten or twelve thousand years old (dated erroneously by Latourette from "the last retreat of the continental ice sheets"—as if melting glaciers had magical cities buried beneath the ice—rather than—more like five or six thousand years ago—from the bandit hijacking of the evolving agrarian village), the sheer adolescent egoism of Christian assertion appears amazingly audacious, although perhaps it is primarily an egoism residing inside an armored *super*egoism provided by metaphysical obsession, an obsession that male-dominated religion shares with male-dominated civilization. That is, we not only have a kind of history shaped by ahistorical myth and "eternal" metaphysics—that is its "objective" sphere—we also have a subjective sphere of personality traits and psychological characteristics—Burton Mack's "mentalities"—shaped essentially by the same force or forces. Institutions shape human consciousness; human consciousness, in turn, shapes—sometimes dangerously strengthens—institutions. Fear builds weapons; weapons incite fear. (Remember how Dorothy Dinnerstein told us that "the prevailing structure of the human family both underlies societal despotism and constricts sexuality, and that these two interpenetrate" or how Lewis Mumford identified the civilized town as a "divine transformer" whose "deadly high-tension currents of godhead were stepped down for human use"?)

As biological beings, as individuals, we really don't know very much. We know, in many respects, amazingly little, perhaps even alarmingly little. And it may be that our anxiety about our ignorance, our wonder and awe in the best sense, and our fear and terror in the worst sense, generates in us a desire to assert that we know not only more than we really do know, but to assert that knowing with an insupportable posture of divine certitude. Why? Because anxiety is hard to live with. It is intensely

40. Pagels, *Adam*, 131.

uncomfortable. Staying indefinitely in The Dark Night of the Soul is not our idea of a successful career or relaxing vacation. Conviction, especially if conveyed authoritatively, relieves anxiety and soothes insecurity. Insecurity is reduced by adoration of the strong man who confidently explains what's what. Metaphysical conviction is the religious and cultural clothing covering the existential nakedness of our anxiety.

We might speculate that the example of spiritual life Jesus left with his followers was not only unforgettable in its ethical audacity but also unacceptable in its evocation of terror. Follow this man into torture and execution? You've got to be kidding! Hence the powerful, immediate slide into saviorism, into ascension, heaven, and the prospect of blissful life eternal—and, in self-justifying posture, a kind of aggressive, stubborn stupidity about cultural transformation, a refusal to recognize how the traumatic institutions of civilization, as Powers and Principalities, seduce compliance in so many ways, certainly including the freedom to metaphysically soar into godly ether so long as actual governance is safely left in state control. The doctrine of the two kingdoms provides relief from the earthly attractions and existential obligations of *malkuta*. Once this doctrine becomes ecclesiastically official, Jesus' tomb is sealed with metaphysical cement and gospel yeast is carefully treated with growth-inhibiting fungicide. Civilization has the "real" Jesus on display on a crucifix, God's relic on Earth. Is it civilization's message to peasant revolutionaries? This could be you.

XIII

Former Jesuit Jack Miles has read God's script, so to speak, with God Himself cast in the central role. In *God: A Biography*, Miles approaches God as a literary character. He says "No character, however, on stage, page, or screen has ever had the reception that God has had. God is more than a household word in the West; he is, welcome or not, a virtual member of the Western family."[41] Perhaps, for what it's worth, we could say that God is the Resident Superego in the Western family and, by extension, the resident superego of all Western institutions, not merely the superego of the church or of Christianity.[42] But as Jack Miles goes on to say:

41. Miles, *God*, 5.

42. In an essay called "The Conscious Id," in my *Green Politics Is Eutopian* (page 107), I quote Marcus Borg's *The God We Never Knew* to the effect that the monarchical model of God confuses God with the superego and that this confusion is a "central dimension of the human predicament from which we need deliverance." But in rereading Lewis Mumford's *The Transformations of Man*, published in 1956, I find (on page 65) that my mentor has a much softer understanding of superego than I do; and I begin to wonder whether Mumford's childhood was so unusually gentle that, for him, superego meant rising above both the "basic biological self" (id) and the "derivative social self" (ego) into an "ideal self" (superego) of spiritually transcendent proportions into which "one must be reborn." I take this softness as a clue. That is, if Mumford's childhood was unusually gentle, then fierce, capricious, authoritarian power was *abnormal* in his understanding. Hence we see not so much his reluctance to call a spade a spade (as in the civilization/"civilization" business referenced earlier) but, rather, his constitutional inability to recognize within civilization the perverse normality Jack Miles will call

Religiously fostered appreciation of the Bible attends centrally and explicitly to the goodness of God. Jews and Christians [with Seyyed Hossein Nasr, we might also say Muslims] have adored God as the origin of all virtue, a well-spring of justice, wisdom, mercy, patience, strength, and love. But peripherally and implicitly, they have also grown accustomed and then attached, over the centuries, to what we may call God's anxiety. God is . . . an amalgam of several personalities in one character. Tension among these personalities makes God difficult, but it also makes him compelling, even addictive. While consciously emulating his virtues, the West has unconsciously assimilated the anxiety-inducing tension between his unity and his multiplicity.[43]

Tension between unity and multiplicity brings to mind the struggle between the Right and Left Hands of God with which Michael Lerner wrestles. But let's put that thought and the path it opens in reserve for the moment.

Miles says "Monotheism recognizes only one God: 'Hear, O Israel, the Lord is our God, the Lord is one.' The Bible insists on nothing about God more than on his unity. . . . [Y]et this same being combines several personalities." Because God is com-posed of several personalities, the "image of the human that derives from him" is open to multiple options.[44] The two major options—the Opposing Hands of God—is where we find Michael Lerner engaged in a cosmic arm wrestle. Meanwhile, Jack Miles, like

God's suicidal violence and His emotional revulsion in regard to the feminine divine. I don't mean to excuse Mumford but to ponder a possible explanation for what seems a major lapse in judgment.

In addition, Mumford—perhaps inadvertently—puts his finger on a powerful misunderstanding that correlates tightly to the civilization/"civilization" problem. That is, superego in Western conscious-ness is closely linked to Mumford's "civilization" (and to the Yahweh Jack Miles is about to unfold for us); but to be "reborn" puts one in a psychological and spiritual space that, as Marcus Borg wisely points out, *liberates* us from superego captivity. (If Mother = id, Father = superego, and Son = ego, then perhaps Daughter integrates id, ego, and superego into something for which we have as yet no name.)

Since writing the paragraphs above, I've read a 1954 essay entitled "The Uprising of Caliban" in Mumford's *Interpretations and Forecasts*. In this essay, Mumford heaps abuse on the id for the violence and slaughter, the extremities of fascism and communism, in the twentieth century. All this is suppos-edly a consequence of the overthrow of superego, an overthrow Mumford attributes to the detached intellect of scientific objectivity, leaving superego disembodied and isolated, easily lured into serving tyranny—a tyranny (coming round full circle) in service to the rapacious id.

I find this brittle and reactionary—and Mumford even supplies evidence for such judgment. On page 340, he says "The id is that part of the spiritual anatomy which Christian theology habitually refers to as the Old Adam; and it is, perhaps, significant that the Old Adam was rediscovered at the end of a century when men blandly supposed that the primitive elements in life had been wiped out by the advance of science and mechanical industry, just as the primitive races were being wiped out—or what was almost the same thing, 'civilized'—by the spread of colonial empires."

So here we have the primitive elements in life (like—I presume—the ancient peasantry) *wiped out* along with primitive races, and we're to believe the *cause* for twentieth-century violence and slaughter was an *upsurge* of id? This would be hilarious if it weren't so painfully illustrative of how incapable (or is it unwilling?) superego is to examine the civilized genocide tucked so righteously and piously within its utopian mythology. (For a series of case studies in male superego strutting toward the First World War, see Barbara Tuchman's *The Proud Tower*.)

43. Miles, *God*, 6.

44. Miles, *God*, 6.

a literary detective, is lurking around backstage, looking at earlier drafts of the script. He's looking backward not forward:

> The God whom ancient Israel worshipped arose as the fusion of a number of the gods whom a nomadic nation had met in its wanderings. A reader interested in tracking this process historically may do so through such impressive technical studies as *Yahweh and the Gods of Canaan* by William Foxwell Albright, *Canaanite Myth and Hebrew Epic* by Albright's student Frank Moore Cross, and *The Early History of God* by Cross's student Mark S. Smith. These are works of controlled imagination as well as massive erudition. But a more literary reader may be prompted by them to ask, "How did all this feel to God?" an absurd question within the methodology of historical reconstruction but an utterly ordinary one—in fact, an indispensable one—for literary appreciation.[45]

Miles goes on to say that:

> In their historical "genealogy" of God, scholars such as Albright, Cross, and Smith find that various divine personalities whom they recognize from extrabiblical sources have left traces on the pages of the Bible. A literary critic who knows their work may read this objective multiplicity back into the character of the Lord God as a literary protagonist, turning their observed inconsistencies imaginatively into God's experienced inner conflict. In this way, the emergence of monotheism from polytheism can be recovered for literature as the story of a single God struggling with himself.[46]

And that:

> If the Bible is finally a work of literature, these historically distinguishable personalities need to be read back into—and then back out of—the one God, the monos theos, who came into being as they fused. After God has been understood in his multiplicity, in short, he needs to be imagined again in his riven and difficult unity.[47]

Eventually, Jack Miles begins exploring the tell-tale traces of divinity in the sand behind God's Hebrew theater:

> Israelite monotheism in its fully developed form, while retaining one personal god—the "god of" Abraham, Isaac, and Jacob—and assigning his functions to its fusion deity, will deny the reality of all other personal gods just as it denied the reality of all high gods but its own. But the emergence of monotheism from polytheism is a matter of selective inclusion as well as wholesale exclusion. It would be wrong, wildly wrong, to suppose that anything ever predicated of

45. Miles, *God*, 20.

46. Miles, *God*, 20-21.

47. Miles, *God*, 21.

any Semitic deity ends up being predicated of Israel's deity—the sole survivor, so to speak. But it would be almost equally wrong to suppose that there is no overlap between Israel's deity and his ancient rivals. In fact, the most coherent way to imagine the Lord God of Israel is as the inclusion of the content of several ancient divine personalities in a single character.[48]

God, says Miles, is "a character with a multiple personality."[49]

Forty pages earlier, Miles puts greater specificity into this transition from polytheism into monotheism (if "transition" is a suitable term; Merlin Stone might well dispute the use of such a smooth and unconflicted word):

> In ancient Mesopotamia [says Miles], creation was often presented as the creator divinity's victory over chaos, chaos being represented as a rival deity, a fearful watery dragon, a flood monster. Imagine the curves of a great river as the living, twisting body of a gigantic snake; imagine that this snake could engulf the land in its watery coils, as the Tigris and Euphrates could indeed do, and you have the mythological mise-en-scene. There is undoubtedly an echo of that mythic battle in the Lord God's punishment of the serpent for tempting the woman, but scarcely more than an echo, for monotheistic editing has tamed the serpent into an opponent scarcely worthy of the Lord God. The ancient mythic materials have been rewritten so thoroughly that the serpent—the third personality absorbed in the emergent divine personality—is no longer a rival god but (recalling the first creation account [in the Bible]) merely one of God's creatures.
>
> As a result of this revision, the serpent's creator cannot escape responsibility for what the serpent does. But as a rarely noticed second result of the same revision, the Lord God will become a character with an interior conversation. He will rebuke the serpent; and when he does so, he will necessarily rebuke himself. What polytheism would allow to be externally directed anger against a rival deity, monotheism—even a monotheism speaking occasionally in the first person plural—must turn into the Lord God's inwardly directed regret. The appearance of divine regret, the first of its many appearances, is the first appearance of the deity as a true literary character as distinct from a mythic force or a mere meaning endowed with an allegorical voice. The peculiar, culturally determined interior life of Western man begins, in a way, with the divided interior life of the deity, and the deity's interior life begins with a creator's regret.[50]

Do we have here—the place where the "culturally determined interior life of Western man begins"—the congealing of superego, immense regret wrapped by denial in explosive wrath, intense guilt sheathed in rigid righteousness?

48. Miles, *God*, 72.

49. Miles, *God*, 72.

50. Miles, *God*, 32.

Before we go to Merlin Stone's backstage investigation and analysis, let's hear what Jack Miles has to say about God's gender or sexual orientation. God may have a fractured personality in a variety of dimensions; but, when it comes to Female Divinity, the Conflicted Old Man can hardly contain his rage. In a chapter entitled "Wife," Miles wonders "whether among the personalities that fuse in the character of God we must recognize a goddess." But, before he tries to answer that query, he says we "should note the uniformly subordinate and disparaged character of women in ancient Israelite society."[51] Miles goes on to say:

> The deeper question is not about whether women ever held power in Israelite society but whether, so to put it, there is a goddess inside Israel's God. Is God female as well as male, a mother as well as a father, a matriarch as well as a patriarch, a wife as well as a husband, and so forth?
>
> Historical criticism has drawn attention to the fact that the ancient Canaanite god El, the sky god whose personality was taken up into that of the Lord God, had a consort, Asherah, who bore monsters to battle El's younger rival, Baal, but was also, very generally, a goddess of fertility and motherhood. By identification with El, Israel's God could, so to speak, have inherited Asherah; and a few verses (a very few, to be sure) survive in which Israel's God seems to be described as male and female in successive lines—thus, by possible implication, as a divine couple. Deuteronomy 32:18, a verse in the Song of Moses, is often cited:
>
>> You were unmindful of the Rock that begot you,
>> and you forgot the God who gave you birth. (RSV)
>
> The verse may originally have ended "and you forgot the *tree* who gave you birth," rock and tree or stone altar and wooden pole standing for the divine couple El (Yahweh) and Asherah. If Yahweh and Asherah were once a couple, however, they seem to be a couple no longer. Yahweh, the Lord, is without spouse, and the text . . . invariably links Asherah with Baal rather than with him. Speaking rather loosely, Yahweh may once have shared Asherah with El; but if so, then when Yahweh became a celibate, the bereft Asherah ended up with Baal.[52]

All of this

> . . . suggests that at whatever point the Lord God became asexual (or ceased to be sexual), he did not—at least not immediately—fuse with his erstwhile consort, becoming in the process equally male and female, an ambisexual being, but rather divorced his consort and attempted to exclude the feminine from

51. Miles, *God*, 262.

52. Miles, *God*, 263-64.

his own character. The exclusion of Asherah must not be seen as, on the Lord's own part, anything less than a violently emotional revulsion.[53]

Miles notes God's "overwhelming revulsion at the thought that a goddess should be permitted to cohabit his House with him," but yet (to repeat an epigraph):

> The human male alone is not the image of God, only the male and the female together. And this duality in the image must somehow be matched by a duality in the original. It is this fact that requires us to speak of the exclusion rather than the mere absence of the feminine from God's character.[54]

In a later chapter ("Does God Lose Interest?"), Miles returns to the question of the feminine—its presence or its absence—in the character of God:

> In the section of Chapter 9 entitled "Wife," we said that the feminine was not merely absent from the developed character of God but had been actively excluded from it. At the creative start, God spoke of himself in the plural and saw himself reflected in the human couple rather than the male. But thereafter the female in the divine male was suppressed, suppressed indeed far more thoroughly than the destroyer in the divine creator. When a goddess was brought into God's temple, his reaction was almost suicidally violent, for when he destroyed Jerusalem, as we have seen, he very nearly destroyed himself.[55]

If Yahweh, for Ched Myers, is the Always Existing Eternal Being known in the West as God (who selected a certain Semitic group as His Chosen People), He is in Jack Miles' literary analysis a bit of an attention-deficit-disorder, aimlessly wandering Middle Eastern god who, after some obscure identity breakdowns and shady personality shuffling, emerged as the thin-skinned, irascible Lord God of the Israelites where, occasionally confronted with even the possibility of a Female Divinity in the neighborhood, He would blow a gasket and become irrationally violent in speech and manner. Where Ched Myers apparently finds (or simply assumes) Serene and Loving Majesty in Yahweh, Jack Miles finds a Dangerous Roily God given to explosive temper tantrums when confronted with any reminder of his Better Half.

Now I am here utilizing some antieurythmic language as a way to jolt the reader (and myself?) out of either the standard religious sanctimonious piety or the standard irreligious glazed indifference. Perfect proportion and cosmic harmony are out the window. Here we get a helpful word from Lewis Mumford:

> Gilgamesh, in the early Babylonian epic, rejected the love of the goddess, Inanna, but readily slew the bull she sent against him. Odysseus, under Calypso's enchantment, lost his initiative; and Samson, by sinking into the arms of Delilah, was shorn of his physical power. Only by spurning his sexuality,

53. Miles, *God*, 265-66.

54. Miles, *God*, 265.

55. Miles, *God*, 405.

pouring all his energies into work, will the hero have the power to perform these superhuman tasks. The pioneers of civilisation are not at home in woman's world; on their typical adventures they leave her behind. If, like Heracles, they boast of having intercourse with fifty women in one night, that boast itself shows that they confused the mere breaking of records with amorous delight—a further proof of their undeveloped erotic life.[56]

Mumford goes on to say:

> Religion, as it comes before us in the early civilisations, is plainly an upsurging of unconscious forces. These divine powers seem to erupt from the hot magma of the human soul: the gods at first have nothing to do with morality or civic duty, with love and justice. So far from being moralisers, the gods are rather pure expressions of lust, ferocity, and wanton energy: the very qualities that civilisation, seemingly for man's own good, seeks to modify and soften, or at least to divert to more pragmatic purposes. Listen to what Horus says to the enemies of his father, Osiris. 'Your arms are tied to your heads, O you evil ones. You are fettered from behind, you are the evil ones to be decapitated—you shall not exist.' This same unrestrained murderous anger belches forth likewise from the mouth of Yahweh: he who unlooses every method of extermination, from sword to plague, upon those who stand in the way of his Chosen People.
>
> One may interpret the insolent powers of these monstrous divinities, at least in part, as attempts to restore by unconscious projection the human vitalities repressed by civilisation: they were likewise a means—irrational but plausible—of creating an active superpersonal authority to make up for the absence of an archaic morality based on consensus, in a mixed urban society filled with newcomers and outsiders who had few shared values and common folkways. Finally the gods, though created independently of this need, lent countenance to social stratifications that nullified the natural harmonies and human solidarities of more primitive cultures.[57]

Well, the insolent powers of monstrous divinities may be less about the restoration of vitalities repressed than about justifying the systemic unrepressed explosion of male violence in behalf of superhuman tasks coupled with spurned sexuality. I no longer trust Mumford's inclination to protect civilization—civilization-without-quotation-marks—from contamination by "civilization," or to glorify superego while scapegoating id.

If suppression of the female was achieved via the power institutions of Western civilization (represented triumphantly in the exclusion of the Female from religious theophanies in all three Abrahamic religions), and if Western civilization globalized has wrought Global Crises of ecocidal magnitude based overwhelmingly on male

56. Mumford, *Transformations*, 49-50.

57. Mumford, *Transformations*, 52.

aggression, then attempting a psychoanalysis of the jealous Father God Almighty may be less foolish, capricious, or whimsical than it may appear at first blush. But who am I to try to strap the Old Guy to a psychotherapeutic couch? Merely a gimpy, two-legged farm boy who once asked "Why are small farms dying?" and who now asks "Why is the whole world dying?" I happen, you see, to have a personal, vested interest in the liberation of life from the demented grip of death, and I'll be—excuse the language— goddamned to go down without a fight—even if it's only on paper.

XIV

One way to look at Michael Lerner's Left and Right Hands of God is, with considerable irony, as something strangely similar to how the second-century Marcion looked at God. According to Justo Gonzalez in *The Story of Christianity*, Marcion believed that the "God and Father of Jesus is not the same as Jehovah, the God of the Old Testament." The "Father of Christians," Gonzalez says of Marcion's conviction, was loving and not vindictive: "This God requires nothing of us, but rather gives everything freely, including salvation. This God does not seek to be obeyed, but to be loved."[58] Kenneth Scott Latourette, in *A History of Christianity*, says Marcion

> . . . maintained that the God of the Old Testament and of the Jews is an evil God. . . . This God, whom he called by the Platonic term *Demiurgos*, a word also employed by the Gnostics, had created the world, with its revolting evils. . . . He also noted that the God of the Old Testament commanded bloody sacrifices to him, and, a God of battles, rejoiced in bloodshed and was vindictive. He taught that this God had given a stern and inflexible law for the governance of men, demanded obedience to it, was rigorous in his enforcement of it, and was arbitrary in his choice of favorites.[59]

Both Gonzalez and Latourette make distinctions between gnostics and Marcionites, but it seems obvious each sees the latter as a peculiar type of the former—i.e., Marcion was a gnostic. Organizationally, of course, gnostics lost the battle for the lead position within Christianity, and the orthodox won. (It's interesting, though, to look at Elizabeth Johnson's construction, or reconstruction, of the Christian Trinity, as we saw in "Going for the Juggler," in light of Elaine Pagels' chapter "God the Father/God the Mother" in *The Gnostic Gospels*. That is, Johnson's female-dominated Trinity correlates quite well with some early gnostic formulations.) But in another chapter ("One God, One Bishop") in *The Gnostic Gospels*, Pagels shows how orthodoxy began to flex its muscles. This is worth quoting at length:

> . . . by the latter part of the second century, when the orthodox insisted upon "one God," they simultaneously validated the system of governance in which

58. Gonzalez, *Story*, 61.

59. Latourette, *History*, 126.

the church is ruled by "one bishop." Gnostic modification of monotheism was taken—and perhaps intended—as an attack upon that system. For when gnostic and orthodox Christians discussed the nature of God, they were at the same time debating the issue of *spiritual authority*.

This issue dominates one of the earliest writings we have from the church at Rome—a letter attributed to Clement, called Bishop of Rome (c. 90-100). As spokesman for the Roman church, Clement wrote to the Christian community in Corinth at a time of crisis: certain leaders of the Corinthian church had been divested of power. Clement says that "a few rash and self-willed people" drove them out of office: "those of no reputation [rose up] against those with reputation, the fools against the wise, the young against the old." Using political language, he calls this "a rebellion" and insists that the deposed leaders be restored to their authority: he warns that they must be feared, respected, and obeyed.

On what grounds? Clement argues that God, the God of Israel, alone rules all things: he is the lord and master whom all must obey; he is the judge who lays down the law, punishing rebels and rewarding the obedient. But how is God's rule actually administered? Here Clement's theology becomes practical: God, he says, delegates his "authority of reign" to "rulers and leaders on earth." Who are these designated rulers? Clement answers that they are bishops, priests, and deacons. Whoever refuses to "bow the neck" and obey church leaders is guilty of insubordination against the divine master himself. Carried away with his argument, Clement warns that whoever disobeys the divinely ordained authorities "receives the death penalty!"

This letter marks a dramatic moment in the history of Christianity. For the first time, we find here an argument for dividing the Christian community between "the clergy" and "the laity." The church is to be organized in terms of a strict order of superiors and subordinates. Even within the clergy, Clement insists on ranking each member, whether bishop, priest, or deacon, "in his own order": each must observe "the rules and commandments" of his position at all times.

Many historians are puzzled by this letter. What, they ask, was the basis for the dispute in Corinth? What *religious* issues were at stake? The letter does not tell us that directly. But this does not mean that the author ignores such issues. I suggest that he makes his own point—his religious point—entirely clear: he intended to establish the Corinthian church on the model of the divine authority. As God reigns in heaven as master, lord, commander, judge, and king, so on earth he delegates his rule to members of the church hierarchy, who serve as generals who command an army of subordinates, kings who rule over "the people"; judges who preside in God's place.

Clement may simply be stating what Roman Christians took for granted—and what Christians outside of Rome, in the early second century, were coming to accept. The chief advocates of this theory, not surprisingly, were the bishops themselves. Only a generation later, another bishop, Ignatius of Antioch in Syria, more than a thousand miles from Rome, passionately defended the same principle. But Ignatius went further than Clement. He defended the three ranks—bishops, priests, and deacons—as a hierarchical order that mirrors the divine hierarchy in heaven. As there is only one God in heaven, Ignatius declares, so there can be only one bishop in the church. "One God, one bishop"—this became the orthodox slogan. Ignatius warns "the laity" to revere, honor, and obey the bishop "as if he were God." For the bishop, standing at the pinnacle of the church hierarchy, presides "in the place of God." Who, then, stands below God? The divine council, Ignatius replies. And as God rules over that council in heaven, so the bishop on earth rules over a council of priests. The heavenly divine council, in turn, stands above the apostles; so, on earth, the priests rule over the deacons—and all three of these rule over "the laity."[60]

I don't know if we could find a clearer illustration of the meaning and implication of "the monarchical model" of God or of how far back in Christian theology the construct goes: as God rules in heaven, so the bishop rules on earth.

XV

Before we visit an interesting modern gnostic—I mean Andrew Harvey—let's remember that we are, in theory, exploring a notion of Dorothy Dinnerstein's: namely, the psychocultural and political manifestations of "mother-raised children" are hugely consequential for our growing Global Crises, that the ancient and accrued distortions of gender may well represent the beating heart of our predicament, a predicament immensely hard to examine precisely because its underlying dynamics are so normative and even "sacred." In this context, we are also looking (in a somewhat wandering way) at earnest proposals from sincere thinkers—Michael Lerner, for instance—proposals or diagrammatic "framings" important to consider in this larger effort. We're looking for linkage between mother-raised children and male domination in a spectrum from everyday behavior to formal governance to religious imagery. So, with that in mind, let's spend a little time testing the strength, so to speak, of God's Left and Right Arms.

As we have seen in section IX of this essay, Lerner's Left Hand of God is the Loving and Kind Hand, while the Right Hand is a Cocked Fist ready to utilize violence in order to overcome always-lurking evil. Lerner's opening paragraphs in his Introduction read like this:

> The unholy alliance of the political Right and Religious Right threatens to destroy the America we love. It also threatens to generate a popular revulsion against God and religion by identifying them with militarism, ecological

60. Pagels, *Gnostic*, 34-35.

irresponsibility, fundamentalist antagonism to science and rational thought, and insensitivity to the needs of the poor and the powerless.

In the following pages, I will explain how a progressive spiritual politics can help rescue this country from its current self-destructive course. By addressing the real spiritual and moral crisis in the daily lives of most Americans, a movement with a progressive spiritual vision would provide an alternate solution to both the intolerant and militarist politics of the Right and the current misguided, visionless, and often spiritually empty politics of the Left.

The first section of this book details the spiritual and psychological needs that the Right was able to address in ways that allowed it to grow powerful and that the Left ignored and misunderstood (thus precipitating its decline) over the past thirty years. In the second section, I'll present a Progressive Spiritual Covenant with America that could advance a progressive political revival in the coming years.[61]

Rabbi Lerner, by his third paragraph, is already wandering in a less-than-convincing direction. That is, he says the Right, over the past thirty years, *has* addressed spiritual and psychological needs, while the Left ignored and misunderstood those needs, even as its politics were misguided, visionless, and spiritually empty.

I would put this quite differently. First of all, the impact of the scientific revolution, especially as it incrementally demolished (or at least increasingly etherealized) the conventional and orthodox conception of God, reached, we might say, a cultural and religious tipping point in the 1960s. From then on, if not earlier, the popular Left began to be without a clear and decisive God concept, while the popular Right began to harden in on its orthodoxy and "fundamentals," even as it became more disbelieving or at least agnostic in regard to science: not only evolution but also its more recent scorn of global warming and climate change.

The Johnson administration represents both a zenith and the nadir of "liberalism" and therefore a zenith and nadir of the popular Left. Its zenith was civil rights legislation, finally breaking the quasi-legal back of racial segregation, and its nadir was the brutal escalation of the war on Vietnam. Antiwar sentiment forced Johnson not to seek a second term; civil rights caused the racist white South to switch party affiliation from Democrat to Republican; Martin Luther King found Chicago more openly hostile and racist than Birmingham; big, white unions sided with the cops who beat antiwar protesters at the Democratic Party convention in Chicago; hippies mocked "The System" in a way disgusting to Archie Bunker; long-haired young people hugged trees; women began to go around without bras; persons with same-sex inclinations started to come out of the closet.

It's not a stretch to say that the civilizational system was under attack from Mexico City to Paris to Prague to Chicago (see Mark Kurlansky's *1968: The Year That Rocked the World* for something of a guided tour and series of case studies), and we

61. Lerner, *Left*, 1.

might say that God came to the rescue of civilization. He came to the rescue by aligning His Right Hand with the most extreme right hands within the Republican Party (and of those within the Democratic Party who jumped ship to the Republicans), pushing out, in the process, virtually all the socially liberal Republicans who stood, for example, for women's rights or environmental protection. God was deployed to save civilization from sinking into a filthy, chaotic sea of humanist, feminist, environmentalist, multicultural paganism. And civilization—put Mumford's quotation marks around the word if you must—has steadily demonstrated its underlying brutality. The Right Hand of God refuses to go down in a way that's not only parallel to but joined at the hip with the refusal of civilization to go down. As Mumford says, civilization's traumatic institutions have survived precisely because of God's protection and the "heavenly sanctions of kingship."

XVI

We'll come back to Michael Lerner in a bit, but let's spend a little time poking around in the upheavals of the 1960s. If there is a person who openly predicted the countercultural explosion of the 1960s, that person (to the best of my knowledge) is Paul Goodman. His book is *Growing Up Absurd*, published in 1960. Goodman says in a chapter called "Social Animal" (the subjects are sex and marriage, with considerable focus on the "Beat Generation") that:

> If the highest aim in life is to achieve a normal marriage and raise healthy children, we can understand the preoccupation with Psychology, for the parents do not have much activity of their own to give rules to the family life. The thousand manuals of sex technique and happy marriage, then, have the touching dignity of evangelical tracts, as is indeed their tone; they teach how to be saved, and there is no other way to be saved.
>
> On the children is lavished an avalanche of attention. They cannot possibly reward so much attention, and the young father, at least, soon gets pretty bored and retires to his Do-It-Yourself. Now it used to be said that middle-class parents frustrate the children more, to meet high standards, but the frustration is acceptable because it leads to an improved status, esteemed by the children; the lower classes, on the contrary, are more permissive; nor would the discipline be accepted, because the father is disesteemed. What then is the effect, in the ranch houses, if the discipline is maintained, because the standard is high, but the status is disesteemed, first by the father himself, who talks cynically about it; then by the mother, who does not respect it; then by the growing children? *Is it possible to maintain and pass on a middle-class standard without belief in its productive and cultural mission?*
>
> I wonder if we are not here describing the specific genesis of a Beat Generation: young men who (1) cannot break away from the father who has been

good to them, but who (2) simply cannot affirm father's values; and (3) there are no other dominant social values to compensate. If this is the case, where now there are thousands of these young men, there will be hundreds of thousands. *The organized system is the breeding ground of a Beat Generation.*[62]

If this is not anticipation of the hippie phenomenon, I don't know what to call it! However, what Goodman fails to see (I'll quote a fairly long paragraph here, complete with parentheses) is that the social problems he delves into are not just confined to boys:

> (I say the "young men and boys" rather than the "young people" because the problems I want to discuss in this book belong primarily, in our society, to the boys: how to be useful and make something of oneself. A girl does not *have* to, she is not expected to, "make something" of herself. Her career does not have to be self-justifying, for she will have children, which is absolutely self-justifying, like any other natural or creative act. With this background, it is less important, for instance, what job an average young woman works at till she is married. The quest for the glamour job is given at least a little substance by its relation to a "better" marriage. Correspondingly, our "youth troubles" are boys' troubles—female delinquency is sexual: "incorrigibility" and unmarried pregnancy. Yet as every woman knows, these problems are intensely interesting to women, for if the boys do not grow to be men, where shall the women find men? If the husband is running the rat race of the organized system, there is not much father for the children.)[63]

There's a lot of substance in Goodman's comments; yet Dorothy Dinnerstein, as we have seen and will continue to see, reveals how deeply poisonous the conventional gender divide really is. (In this sense, Dinnerstein's remark about Norman O. Brown, that "one cannot imagine Brown's emotionally hermaphroditic men burping and diapering babies," may fit Paul Goodman too.)

But I think we have to treat Goodman as Dinnerstein treats Brown: honoring him for keen and crucial insights, not giving him a pass for anything misleading or stupid. That said, we'll listen again to Goodman's actual speech rather than an expurgation. Here he is, talking about conflicts between Liberty and Equality, Science and Faith, Technology and Syndicalism (these are Goodman's capitalizations), and he says

> . . . experience has taught that the failure in one of these ideals at once entails failure in others. For instance, failure in social justice weakens political freedom, and this compromises scientific and religious autonomy. "If we continue to be without a socialist movement," says Frank Marquart, "we may end up without a labor movement." The setback of progressive education makes the

---

62. Goodman, *Growing*, 122-23.
63. Goodman, *Growing*, 13.

compulsory school system more hopeless, and this now threatens permissiveness and sexual freedom; and so forth.[64]

Note that Goodman doesn't say socialism needs the labor movement so much as *the labor movement may die without socialism*! Once again, Goodman—or Frank Marquart—was amazingly prophetic. As I write (late February of 2011), the newly elected Republican governor in Wisconsin and the Republican state legislature are attempting to break public sector unions—with, it must be added, unprecedented public protest in and around the state capitol. Yet it's true that lack of socialist comprehension has been at the core of union disintegration in the years and decades after 1968. (Could deindustrialization have occurred without the prior empire alignment of unions?) Governor Scott Walker is only providing a final blow to a severely weakened set of far-from-radical institutions.[65]

To some extent, union disintegration was the result of libertarian, countercultural energy undermining what Michael Lerner calls the "racist, sexist, and homophobic attitudes that had been part of the unconscious structure of Western societies for millennia" as they were "exposed and challenged in unprecedented ways" by the new social movements and cultural upheavals of the '60s and '70s.[66] (We can add to Lerner's list another threat to convention: the dawning realization that Western affluence is not only ecologically unsustainable, but its unsustainability is in urgent need of radical political attention. This implies, and to some extent necessitates, a "going backwards"—i.e., select technological retrogressions guided by ethical considerations and ecological reconciliation—for which we are not only unprepared psychologically, but for which our submersion in affluent "progress" has taught us is as obsolete as the spinning wheel and as extinct as the passenger pigeon. That is, we'll willingly consent to a "going backward" only if "retrogression" is culturally lubricated by the undoing of societal despotism and constricted sexuality. The way out of global crisis is a kind of Green "backwardness" infused with spiritual liberation in which gender reconciliation and sexual expressiveness are core dynamics. Of course those are precisely the dynamics feared and hated by the Right Hand of God and viewed with acute anxiety by the Left Hand. But only with the embrace of these dynamics will we begin to realize that the "backwardness" we've been taught to fear is a psychoreligious device, a civilized construct, that has kept us in the dominion of death in life.)

The lack of socialist—and psychoanalytical—comprehension is resulting in an attempt by the Right to crack unions entirely. The result is likely to be powerfully

64. Goodman, *Growing*, 226-27.

65. See the collected essays in *A Whole Which Is Greater: Why the Wisconsin "Uprising" Failed*, edited by David Kast and myself. The essay "Who's Awake in Clark County?" by Mike McCabe is the most pertinent in regard to the atrophy of unions. See also McCabe's *Blue Jeans in High Places*, published in 2014. And now—late winter of 2015—the Wisconsin state legislature has passed a "right to work" dismemberment of *private sector unions*, a bill Governor Walker (with presidential aspirations) quickly signed into law.

66. Lerner, *Left*, 168.

paradoxical, with the Left—hopefully—waking up from its affluent, utopian somnolence to discover its eutopian backbone is in urgent need of exercise and strengthening. (Of course this political awakening is largely led, not by white men, but by people of color, like Kshama Sawant of Seattle and William Barber of North Carolina.) Socialism, especially in the form advocated by R. H. Tawney, is a ripe, rich fruit waiting to be plucked and eaten. But it takes spiritual strength—spiritual transformation—to reach that fruit.

Dinnerstein, meanwhile, focuses attention on the failure of young men in the New Left to join women as "unequivocally equal collaborators." She says "This is a necessity that mother-raised men find it painfully hard to accept, and that mother-raised women find it intolerably bruising to urge upon them."[67] Dinnerstein, in her final chapter, goes over the same ground Goodman has gone over. But she draws a different conclusion than Goodman in regard to the relationship between women and men. She says of the countercultural upheaval that it

> . . . has to be seen as part of a wider surge of revulsion against contemporary civilization, a revulsion that took new, acute form in a new generation which had grown up in a world silently and intangibly permeated with the possibility that civilization may not, after all, extend into the indefinite future, and for whom a kind of bone-marrow detachment from the past became possible. *What this mood of revulsion and detachment did at its first peak was force the beginning of a redefinition, by young men themselves, of the traditional male role.*
>
> In the milieu from which the new feminism springs, men tended (mainly tacitly) to reject many aspects of traditional masculine responsibility and to usurp many aspects of traditional feminine authority. At the same time, they remained understandably unwilling to relinquish traditional male privilege. This left women stripped of old forms of support, respect, and protection, and of old outlets for self-assertion, but still as disparaged, subordinated, and exploited as ever. Male leadership of historic endeavor necessarily became less tolerable as that endeavor came to embrace what had always been female areas of expertise. It was one thing for women busy with their own traditional responsibilities to enjoy vicarious participation in public effort at which they themselves had no trained competence and in relation to which their own ventilation of counter-considerations formed one side of a vital balance. It is quite another thing to expect them to take part as menial assistants in a public effort for certain features of which they themselves are by tradition and training clearly better qualified than those they assist, and in relation to which they have no autonomous, unique counterbalancing role to play.[68]

Dinnerstein also says that

67. Dinnerstein, *Mermaid*, 272.
68. Dinnerstein, *Mermaid*, 268.

... women have always informally and deeply known, and been heavily relied upon ... to affirm on an everyday, folk-knowledge level—for example, that personal truth, one's own intuitive grasp of what is going on, is ignored at one's own grave risk; that large-scale politics are pompous and farcical; that science and logic are a limited and overrated part of our array of techniques for exploring reality; that face-to-face relations are in a basic sense the point of life; that flowers, gossip, the smell of food, the smiling of babies, embody and symbolize central human values—men now seized from their hands and made into a big and characteristically overblown deal, a newly discovered historic tool too significant for women to wield except as men's assistants.[69]

Nevertheless, says Dinnerstein, there were and are "two streams of feeling embodied in this burst of consciousness [that] were and remain largely unreconciled."[70] These two streams are a "rebirth of broad historic concern" and an "explosively accelerated public reformulation of the personalistic, here-and-now-oriented trend that had begun after Hiroshima."[71] Out of all this came

... certain general principles: that expressive, aesthetic, humanistic values must shape the new world; that eroticism must permeate history, not be encapsulated in genital sex; that first-hand emotionally vivid experience, not theory-dominated policy which violates such experience, must shape social action.

Nobody knows, of course, how such principles can be implemented, given (a) the nature of normal human psychopathology and (b) the centralized economic-political structures on which our high technology seems to depend. Indeed, even to approach such knowledge—to diagnose that pathology, or to start finding out how much centralization is really necessary and which benefits of high technology we are willing to relinquish for the sake of smaller-scale more humanly flexible societal forms—is dauntingly difficult.[72]

What's dauntingly difficult is not so much the formulation of corrective policy—elements of that are pretty well in hand, at least intellectually—as the seemingly unmovable "sexual arrangements and human malaise" embedded in gender structure, civilized institutions, and in Abrahamic religious certitudes. To get to this "new world" of smaller-scale humanly flexible societal norms means achieving release from the immobilizing energy field of the prevailing restrictive normality that's both civilizational and religious. It is this subjective psychocultural bondage we are here addressing. Its most righteous face is embodied in the political Right; but much of the liberal Left is sitting in a muddled state of dead-weight bewilderment, unwilling to struggle through

69. Dinnerstein, *Mermaid*, 267.
70. Dinnerstein, *Mermaid*, 264.
71. Dinnerstein, *Mermaid*, 263.
72. Dinnerstein, *Mermaid*, 264.

the moral constrictions of inherited religious understandings and cultural conventions. Much of this bewilderment, as weird, perhaps, as it might at first appear, is due to the collapse of God. As George Lakoff says in his *Don't Think of an Elephant!*: "One of the problems is that the progressive religious community, particularly progressive Christianity, doesn't really know how to express its own theology in a way that makes its politics clear, whereas conservative Christians do know the direct link between their theology and their politics."[73]

I differ with Lakoff when he says the progressive religious community doesn't know *how to express* its theology in a way that makes its politics clear. I would say the muddled state of progressive politics is a consequence *of the collapse* of orthodox spiritual authority and the subsequent confusion that is bound to follow (i.e., the Dark Night of the Soul) before a new and richer clarity can be achieved. You can't very well express what you are still unable (or unwilling) to formulate. (I say "unwilling" because I see on the Left an enormous amount of risk-averse intellectual laziness packed in don't-rock-the-boat morality. It is this timid—but also stubborn—morality that accounts for much of the intellectual, political, and spiritual sluggardness endemic in our time.) Dorothy Dinnerstein has an observation on that problem, too:

> The fading away of God the Father, the righteous judge, should in principle motivate his lopsidedly developed offspring to learn how to judge and govern themselves, but so far this has not happened. The loss of supernatural moral guidance in the light of scientific reason has not made people more grown-up; it has only unleashed the amoral greed of infancy.
>
> Inextricable from the notion that nature is our semi-sentient early mother is the notion that she is inherently inexhaustible, that if she does not provide everything we would like to have it is because she does not want to, that her treasure is infinite and can if necessary be taken by force. This view of Mother Earth is in turn identical with the view of woman as Earth Mother, a bottomless source of richness, a being not human enough to have needs of an importance as primary, as self-evident, as the importance of our own needs, but voluntary and conscious enough so that if she does not give us what we expect she is withholding it on purpose and we are justified in getting it from her any way we can. The murderous infantilism of our relation to nature follows inexorably from the murderous infantilism of our sexual arrangements. To outgrow the one we must outgrow the other.[74]

Well, yes to the diagnosis of amoral greed, although a lot of amoral greed is built into the normality of our civilized and functionally imperialist standard of living. (Aren't we all to celebrate a continually growing economy?) Even deeper is fear of violating inherited norms of morality and how we compensate for that fear: if we can't have voluptuous life, we can at least accumulate lots of stuff. (This is Psychoanalysis

73. Lakoff, *Don't*, 102.

74. Dinnerstein, *Mermaid*, 109-10.

101.) But we also have to realize that superego has traditionally kept id in a state of "infantile" captivity; the "loss of supernatural moral guidance" therefore opens the infantile playpen, which may be another way to describe the "democratization" of aristocratic self-indulgence—a long-standing merger of greed and rationalized violence. To democratize aristocratic entitlement is to unleash amoral greed as a common standard. Cultures based on "that's enough" have been discredited and extinguished. To have the supernatural moral guidance of God the Father in a state of slow disintegration doesn't automatically result in the discovery (or rediscovery) of subsistent eutopian Spirit. The transition from God to Spirit, from civilization to Green culture—a transition we have already begun to enter—is difficult, jumbled, and confused. The disintegration of theism will resolve itself in a rich and complex pantheism or panentheism; but the prolonged, bitter, painful, alienated and alienating intermediate zone is a weird mirror reflection of sterile atheism and rigid fundamentalism, grim commercial meaninglessness and cultural dissatisfaction. The cage is falling apart; yet—for all our dissatisfactions and yearnings—we're afraid of the freedom that's become urgently necessary. We don't know how to ethically appropriate that freedom; traditional morality holds us back.

Dinnerstein's larger subject, of course, is the malaise deriving from the lopsidedly developed gender psychology, culture, economics, and politics arising from mother-raised children. But she doesn't connect God the Father to the disastrous greed of our economic relation to nature. Yet *civilization* (the monarchical model) is that connection. Aristocracy is our long-standing standard of envy and entitlement. As Mumford and Brown teach, the systematic expropriation of nature's bounty and the authoritarian control of human lives (including our sexual lives) are exactly what the traumatic institutions of civilization are built to achieve and perpetuate. This is the psychodynamic legacy of civility, the murderous infantilism of an aristocratic "standard of living" exploded to "democratic" and global dimensions. To outgrow this murderous infantilism—from rape to militarism to mindless consumerism to ecological plunder—is to move from utopia to eutopia, from hierarchical authoritarianism (even if disguised as "democratic" capitalist consumerism) to a decentralized blend of the socialized large-scale and the private, cooperative, and communal small-scale. But the shedding of envy and resentment means that God the Father, the "righteous" superego judge, has more stages of fading and levels of shrinking to pass through before we're ready for the liberation we yearn for but reflexively resist.

XVII

We can begin to zero in on why Michael Lerner's book—although sincere, and in some descriptive ways wonderfully insightful—is reduced to a kind of moralistic carping precisely because it ties progressive spiritual politics to God, Yahweh, or, in Lerner's usage, YHVH:

From my standpoint, YHVH, the God of the universe, is the force of trans-formation that makes possible the healing of the world, the shift from what is to what ought to be. The good news of Judaism, Christianity, and many other spiritual traditions is that the circumstances of the world are not fixed, that the world can be changed and healed, and that this is precisely our task. And what makes that change possible, is that a God exists in the universe in Whose image we are made, and our task is to be partners with that God in the transformation of the world.[75]

Well, Michael Lerner depicts God or Yahweh much as Ched Myers does. Their God is eternal, God of the universe. This is not a hobo God, such as Jack Miles tracks through the blowing sand and prickly thorn bushes of the Middle East. Lerner's God, like My-ers', is metaphysically ahistorical while posing as suprahistorical. Theism of this sort inflates an accrued cultural construct (God, Yahweh, YHVH) to an always-existing Supreme Being and thereby asserts the foundational nature of this always-existing Su-preme Being in a manner exactly like (for instance) Augustine's use of Adam's semen by which to propound a doctrine of original sin. Mythic construct becomes historical fact. Factual—we might even say "scientific"—analysis and assertion, in both cases, rests on a base of mythological, ahistorical conviction representing itself as supra-historical truth. Here's Lerner again, this time in a carefully laundered version of the Hebrew Exodus:

The central story of the Torah is that of a people who are enslaved and then through divine intervention freed from slavery. Its message is one of hope: we *can* overcome oppression, the world can be transformed. In Judaism, the force that makes change possible is YHVH, the God-force of the universe. This God-force, a force of healing and transformation (*tikkun*), is the ulti-mate reality of the universe, the force that has shaped the universe from the start, the truth whose will toward goodness is manifested in the command to "pursue justice," to "love one's neighbor as oneself," and never to "oppress the stranger." This God is a loving being whose essential nature is compassionate, caring, forgiving, generous, and peace loving, even though God can at times be angry at the persistence of injustice and our indifference to the suffering we cause by participating in oppressive social or political systems. God wants us to care not only for ourselves but for everyone on the planet because we have all been created in the divine image. God needs us as partners in the heal-ing and transformation of the world and as stewards of the well-being of the planet, and sometimes gets irritated or upset when we misuse God or Torah or Judaism as a vehicle to escape doing what we know we must do to heal the world. Although ultimately God cares for us, has compassion for our straying from our mission, God desperately needs us to get back on the path of healing the world, even with all our imperfections and weaknesses, as long as we show

75. Lerner, *Left*, 110.

compassion for others. This is how God is understood from the standpoint of the Left Hand of God.[76]

I'm not sure what Michael Lerner intends by "Torah." Does he mean the entire body of Jewish biblical literature or the first five books of the Bible? It's true that the later prophets said wise and compassionate things; but to read the "central story" of Exodus through Joshua is to witness the acts of a God who not only kills but who kills the populations of *entire cities* and who *commands massacre and extermination*, even while minutely detailing the obligations toward and deference due the Levites, the priestly class of the Israelites.[77]

We have, in Lerner's passage above, the equivalent of a warm and fuzzy Sunday School lesson, as devoid of scriptural detail and historical realism as it is larded with syrupy sentimentality. If *this* is the Left Hand of God, the core understanding needed for progressive spiritual politics, we are being asked to bite as deeply into the apple of fantasy denial as when America is celebrated for its spread of democracy from shore to shore, with liberty and justice for all, with no mention made of conquest, extermination of Native peoples, or the brutal enslavement of black Africans. And then Lerner carps about the Left's capacity to ignore and misunderstand America's spiritual and psychological needs!

76. Lerner, *Left*, 83.

77. Chapter 2 in W. Michael Slattery's *Jesus the Warrior?* is entitled "War & Inter-Group Lethal Violence in the Hebrew Scriptures." In that chapter, Slattery says "That holy war in the Hebrew scriptures focused on the centrality of YHWH (i.e., Yahweh) in the lives of the ancient Israelites cannot be overstated." In that chapter's final paragraph, on page 51, Slattery says: "In conclusion, we may observe the following principal tenets on the treatment of war and lethal violence in the Hebrew scriptures. The earlier scriptures of Exodus, Joshua, Judges and I and II Samuel implicitly accept the use of war and refrain from moral questioning of its validity because they essentially accept that war is conducted at the behest and direction of YHWH. It is YHWH who delivers the enemies of the Israelites into defeat and it is YHWH who is the actual warrior; the Israelites are merely the agents or instruments for enactment of the will of YHWH. That the practice of the brutal ban was employed by the Israelites at the direction of YHWH cannot be contested in terms of scriptural interpretation. . . ." But what, exactly, is the meaning of this word "ban"? Slattery explains on page 42: "Deuteronomy 20 . . . presents a provocative case of total annihilation of Israelite enemies (Hittites, Amorites, Canaanites, Perizzites, Hivites, and Jebusites) who, prior to the Israelite immigration, had occupied and resided on the land that Israel claimed was being given to them by their God. This is the ban oft referenced in the Hebrew scriptures. Under the ban, every living enemy of Israel—all men, women, children, inclusive even of living animals—was to be put to the sword, unlike the possible negotiated peace with Israel's enemies outside of this land where all the men were killed and the women, children, and livestock were placed in forced slavery, when the Israelites fought and beat them." Where is God's Left Hand in this picture?

Meanwhile, Walter Wink, on page 84 of *The Powers That Be*, says "The violence of the Old Testament has always been a scandal to Christianity. The church has usually ducked the issue, either by allegorizing the Old Testament or by rejecting it. Biblical scholar Raymund Schwager points out that there are six hundred passages of explicit violence in the Hebrew Bible, one thousand verses where God's own violent actions of punishment are described, a hundred passages where Yahweh expressly commands others to kill people, and several stories where God irrationally kills or tries to kill for no apparent reason (for example, Exod. 4:24-26). Violence, Schwager concludes, is easily the most often mentioned activity in the Hebrew Bible."

This is altogether too disingenuous. It's not that the absence of a clear and defining spiritual narrative on the Left isn't important and even crucial. It *is* important and crucial. But when Lerner talks about the "deep-seated sociohistorical and psychological reasons why the Left, and particularly male leftists, are fearful of and resistant to a progressive spirituality,"[78] he would do well to follow his subsequent analysis (I'll quote it in a moment) of how girls and boys are raised, rather than complain about "the Left's hostility toward religion"[79]:

> Despite all the advances of the past century, our culture continues to inculcate patriarchal values as it educates and socializes its children. It continues to value strength over compassion, power over vulnerability, "hardness" over "softness," and to view the first of each of these pairs as appropriate for men and the second as appropriate for women.
>
> As psychologists have pointed out, parents work hard, consciously as well as unconsciously, to ensure that boys develop the masculine traits they will need to succeed. Mothers, who are usually our first care-givers and thus embody the nurturing traits of femininity for us, tend to push sons away from them earlier than they do daughters so that boys will learn independence, a quality we assign to men.
>
> Boys learn early, from their own parents, from TV, and from the surrounding society, that to be considered a man they must strongly disidentify with their mothers and suppress the "feminine" inside of them. Becoming the school-yard bully, greeting a friend by giving him a punch in the arm, focusing on guns and superheros and video games that feature war and conquest and killing, emphasizing victory in competitive sports, making fun of girls— all these are ways that preadolescent and adolescent boys learn to repress that part of them that actually wants very much to run back to mother; to be accepted by her, embraced by her, and even to be like her.
>
> Girls, meanwhile, are given the mixed message that they should identify with their mothers and yet that they should not value that identity. This mixed message causes serious self-esteem problems in preadolescent girls, manifested in falling grades, eating disorders, and other self-destructive behaviors.
>
> Given this culture, it's understandable why so many of the politicians and pundits of the Left—women as well as men—gravitate toward worldviews that will make them look hard, tough, and powerful. No wonder, then, that so many on the Left find spirituality, religion, and even words like *love, caring, kindness,* and *generosity* so very threatening. These Leftists have already put themselves in the position of championing causes like peace ("sissies who are scared to fight"), the environment ("tree huggers") and social justice ("liberal do-gooders") that the Right puts down as soft and girlish. From a marketing standpoint, many Leftists believe, the central challenge in a patriarchal society

78. Lerner, *Left,* 153-54.

79. Lerner, *Left,* 158.

is to create an approach to politics that will appeal to men, and that means showing them that they are not going to be too vulnerable to the charges of softness. They feel the sting when California's governor, Arnold Schwarzenegger, decries the "girlie men" of the Left.

For many on the Left, the solution seems obvious: Cling with tenacious ferocity to the world of science, with its "hard facts," and to a scientism that dismisses spirituality and religion as lacking the hard foundation that facts provide. Distance yourself from anything that suggests emotionality and vulnerability. Build your strategies around the accumulation of power, not around the maximizing of loving experiences. Stay away from the talk of awe and wonder about nature or about unnecessary suffering, and instead quantify, quantify, quantify. Show that you've got measurements that can back your case, that you are not relying on any of that silly girlish stuff like feelings and intuitions—forms of knowing that cannot be verified through empirical observation and confirmed through redoing the experiment under controlled circumstances. Show them you are tough.[80]

Well, there's a lot in those paragraphs that's solid and that dovetails nicely with Dorothy Dinnerstein's analysis, especially her childhood gender observations. Yet the problem with Lerner's overall outlook is that he never calls God or Yahweh or YHVH "He." Lerner omits the gender identity of the Torah God while dressing this ferocious male God in a motherly skirt of all-embracing kindness. (Incidentally, to render Yahweh as YHVH is a condensation called tetragram. It's done because the full name of God is considered too sacred to pronounce.) This divine cross-dressing helps explain the pleading sentimentality in the "central story" passage previously quoted, where the "God-force" is the "ultimate reality of the universe," the force that "has shaped the universe from the start," a force that's also a "loving being whose essential nature is compassionate, caring," and so on. Although "God can at times be angry," irritated or upset, (He) *desperately needs us* to get back on the path. But which path is that, exactly?

It's one thing to hit leftists for an obsession with scientific "hard facts"; that's a fair accusation, especially with the technofix crowd; but it's off the mark to imply (as I think Lerner does imply) that rigorous scholarship shouldn't get in the way of "feelings and intuitions." (This is exactly the defensiveness of fundamentalism: don't ever allow honest scholarship to upset sacred mythology.) When I see what he's doing—dressing the fire-breathing Yahweh in a pretty pink apron, cinching up a feminine sidesaddle on a Trojan horse—I can't help concluding there's something deeply conflicted and unresolved in Lerner's Left Hand analysis. His sentimentality is a kind of intellectual quicksand in which he is himself stuck.

The reality is that we are in the midst of a powerfully transformative process that could go any one of three major directions: global catastrophe, aristocratic restoration,

80. Lerner, *Left*, 154-55.

or Green socialism. The wackiest of the wacky Right actually yearn for catastrophe: catastrophe is a key element in their religious script. The more cynical and calculating, including the *Realpolitik* atheists among them who are contemptuous of democracy, seem to be angling for aristocratic restoration. Meanwhile, an unformed turbulence, as yet without explicit narrative, is churning in human beings around the world. (As I write, in February of 2011, Egypt is in the midst of a huge popular uprising in the wake of another such uprising in Tunisia—the so-called Arab Spring.) If the dust eventually settles in favor of Green socialism, a new spirituality with a reformulated conception of the sacred will come into popular understanding and common practice. It will be servanthood and stewardship, but it will not be YHVH or Yahweh or any other orthodox depiction of God. It will not be a house built on a foundation of sentimental quicksand.

If the Right Hand of God is hard and brutal, the Left Hand is soft and sentimental. The task is not to replace the former with the latter. The first represents fierce male dominance, the second represents cloying female deference. As gender projections, they accurately depict Dorothy Dinnerstein's "lopsidedly developed offspring." The task is to dissolve *both* in favor of fuller understanding—a more mature understanding, historically deep, neither brutal nor sentimental. Mother, Father, Son, and Daughter—while still mythological and therefore open to abuse—restores the suppressed Mother, puts the (wildly inflated) Father in his sequential place, acknowledges the Son, and welcomes the Daughter. With this configuration, we get to keep gender in our mythological depiction of the divine; but it'll not be necessary—as a recent political aphorism has it—to put lipstick on a pig.

XVIII

There are odd and endearing eruptions in this ongoing struggle of unfinished gnostic/orthodox conflict. Andrew Harvey, for instance, author of *Son of Man: The Mystical Path to Christ*, is a modern gnostic who's a virtual fireworks display of gnostic articulations ("this new mystical understanding of Mary as complete and full divine Mother and of Christ as the Sacred Androgyne-Divine-Child, born of the total union of the complete Father and fully recognized and fully celebrated divine Mother"[81]) even as he recognizes and affirms the transformational intent of the kingdom of God proclamation. In a set of paragraphs explicating Jesus' injunction to love enemies, Harvey says:

> Only such an unconditional love of all beings—the love that Jesus himself had—could make anyone transparent enough for the Spirit to blaze through them at all moments; only such an unconditional love of all beings could transform anyone into an instrument of the Kingdom in the real and give

81. Harvey, *Son*, 173.

whoever practiced it the undivided consciousness and unshakable inner strength to fight peacefully for the establishment of the Kingdom without being exhausted by suffering or hatred. When philosophical and political commentators patronize Jesus' vision of forgiving one's enemies as "utopian," they do so from a far lower level of awareness than the one Jesus is trying to raise humanity to; they do not know what an awakened mystic like Jesus knows about the power of the Spirit to transform all things and so they imagine that their "bitter experience" is wisdom.

For Jesus, however, for one who has seen the Kingdom and known it as his only and final reality, the only ultimately "practical" politics must be one that changes definitively the consciousness of the human race; for only such a change can significantly alter the conditions of cyclical violence that entrap all societies and deform all eras of history. A political vision that accepts human evil and hatred in the name of "sober pragmatism" in fact keeps that evil and hatred alive.

Jesus teaching of loving one's enemies is not the cry of a utopian dreamer; it is the announcement of a law of transformation, a law of mystical evolution that everyone needs to practice if the race is to have a chance to create those conditions of authentic peace and harmony in which the Kingdom can unveil itself. Jesus is always realistic; but his realism is that of the awakened heart; it is the realism of the highest dimension of reality and so the most astute and demanding realism imaginable.[82]

I don't know if Ched Myers would roll his eyes over Jesus as "an awakened mystic"; but Myers' analysis of the Jesus depicted in Mark's gospel is in perfect accord with Andrew Harvey's assertion that "the only ultimately 'practical' politics must be one that changes definitively the consciousness of the human race." The "remarkable affinity between [Mark's] portrait of the messianic socio-political strategy [of Jesus] and Gandhi's satyagraha,"[83] says Myers, is nothing less than a "concern to apply the kingdom to the whole of public life."[84] On the other hand (God's Right Hand?), as Harvey points out, the "doctrine of 'original sin,' after all, can offer a kind of depressive comfort to those too passive or too despairing or too lazy to invite and pursue awakening."[85]

Passive, despairing, lazy (might we add smugly self-contented?)—these are certainly descriptions that apply to human psychology and human behavior, although we always need to bear in mind that the frenetic energy of empire builders, the performers of superhuman tasks with undeveloped erotic lives (as Mumford said), also originates in dread of spiritual vulnerability, manifesting manic rather than

82. Harvey, *Son*, 73-74.

83. Myers, *Binding*, 184.

84. Myers, *Binding*, 183-84.

85. Harvey, *Son*, 18.

catatonic escapism. Ched Myers has some pertinent comments on this dynamic of ethical self-containment:

> John H. Yoder's epochal work, *The Politics of Jesus* (1972) . . . influenced a whole generation of radical Christians in the U.S.A. This study *did* attempt a more systematic hermeneutic reconstruction, though it is more important for its theoretics than for its actual exegesis. Yoder launched a broadside attack on the conventional wisdom of modern liberal Protestant social ethics in its attitudes toward scripture. The mainstream view held that a reading of the New Testament might well yield broad ethical or political principles, such as "economic justice" or "human dignity"; it should not, however, be looked to for practical instructions on how to achieve these objectives in our modern social systems. Any *direct* appropriations were said to be naïve; in fact, this meant that it was up to the modern social ethicist to "translate" the lofty abstractions of the New Testament into contemporary imperatives. . . .
>
> For Yoder the crux of the matter was Jesus' practice of "pacifism," the New Testament evidence of which liberal scholars concede but dismiss as irrelevant to the modern situation. Jesus injunction to nonviolence is rejected either as a "special" dispensation based upon his mistaken eschatological view of history (the so-called interim ethic), or as a well-intentioned but misguided perfectionism that could only wreak havoc in the real political world (the position of the Niebuhrian "realists").[86]

But Myers also says:

> Our analysis of the structural characteristics of the global metropolitan-sponsored system of militarism persuades us that armed revolutionary struggle, although it may in the short term liberate political space, in the long term only strengthens the dominant system as a whole, and hence those who control it. To use an economic analogy from liberation theology, it is like trying to solve the problem of Third World dependence through redirected capitalist "development." This is a reformist strategy, attacking symptoms rather than causes, and in the long run serves only to strengthen the international capitalist system. Similarly, recent history suggests that liberation movements that are fundamentally military in character can never fully eradicate the infrastructures of an oppressive system that was itself founded and perpetuated by a military elite. In a world ruled by the logic of militarism, armed struggle becomes counterrevolutionary.[87]

What links the exotic but brilliant Harvey with the prosaic but profound Myers is a conviction that liberation from structures of oppression is the political *and* spiritual goal of Jesus; the "kingdom of God" is the name of his "program" (at minimum a

86. Myers, *Binding*, 460-61.

87. Myers, *Binding*, 453.

strategy) for effectuating that goal. In Myers' construction, the "kingdom" is to apply to the whole of public life; in Harvey's, this application depends on spiritual changes in the consciousness of the human race. If "apocalypse" means a disclosing, a revelation, then the uncovering of contradictions and hypocrisies within our governing mythologies, in both religious and civilizational aspects, is our apocalyptic circumstance. It is the "end times" crisis of our historical and evolutionary moment that compels us to remove the mythic scales from our eyes and see—perhaps for the first time—the astonishing political practicality, the urgent ecological necessity, of embracing Jesus' vision. *Apocalypse does not mean End Times*. Rather, it means *an uncovering of the dynamics that have brought us to End Times* and a disclosing of the spiritual practicalities that will bring us to a healing transformation. There's even a term—catachresis—for the "incorrect use of a word or words, as by misapplication of terminology." So says *Webster's*. "Catachresis" applies perfectly to the conventional use, the incorrect use, of "apocalypse." For those who have no desire for the actualization of End Times, turning to the apocalyptic and embracing it with passion may be the only protection against End Times.

In the face of orthodox theology, which unbendingly repudiates any possibility of the kingdom of God on Earth, we who say otherwise need to articulate on what basis of spiritual understanding we refuse that repudiation. It comes down to eutopia versus utopia, *pagus* versus *civis*, Earth culture versus civilizational hegemony (with its carefully domesticated otherworldly authorized religion providing divine protection). It comes down to our understanding of the sacred and the spiritual, of who or what Spirit is—of where we look for or encounter Spirit. It comes down to whether we are evolutionary indigenous redeemed or extraterrestrial tourist aliens waiting for a one-way ticket elsewhere.

Civilization globalized creates massive alienation from *pagus*. Even more: civilization globalized, with its traumatic diseases, brings us to the prospect of End Times. The repudiation of the kingdom of God on Earth is related to—is finally an expression of—a theology that's located its spiritual and psychic center in the heavenly City of God. It is an Augustinian construct and otherworldly perspective, with the peasant Jesus forcibly dressed in the metaphysical clothing of Plato. But the Age of the Daughter is the Age of the Holy Spirit, who integrates id, superego and ego, who draws into Herself all aspects of radiant goodness made manifest in the previous three epochs, who winnows out the genetically modified otherworldly chaff from the wholesome earthly wheat.

This movement, this integration, this winnowing, terminates civilizational hegemony, cures the diseases and resolves the traumas, shares the wealth at a level accommodating ecological health and ethical well-being, as it resurrects cultural evolution free of domination. Getting to *this* place in our everyday consciousness and political conduct is to enter a new metaphysical time zone. To learn what this is, what it means for our daily lives, requires that we go beyond the prevailing orthodox conventions.

Christian orthodoxy will get its clock cleaned in the Daughter's age: the orthodox sense of time, including the "fallen" time of civilizational estrangement and spiritual alienation, will give up its righteous arrogance, its unabashed conviction of superiority and supremacy.

Spirit has been—and is—infecting the biological human soul. *Malkuta* redeems us as bodies. We've eaten the Son of God. We've ingested Jesus, a Jewish peasant who embodied such purity of vision that it has spread into us with the digestion of his spiritual body. We've been infected with the kingdom of God. To deny this is to refuse the psychomythological meaning of Eucharist. It is a sin against the Holy Spirit. It's a refusal to recognize Daughter, a refusal to live in creation.

The "conservative," the "liberal," and the atheist may scorn such a view, but those who have broken through to depth psychoanalytical comprehension are able to recognize and embrace the hidden-in-plain-view meaning of Eucharist: the spiritual transformation and political liberation of human life from the authoritarian dictates of an absent God and an overbearingly present (and deadly violent) dominant minority of self-righteous men. *Pagus* redeemed: *that* is the meaning in human history and evolutionary unfolding of the "resurrection" of a spiritually revolutionary peasant legally murdered by the collusion of religious and civilizational powers.

To take Ched Myers and Andrew Harvey seriously is to do whatever one can to be in on the transformative unfolding of the kingdom of God, the blooming of the *malkuta* of the Goddess. To not take this seriously is to keep one's weight—however great or insignificant that weight may be—inside the momentum of End Times catastrophe, even if that weight consists of nothing more than skeptical indifference, aloof passivity, or oblivious consumerism. These are some of the faces of our possession.

XIX

Now I am a person (if it even needs to be repeated) whose politics aligns in general with what Michael Lerner calls the Left Hand of God. Generally, when it comes to the Right Hand of God, I will be found carrying a wrecking bar and heavy maul, actively employed in the eternal deconstruction business, with plaster dust and fragments of framing lumber scattered all around.

But at the risk of getting trapped in the image of Lerner's Right and Left Hands, I have to say that Left and Right are not ambidextrously equal. The Right may have an ancient root running all the way back to what Mumford calls the hunting chieftain, and the Left a root that runs to the gatherer-becoming-a-horticulturist. But the Right's real power lies in its longstanding alliance between God and Civilization. This is not an alliance created by a pleading or yearning God who wants or needs us, who may get a bit upset now and then and who takes time out to cool off, but is, instead, a fierce killer God who, in behalf of a Chosen People, will exterminate the enemy (even if the "enemy" just happens to be people living where the killer God has His eye on some choice real estate) and then have stoned to death those of His own Chosen People who violate His rigid rules and sacred order. This is a Male God who, as Jack Miles has shown us, goes ballistic over the mere mention of a goddess, much less a Goddess. If this God has a Left Hand, it is a shriveled stump, dysfunctional, a source of embarrassment and rage.

So, in this country, the Right has this civilized Male God fierceness at its back. This is the mental or mythological world we have inherited and that we inhabit. Christian America worships Yahweh of ancient Israel. This is the core American heritage, our Manifest Destiny, our exceptional one-armed God of righteous conquest. We have to conquer—perhaps destroy—the world in order to save it. Yahweh of Jericho remains America's Chieftain God.

What Michael Lerner calls the Left is to some extent made up of dropouts or refugees from the Right who have fled because of nasty racism or ugly discrimination. They may have dropped out because of physical science understanding or solid scholarship in the fields of history and economics or because of gospel ethics or for other reasons too elusive to document. But just as the American working class never got it sufficiently together to create a socialist political party before unions began collapsing, so the post-'60s Left is less a unified alliance with a coherent worldview than a hodgepodge crazy quilt of disparate "interest groups": ethnic minorities (i.e., people of color), remnants of the bedraggled labor movement, feminists, environmentalists, the gay community, and a fairly amorphous body of ethical "liberals" who find, for various reasons, the Right's agenda repulsive. In terms of religious conviction, there is in this leftist cluster a huge range of belief and unbelief, from totally conventional Catholics, Protestants, Jews, Muslims and Buddhists to atheists and so-called neopagans. Unlike the Right, there is on the Left no unified concept of the divine. This is due to two fundamental realities: first, the Right is the primary carrier of the core Judeo-Christian construction of God; second, a new construct has not been articulated, accepted, or assimilated even as the prevailing construct is a battered old heavyweight with cauliflower ears. We may disbelieve in the bloody, tribal *civis* God, but we're so stuck in *civis* institutions and in the mentality those institutions have instilled in us, that we are oblivious to the finding of Spirit in rediscovered *pagus*.

Meanwhile, the civilized Male God trajectory, with its astonishing, unreflective sense of entitlement, is, in Wade Davis's image, a fire burning over the Earth. It consists of the traumatic institutions of civilization fully globalized, in apparent league with the irresistible will of the God of the Universe. The disparate Left represents an unmistakable demographic majority. But the Right, with its greater focus and concentrated center, sensing (as we all do) the catastrophic energy in everything from nuclear weapons to climate change to overpopulation to species extinctions to fracking to "dead zone" toxins and pollutants, led and agitated by demagogues, demonic corporate "persons" and billionaire industrialists, is working feverishly to confuse, fracture, hamstring, demoralize, and depress the Left to the point where democracy, if it survives, will resemble the "democracy" of apartheid South Africa or modern Israel or, perhaps more accurately, a "legal person" Magna Carta for aristocratic corporations, a country of and for corporate barons, complete with logo and livery.

And yet there is on the popular or everyday Right an impatience toward and irritation with the Left for the latter's cloying and big-eyed emotional neediness, its "please now be nice" painfully smiling pleading. It is no accident that this political dynamic—tough Daddy Party, supplicating Mommy Party—just happens to overlay with near perfection the conventional male-female dynamic laid out by Dorothy Dinnerstein. (See the beautifully done Irish novel *The Countrywoman*, by Paul Smith, for a luminous fictional illustration of the dynamic.) The Right represents the historic collusion of kingship and God, civilization and the Judeo-Christian tradition. The Right, precisely because of its endemic righteousness, can hardly help but see the Left as baby-faced scum that God's green Earth would be better off without. (Don't laugh; this was precisely Hitler's dream: civilization cleansed of all racial and ideological filth.)

Achieving decentralized and federated Green socialism—which I take to be the only humane and ecologically sensible way out of our predicament—is not simply a matter of putting policy flesh on political principles like "social justice" or "ecological responsibility" or "economic fairness." This is where the Left is both inhibited and sentimental. The requisite transformation is not just about political policy or abstract moral conversion. If the roots of this crisis are as psychologically deep as Dorothy Dinnerstein believes they are—a belief I share—then Green socialism will be possible only when we are bold enough to become transformed persons—transformed precisely because we've become bold and brave enough to address what Dorothy Dinnerstein calls our sexual arrangements and human malaise. It's precisely in this difficult area where a fresh spiritual construct must take shape and enable our liberation.

But all this leads us inexorably into a nest of very difficult questions. If we are looking for the origins of our motives, of what inspires and encourages our actions on the one hand and what constrains and restricts them on the other, we are, of course, going to have to look *within* in a personal and psychological sense even as we are going to have to look *without* in terms of society, culture, religion, and history. It's not only external chains that need breaking, but also the chains we've internalized—and these internal chains are hard to break precisely because they're normative. We've been taught *civis* morality and the immorality of *pagus*. As utopian citizens and civilized consumers, we reflexively balk at stepping into the eutopian freedom of the redeemed *pagus*. It's too exotic and much too strange for our refined temperaments. *Pagus* smacks of blasphemy and sin. Its opprobrium has long-standing religious and cultural sanction.

Merlin Stone, in "The Daughters of Eve," her final chapter in *When God Was a Woman*, quotes meaningfully from a speech given by Abby Foster, in 1853:

"You may tell me that it is a woman who forms the mind of a child, but I
charge it back again, that it is the minister, who forms the mind of the woman.
It is he who makes the mother what she is, therefore her teaching of the child
is only conveying the instructions of the pulpit at second hand."[88]

This passage conveys not only the interlocking dynamics of inner and outer, it also
exposes the influence of prevailing religious authority in a self-perpetuating form of
gender dominance and submission. We may yearn for the core platform principles
of Mommy Party, but it's the overbearing (im)moral authority of Big Daddy which
compels us to stand straight and salute.

Perhaps we're ready to go back to "Norma A. Brown"—our very own Dorothy
Dinnerstein.

XX

In a section of *The Mermaid and the Minotaur* entitled "Some Evolutionary Considerations," Dinnerstein lays out the foundation of her analysis. She says the "biological
factors historically responsible for our traditional sexual arrangements"[89] are to a
large extent related to the development of bipedal locomotion in our early ancestors,
freeing the hands for the discovery and sustained use of tools. Here, with tools and increasingly complex language, human beings begin to move out of complete encapsulation within nature as given and toward the steady growth of an increasingly complex
transmissible culture, an accrued and enlarging body of shared social intelligence and
collective behavior that seems to distinguish human beings, both male and female,
from other creatures on Earth.

With upright posture, says Dinnerstein (who quotes anthropologist Sherwood
Washburn), the size of the female birth canal was altered—actually constricted—by
this upright posture, so babies (with large brains) had to be born at an earlier stage
of development than babies of other primates. Just at that "moment" when upright
posture and (it is presumed) a growing capacity for language are achieved, men (with
hunting tools) are cooperatively exploring and jointly exploiting a larger physical terrain while women (with domestic tools) are increasingly limited in their mobility by
extended child care. All this, she says, put the "female in a strange bind":

She is the only female, so far as we know, capable of thinking up and bringing
about a world wider than the one she sees around her (and her subversive
tendency to keep trying to use this capacity is recorded, resentfully, in Eve
and Pandora myths). She thus seems, of all females, the one least fitted to live
in a world narrower than the one she sees around her. And yet, for reasons
inherent in her evolutionary history, she has been, of all females, the one most

88. Stone, *When*, 235.

89. Dinnerstein, *Mermaid*, 16-17.

fated to do so. Her young are born less mature than those of related mammals; they require more physical care for a relatively longer time; they have much more to learn before they can function without adult supervision. Without contraception, she must spend most of her vigorous adult life pregnant or lactating. Given these handicaps to wide-ranging mobility, she has been the logical keeper of the hearth and doer of domestic tasks, and also (usually in collaboration with other females) the logical guardian and educator of the slow-maturing toddler.

As a result, until quite recent technological developments opened new possibilities (so far largely unused), most of the world's women have been obliged to invest major energy in the biological task of perpetuating the species. This reproductive task has tended to make them specialists in the exercise of certain essential human capacities, capacities crucial for empathic care of the very young and for maintenance of the social-emotional arrangements that sustain everyday primary-group life. At the same time, it has tended to prevent them from exercising certain other essential human capacities, capacities for demanding, sustained enterprise that extends beyond (and can violate) close interpersonal concerns. It has limited their opportunity, in other words, to contribute to those aspects of the growth of our species' cumulatively pooled achievement that change the gross, overt shape of our shared reality: to make history.[90]

In essence, Dorothy Dinnerstein is asserting that gender cleavage between male and female cultural realms can be traced, at least in part, to the upright posture of our ancient ancestors; that these separate gender realms (though not without tension or conflict) had sufficient practical symbiosis and sexual reciprocity for thousands of years so the cultural project (including species reproduction) worked; but now the male/female "division of labor"—that males go out to make history while females stay home to rear babies—has, in the modern world, revealed its toxic lopsidedness, its unbalanced emotional and spiritual underpinnings, to the point where all higher life forms (including our own) are in peril from the externalized consequences of this imbalance. (Taking a hint from Dinnerstein's evocation of Eve, in the passage above, we might consider that Eve, as serpent-deluded bimbo, is a projection of male resentment created because women made a breakthrough, a budding liberation, in the complex village dynamic shaped—and given feminine spiritual ambience—by the extensive practice of horticulture. That is, the precivilized agrarian village may represent the first women's liberation movement, a successful attempt to achieve equalitarian status with men, an attempt whose back was broken by the unholy alliance of God and king—the feral founding of civilization.)

All this, so far, is flat-footed and reasonably factual. But Dinnerstein says that

90. Dinnerstein, *Mermaid*, 20-21.

... what at this point mainly keeps the arrangement going is not its longstanding biotechnological function, which it has largely outlived, but the defensive psychological function (perhaps nearly as longstanding, since our hominid ancestors were mentally complex beings) that it still serves. When enough of us are clearly enough aware of this function, it will disintegrate; and its disintegration, in turn, will undermine certain time-honored modes of interaction—deadly, but cozily familiar—which now govern our intimate everyday relations with each other and with the natural environment.

What must be seen from the outset is that the trouble people have in thinking about our male-female symbiosis is not primarily intellectual trouble. Thought in this region (even for thinkers who are committed to the project of sexual liberty) is inevitably slowed down by fear: we are thinking about a question whose answer is bound to melt the ground under our feet. It is dangerous, uncomfortable ground, and it is high time we stepped off it; still, it is the ground we stand on now, the only ground we know.[91]

The *psychological* problems start, so to speak, as the skin of gender convention and boundaries of sexual prerogative begin to be probed and palpated. Suddenly we realize, despite aggravation, tension and conflict, just how powerfully self-perpetuating these ancient encapsulations are, how our identities are rooted in these encapsulations, and how reflexively resistant we are to having these venerable patterns modified, challenged, or openly exposed. (I am reminded of a statement made by former Senator Theodore Bilbo—I quote it on page 41 in *Green Politics Is Eutopian*—of how it would be better for the human race to be exterminated by the atomic bomb than to permit marriage across racial lines. Was Bilbo merely echoing God's "overwhelming revulsion" that Jack Miles told us about?)

Because we turn away so quickly from examining the "sacredness" of our gender arrangements, because the entire area is so loaded with thwarted emotional needs and repressed sexual energy, it's difficult to examine the terrain in private much less explore analyses in public. As Dorothy Dinnerstein warned us early on, this material is emotionally threatening, even to the point where she was threatened by it herself. But, perhaps with perverse stubbornness, let's give it a shot. What do we have to lose? If this is the eutopian gateway to our liberation, it's suicidal cowardice to refuse the port of entry.

XXI

I don't think Dorothy Dinnerstein has a relentless single-factor analysis, although a superficial reading of *Mermaid and Minotaur* might create such an impression. Dinnerstein *does* put a lot of eggs in the mother-raised-children basket; but she methodically peels those eggs like proverbial onions: layer after layer of subtle meaning

91. Dinnerstein, *Mermaid*, 23-24.

and surprising implication. She nails Norman O. Brown, as we have seen, for his implicit male bias—an assessment that, in my estimation, is quite accurate—and, having stunned Brown, she goes right after Freud. This is not, however, any knee-jerk sort of ball-busting, man-hating snarl. This is upfront, straightforward wrestling in the mudpit of existential meaning. All in all, Dinnerstein venerates both Freud and Brown for their brilliant breakthroughs in human psychology and for the application of those breakthroughs as they pertain both to the human past and to the human (and ecological) future. (Not at all incidentally, Dinnerstein also honors Lewis Mumford for his deep and comprehensive analysis of the "megamachine." Herbert Marcuse gets a respectful nod. But Simone de Beauvoir is her heroine.)

Whatever other factors there may be to complicate the analysis, Dinnerstein traces the big factor back to our ancient ancestors, whose upright posture narrowed the birth canal at a time when the human brain—and therefore the human head—was getting bigger. This necessitated a longer period of extended care for helpless infants. This extended care fell overwhelmingly to women, over a prolonged period of time, even as male upright posture freed the hands for the use of rudimentary weapons in the pursuit of animals for food—and, probably, for unfriendly contact with bands of other male hunters perceived as rivals. A cultural cleavage was not only developing but widening—"outer" man, "inner" woman—even as children, with their prolonged childhood, were submerged in extended female presence. It's here where anthropology begins to give way to psychology. If there is a place where Dinnerstein dives in and comes up with treasure, it's in this childhood submersion in prolonged female presence.

I am not going to repeat her arguments, her subtle findings. (If you haven't read her book, go do it. It's a big bone worth a lot of gnawing.) But in the end she says that male dominance, with all its pathologies, is related to and rooted in this prolonged baby bath of overwhelming female presence, and that female deference, with all *its* pathologies, is floating in the same tub. Although she says the "'practical' bases for asymmetric human sexual privilege have clearly started to crumble," she also says:

> What remains very much intact, however, is its deepest emotional basis: A central psychological asymmetry between the sexes, laid down in the first months, and consolidated in the first years, of life, is built into the primary-group arrangement that Washburn . . . describes as the "fundamental pattern . . . [of human] social organization." This central asymmetry, which drives men to insist on unilateral sexual prerogative and inclines women to consent to their insistence, will endure as a powerful force until the "fundamental pattern" is outgrown—until, that is, the female monopoly of child care is broken.[92]

Dinnerstein explains how psychological asymmetry between the sexes takes shape:

92. Dinnerstein, *Mermaid*, 39-40.

Early rage at the first parent, in other words, is typically used by the "masculine" boy during Oedipal period to *consolidate* his tie with his own sex by establishing a principled independence, a more or less derogatory distance, from women. And it is typically used by the "feminine" girl in this same period to *loosen* her tie with her own sex by establishing a worshipful, dependent stance toward men. Just when that boy is learning to keep his feelings for the mother under control, that girl (precisely because her first emotional problems also centered on the mother) is learning to over-idealize the father. This contrast, of course, heavily supports asymmetry of sexual privilege.[93]

If we are to survive, she says, and not blow the world to hell, we must deal honestly and bravely with this gendered asymmetry. What Dinnerstein doesn't do is adequately explore the Oedipal dynamic of boys learning to keep their feelings for their mothers under control. That is, the blockage of sexual access to the mother—the watershed event of weaning whereby boys turn from mother to consolidate ties with males—also dams up male sexual energy, a blockage compounded when access to other females is also prohibited. When sexual access to a female is finally allowed, via strict rules of conduct and lifetime commitment, it should come as no surprise that militant male protection of that access would inevitably follow. That is, if a male "protects" "his" female from other males, the female in turn utilizes the same "protective" energy to secure a reliable provider for herself and her children. Hence long-term pair-bonding (monogamy) is built on a base of tightly channeled sexual desire that satisfies short-term desire but prevents it from exploration or growth in the long-term. If tender erotic encounter is one of the means by which males and females meet equally as persons—both meet and grow—the reduction of such encounter to rote roles of genital release, perhaps driven primarily by the male need for testicular discharge, seriously narrows the scope of human fulfillment, leading to all manner of resigned "sublimations" that accrue over time as lethal power organizations. In a section called "Male-Female Collaboration to Keep History Mad," Dinnerstein says that:

> Freud called woman "the enemy of civilization," and in a sense this is true. But he radically oversimplified. She is the loyal opponent, the indispensable defanged and domesticated critic, of what he himself identified as the essential, and imminently lethal, sickness of civilization. Without her sabotage, civilization as it is could not go on. This sabotage is harmless to what it purports to assault. Indeed it dissipates what could be effectively explosive feeling, discharges potentially subversive emotional energy in frivolous and impotent, homey and comfortable, ways. It farts away internal pressure that would otherwise shatter the social system. She is not civilization's enemy: she is its court jester, without whose jibes the court would collapse.[94]

93. Dinnerstein, *Mermaid*, 53.
94. Dinnerstein, *Mermaid*, 225.

What Dinnerstein means by woman-as-court-jester is that "When she goes too far, man lets her know; and, like the jester, she backs down, for she is not a true enemy but a house-trained menial, willingly ruled by the power she mocks." The jester's jibes "ventilate the intuition . . . that the human process of self-creation is in essential ways destructive":

> He is capable of the intuition, and articulates it now and then, here and there. She is capable of history-making, and engages in it now and then, here and there. But if he allowed himself more generally to dwell upon the intuition, to give it full status in his pattern of conscious concerns, he could not go on making the kind of history he makes. And if she immersed herself more generally in that kind of history, she would have to bury the intuition.
>
> Not only is this intuition, this body of misgivings and reservations, too well-developed in woman to be pushed under as men push it under. She is also unwilling to bury it. Her unwillingness rests in part on a sense of responsibility, a fear of what the world would be like if the perspective that she embodies were lost to all of us: she knows, and man knows too—hence his enraged alarm at the prospect of her entering history—that the side of life she protects, maintains, and stands up for is the side that keeps the world at least partly sane. Both need to have this side of life affirmed. But her unwillingness rests also on the darker need, which she also shares with man, to keep the world mainly mad. It is this darker need, more then the sunnier one (for the sunnier one could be fulfilled in other ways. and on some level we all know that), which makes him honor her, even while deriding her, in her role as jester, and which underlies much of his angry fear when she starts to withdraw from this role. . . .
>
> Woman cannot enter history, then, without shattering the collaboration between herself and man that maintains our present way of "coping" with what Freud calls civilization's discontents. What will happen when the split in sensibility that the two sexes now work together to preserve breaks down, melts away? We cannot be sure what will happen. We can be sure only that so long as this split is preserved the mad megamachine of which Mumford writes will inexorably grow and proliferate, destroying and displacing the flawed but still vigorous human life on which it feeds.[95]

In Dorothy Dinnerstein's analysis, nothing less than gender equality in infant child care contains the formative psychological power by which children could grow into adulthood without the deformities created by excessive female presence in infancy. Such equality would radically reduce gender fixations and sexual distortions attendant on mother-raised children. Her argument is complex and nuanced; I am merely lifting a few passages and summarizing.

---

95. Dinnerstein, *Mermaid*, 225-27.

What's *not* adequately dealt with in her book is what's meant by the "project of sexual liberty"; and if it were just a project of gender *equality*, there would be no reason to raise the question. But sexual *liberty* suggests something more intimate than "equality"; it suggests something missing or repressed in the intimacy of our sexual lives, that the "project" is not only about a man's hand on the cradle and a woman's on the ship-of-state's helm, but where, how, when, and under what conditions women and men may put their hands on each other's bodies. Dinnerstein suggests, but she does not describe or really even attempt to describe, what kind of liberation is necessary for our constricted sexual energy, what that liberty might look like or what its cultural consequence might be.

This is such a dense and loaded knot that few of us are willing to try to pry it open. It is instantly personal, profoundly and unavoidably so. It's rife with risk and conflict. Is this the heart of what Dorothy Dinnerstein warned us is so emotionally threatening? Let's not forget God's rage over the nearness of a Female deity or that it was in regard to inter-racial sex that Senator Bilbo wished for the atomic bomb. So let's not pretend that there's only a trivial amount of psychic energy tied up in the attractions—and the constraints—of erotic intimacy.

Now one could say that, somehow, naturalistically, humanity will just slide into the desired equality as necessity for equality reaches a watershed point of threatened survival. That is, "equality" *will just happen* as automatic adjustment to gravely pressing need, without internal struggle, intellectual courage, or spiritual transformation. On the other extreme, we *could be forced* to recognize our predicament and, by acts of sheer moral will, reorganize our sexual behavior and gender arrangements accordingly. While there may be elements of both natural change and moral enforcement in the offing, I don't think that exhausts the analysis.

Dinnerstein warns repeatedly about "acute discomfort," saying her book is "emotionally threatening" and will "enrage the reader." Part of what she means is how deeply we—both men and women—are locked into inherited gender roles, sexual identities, and bubbles of exclusive intimacy; therefore how difficult it is for us to examine that lockage or break free of it. But she only brushes up against our actual erotic conduct—as if the changes she says are so elemental and vital (shared parenting in particular) do not in some ways imply serious modifications in how we express our sexuality from childhood through old age. It's not just that males need to rock the cradle so females can more fully engage the public sphere—i.e., "make history." That part is both true and necessary. But something is missing or seriously understated in Dinnerstein's prescription: a fuller and freer exploration of transformed erotic behavior and where, culturally speaking, such transformation would enable us to go. That is, we're back to the question of how prevailing sexual morality locks us into the utopian worldview, how it obstructs entrance into the eutopian worldview. But facing this possibility, even speculating on what changes might be involved in the transition from utopia to eutopia, activates some of our deepest fears and walls up our conditioned resistances. Both women and men are locked into a kind of "mono-theism" of monogamy possessiveness buttressed by an intimidating array of cultural supports, legal prohibitions, and religious ultimatums. You belong to me, and I belong to you. Fear, jealousy, and possessiveness may in principle be recognized as negative emotions; but these "negative emotions" are nevertheless seen as having an acutely positive function in protecting the sanctity of marriage, the stability of the family, and even the righteousness of private property.

Paul Goodman was something of a sexual libertarian. In his wise *Growing Up Absurd*, he paints a picture of how the accrued nature of our pinched private lives adds up to a perverse social and political collectivity whose deadliness just keeps growing. (There are two layers of quotation here. The first is straightforward text from *Growing Up Absurd*; the second is Goodman quoting himself from an earlier work, *Gestalt Therapy*.):

> In our truly remarkable and unexampled civil peace, where there are rarely fist fights; where no one is born, is gravely ill, or dies; where meat is eaten but no one sees an animal slaughtered; where scores of millions of cars, trains, elevators, and airplanes go their scheduled way and there is rarely a crash; where an immense production proceeds in orderly efficiency and the shelves are duly cleared—and *nevertheless* none of this comes to joy or tragic grief or any other final good—it is not surprising if there are explosions. They occur at the boundaries of the organized system of society: in juvenile gang fights, in prison riots, in foreign wars:
>
> "These conditions are almost specific for the excitement of primary mas-ochism. There is continual stimulation and only partial release of tension, an unbearable heightening of the unaware tensions—unaware because people do not know what they want, nor how to get it. The desire for final satisfaction, for orgasm, is interpreted as the wish for total self-destruction. It is inevitable, then, that there should be a public dream of universal disaster, with vast ex-plosions, fires, and electric shocks; and people pool their efforts to bring this apocalypse to an actuality.
>
> "At the same time all overt expression of destructiveness, annihilation, anger, combatativeness, is suppressed in the interests of civil order. Also, the feeling of anger is inhibited and even repressed. People are sensible, tolerant, polite, and co-operative in being pushed around. But the occasions of anger are by no means minimized. On the contrary, when the larger movements of initiative are circumscribed in the competitive routines of offices, bureaucra-cies, and factories, there is petty friction, hurt feelings, being crossed. Small anger is continually generated, never discharged; big anger, that goes with big initiative, is repressed.
>
> "Therefore the angry situation is projected afar. People must find big dis-tant causes to explain the pressure of anger that is certainly not explicable by

petty frustrations. It is necessary to have something worthy of the hatred that is unaware felt for oneself. In brief, one is angry with the Enemy."[96]

One might say Goodman's analysis minimizes greed or how anger for the Enemy conveniently disguises greed—as in the long-standing, dreadful American posture with Iraq. (As the sardonic aphorism puts it: How did *our* oil get under *your* sand?) But that pent-up "small anger" gets compacted, enlarged, and projected afar is certainly true. For the enemy to be "worthy" of hatred requires that he be heavily invested with evil. For this, a righteous religious conviction is always helpful and probably necessary. Our tiny, individual tensions, our subjective wrappings of negative emotions, get politically and religiously pooled into big, distant causes worthy of our hatred. We *protect* our negative emotions from interpersonal therapeutic resolution by projecting them outward onto an enemy and discharging them as political violence justified by moral and religious superiority. Afraid to make love, we make war instead.

Now, in contrast to Goodman's sexual frankness, it may be that Dorothy Dinnerstein resists being descriptive about "erotic relations" because men often want the fun and juicy part of sex, the ripe voluptuousness, but not the extended or prolonged intimacy—not to speak of the baby burping, squalling, and diapering Dinnerstein mentions in relation to Norman O. Brown's "ideal emotionally androgynous humanity." This is real. But stopping there also avoids the subject.[97]

Achieving a fuller and more complex erotic life requires enduring the anxiety, stress, and pain of having what we might call our ectomorphic cultural clothing stripped away, sort of reversing the Garden of Eden expulsion story: learning again to be naked and endogenous. I think this means not terrifying children with negative judgments in regard to body exploration; some sort of culturally sanctioned tender and gentle sexual initiation for adolescents; protected physical and psychic space for

---

96. Goodman, *Growing*, 209-10.

97. Yes, even here, shielded and protected by a qualifying footnote, I find it emotionally threatening—exactly as Dorothy Dinnerstein forecast—to probe the possibility and necessity of erotic complexity. But what if permanent, oath-committed monogamy is really a sexual property contract similar to a real estate arrangement? What if Aldo Leopold's famous aphorism—"land as a community to which we belong" (page xviii in the Foreword to *A Sand County Almanac*)—requires cooperative erotic complexity to be achievable? What if so much male aggression, including aggression righteously disguised as "defense," is—like rape—the product of systemic erotic frustration? If men in particular need freer and fuller erotic access to women, with all the tension-reducing bodily satisfactions and emotional gentling such access entails, what are the changes in male character and male behavior needed as preconditions to facilitate such access? What's the role and responsibility of women in achieving such transformation? Is there a collective female "conspiracy" (at an unconscious level) to keep men erotically frustrated so that male energy might be channeled into family-based productive labor? Dorothy Dinnerstein certainly is correct about the need for men taking greater care of infants and children. Yes to that. But that's not only a necessity; it's also a consequence—a consequence of achieving an actual workable, livable erotic complexity in community. And if all this seems impossible, ridiculous and downright stupid, I have for the objectors a very simple question: What else is there of sufficient importance, depth, and magnitude by which we humans might avert the global catastrophe our species is in process of achieving? I ask this in all earnestness.

the young in love; a more communal atmosphere for child care and adult interaction; patterns of more complex marriage for the mature—well, not only for those with grey hair, for if Dorothy Dinnerstein is correct about the need for and importance of a communal environment for child rearing, then complex marriage must involve young mothers and fathers. But this is not about rampant "free" sex, just as it's not about locked-in-for-life monogamy with its literal feeling of voluntary incarceration. To grow we must feel free to grow, able to engage in intimate encounters facilitating growth. We need the freedom to fall in love without feelings of guilt and betrayal for those we already love. We need a more complex and inclusive love constellation.

To transform our overall behavior in a political macro sense requires a simultaneous transformation in a personal micro sense. Our inner value structure reflects the outer political, economic, and religious structures in ways we are only beginning to perceive. To think we can radically change the overall economy in the direction of Green socialism without radical change in our inner, "private" lives is an illusion. The enlarging influence and power of the Right may more accurately reflect the incapacity or unwillingness of the Left to move beyond its conventional comfort zone: the Right accrues power as the Left is afraid to articulate its new understandings, which includes the exploration of richer intimacy. This fear is linked to an unwillingness to confront America's empire machinations or face the "lifestyle" implications and consequences of global warming and climate change. To really "go Green" is certainly to embrace reform by retrogression (as Carl Jung explains in chapter VIII of his *Memories, Dreams, Reflections* or as I quote him on pages 7 and 8 in *Nature's Unruly Mob*); but such reformation requires an accompanying gender reconciliation in which erotic intimacy provides a vivacious glow of bodily satisfaction and emotional fulfillment. To willingly—even joyfully—go "backward," we need the facilitating lubrication of erotic intimacy in a mode of spiritual wholeness and gender reconciliation. Greater simplicity will be normal with the satisfactions of loving erotic intimacy. Devoid of the emotional courage and intellectual strength a more complex and open-ended intimacy would stimulate, we are reluctant to give up the security we already do have, even as we uneasily realize that our current forms of material and institutional security are unsustainable. Well, worse than unsustainable: murderous and catastrophic. If civilization is the unsustainable means by which the collective unconscious of cultural evolution has brought us to a point of freedom from the constraints of traditional gender arrangements, the next step requires conscious, voluntary courage. A good part of what's holding us back from this courageous step is the absence of an understanding of the sacred appropriate to the crisis, an absence reducing the Mommy Party to the status of a court jester that—as Dorothy Dinnerstein says generally of women—"farts away internal pressure that would otherwise shatter the social system." (Here's where the mythic enlargement of Trinity to Mandala has immense enabling power.)

If we really want to hunker down and explore our acute discomfort, experience at close range what feels emotionally threatening and do something more than dance around the edges of what can elicit possessive rage, we need look no further than our own erotic lives. In my estimation, this is a gate, the eye of one of the needles through which we need to crawl if we have any hope of getting to Dorothy Dinnerstein's desired world. "Heaven" is comprised of *fulfilled* bodies, bodies largely free of fear, not bodies squirming with undischarged, unrealized, or unexpressed needs and thwarted desires. It's true that renunciation is an important moral principle we all need at times to practice; but it's also a negative form of discipline whose function is to achieve a positive outcome. *Permanent* renunciation may be the morality of otherworldly fixation; the "kingdom of God" requires a maximum degree of bodily fulfillment. If the "kingdom" is to become manifest on Earth, then it's *here* where we must learn what fulfillment means. As John Ruskin said, there is no wealth but life—to which we might add: life not lived gives us "the feeling of no chance in the past, no prospect for the future, no recourse in the present; whence the drive to disaster. It is a religious crisis."[98] Civilization imposed systemic repression on the bulk of the impounded population; otherworldly religion not only made acquiescence to that repression spiritually obligatory, it also proclaimed that Original Sin prevents any reprieve. Therefore we are stuck in ruts from which escape is deemed immoral.

Religious orthodoxy and civilized mythology combine to obstruct an accurate understanding of the past; without a wholesome grounding in the deep past, without understanding the traumatic institutions and diseases of Class and War, without grasping what it's meant to delete the Mother, our present is driven by civilizational bullying and religious fear mongering; therefore the future is bound to be a future of disaster, precisely because it's built on a foundation of evasion, avoidance, suppression, and misrepresentation. This *is* a religious crisis, as Goodman says; but it's a crisis that requires breaking through to a *real* past by means of a disclosing *apokalypsis*, an integration that puts civilized history in its evolutionary place and the Abrahamic religions in proper mythological perspective. If the project of sexual liberty needs gender equality at the cradle, it also means men must achieve reconciliation with women in an intimate, erotic sense—just as God the Father needs historical confrontation, psychoanalytical mediation, and mythological reconciliation with the Mother Goddess.

Let's not forget that Yahweh is a *jealous* God, a *possessive* God, a God fully capable of commanding righteous *genocide*. If we are entitled to act in the image and manner of this Right-Handed God, then our jealousy, possessiveness, and even our acts of genocide are fully rational and spiritually justified, perhaps even morally obligatory. I'm not saying that jealousy will evaporate or possessiveness disappear when God the Father goes off for divine psychotherapy. Nor am I saying that jealousy and possessiveness reside only in the male camp. But we have to stop treating jealousy and possessiveness as if they were divine mandates swung like smoking censers, wafting the poisonous incense of our injured self-righteousness. We will have to learn to live and let live, accept some bruises, and forgive as the actual conduct of life, not as

98. Goodman, *Growing*, 211.

long-suffering Sunday sacrifices made nobly in behalf of moral principles worn like billboards to advertise our capacity to endure pain and signify our eternal victimhood.

Or are our prevailing sexual and gender arrangements so sacred we will offer them as holy sacrifices to thermonuclear holocaust? Is Senator Bilbo our most prescient prophet?

XXII

Having used, somewhat provocatively, the word "sacred" to describe our sexual and gender arrangements, let's give that idea some legs by attending to a section of Merlin Stone's *When God Was a Woman*, "Dawn in the Gravettian Garden of Eden." Here Stone is groping for "the conjectural foundation of the religion of the Goddess as it emerged in the later Neolithic Age of the Near East." She says "Theories on the origins of the Goddess in this period are founded on the juxtaposition of mother-kinship customs to ancestor worship. They are based upon three separate lines of evidence."[99] These three lines are: the female as the giver of life; ancestor worship linked to matrilineal descent; the numerous sculptures of women and female figurines discovered in archaeological digs.

We are, of course, talking about the huge transition from paleolithic hunting and gathering culture—heavily squeezed by the last Ice Age—to early neolithic horticulture created by women gatherers who slowly but steadily developed the requisite practices by which an enlarging human community could be wholesomely fed. William H. McNeill's massive study *The Rise of the West: A History of the Human Community* goes into detail:

> A widespread shift in human relations brought about by the transition from hunting to agriculture seems also to have affected Neolithic cults. In proportion as women became the major suppliers of food for the community, their independence and authority probably increased; and various survivals in historic times suggest that matrilineal family systems prevailed in many Neolithic communities. Correspondingly, the spread of agriculture was connected everywhere with the rise of female priestesses and deities to prominence. The earth itself was apparently conceived as a woman—the prototype for the Great Mother of later religions—and the numerous female figurines which have been unearthed from Neolithic sites may have been intended as representations of the fruitful earth goddess.[100]

McNeill goes on to paint more detail into this picture:

> In agricultural communities, male leadership in the hunt ceased to be of much importance. As the discipline of the hunting band decayed, the political

99. Stone, *When*, 10.
100. McNeill, *Rise*, 35.

institutions of the earliest village settlements perhaps approximated the anarchism which has remained ever since the ideal of peaceful peasantries all round the earth. . . . The strong hunter and man of prowess, his occupation gone or relegated to the margins of social life, lost the unambiguous primacy which had once been his; while the comparatively tight personal subordination to a leader necessary to the success of a hunting party could be relaxed in proportion as grain fields became the center around which life revolved.

Among predominantly pastoral peoples, however, religious political institutions took a quite different turn. To protect the flocks from animal predators required the same courage and social discipline which hunters had always needed. Among pastoralists, likewise, the principal economic activity—focused, as among the earliest hunters, on a parasitic relation to animals—continued to be the special preserve of menfolk. Hence a system of patrilineal families, united into kinship groups under the authority of a chieftain responsible for daily decisions as to where to seek pasture, best fitted the conditions of pastoral life. In addition, pastoralists were likely to accord importance to the practices and discipline of war. After all, violent seizure of someone else's animals or pasture grounds was the easiest and speediest way to wealth and might be the only means of survival in a year of scant vegetation.

Such warlikeness was entirely alien to communities tilling the soil. Archeological remains from early Neolithic villages suggest remarkably peaceable societies. As long as cultivable land was plentiful, and as long as the labor of a single household could not produce a significant surplus, there can have been little incentive to war. Traditions of violence and hunting-party organization presumably withered in such societies, to be revived only *when pastoral conquest superimposed upon peaceable villagers the elements of warlike organization from which civilized political institutions without exception descend.*[101] (Emphasis added)

Merlin Stone talks about the "appearance of the invading northerners, who from all accounts had established patrilineal, patriarchal customs and the worship of a supreme male deity sometime before their arrival in the Goddess-worshiping areas"[102]—and she includes among these invaders the ruling priestly class of the Hebrews, the Levites.

Meanwhile, let's note that Jack Miles makes a passing comment about "Near Eastern goddesses [who] are so often utterly ferocious."[103] But how are we to reconcile the characterization of agrarian village peacefulness that William McNeill has just spoken of ("warlikeness was entirely alien to communities tilling the soil") with allegations of Middle Eastern goddesses who are utterly ferocious? I confess to a certain puzzlement here; but let's look at this to the best of our ability. Let's start, somewhat crookedly, with Benedictine nun Joan Chittister.

101. McNeill, *Rise*, 37-38.

102. Stone, *When*, 61.

103. Miles, *God*, 267.

In "A Conversation with the Speakers," at the end of *God at 2000*, Sister Joan answers a question about the "concept of goddess":

> I will say something, and you will probably be shocked by my answer. I get no mileage out of goddess at all. Zero. I struggled with it. I saw it happening in the literature. I knew its intention. But I saw it as the other side of heresy.
>
> First, the connotations of goddess, at least in my classical education, are Greek. They did not inspire me. The notion of a goddess who ate her own children was not an allusion I could live spiritually and grow from. . . . I know we need a change, but—and I am being as honest as I can with you—goddess does not do it for me. It works for some women. I am happy about that. They are not going down an ancient or distorting path. But if your question is a personal one for me, goddess does not work.[104]

I have to say this seems like saying China doesn't work or there's no mileage in penicillin. It's historically absurd. (And what does "the other side of heresy" mean? Does Sister Joan detect tampering with orthodox Trinity?) To acknowledge the Mother (i.e., "the goddess" or Goddess) is to recognize the historical fact of (at minimum) a prolonged phase of cultural evolution before the imposition of civilized aristocracy, a time before Father sent Mother into exile and suppressed any mention of Her existence. To not acknowledge Mother in the religious history of the human race is disingenuous to the point of being ridiculous. It's tantamount to saying the precivilized period of the agrarian village doesn't matter—which is the liberal equivalent of the fundamentalist assertion that such a period never occurred. But it also seems that Joan Chittister, like many Catholic women religious, chooses to remain orthodox even as she bends orthodoxy *almost* to the breaking point. (Is Chittister representing Dinnerstein's description of the court jester as loyal opponent, the "indispensable defanged and domesticated critic"?)

Yet here, too, is Barbara Ehrenreich, in *Blood Rites: Origins and History of the Passions of War*, complaining that "there has been consistent misrepresentation of the archaic goddess . . . in the direction of downplaying her more savage predilections," a misrepresentation Ehrenreich blames on "contemporary feminist scholars [who] have been particularly energetic in their efforts to rehabilitate the archaic goddess as a thoroughly gentle and 'feminine' figure."[105] Ehrenreich devotes chapter 6 in her book to the subject "When the Predator Had a Woman's Face."

But before we dip into Ehrenreich's bloody rites, let's clarify a core term. That term is "predator beast." She means that "our peculiar and ambivalent relationship to violence is rooted in a primordial experience that we have managed, as a species, to almost entirely repress." What is this repressed experience? It's the "experience, not

---

104. Chittister, *God*, 148.
105. Ehrenreich, *Blood*, 101.

of hunting, but of being preyed upon by animals that were initially far more skillful hunters than ourselves."[106] Ehrenreich opens her analysis like this:

> Some of the earliest deities worshipped by humans were female, but they were hardly the nurturing "earth mothers" imagined by so many later scholars, both male and female. The archaic goddess unearthed from Mediterranean and Mesopotamian ruins or recalled in Mesoamerican mythology is far more likely to hold a snake in her clenched fist than a child in her arms. Only rarely a mother and seldom a wife, she reigned in the company of her lion, serpent, or leopard familiars. She was a huntress, a consumer of sacrificial offerings, and, most strikingly, an anthropomorphized version of the predator beast.
>
> In Anatolia the predator goddess is Cybele, the commander of lions. In Egypt she is Sekmet, portrayed as a lioness whose "mane smoked with fire, her back had the colour of blood, her countenance glowed like the sun, her eyes shone with fire." In India she is Durga, also known as Kali, who rides on a tiger and is associated in Brahmanic texts, with an actual forest region infested with lions and tigers. In Sumer she is Innanna, one of whose names was Labbatu, or lioness, and who is often shown standing with her feet planted on the backs of two imperious lions. In Canaan she is Astarte, who is depicted similarly, on a lion's back. In Mycenae she is flanked by lions; at Catal Huyuk she sits between leopards. In Crete she is shown playing with lions or standing on a lion-flanked mountain before a worshipping youth. In the Homeric epic, she is Artemis, of whom the poet says:
>
> > Zeus has made you a lion among women, and given you leave
> > to kill any at your pleasure.[107]

Ehrenreich goes on to say

> . . . there was a time, apparently in many disparate cultures, when imagination gave the beast a human female form. In this chapter, we consider the "feminine" imagery of the predator beast, as suggested by archaic predator goddesses, and speculate on what it meant and why it eventually faded. The data are scant, and the literature is either frustratingly speculative or tainted with romantic notions of femininity from historical times. But it does seem likely that the ascension of "mankind" to the status of predator was followed, near to historical times, by the descent of woman in the opposite direction: from someone who could be imagined as possessing lethal force to a creature more commonly conceived as prey.[108]

---

106. Ehrenreich, *Blood*, 22.

107. Ehrenreich, *Blood*, 97-98.

108. Ehrenreich, *Blood*, 98.

So where did this feminine imagery as predator beast originate? Well, let's note Dorothy Dinnerstein saying that "On a primitive feeling level, female authority is far more awesome to all of us."[109] And she—Dinnerstein—goes on to say:

> The mother, then—like nature, which sends blizzards and locusts as well as sunshine and strawberries—is perceived as capricious, sometimes actively malevolent. Her body is the first important piece of the physical world we encounter, and the events for which she seems responsible the first instances of fate. Hence Mother Nature, with her hurricane daughters Alice, Betty, Clara, Debbie, Edna. Hence that fickle female Lady Luck.[110]

(We're going to allow Barbara Ehrenreich her say here; but let's bear in mind Dinnerstein's admonition regarding the *perceived* overbearing nature of the mother in the unconscious of mother-raised children, a nature she calls, at different times, a "carnal scapegoat-idol" and a "dirty goddess."[111] But don't think that Dinnerstein is *blaming* women for our overarching gender predicament. Her mode of analysis is the complex dynamics of gender, even as her conclusions may be acutely unsettling. We might consider both Ehrenreich's predator beast and Dinnerstein's mother-raised-children dynamic as rooted in the far distant, precivilized past. That is, they're psychic constructs emerging out of *pagus*, which helps explain the negativity attached to each.)

According to Ehrenreich, "scholars have tended to associate goddess worship with agriculture, and the goddess with the 'life-giving' earth."[112] But in a variety of religions and cultures (she names the Aztecs, ancient Greeks, Egyptians, and Sumerians), a "female deity presides over the hunt and wild animals in general."[113] She says that "early goddesses revealed a predatory, even bestial, side":

> No doubt the dark side of the goddess was exaggerated by later adherents of patriarchal religions, just as the "wise woman" of pre-Christian European tradition was discredited by the late-medieval church as a witch. But there is reason to think that the "real" goddess, as known to her original worshippers, deserved at least some of her later reputation for bloodthirstiness.[114]

"If there has been consistent misrepresentation of the archaic goddess," Ehrenreich continues, "it has been in the direction of downplaying her more savage predilections":

> By classical times, and certainly in our own time, the associations between masculinity and violence, femininity and nonviolence, had hardened into dogma. The primordial goddess—huntress of beasts and consumer of blood—had

---

109. Dinnerstein, *Mermaid*, 87.

110. Dinnerstein, *Mermaid*, 95.

111. Dinnerstein, *Mermaid*, 124, 147.

112. Ehrenreich, *Blood*, 99.

113. Ehrenreich, *Blood*, 99.

114. Ehrenreich, *Blood*, 100.

to be prettified as a seductress, like Aphrodite, or a motherly figure with a passion for gardening, like Demeter or Ceres.[115]

From there, Ehrenreich looks for an explanation of what she calls "the link between the predator beast and the human female."[116] She finds that link in menstruation, in the cyclical shedding of blood. At first she says "Some cultures make a conscious and explicit connection between women's natural vaginal bleeding—both menstrual and postpartum—and acts of ritual bloodletting usually reserved for males,"[117] but then she hints at the vagina as a "blood-smeared mouth"[118] associated with violence and potency. She asks if there could

> . . . have been some real event or trend that brought an end to the predator goddess's reign and ushered in the era of the male warrior-hero? If so, it must have occurred long before the Neolithic revolution brought forth settled agricultural communities, because whatever happened, happened almost worldwide, and it happened also among peoples who continued to make their living exclusively as hunter-gatherers. . . .
>
> One possible candidate for this crucial "event" is a change in hunting strategies.[119]

What she means by a change in hunting strategies is that hunting, due to declines in big game populations, became an activity of male stalking rather than a practice of "noisy assemblages that included women and children."[120] This change created, she says,

> . . . a new sexual division of labor and, with it, a general demotion of the female sex. Instead of the communal hunt undertaken by the whole band, there was now the male hunters' sub-band, with women relegated to the less glamorous job of processing the meat (as well as the skin, bones, and other useful animal products) brought back by men. If so, this might help explain the general decline in depictions of human females in the art of the Upper (or more recent) Paleolithic. On the eve of the Neolithic, the human male was probably a good, goddess-fearing soul. But he held the spear, the sling, and the bow, all firmly in his hand.
>
> In surviving hunting-gathering cultures, not only are women expected to remain behind while men hunt; they are often barred from contact with men's weapons or other "magic" items. Possibly, with the historic change to a male-only hunting strategy, violence in general began to be seen as the exclusive

115. Ehrenreich, *Blood*, 101.

116. Ehrenreich, *Blood*, 104.

117. Ehrenreich, *Blood*, 106.

118. Ehrenreich, *Blood*, 107.

119. Ehrenreich, *Blood*, 110.

120. Ehrenreich, *Blood*, 110.

prerogative of males. Even women's involuntary bloodshed must, in most traditional societies, be thoroughly kept from sight. In the patriarchal era, as anthropologist Nancy Jay has written, the blood shed by men in sacrifice or war is powerful and redeeming, while the blood shed by women becomes a dangerous pollutant.[121]

Monstrous females, Ehrenreich concludes,

> . . . had no place in the patriarchal order, which attempted to efface every vestige of the archaic association between the human female and the predator beast. Henceforth, for the most part, males alone would be privileged to reenact the transformation from prey to predator. Deprived, in most cases, of a blood rite of initiation, females would have no ritual escape from the child's status as prey. . . .
>
> By assigning the triumphant-predator status to males alone, humans have helped themselves to "forget" that nightmarish prehistory in which they were all, male and female, prey to larger, stronger animals. Insofar as males have been the human "norm" and females the deviation, weakness and vulnerability could be seen as something aberrant and incidental to the story of humankind. Gender, in other words, is an idea that conveniently obliterates our common past as prey, and states that the predator status is innate and "natural"—at least to men.[122]

Perhaps Ehrenreich's cautionary tale is legitimately warning us against a sentimental view of precivilized history.[123] But let's also note that her pantheon of Monstrous Females, as far as I can see, is representative of religious energies (i.e., psychic power-and-fear projections) in the early period of civilization, even as she surmises that the *end* of the "predator goddess's reign" occurred long *before* the "Neolithic revolution brought forth settled agricultural communities." That means (or at least suggests) that Monstrous Females were, at most, early civilized relics of paleolithic culture and/or a carry-over of (male?) psychic projection having to do with what Dinnerstein calls "dirty goddess" and "carnal scapegoat-idol." What we *can* say with some certainty—until there is new and convincing scholarship on the subject—is that the "remarkably peaceful societies" McNeill tells of in regard to neolithic villages bear little if any resemblance to the bloodcurdling, bloody-mouthed, violent, vicious goddesses Ehrenreich describes. And while it may be true that unconscious trauma, stemming from ancient encounters with predator beasts, continue at a deep level in our collective psychic and cultural life, let's also bear in mind Dinnerstein's exposition of

---

121. Ehrenreich, *Blood*, 111.

122. Ehrenreich, *Blood*, 113–14.

123. See also George Monbiot's *Feral*, especially—chapter 5—"The Never-spotted Leopard."

the "link between societal despotism, female rule over childhood, and male rule over the historical process"[124]:

> *The crucial psychological fact is that all of us, female as well as male, fear the will of woman.* Man's dominion over what we think of as the world rests on a terror that we all feel: the terror of sinking back wholly into the helplessness of infancy. As the folk saying insists, there is another realm that interpenetrates all too intimately with what is formally recognized as the world: a realm already ruled, despotically enough, by the hand that rocks the cradle.
>
> Female will is embedded in female power, which is under present conditions the earliest and profoundest prototype of absolute power. It emanates, at the outset, from a boundless, all-embracing presence. We live by its grace while our lives are most fragile. We grow human within its aura. Its reign is total, all-pervasive, throughout our most vulnerable, and most fatefully impressionable, years. Power of this kind, concentrated in one sex and exerted at the outset over both, is far too potent and dangerous a force to be allowed free sway in adult life. To contain it, to keep it under control and harness it to chosen purposes, is a vital need, a vital task, for every mother-raised human.
>
> The weight of this emotional fact is so familiar to us, we carry it so universally and its pressure is so numbing, that to be vividly aware of how it crushes us—or to imagine not being crushed by it—is almost impossible. We can refer to it with the elliptical offhand intensity of that folk saying, or describe it with the sustained poetic lucidity of de Beauvoir, and still never focus on how the possibility of living free of it can be concretely realized.
>
> Pre-Christian goddesses, de Beauvoir says, "were cruel, capricious, lustful; in giving birth to men they made men their slaves. Under Christianity, life and death depend only on God, and man, once out of the maternal body, has escaped that body forever. For the destiny of his soul is played out in regions where the mother's powers are abolished . . ." But having said this (and she says it in many ways), de Beauvoir rests her case. Her implication is that in the very act of recognizing its truth, we will have started to surmount it, and of course she is right. What I am adding is that having started we must carry through what we have begun; and that to do so we must look hard at what is very hard to look at: the precise feature of childhood whose existence makes the adult situation de Beauvoir describes inevitable, and the consequent necessity for female abdication of unilateral rule over childhood, which she stopped short of facing.[125]

There are thirteen pages of small print in the Bibliography of Barbara Ehrenreich's *Blood Rites*. Dorothy Dinnerstein's name doesn't appear there. Perhaps Dinnerstein's analysis was perceived by Ehrenreich as too intangible, too "psychological," to be worthy of consideration. But I'm reminded of Lewis Mumford's remark in "Utopia, the City, and

---

124. Dinnerstein, *Mermaid*, 163.
125. Dinnerstein, *Mermaid*, 161-62.

the Machine"—one of many brilliant essays in *Interpretations and Forecasts*—where he points out that the "machine" of early civilizations left no direct archaeological record, because that "machine" was composed of regimented human beings acting as slaves. One could therefore infer that such a "machine" never existed—where are its parts?—but that would leave, for instance, the Egyptian pyramids as a bit of cosmic puzzle. (Were they dropped out of the sky by space aliens?) But, as Dinnerstein says, it's our job to look hard at what is hard to look at—not so much because it's "invisible" as it is so utterly *normal*: the extent to which female will is the earliest and most profound prototype of absolute power, and therefore (we must surmise) the *psychological* reservoir out of which Monstrous Female goddesses at least in part arose.

Well, let's see what Merlin Stone has to say about this same subject, more or less. In a chapter called "If the King Did Not Weep," we hear what happened when a queen took a young man as consort:

> The sacred sexual union with the high priestess gave the male consort a privileged position. According to Professor Saggs, in historic Sumer and Babylon, after the sacred marriage the Goddess "fixed the destiny" of the king for the coming year. But in earlier days this position of kingship was far from permanent. The male chosen held his royal rights for a specific period of time. At the end of this time (perhaps a year since the ceremony was celebrated annually, but other records seem to suggest possibly a longer period in certain areas), this youth was then ritually sacrificed.[126]

Stone also says that:

> The subject of the annual death of the son/lover of the Goddess interests us here because it appears to be a direct outgrowth of the original rituals and customs of the early female religion. It symbolizes one of the most ancient practices recorded—the ritual sacrifice of an annual "king," consort of the high priestess.[127]

She goes on to conclude her chapter by saying

> . . . the mass of evidence makes it clear that Ishtar, as well as other versions of the Goddess throughout the Near and Middle East, was described as "the fountainhead of the power and prestige of the king" because it was actually required that the king become the sexual consort of the high priestess, incarnation of the Goddess on earth, who probably held the rights to the royal throne through matrilineal descent.
>
> The custom of ritual regicide disappeared as the patrilineal tribes gained dominance. The numerous copies of the legend of Gilgamesh, in various languages, may have been used to further this purpose. Permanent hereditary

126. Stone, *When*, 133.

127. Stone, *When*, 132.

kingship became the rule and as the male deity gained supremacy, the role of the benefactor of the divine right to the throne was eventually shifted over to him, a concept of the rights of royalty that survives even today.

There can be little doubt that the original customs of ritual regicide, and the political position of the high priestess, presented a major obstacle to the desire of the northern conquerors for a permanent kingship and more total control of government.[128]

What Merlin Stone's analysis suggests is the possibility—I want to stress *possibility*—that the social and cultural conditions surrounding the religious practices described in her book represent a culmination in the economic size and cultural complexity of village life on the cusp of civilization. That is, if the prestige and power of women grew right along with the growth and complexity of settled village life, partly as a consequence of horticultural abundance, then the ritual "sacred marriage" of a young man to the queen or high priestess, and his ritual murder or "sacrifice" a year or so later, was a way—certainly an alarming and brutal way—to tamp down or hold back a kind of authoritarian rule that an unrestrained male king, acting without limitation or restriction, might have imposed on the entire community. All this, says Stone, may have been a way of protecting "the sexual customs of the Goddess":

> In the worship of the female deity, sex was Her gift to humanity. It was sacred and holy. She was the Goddess of Sexual Love and Procreation. But in the religions of today we find an almost totally reversed attitude. Sex, especially non-marital sex, is considered to be somewhat naughty, dirty, even sinful. Yet rather than calling the earliest religions, which embraced such an open acceptance of all human sexuality, "fertility-cults," we might consider the religions of today as strange in that they seem to associate shame and even sin with the very process of conceiving new human life. Perhaps centuries from now scholars and historians will be classifying them as "sterility-cults."[129]

Stone also says the "temples of the Goddess in Neolithic and Chalcolithic periods appear to have been the core of the community, apparently owning the land, the herds of animals and most material property." But she insists that a "nominal leader does not infer monarchy. In fact, several documents and myths suggest that Neolithic and early historic Goddess-worshiping communities were governed by assemblies, probably composed of the elders of the community":

> Professor Thorkild Jacobsen of the University of Chicago has influenced many other archaeologists and historians on this subject. His theory, based on the fact that the earliest Sumerian myths included both female and male deities in the decision-making assemblies of heaven, suggests that such participation of women in leadership was very likely a reflection of the societies that wrote

128. Stone, *When*, 151-52.
129. Stone, *When*, 154-55.

the legends, both women and men taking part in community government. We may even regard the concept of monotheism, so often presented as a more civilized or sophisticated type of religion, as reflecting the political ideology that places all power in a single dominant person, while polytheism, especially as represented in the image of divine assembles, perhaps symbolized a more communal attitude in the societies that developed and followed this type of theological thought.[130]

Do we recall what Elaine Pagels said to us regarding "spiritual authority"? That first Clement and then Ignatius taught "One God, one bishop":

> And as God rules over that council in heaven, so the bishop on earth rules over a council of priests. The heavenly divine council, in turn, stands above the apostles; so, on earth, the priests rule over the deacons—and all three of these rule over "the laity."

What if Professor Thorkild Jacobsen and Merlin Stone are correct? What if the monarchical model of God justifies both monotheism and male domination, both heaven and harem? What if female will, the "earliest and profoundest prototype of absolute power" for all mother-raised children, is "too potent and dangerous," as Dorothy Dinnerstein asserts, to be "allowed free sway in adult life"? What if males, in (largely) unconscious dread of this power, once they achieve supreme power in monotheistic and civilizational ways, proceed to deploy policies and enact practices that bring us to the lip of global abyss? Who or what, exactly, is the psychodynamic "divinity" of this extermination-in-waiting?

XXIII

So here, with Ehrenreich and Stone, we may be seeing the sordid side of the Goddess. Perhaps that's so. Nevertheless, let's face it, even at Her worst She's no more ferocious than Yahweh. So let's not pretend that Mama's a dirty bitch but Daddy's a gentle hero, or that Mother isn't locked in the cellar of Western history while Father is busily making the world safe for democracy. Refusal to acknowledge the incarcerated Mother gives Father free rein in His *Realpolitik* aggressions. No matter what it is—fair or foul, benign or brutal—our history, and the divinities of our history, have to be faced and acknowledged for what they represent, neither idealized nor repressed. If we wish to be free of these obsessions, we must see them for what they are. They must undergo "apocalyptic" disclosure. This is why I say—even while insisting on Mother, Father, Son, and Daughter as unavoidable "divine" sequence—that these are dangerous constructs, easily deployed in behalf of power, advantage, murder, and mayhem. The real and necessary task is always to sink, in our human unknowing, into the embrace of underlying Spirit, who may well defy any and all categorization as Mother, Father, Son,

130. Stone, *When*, 130-31.

or Daughter. As human creatures in an incredibly complex evolutionary process, we have in the end no choice but to trust in the benevolence of underlying Spirit. There really is no rational option. (Get a one-way ticket to Venus or Mars?) I believe this sinking into Spirit is what Jesus did repeatedly, with a willing wholeness that remains a major example and powerful model for human yearning. Take away the accrued otherworldly excrescences, the theological claptrap of Christianity, and Jesus emerges more—not less—spiritually astonishing. Here is a peasant who conveys a spiritual approach for the dissolving of civilizational oppression and religious hypocrisy: put down the weapons and dare to live with humility, compassion, and vulnerability. We can move in that astonishingly brave atmosphere as we sink into Spirit, as we embrace the corresponding ethical principles of radical stewardship and radical servanthood, finding in openness and humility what is otherwise closed to us by doctrinal assertiveness, creedal pride, gender superiority, and sexual evasion.

But then we also see the extent to which Christian intellectuals who, one presumes, consider themselves on the cutting edge of creative thinking while remaining in a conventional Trinitarian box. We've seen this with Elizabeth Johnson and Andrew Harvey. Karen Armstrong, in *The Battle for God*, touches into the same turf when she says of Isaac Newton that he

> . . . was unable to appreciate that the dogma of the Trinity had been devised by the Greek Orthodox theologians of the fourth century precisely as *mythos*, similar to that later created by the Jewish Kabbalists. As Gregory of Nyssa had explained, the three *hypostases* of Father, Son, and Spirit were not objective facts but simply "terms that we use" to express the way in which the "unnameable and unspeakable" divine nature (*ousia*) adapts itself to the limitations of our human minds. It made no sense outside the cultic context of prayer, contemplation, and liturgy. But Newton could only see the Trinity in rational terms, had no understanding of the role of myth, and was therefore obliged to jettison the doctrine. The difficulty that many Western Christians today experience with trinitarian theology shows that they share Newton's bias in favor of reason.[131]

This allegation—that Newton had no understanding of the role of myth—needs elaboration. Here's Armstrong from her Introduction, explaining her understanding of *mythos* and *logos*. Let's start with *logos*:

> Unlike myth, *logos* must relate exactly to facts and correspond to external realities if it is to be effective. It must work efficiently in the mundane world. We use this logical, discursive reasoning when we have to make things happen, get something done, or persuade other people to adopt a particular course of action. *Logos* is practical. Unlike myth, which looks back to the beginnings and to the foundations, *logos* forges ahead and tries to find something new:

131. Armstrong, *Battle*, 69.

to elaborate on old insights, achieve a greater control over our environment, discover something fresh, and invent something novel.[132]

Let's look at this. First, the neat *mythos/logos* duality just happens to reflect the two-kingdom church/state combination rather well; both are constructions in need of serious attention. To zero in on one thing, Armstrong says *logos* is logical, practical and forward looking, while myth looks to beginnings and foundations. Well, pardon me, if anything's clarified our vision in regard to beginnings and foundations, it's been the *logos* of astronomy, geology, biology, anthropology, and archaeology. *Mythos*, meanwhile, certainly so in the fundamentalist camp (which is orthodoxy in a corner created by its embrace of *mythos* posturing as *logos*), has been throwing a giant hissy fit because its suppositions and abstractions have been evaporated by a burst of scholarly sunshine and intellectual fresh air. But let's hear more from Karen Armstrong:

> We tend to assume that the people of the past were (more or less) like us, but in fact their spiritual lives were rather different. In particular, they evolved two ways of thinking, speaking, and acquiring knowledge, which scholars have called *mythos* and *logos*. Both were essential; they were regarded as complementary ways of arriving at truth, and each had its special area of competence. Myth was regarded as primary; it was concerned with what was thought to be timeless and constant in our existence. Myth looked back to the origins of life, to the foundations of culture, and to the deepest levels of the human mind. Myth was not concerned with practical matters, but with meaning. Unless we find some significance in our lives, we mortal men and women fall very easily into despair. The *mythos* of a society provided people with a context that made sense of their day-to-day lives; it directed their attention to the eternal and the universal. It was also rooted in what we would call the unconscious mind. The various mythological stories, which were not intended to be taken literally, were an ancient form of psychology. When people told stories about heroes who descended into the underworld, struggled through labyrinths, or fought with monsters, they were bringing to light the obscure regions of the subconscious realm, which is not accessible to purely rational investigation, but which has a profound effect upon our experience and behavior. Because of the dearth of myth in our modern society, we have had to evolve the science of psychoanalysis to help us to deal with our inner world.
>
> Myth could not be demonstrated by rational proof; its insights were more intuitive, similar to those of art, music, poetry, or sculpture. Myth only became a reality when it was embodied in cult, rituals, and ceremonies which worked aesthetically upon worshippers, evoking within them a sense of sacred significance and enabling them to apprehend the deeper currents of existence. Myth and cult were so inseparable that it is a matter of scholarly debate which came first: the mythical narrative or the rituals attached to it. Myth was also

132. Armstrong, *Battle*, xiv-xv.

associated with mysticism, the descent into the psyche by means of structured disciplines of focus and concentration which have been evolved in all cultures as a means of acquiring intuitive insight. Without a cult or mystical practice, the myths of religion would make no sense. They would remain abstract and seem incredible, in rather the same way as a musical score remains opaque to most of us and needs to be interpreted instrumentally before we can appreciate its beauty.

In the premodern world, people had a different view of history. They were less concerned than we are in what actually happened, but more concerned with the meaning of an event. Historical incidents were not seen as unique occurrences, set in a far-off time, but were thought to be external manifestations of constant, timeless realities.[133]

In my estimation, this is a lucid articulation of modern liberal obfuscation, obscuring rather than clarifying, evoking real subjects but dressing the "intuitive" in fluff. As we have seen with Elaine Pagels' explication of Clement and Ignatius (or as we can find in Pagels' *Adam, Eve, and the Serpent,* in regard to Augustine), *mythos* was taken *literally* by the early church fathers:

The majority of orthodox Christians in the first and second centuries, like most Jews and Christians ever since, read the Scriptures . . . primarily as practical guides to moral living. They read the Genesis story, in particular, as *history with a moral*: that is, they regarded Adam and Eve as actual historical persons, the venerable ancestors of our race; and from the story of their disobedience, orthodox interpreters drew practical lessons in moral behavior. Tertullian, for example, took Genesis 3 as an opportunity to warn his "sisters in Christ" that even the best of them were, in effect, Eve's co-conspirators:

"You are the devil's gateway. . . you are she who persuaded him whom the devil did not dare attack. . . . Do you not know that every one of you is an Eve? The sentence of God on your sex lives on in this age; the guilt, of necessity, lives on too."[134]

Doesn't this show that a great deal of theological assertion derives from orthodox church fathers taking *mythos* as historical fact? Augustine's doctrine of original sin rests in Adam's testicles:

Augustine declares . . . that the whole human race inherited from Adam a nature irreversibly damaged by sin. "For we all were in that one man, since all of us were that one man who fell into sin through the woman who was made from him." . . . That semen itself, Augustine argues, already "shackled by the bond of death," transmits the damage incurred by sin.[135]

133. Armstrong, *Battle*, xiii-xiv.

134. Pagels, *Adam*, 62-63.

135. Pagels, *Adam*, 109.

Pagels says explicitly that it was *gnostic* Christians who "castigated the orthodox for making the mistake of reading the Scriptures—and especially Genesis—literally, and thereby missing its 'deeper meaning.'"[136] (And, lest we forget, the gnostics *lost* the theological fight with the orthodox.) She also asks:

> Why did Catholic Christianity adopt Augustine's paradoxical—some would say preposterous—views? Some historians suggest that such beliefs validate the church's authority, for if the human condition is a disease, Catholic Christianity, acting as the Good Physician, offers the spiritual medication and the discipline that alone can cure it. No doubt Augustine's views did serve the interests of the emerging imperial church and the Christian state. . . .
>
> For what Augustine says, in simplest terms, is this: human beings cannot be trusted to govern themselves, because our very nature—indeed, *all* of nature—has become corrupt as the result of Adam's sin.[137]

Through her device of packing what's "timeless and constant" into myth (while simultaneously making myth "not concerned with practical matters"), Armstrong can say that historical incidences are only "external manifestations of constant, timeless realities." This serves to dehistoricize myth and make metaphysical assertion untouchable by historical analysis or psychoanalytical critique. Thus myth gets to float in a cloud of timeless Platonic idealism, ungrounded from practical matters and unsullied by temporal dirt.

No. Absolutely not. Myth is not this clean, gossamer will-o'-the-wisp drifting beyond the grasping, grubby hands of sordid-minded history. Myth serves human purposes, even if those purposes originate in obscure regions of the subconscious: and, not too incidentally, we are *not* entitled to our myths just because they serve as an antidote to despair. Truth has to look reality in the face. That's its spiritual job. If reality is not benevolent, we have to face the facts. Psychoanalysis—at least the kind of psychoanalytical thinking I know of and respect from Norman O. Brown and Dorothy Dinnerstein—pulls very real "practical matters" out of the mystical hat of myth and demonstrates that myth is not just flowers and butterflies but also venom and claws. This is exactly what I meant when I said Ched Myers and Michael Lerner take ahistorical metaphysical assertion and present it as suprahistorical divine reality. This may be what is sometimes called misplaced concreteness. But truth sets us free. Revelation means disclosure. Although we may prefer the provisional comfort of falsity—there invariably are moments in our personal lives when sliding around the edges of jagged truth seems ambiguously preferable—we are sealing our collective doom by embracing evasive thinking, particularly in religion, politics, and economics. It's one thing to avoid an unnecessary harshness in behalf of an immediate personal kindness, but it's

---

136. Pagels, *Adam*, 63.

137. Pagels, *Adam*, 145.

completely inappropriate to protect religious mythology or political ideology on that basis. Myth, on that level, becomes the foundation of institutional sin.

In this vein, it's necessary to reconsider the meaning of the religious/scientific divide associated with Copernicus onward. So many of the great scientific minds in the Enlightenment pantheon (people like Galileo, Descartes, and Newton) were prevented from finding a more supple spirituality in the workings of nature—prevented by the hegemony of Christian orthodoxy and the extent to which that orthodoxy demanded what had to be believed. Governed by a social and cultural authoritarianism in behalf of the Supreme Being or the Creator of the Universe or inherited Christian Truth, these acute observers were forced to see nature despiritualized—prevented from recognizing the spiritual within nature—because to find Spirit *within* nature was tantamount to paganism, and paganism had an ancient pedigree of evil, something to be avoided at all cost. Therefore, nature had to be dead, lifeless, a mere cause-and-effect mechanism. The deadness of nature was the spiritual (and therefore intellectual) consequence of original sin. The deity associated with fallen nature was Satan. If inquisitorial torture was used by the church to compel religious wickedness to confess, science inherited from the church both a technical procedure and a "spiritual" approach by which to elicit nature's stubborn secrets.[138]

To say, therefore, that the Enlightenment was the product of perverse minds may be true, to some degree; but the basis of that perversity was—and remains—an underlying authoritarian power of religious assertion denying indwelling Spirit in nature. (Only humans are made in the image of God, and that image was permanently damaged by original sin.) We can get a sense of how deeply orthodox religion was tied into the social status quo by attending to this commentary on Edmund Burke from *The True and Only Heaven* by Christopher Lasch:

> A brilliant debater, Burke nevertheless preferred silence to the noise of debate or, in his favorite image, the decent clothing of custom to the "nakedness" he associated with reason. He praised religion as the "basis of civil society" but deplored theological controversy. Modern Christians, he wrote, took "their

138. Here's what Fritjof Capra says on page 22 of *The Web of Life*: "The Romantic view of nature as 'one great harmonious whole,' as Goethe put it, led some scientists of that period to extend their search for wholeness to the entire planet and see the Earth as an integrated whole, a living being. The view of the Earth as being alive, of course, has a long tradition. Mythical images of the Earth Mother are among the oldest in human religious history. Gaia, the Earth Goddess, was revered as the supreme deity in early, pre-Hellenic Greece. Earlier still, from the Neolithic through the Bronze Ages, the societies of 'Old Europe' worshiped numerous female deities as incarnations of Mother Earth.

"The idea of the Earth as a living, spiritual being continued to flourish throughout the Middle Ages and the Renaissance, until the whole medieval outlook was replaced by the Cartesian image of the world as a machine. So when scientists in the eighteenth century began to visualize the Earth as a living being, they revived an ancient tradition that had been dormant for only a relatively brief period."

What Capra's summation overlooks is the deeply potent Judeo-Christian doctrine of the fallenness of nature, nature's corruption, or how Augustine's City of God imagery established *pagus* as the wicked Other. Earth as living being hadn't so much been "dormant" as it had been religiously suppressed.

religion as an habit, and upon authority, and not by disputation." When he spoke of Christianity as "the one great source of civilization amongst us," he added that "throwing off" Christianity would "uncover our nakedness." In his tribute to Marie Antoinette, he spoke in the same way of "chivalry." Those who took the position that a "queen is but a woman" stripped away the "pleasing illusions which made power gentle and obedience liberal, which harmonized the different shades of life, and which by a bland assimilation incorporated into politics the sentiments which beautify and soften private society." Note that Burke did not deny the truth of the assertion that "a queen is but a woman, a woman is but an animal,—and an animal not of the highest order." He denied only that it was safe to dispense with the "pleasing illusion" that things were otherwise, According to the "mechanical philosophy" of the Enlightenment, "all the decent drapery of life is to be rudely torn off. All the superadded ideas, furnished from the wardrobe of a moral imagination, which the heart owns and the understanding ratifies, as necessary to cover the defects of our naked, shivering nature, and to raise it to dignity in our own estimation, are to be exploded, as a ridiculous, absurd, and antiquated fashion."

Burke capped his defense of prejudice with the same figure. To "cast away the coat of prejudice," he argued, would "leave nothing but the naked reason."[139]

Well, it seems that exposure to "naked reason" could go a number of ways. One way is to proceed humbly unclothed into the Cloud of Unknowing and consent, even in embarrassment and pain, to be dissolved—or hope to be dissolved—of cloying illusions. Another is to look at the world as a nearly bottomless repository of "resources" we are entitled to grab with greed proportionate to the "dignity in our own estimation"—i.e., God says the fallen Earth is ours to use as we see fit, so let's get at it. Yet another is to refuse to "cast away the coat of prejudice" because, in all frankness, we don't wish to contemplate—i.e., we don't wish to acknowledge—the "defects of our naked, shivering nature." This does nothing to lovingly guide liberated reason toward humility but, in fact, enables its opposite—which is perverse pride.[140]

---

139. Lasch, *True*, 130-31.

140. Edmund Burke, though twenty years younger, was nevertheless a friend and conversational associate of Samuel Johnson. In John Wain's biography of Johnson (simply called *Samuel Johnson*), we find, on page 167, that, as Johnson saw it, the "Church to which he belonged had elaborated its doctrines, and worked out its procedures through centuries of trial and error and debate, and had achieved a consensus on which the individual mind could repose. Just as, in his historical writings, he shows impatience with the preaching tinkers and tailors of the seventeenth-century Commonwealth, so he wishes also to show obedience to central custom and tradition."

But Wain shows that Johnson's mind was, in an important way, not at all in repose. He says of Johnson, on pages 202 and 203, that sexual relationships were for Johnson "treacherous ground," that sexual desires were "represented by his religion as leading straight to hell-fire," and that he "did everything he could to smother them": "In a mind more happily constituted, religious belief might have provided the emotional sustenance it forbade him to seek in women. As a religious man Johnson had in theory the possibility of a comforting and uplifting relationship with his God. But this relationship,

There is a reasonably good chapter ("Science and Religion: The Great Divorce") in an otherwise mediocre book called *What the Bleep Do We (K)now!?* It has a brief section on Francis Bacon, one paragraph of which reads like this:

> As Fritjof Capra has pointed out, Bacon viewed the scientific enterprise in terms that were "often outright vicious." Nature had to be "hounded in her wanderings," "bound into service," and "made a slave." The job of the scientist was to "torture nature's secrets from her." Unfortunately, this attitude that sought to extract knowledge in order to control and dominate nature (described as a "her") has become a guiding principle of Western science. Bacon summed it up in a phrase we all learned in school: "Knowledge is Power."[141]

But this "guiding principle" was precisely the inquisitional practice of the church at the height of its power—in regard, that is, to heresy, unbelief, and false understanding. Should we be shocked that science picked up and refined this inquisitorial methodology? We will be shocked only to the extent that we are oblivious (willfully or otherwise) of the institutional—religious—history out of which science emerged.

Norman O. Brown, in a discussion of modern science, says an aggressive and dominating attitude toward nature is a "disease in consciousness. In more technical psychoanalytical terms, the issue is not the conscious structure of science, but the unconscious premises of science; the trouble is in the unconscious strata of the scientific ego, in the scientific character-structure."[142] These "unconscious premises" are rooted not only in the inquisitorial church but also in the sanctimonious brutality of civilizational self-absorption, in the dignity of our civilized self-estimation. To protect these self-serving premises, this *mythos*, from being stripped away is to participate in

---

for various reasons, was associated in his mind with guilt and terror. Whatever Johnson's religion did for him, it did not make him happy in this mortal life."

Wain says that Johnson "dreaded the judgment of God" (page 219) and feared "that God whose dreadful vengeance he dreaded with every fiber of his being" (page 287). So it seems perfectly reasonable to say that Johnson's religious *and* political orthodoxy was held firmly in place by the power of his fear of God and that this fear had a strong linkage to his erotic proclivities. Nor do I think it a stretch to suggest that Johnson's reflexive smothering of his sexual urges bears a close connection with what Wain, on page 281, calls "Johnson's anti-populist feeling": "The notion of popular intervention in government policy meant nothing to him but stark mob rule. It recalled the preaching tinkers and cobblers, the ragged philosophers of the seventeenth century, the rabble of fanatics who had done so much harm to the fabric of English life."

Repression, as Norman O. Brown consistently reminds us, may have at its core the suppression of sexual desire, but its controlling energy infiltrates and spreads to other areas of life where eruption "from below" seeks liberation, realization, and actualization. Thus God, with the power (and inclination) to impose eternal damnation, is the keystone of the two-kingdom arch whose legs are Church and State. Therefore it should come as no surprise that democracy, the discovery of an exceedingly more gentle, loving and forgiving divinity, and the steady unfolding of a richer and more fulfilling sexuality should all emerge simultaneously. All this, in turn, is a prerequisite for a far deeper ecological sensitivity and humanitarian sensibility whereby the realization of a globalized Green economy actually becomes possible.

141. Arntz, *What*, 16.

142. Brown, *Life*, 317.

the harmless sabotage of the court jester, as Dorothy Dinnerstein pointed out. I repeat a portion of an earlier quotation:

> This sabotage is harmless to what it purports to assault. Indeed it dissipates what could be effectively explosive feeling, discharges potentially subversive emotional energy in frivolous and impotent, homey and comfortable, ways. It farts away internal pressure that would otherwise shatter the social system.

In other words, and to bend the analysis in terms of this essay, the "mystical" patronizing of *logos*, such as Karen Armstrong indulges in, only serves to evade the historical fact that Christian *mythos* has used ecclesiastical "*logos*" as a club to beat *pagus* into submission to *civis*. That science would follow in the church's *pagus*-hating footsteps should come as no surprise.

XXIV

Merlin Stone explains her keen interest in feminine forms of divinity by having become aware of the almost total absence of such feminine forms in the Judeo-Christian tradition, and by realizing that where goddesses were part of Western history (the ancient religions of Greece and Rome, for instance), they were decorative, wicked, fickle, or foolish.

Certainly it was true for me, raised in the United Church of Christ, that the divine was completely Male. The absolute central pillar of the eternal and divine, Creator of the Universe, was God the Father. There was no question about that or any alternative to it. Catholics may have retained a sentimental adoration and unbiblical worship of Mary as Mother of God—"The only two formal exercises of papal infallibility in modern times have been definitions of Marian dogmas—of her Immaculate Conception by Pius IX and of her Assumption into Heaven by Pius XII"[143]—but most Protestants probably saw such exercises as throwbacks to pre-Christian paganism. Garry Wills goes on from his remarks regarding Marian dogmas to say:

> One reason the Virgin is semideifed in this way is that "feminine" functions of God—formation and nurturing of the church—are not assigned to the Father and Son, whose relationship is symbolically male. Some feminist theologians oppose this monopoly of male analogues by suggesting that Father and son be replaced by mother and daughter, which retains a gender monopoly by simply reversing it. The historical circumstances of New Testament revelation make that an arbitrary revisionism. The better course is to welcome a female analogy for God, but assign it to the third person of the Trinity. . . . The pronoun for the Spirit should be She, which will make clear that many of the functions

143. Wills, *Papal*, 205.

assigned to Mary (as a symbol of the church, or its protector) truly belong to the Trinity in its female analogue. One should pray to Her as well as to Him.[144]

This is an interesting passage in a number of ways. First, it correctly identifies the reversal of gender monopoly (as we have seen from Elizabeth Johnson) as an "arbitrary revisionism." Well, it's not exactly arbitrary—it's no mere caprice—yet such a reversal serves as historical erasure of something supposedly eternal and in principle unchanging and unchangeable: God the Father Almighty. That is, male domination in Western civilization would be inexplicable without a Father God in overarching authority. (Since we are a religious species, how could there be male domination without divine sanction?) The revisionist construct is historically absurd. Second, Wills' advocacy—the pronoun for Spirit should be She—is "liberal" in that it accords femininity to Spirit; but it obviously does so with a great deal of caution, as can be seen in the sudden dropping of capitalization—"suggesting that Father and son be replaced by mother and daughter"—in a manner that voluntarily (and temporarily) demotes "son" (not Son) so that refusal to promote "mother and daughter" (not Mother or Daughter) isn't so glaringly obvious. (Of course Father continues to be Father.) So while it's possible to say Wills' stance represents a loosening or liberalization of gender rigidity, it's really quite timid. If he had kept Son after Father, put Mother in front of Father and Daughter after Son, Wills would share Joachim's construct enlarged. But one can't get to that understanding while remaining an orthodox Trinitarian. Trinity locks out the Mother, even as some liberals try to slip a little femininity into Holy Spirit. That is, orthodox mythology (even if given a liberal twist) continues to evade the obvious correction. It is precisely this religious correction that's key to a simultaneous civilizational correction: civilization has buried the feminine agrarian village in a manner directly analogous to how the Abrahamic religions have eradicated the feminine from divinity. Fundamentalism is the mythic completeness of this eradication. Correction to Mandala is the mythic key to our survival. Recognizing Mandala—Mother, Father, Son, and Daughter—is, in strict etymology, apocalyptic. That is, it *uncovers* the hidden and *incorporates what was hidden* into our understanding of the past, into our anticipation of the future. It heals a great, festering wound and restores us to spiritual wholeness.

XXV

The mother-raised-children dynamic Dorothy Dinnerstein unfolds as a core cause of our enlarging deadly crises—world-shaping men who presume male entitlement, child-rearing women who defer to men who run the world—has achieved such "archetypal" form and normative power that we can see it projected in religious imagery and historical mythology. This imagery and mythology "divinizes" the exercise of

144. Wills, *Papal*, 218.

male power. Yet discerning the psychomythology of gender, as displayed in religious theophany, is now virtual child's play, given what we know of how gendered images have functioned (and continue to function) in the collective human mind and in history. It cannot be accidental that the period of neolithic horticulture corresponds to the enlargement of Goddess or Mother, a period largely free of weapons or violence, while God as jealous and wrathful Father emerged as a consequence of male power consolidation in the formation of civilization's traumatic institutions.

I think it fair to say, insofar as we are in a state of psychological and political bewilderment about these gender dynamics, such bewilderment reflects the psychological distress (including distress manifesting as evasion or denial) about disturbed gender comfort and sexual-arrangement familiarity, such as Dorothy Dinnerstein alerts us to, for women as well as men. To disturb these arrangements causes acute anxiety. For those of us raised in the traditional Sunday Schools of the Judeo-Christian West, our foundational religious stories about the origin of the world generally and the origin of the human race specifically, told us nothing of life before God created the world because, according to those stories, there was no life (except God's life) prior to that creation; and, as various biblical literalists with a taste for mathematics have tried over the centuries to calculate, that creation occurred only about six thousand years ago. Biblical mathematics aside, the religious view I grew up with did not differ appreciably from that held by the majority of orthodox Christians in the first and second centuries; that is, echoing Elaine Pagels, I regarded Adam and Eve as actual historical persons, the venerable ancestors of our race, exactly as the early church fathers did.

The literal view and its associated gender formations retain sufficient political strength in contemporary American society to prevent a fuller embrace and assimilation of scientific understanding. By "scientific" I mean an open exploration and honest acknowledgment of origins beyond the mythological shroud of biblical literalism. To get beyond the shroud, for people intent on wrestling with deeper realities, means coming to grips with the nature of the divine (including its possible absence, at least in conventional terms) as well as with the gender attributes of the divine.

It's hard to overemphasize the extent to which the precivilized past has been blocked from cultural consciousness by the sustained impact of civilized history (which teaches that precivilized life was at best contemptible) and religious mythology (which teaches either that there is no such thing as life before Genesis or that myth itself will teach us what we need to know about beginnings and foundations). Each, as we have seen, is enveloped in a *mythos* that obstructs and denies—or, at minimum, belittles and patronizes—the creativity of women and the significance of the Mother Goddess right up to (and even, for a while, blended in with) the establishment of male power in both secular and religious structures. I am keenly aware how breaking through this blockage in my life was accompanied by a struggle with fear, a fear emanating from childhood conditioning (far more religious than secular) that said beliefs or understandings in violation of Genesis were evil. Not just wrong—*evil.*

This diffuse sense of evil is now discernible as the dreadful negativity regarding the feminine that continues to radiate out of ferocious and even vicious Father God constructs, a massive projection of male (and female) anxiety in regard to traditional gender arrangements. The collapse of God in the modern "liberal" world does not so much open human consciousness to the sweet side of God's Left Hand, as Michael Lerner would have it, as it opens manicured male history to the abused and neglected precivilized past, to the Mother locked—to this day—in the religious dungeon. To talk of God's Left Hand while ignoring this history is dishonest at best. (The Left Hand belongs to the impounded Goddess, not to the rampant God.) The alarm of those still captivated by the Right Hand—held, as it were, in a demonic trance—becomes increasingly reactionary, shrill, and ferocious. This alarm will become more blatant in the political realm as civilization undergoes the fracking of its mythology. This shrinking Right Hand sees itself, as it faces demographic contraction and ecological constriction, a threatened island of godly righteousness in a rising sea of demonic paganism. Since the retaliatory viciousness of civilization is sanctified by God, as the slaughter of Jericho was not merely sanctified by Yahweh but commanded by Him, overpowering violence will once again believe it can achieve peace and decency. The good God will smash the wicked Devil. The *civis* of God will triumph over Satan's *pagus*.

We are facing the brutal collapse of male-dominated religion simultaneously with the breakdown of civilization's unsustainable utopian globalization: the end of male domination, the radical shrinkage of civilization's traumatic institutions. And in its place?

XXVI

We are in the midst of realizing and coming to grips with an astonishing "neglect" in the realm of the feminine divine. That is, the exclusion of Mother from a totally Male God construct is now obvious to all with even a passing knowledge of human history. Meanwhile, we are entering—we have entered—breakdown of the patriarchal establishments that are the internal weight-bearing beams of the entire civilizational project. Biblical literalism and Christian fundamentalism are mythic frameworks whose maintenance is part of American Right-Hand-of-God empire, which is the present global hegemony of civilizational hubris. Orthodox Christianity religiously protects the God-given rights of civilization's traumatic institutions. This project has reached its terminus. The outcome could be total devastation or aristocratic restoration or a breaking beyond civilizational/theocratic/fundamentalist mythology to a radically new reformulation of folk evolution culturally modified and spiritually purified by virtue of the realization of how gender distortions and sexual inequalities, concentrated and intensified by civilizational structures and frozen into place by explicitly male religious theophanies, have brought us to the brink of the ecological wreckage of the Earth on which our species has evolved. It's either City of God dystopia or the eutopia of *malkuta*.

This means we have to explore and come to spiritual grips with the excluded feminine in religious theophany. Theophany and behavior are reciprocally reflective. One shapes the other, just as societal despotism and constricted sexuality shape each other. Here is where Dorothy Dinnerstein's mother-raised children represents the place where the rubber really hits the road and where the gender ramifications of horticulture, agriculture, and the civilizational control and expropriation of agriculture must be grasped if a reformulation of folk evolution is to be achieved. The resurrection and restoration of folk evolution will renew, reinvigorate, and reconceptualize the women's liberation movement as initially represented in the precivilized agrarian village. If Mother represents the first women's movement, Daughter inaugurates the second.

Whatever the truth about prepatriarchal goddesses—benign fecundity personified or terrifying ferocity embodied or some bewildering mixture—we can now begin to read religious mythology as the mass psychic projection of gender arrangements and sexual repressions, perhaps with a bit of "predator beast" dread thrown in. But, if we are to achieve liberation from the distortions codified within these arrangements, liberation in the direction of practical equality (men with hands gently on the cradle, women firmly engaged in the public sphere), we will need a religious mythology, a divine pantheon, representing and encoding that equality and reconciliation. Of course, I think we have such a pantheon, thanks to Joachim of Floris, who took the wonderfully radical step—the wonderfully insightful and spiritual step—of grounding Christian theophany in history, thereby showing that religious representation correlates to historical period or phase. The formulation Mother-Father-Son-Daughter is a crucial corrective in a number of dimensions—historical, cultural, psychological, and religious—even as it could be twisted by and by into yet another dreadful hegemony. But, as Henry Thoreau said, one world at a time.

In actual spiritual practice (as opposed to doctrine, dogma, creed, liturgy, ritual, and all the rest), there is no substitute for humble self-immolation in the cloud of Taoist unknowing. Perhaps it's the compost pile of unknowing, for we are creatures of Earth, little stalks or bulbs of pulsing protoplasm, inexplicably alive, conscious and aware, destined to die and disintegrate as surely as our "personal" arrival as conscious beings is a mystery we cannot understand. (What *is* this consciousness we not only are born with, but whose spiritual cultivation is our ultimate life task? Once again, we'll learn as we cultivate our way down the Eightfold Path of right belief, resolve, speech, action, livelihood, effort, thought and meditation, as we listen in our hearts to the sermon on the mount.) We are more like walking compost than drifting clouds. To attempt to touch or know this underlying, creative power—call it Life or Tao or God or Goddess or Spirit—may well be the most profound work a person can do. We can call this prayer or meditation or contemplation or simple stillness—but it's this inner state of humble "emptiness" that can gentle our egos, dissolve our jealousies, purify our ambitions, prune our distractions, and make us want to feel at one (and at peace) with the underlying, creative force—therefore allowing us to face death without fear, realizing that death is how we are folded back into underlying mystery. (Whatever enables our consciousness to "exist" presumably has the capacity to welcome us home, whatever that may be.) As terrestrial beings who yearn for fulfillment, a significant portion of which is earthy, emotional, physical and sexual, equality and reconciliation at the depth proposed by Dorothy Dinnerstein requires a freer, more wholesome and self-regulated erotic life and a more complex interpersonal bonding: perhaps relational mandalas rather than marriage monotheism—all in a far more relaxed world of gardens, orchards, small fields, clean rivers, swimming holes, wood smoke, and mature forests. Our physical environment reflects our spiritual state of being. Ecological recovery will follow our spiritual healing.

XXVII

I don't want to conclude this cantankerous essay without apologizing to those whose shins I've kicked pretty hard. First, Michael Lerner whose Left and Right Hands of God have provided me a framing at which to hammer. Second, Ched Myers whose unfolding of Mark's Jesus reveals a man of truly awesome and stunningly brave humanity. (However it came about that the Jesus story got top billing in the Western world—a story, quite obviously, that has spread around the globe—it remains a story of amazing power and transformative capacity—and also a story that now needs to be newly internalized with greater mythological understanding. We can learn to read the Jesus story as *pagus* confronting *civis* with a spiritual revolution based on *malkuta*, and not continue to funnel Jesus through the *civis* theology of Constantine and Augustine. It's time to end the intellectual monopoly of civilizational theology.) Third, Karen Armstrong whose many books on world religions have immeasurably helped to humanize the "other." Fourth, with something close to grief and shame, Lewis Mumford, for he (along with Norman O. Brown) was one of two angels with flaming intellectual swords who showed me where and how to enter Eden. (The path in the general direction of Eden had already been roughly paced out by Paul Goodman. He was my first competent guide, back in the roll-your-own 1960s.)

But Mumford, in regard to civilization/"civilization," ducked the issue, refused to face the unavoidable conclusion to his own analysis, and acted evasively—and this realization hurts. Intellectually, I can't pretend to call back or explain away this dreadful judgment, even as it may be true (as I yearningly suggest in the footnote on page 210) that Mumford's sense of superego reveals an unusual gentleness preventing him from recognizing, with unflinching etymological honesty, the raw and brutal truth in regard to civilization. But superego's history is more cruel and complex than a lofty "ideal self" into which "one must be reborn." Perhaps Mumford's understanding will prove true in the future as id, superego, and ego merge into something far more free and wholesome; but our inherited construct is loaded with harsh judgment and vicious violence. In the end, Mumford is simply too good a historian—even a grand historian—to be allowed to slip the civilization/"civilization" wool over his own eyes as well as over ours.

However, my deepest teacher remains the gritty guy from Nazareth, the stubborn, exuberant Jewish peasant: for here was gentleness, earthy gentleness welded to unbendable spiritual strength, such that no fabrication or misrepresentation of truth, no ily twist of possible exculpatory mythology, got past him undetected and unanswered, if only by the refusal of silence. He looked *civis* in the eye and said out loud what he saw there. Civilized theologians ever since have been explaining what Jesus really meant to say.

Well, Jesus is by no means responsible for my false conclusions or erroneous judgments; but he—perhaps I should say his story—did teach me something about responsibility in the face of evasion or caviling: namely, that truth can cut a deep wound in the righteous hide of mythological sanctimony—as well as cause the wounder to get nailed for an open breach of exactly the kind of civility propounded by Edmund Burke: that religion is the "basis of civil society," a habit taken upon by authority and not by disputation. (In his own way, Burke may have spoken with sincerity, but his view is anything but profound. Jesus, I believe, would not have been awed in the least by Burke's shallow religious convention: it was the very complacency Jesus stood against, if one is to believe the gospels, and one of the chief reasons for his murder. *Malkuta*, like PTSD, is not for sissies or empire apologists.) I am a flawed and querulous human being, but I crave the kingdom of God on Earth, which is what Jesus set out to enact and achieve. The redemption of nature is the redemption of *pagus* is the redemption of the village of the Mother. It is the finest, most hopeful and wholesome story of human transformation that I know. Both Ched Myers and Andrew Harvey recognize the global and universal dimensions of that effort, and I honor their recognition.

All this may legitimately raise the question: how did Jesus come by such extraordinary groundedness? It's easy to see how God (as Karen Armstrong says of "Kant's God"—a mere "afterthought, tacked onto the human condition"[145]) gets wheeled out to explain the "Jesus" situation: "Son of God," "virgin birth," "ascended into heaven," and "life everlasting." Before you can say "kingdom of God," Jesus is wrapped in sumptuous purple robes and whisked away to heavenly harmlessness, the orthodox and gnostic get into a knock-down, drag-out fight over metaphysical conjecture, Constantine the cat toys with a flock of Christian bishops, and Augustine (his personal life history a parody of Jack Miles' psychologically conflicted Yahweh) thunders multimillennial theological bolts of dogmatic lightning while standing on a smoking Olympus of biblical folk tale and carefully groomed myth. Millions of people come to ritually chant the two kingdom liturgy while civilization, with its diseases and traumatic institutions, blessed by Augustine and gilded by the mythology of Platonic Christian-

---

145. Armstrong, *Battle*, 74.

ity, pushes earthly Creation closer and closer to ecocide. Holy Roman Catastrophe. Predatory civilization wearing the mask of an otherworldly "Christ." This Christ is also Anti-Christ.

Ched Myers has done a great and salutary thing by putting Jesus back on Earth. But the question of the divine may be irresolvable. There's so much we don't know and perhaps can't know, at least by the conventional protocols of rationality. We certainly can and do say lots of things about what we *believe*, but most of this will remain in a separate ontological basket from what we actually *know*. I don't mean to snarl at Michael Lerner's pleading for "feelings and intuitions" (there's even a dictionary entry for "ontologism," which is "the philosophical doctrine that the knowledge of God is immediate and intuitive, and that all other knowledge is dependent upon this"), for it seems true that we humans, even the supposedly hard-nosed "quantify" types, are heavily governed by feelings and intuitions. (The forceful repudiation of intuition is itself an intense expression of feeling.) It therefore follows that intuition is, if not the only, at least the primary avenue by which we are engulfed in awe and wonder. We may conclude from such experience that we have been touched by the divine. We may also conclude that this "touching" proves, from a subjective perspective, that the divine has a reality independent and distinct from our temporal being, beyond the boundary of normal consciousness—whatever that may be. We may (as I do) call this frustratingly Hidden Something by the name Spirit. But we have no right to name it Everlasting God and no authority (other than poetic license, which is how I take the *Tao Te Ching*) to teach or describe its ontology as cosmic. (How would we know?) We are creatures of evolution on Earth. We are in and of the incredible network of Life on Earth. Our divinity is the Spirit of evolution. If there is divinity in a larger cosmic sense, our awe in starlight may or may not be a viable ontologism.

Spirit—now you see Her, now you don't—has been a very slippery subject—or object: God as tiny pea hidden under one of the swiftly shifted Abrahamic cups. Guess which cup—Jewish? Christian? Moslem?—God prefers to hide under. Is it the Yahweh cup? The God cup? The Allah cup? Here's where I balk and accuse folks like Ched Myers and Michael Lerner, despite their otherwise excellent analyses, of playing a Guess Who shell game. Please don't tell us that Yahweh or YHVH is so purely God or The Ultimate Reality of the Universe that all other understandings are limited or false, or that Yahweh doesn't have a terribly complicated cultural and even political genealogy with a huge wardrobe of bony skeletons in His closet. And please don't try to tell us that your orthodox, ahistorical assertions about Yahweh represent the core of transformative cosmic energy, the starting point for progressive spiritual politics. I believe such assertions to be rocking back and forth on the cracked egg of an idolatry still in thrall to a tribal god, not to speak of a totally outrageous and completely unacceptable oblivion regarding the suppression of the feminine divine in all three Abrahamic religions. This is Daddy fixation, superego captivity, civilizational capitulation. The remedy may be a long and shivering shower in the Cloud of Unknowing.

The Right Hand of conviction comes off as brutal and domineering. The Left Hand comes off as clingy and cloying. In the end, we need to shake the brittle, toxic dust off the Right Hand, and scrape the smelly, sticky goo off the Left. To paraphrase the cracker-barrel theology of Harry Truman: If you can't stand living inside the Cloud of Unknowing, don't pretend to be a classically trained theological weatherman. The "healing of the world" that both Ched Myers and Michael Lerner want will come as gentle, life-bringing rain from the Cloud of Unknowing, and no gang of professional Theological Doctors, with their beautiful carpetbags full of doctrinal scalpels and creedal forceps, will ever be able to tell us how this Cloud actually functions. They may even be shocked by the birth of Daughter.

XXVIII

The kingdom of God is Green. That much is easy to conclude from a close—and critical—reading of the gospels. The gospels are not a how-to manual for building Christian Civilization. *Malkuta* is composed of spiritually transformed human beings who dare to remove the hair shirt of orthodoxy. It is libertarian, democratic, ecological, and socialist. Its ethical groundedness will restore and resurrect rural culture even as it will make villages, towns, and small cities glow with creative vigor. The theophany it conjures is Mother, Father, Son and Daughter, even as everybody's *real* spiritual task is to stand still long enough to locate and sink into ineffable Spirit—who may be Mother, Father, Son or Daughter at any particular moment, time or place, but who is not confined or restricted to any of these designations at any particular moment, time, or place. As Jesus told the tough, in-your-face Samaritan woman at the well (John 4:5-24), the issue is no longer mountain or temple but, instead, Spirit and Truth. We all need living water from that deep well. We have much to learn from Buddhists about exploring that well in concentrated inwardness and disciplined silence.

Perhaps the deeper meaning of the transfiguration-on-the-mountain story (Mark 9:2-8) is that Jesus lived as fully inside the Cloud of Unknowing as any human being before or since. It's there—that's how—he powerfully bonded with the earthy "eternity" of Spirit. Our challenge is, as always, to join in on that transfiguration, to the fullest extent of our capacity and focus and courage. It is our essential spiritual task. But for that we need a bravery that is a daring—perhaps even a reckless—letting go.

14

Rechanneling NPR's Superego

I HEARD "CHANNELING THE Republican id" on the radio while driving and made a mental note to think about it later. Traffic was a bit heavy in the countryside. Reflecting on the politically oriented psychoanalytical wisdom of National Public Radio had to wait for a more opportune moment. My attention had a prior commitment. A deer might jump out onto the road. Or a rabbit, squirrel, skunk, or porcupine—although skunks and porcupines don't jump.

Well, "channeling the Republican id" was uttered last Friday (August 19, 2011) on NPR's two-guest section of "All Things Considered"—two articulate men commenting on the week's news. The phrase was employed to describe Texas Governor Rick Perry's entry into the Republican presidential primary, specifically that Perry said he doesn't believe in evolution or global warming, thus aligning himself with science-denial on the Right. This alignment with denial supposedly has some channeling arrangement with "Republican id."

Although the allusion is seriously flawed—or, more accurately, utterly false—it's also blithely typical. That is, Rick Perry's pandering to deniers of evolution and climate change wasn't directed toward the Republican *id*, but at the Republican *superego*. This misdirection is perfectly normal. And it's not as trivial as it may appear.

Denying evolution and global warming has nothing whatsoever to do with id. Such denial is linked to alignment with so-called "traditional values"; and, as "traditional values" are tied to "conservative" religious conviction and to a monarchical image of God, they are inherently in the domain of superego.

Relatively highbrow NPR talking heads can verbally roll their eyes at Perry's calculated obsequiousness (the commentator on the Right said "channeling the Republican id" first, then the Left guy agreed and repeated it); but we simply have to ask: Why the misidentified id instead of the obvious superego? What's really going on? Is this lack of familiarity with the terms? Did these guys flunk Psychoanalysis 101? Is there something here of greater significance?

Its significance is simple but profound. It's always legitimate to make fun of or scapegoat the id, which construct indicates something pretty dumb or doltish, perhaps even stupidly brutal. But it's a risky breach of propriety to identify the alert, smart, and supersensitive superego with anything stupid or nasty. Why? Because superego is supposedly the human portal to the divine, the "ideal self" into which one is to be reborn. It's through the superego that God directs or corrects human behavior, behavior that's to be in alignment with divine will. It's via the superego where humans are to communicate with the divine or, at least, where God's will is transmitted to the human mind, particularly to the assertive, aggressive, and worldly successful male mind. (Remember Mumford's remark in the previous essay regarding the "deadly high-tension currents of godhead . . . stepped down for human use"?) Nothing is more emblematic of unblemished superego than the successful, top-tier male who commands our attention and directs our behavior. All this is commonly understood. Therefore it's okay to smirk at the pandering, but only if the smirk is deliberately facing in the proper (i.e., the wrong) direction.

I say "deliberately" facing in the wrong direction. "Deliberately" is true, but in a borderline sense. That is, this (mis)use of id is part of a package of conventional semantic evasion and inversion (certainly including a construct like "pagan"), words so commonly and reflexively misused that those who utter this venerable nonsense can do so with apparent complete sincerity. Such sincerity is integral to good standing in polite and privileged society. One does not shout "Empire criminals!" in the Oval Office, on Wall Street, or at the Pentagon. It's just not done. Just as one would think twice about pointing out to gorgeously robed ecclesiastics (Matthew 23:4-6) that Jesus was murdered, not by any ragtag band of Jewish "pagans," but by the most highly civilized people of his time and place. And it's not as if this evasive scapegoating lacks consequence: in the fourth gospel, John the Evangelist repeatedly fingers "the Jews" for Jesus' crucifixion, and there's a crooked but discernible path that leads eventually to Auschwitz. The Holocaust was the scapegoating outcome of *civis* exoneration for Jesus' crucifixion.

This deflection from superego to id may occur at the borderline of consciousness, although I suppose the next question is: borderline between what and what? I hesitate to invoke the unconscious here, for the unconscious lives primarily in the id. (Or is it vice-versa?) But, since deflection is a function of socially learned denial (or reflexive evasion), the borderline would seem to lie between superego and ego, between upper class and middle class. (I am, of course, suggesting a correlation between upper class and superego, middle class and ego, lower class and id, and that deference to authority is always looking up.) Superego, like God, is always up. Id, like the Devil, is always down. Ego lives between these opposites, but is always looking up, waiting for moral trickle-down from above, even while casting surreptitious and wistful glances down at id.

This spirals us willy-nilly to the core contradiction within civilization. On the one hand, it's a cultural given that civilization consists of the highest, finest, most refined aspirations and achievements of the human race. This accrued refinement is why it's perfectly apt to identify the civilized elite with superego (king, priest, commander, banker, financier, lawyer, and so on—all those who've risen to some level of *civis* importance), and also why civilization is the organizational and institutional embodiment of concentrated superego. (Not that the bulk of those who vote Republican are themselves elite. Not at all. Most are simply in alignment with the conventionally tough, righteous image of God the Father: Republicans aren't the "Daddy Party" for no reason. Therefore it may be the case that "channeling the Republican id" alludes, in a sarcastic way, to the dorks and chumps who consistently vote for the party whose policies serve to beggar the chumps and dorks. It may be the latter to whom id is contemptuously assigned.)

Just as civilization wears a thin, synthetic robe of genetically modified "democracy," so (precisely because we believe we are a "democracy" and because elections remain, for the time being, the means by which superego "leaders" are chosen) it's crucial for the middle class to be swept along in this synthetic exercise. Since God has apparently consented (with apparent reluctance) to democratic procedure, to this improbable experiment involving bottom-feeding commoners, it's crucial the middle class vote for the party with the strongest superego in order to show God that His reluctant consent is duly recognized and honored.

The core system of civilization is a multimillennial male power projection based on violence and theft. We might say that the Protestant Reformation facilitated a major superego migration from upper class to middle class, even trickling down to the hard-hat, flag-decal working class. By becoming civilized and capitalist, these deeply alienated peasants and pagans—I'm speaking in terms of cultural evolution—began to wear the factory-made armor of the City of God, and this violence and theft economic enterprise has always been disguised as Good Works, rationalized as God's Will, dressed in the spiritual robes of necessity and sanctification. Superego wears these protective and sanctifying robes. One Nation Under God.

In other words, superego is the chief psychospiritual repository of this immense fraud, this mythic cloak, and the elite are (I would say "by definition") inside this cloak and dagger repository. (It's telling that those elected to high office do not come "into service" but, rather, "into power.") Everybody who wishes to be a "player" implicitly recognizes the power fraud is not to be exposed. Anyone who boldly exposes it—Noam Chomsky may well be America's chief fraud exposer—is shunned, mocked, and scorned. Chomsky has made a career, so to speak, of breaking the unspoken rules.

For housetrained NPR commentators to agree that Rick Perry channels the Republican id is witty and even a touch naughty, which naughtiness adds color and a touch of spice to the wit. It alludes to something important, powerful, and real; but it does so in a smirky manner that preserves the fiction and the fraud—playing with dangerous truth, but keeping it safely under control.

In his *Death of the Liberal Class*, Chris Hedges says it's all about "not offending the status quo." He means by this that the "liberal class and the institutions it controls [have] succumbed to opportunism and finally to fear."[1] While that seems true, as far as it goes, it's not true enough.

1. Hedges, *Death*, 140.

Human beings have always been inclined to identify with their core community and to refrain from offending it. Basic decency needs and expects this. At a certain level, the coherence and stability of any group depends on restraint and solidarity. Cultural life could not go on without it. But "cultural life" in all its preindustrial forms has pretty well been demolished; in its place has come political identification with civilized institutions. As "folk" atrophied, "civilized" assumed the vacated cultural space. Our task, the task we're faced with, is the restoration of folk evolution, the recreation of folk culture willing and able to absorb civilization, prune its brutal arrogance and righteous violence, and create a way of life that integrates the best of both worlds. This requires seeing beneath the cloak and confiscating the dagger. But to do this is to offend the civilizational status quo and the Constantinian accommodation that protects it. We always need to bear in mind that civilization organized human life in a radically different way than the indigenous or folk. Distinct class separation is reflected in the correspondingly distinct psychological attributes of superego, ego and id, and these attributes have religious significance. The only entity or force capable of successfully mediating integration of that segregated trinity is spiritual in nature, and integration can only be achieved by cracking the mythic equation. Apocalyptic disclosing requires *spiritual* discernment of the myths that blinker our understanding of both religion and civilization, and it's spiritual *discernment*—or what we might call psychomythological awakening—that is and will be the basis of political transformation. There will be no Green commonwealth without an underlying spiritual conversion to servanthood and stewardship, and this requires integration of id, superego, and ego. To get to Green culture means walking through the burning hoop of superego righteousness.

What Hedges calls "liberal institutions"—let's say the university—tended to push the boundaries of what was intellectually and socially acceptable. The most expansive growth in liberal institutions happened as rigid governing institutions were breached by upsurging folk energy, as pioneer "democracy" rocked the civilized boat. (But also by "settling" vast areas of so-called "wilderness"—i.e., land inhabited by "primitive" cultures deemed backward, wicked, and expendable. These Jeffersonian/Jacksonian "democratic" pioneers were pushing back the "savage" and the "pagan" while advancing the "Christian" and the "civilized," even if they did so to some degree unwittingly.) I am referencing fairly recent American history here. The only good Indian is a dead Indian. Bringing godly civilization to the wicked wilderness.

Once this huge upsurge/migration was consolidated under comprehensive governing institutions—that is, once the continental "United States" was firmly secured and its indigenous "primitivity" suppressed—"liberal" institutions at first expanded (let's say until 1968, to put a somewhat arbitrary date in play) and then they began to constrict and atrophy as they were coerced into status quo normality and conformity. (How were they coerced? The main bodies of white resistance to civilized institutions, coming from a folk or working-class base, were the farmers of late nineteenth-century populism and the industrial workers who, a few decades later, achieved the formation of unions. Farmers were defeated electorally, and the rural culture of small farms steadily decayed thereafter. Industrial workers betrayed their own movement by racism, by choosing affluent consumption over human solidarity and ecological respect, by alignment with commercial empire hubris—as the hard hats with flag decals demonstrated in the 1960s. That is, a combination of massive agribusiness and massive industrial corporations destroyed the agricultural and craft occupations crucial to the health and maintenance of folk culture. And, with the atrophy of folk culture, the psychic shift to empire identity proceeded as it were invisibly but inexorably.)

Hedges rails against "liberals" for their lack of moral courage; but he doesn't seem to realize that a civilizational watershed was passed more or less in our lifetimes—perhaps as early as the 1890s—or that the kool-aid "liberals" have drunk is the undiluted elixir of inherited civility. "Liberals" have typically been gung-ho for "progressive" civilization, and they've ambiguously achieved their wish. The folk, the "primitive," indigenous, and peasant have all been stuffed into the trash can of history. Folk energy (the agrarian populism of the late nineteenth century or the working-class union organizing of the 1930s) has been suffocated, tamed, subdued, and redirected by the hegemony of civilized institutions. Superego grabbed id by the ears and made it conform to superego standards. Superego taught id to sit still at school and be on time at the factory. America now lives off deindustrialization and corporate agribusiness. Real Americans hate unions and shop for groceries at Sam's Club. What's not to like about the corporate utopia? It provides the greatest shopping opportunities in the history of the world, with nothing to fear from atomic weaponry or climate change.

Hedges seems to have a conservative set of religious convictions empowering his iconoclasm. For those with that sort of religious conviction, there isn't much earthy, gritty ethical traction by which to intellectually deconstruct our plight and predicament. Once again it's original sin that makes deconstruction implausible. Well, no: original sin does provide Hedges with a construct by which he *can* vigorously critique modern institutions—institutions are sinful precisely because of original sin—but the same construct prevents him from any hope of transformation since sin cannot be overcome because it's so deeply embedded in human character. Both "liberals" and "conservatives" are so blinded by utopian mythology—either religious or civilizational or some cocktail mixture of the two—that they simply can't see with eyes of eutopian clarity. It seems to take a painful exploration—religious, historical, psychoanalytical—before it's possible to come to a place where the criminality of civilization combined with the complicit criminality of religious orthodoxy becomes obvious—painfully and even unbearably obvious. Veneration of civilization is by no means an easy illusion to break or overcome, especially with Augustine as the illustrious protector of that merged veneration.[2]

2. Hedges, on page 84 of his book, says "Faith in human institutions was at the core of the Social Gospel, a Christian movement articulated at the turn of the century in books such as *Christianity and the Social Crisis*, published in 1907, and *Theology for the Social Gospel*, published a decade later,

Civilization is a predatory spider that stings "liberal institutions" into numb mythological subjection. But railing at moral cowards comes off more as a guilt hammer than an exercise in spiritual edification. Without helping people recognize what civilization actually is—violence and theft, Class and War, traumatic institutions—or that globalization ramifies as weapons of mass destruction, climate change, human overpopulation and species' extinctions, haranguing is counterproductive, although it's difficult to refrain from taking a well-aimed swipe at the housetrained talking heads on occasion. We all need a little physical exercise from time to time.

Well, the liberal church—to be blunt, to get right at the core of the problem—has yet to arrive at a more experiential and humble understanding of the divine. (See the epigraphs that open this book for a gestalt of our predicament.) Having had the traditional image of God exploded or imploded by science especially, liberals are groping in the dark for a newer, richer, and fuller understanding of the sacred or the divine— although it seems that many liberals, while acknowledging the explosion or implosion of biblical story, are determined to assert that "the story may have been hammered, but God is still God," as if "God" is not an image arrived at by and through story. But this both suggests and confirms the sustained power of religious image. The story may no longer be plausible, but the genie continues to hover over the much-rubbed lamp.

"Conservatives," meanwhile, have hardened orthodoxy in the forge of literalism and on the anvil of denial; and—*because they're organized*—they have steadily accumulated political power in the direction of an authoritarian, interventionist control consistent with their authoritarian, interventionist image of God. Or, alternatively, because liberals have—with guilty ambivalence—moved away from authoritarianism without letting go of the inherited authoritarian God image, their muddled politics accurately reflects their religious confusion. This is exactly why "channeling the Republican id" is so intellectually false. Well, it's worse than false; it's reflexively *protective*

---

both of them written by the leading proponent of the movement, Walter Rauschenbusch. The Social Gospel replaced a preoccupation with damnation and sin with a belief in human progress." On page 85, Hedges says "The Social Gospel secularized traditional Christian eschatology and fused it with the utopian visions of material progress embraced by the wider liberal class." He then goes on to say on page 87 that "The Swiss theologian Karl Barth, in *The Epistle to the Romans* (*Der Romerbrief*), published in 1918, tore apart the Social Gospel's naïve belief that human beings could link the will of God to human endeavors. Christians, Barth argued, could neither envision nor create the kingdom of heaven on earth. The liberal church never found an adequate response to Barth's critique. It retreated into a vague embrace of humanism and self-absorbed forms of spirituality." Here Hedges dismisses the "Social Gospel" in terms I believe inaccurate and inappropriate. "Faith in human institutions," "belief in human progress," and "utopian visions of material progress" are straw dummies. They represent a theologically "conservative" (i.e., reactionary) position. There may well be uncertainty in Social Gospel theology; but finding the eutopian path out of utopian hegemony doesn't happen in a year, a decade, or even a century. The question is—does Chris Hedges believe the kingdom of God is never to be realized on Earth? Is he in alignment with Augustine? When he advocates "rebellion" (it's the title of his final chapter, headed by an epigraph from Albert Camus stressing that revolt must be devoid of hope), he also says, on page 201, that we are "living through one of civilization's seismic reversals." I believe we are living in a period of civilization's *culmination* as utopia unfolds as dystopia. This is not reversal. This is inevitable outcome. By saying "reversal," Hedges is indicating he's still a civilized man.

of falsity. This falseness isn't a "mistake." It's a mythological protection racket shrouded in taboo. Our problem, both religiously and civilizationally, is a total surfeit of super-ego righteousness with its accompanying superego psychosis of obsessive control. It's this mythology—aggressively utopian in secular articulation, passively otherworldly in religious expression—that has us collectively in its grip. It's the mythic rudder of Christian Civilization.

Chris Hedges would do well to lay off his admiration of Karl Barth and Rein-hold Niebuhr—because their orthodox two-kingdom Augustinianism insists there's no way to "link the will of God to human endeavors" or to envision the kingdom of God on Earth—and read instead Lewis Mumford, Norman O. Brown, Paul Goodman, Elaine Pagels, Dorothy Dinnerstein, and Thomas Berry. If Hedges is so stuck on an otherworldly authoritarian God who won't allow the kingdom of God to be linked to human endeavor—because original sin has doomed us—he should quit whining about what civilization is accomplishing on Earth, get dressed in sackcloth, and go play in the ashes.[3]

3. Chris Hedges obviously aggravates me with his brash but bleak hopelessness. Yet his overall analysis is so acute that sheer respect for his integrity compels me to this footnote.

I admire Hedges' ethical combativeness. But his implicit Augustinian worldview contributes immensely to the bleakness he radiates and the powerlessness he projects. He seems to believe the Augustinian worldview is the finest, most comprehensive understanding possible. It's almost as if Hedges channels the Old Testament Job who (with Yahweh's consent) is first ruined economically by Satan (plus all Job's children are killed) and then he's "struck down with malignant ulcers from the sole of his foot to the top of his head." By the middle of the second chapter, Job is sitting in an ashpit, scraping his awful sores with a shard of broken pottery, as his wife counsels him to "Curse God, and die."

I think there are two issues here, which are (of course) the issues in these essays. They are, in order, civilization as the template for our current culminating disasters—disasters that Chris Hedges sees with great acuity—and the role Augustinian Christianity has played as the enabling Bride of Caesar—a role Chris Hedges apparently accepts as the will of God. With one eye, Hedges clearly sees the disasters; but the other eye seems plastered shut with Job's ashes and bandaged with an Augustinian eye patch. If Chris Hedges would remove the bandage and wash the ashes from his eye, he might just discern the beauty of Spirit's hope and realize that the repudiation of the kingdom of God was a political requirement in the dowry negotiations between Constantine and the Christian bishops. Christians got a foot in the palace. The Roman Empire got a religion whose social vision had shrunk to pious powerlessness. Orthodox Christianity became Caesar's concubine.

15

A Curious Little Footpath

Following in the Footsteps of Marcus Borg
and John Dominic Crossan

ALL IN ALL, THE 2006 book by Marcus Borg and John Dominic Crossan—*The Last Week: A Day-by-Day Account of Jesus's Final Week in Jerusalem*—is an exciting commentary on the centrality of the kingdom of God proclamation in Mark's gospel. The book's language is deceptively simple, but the spiritual furrow it cuts is beautifully deep. It is, I would say, an important contribution to the spiritual revolution going on within Christianity—a revolution that, when the dust settles, will reveal a wonderfully earthy Jesus and a far more comprehensive Green spirituality. Jesus will be—not less—even more spiritually significant when Trinity enlarges to Mandala, although that enlargement is not the theme or purpose of Borg and Crossan.

But, of course, being who I am, I am less inclined to heap praise on the praiseworthy than to pry open what seems obscure and, perhaps, misleading. The larger issue may be what Borg and Crossan mean, or don't mean, by "God." This is naturally problematic, for God (or do I say "God"?) is by definition elusive and beyond definition. Yet any talk of or reference to God implies inevitable definiteness, for we are obliged to mean *something* and not *nothing*—unless the word is compulsively repeated until its very repetition makes it meaningless gibberish.

"God," however, is too big a mountain for me to climb. I don't seem to have the requisite climbing gear or an aptitude for thin air. So what I want to do here is wander down a curious little footpath, surprisingly unused and oddly inviting. This curious footpath occurs in chapter eight, "Easter Sunday," in a subsection called "History or Parable?"

What Borg and Crossan talk about here is meaning in the form of parables versus taking Bible stories factually. They are gentle toward those who cling to Bible stories as factual, even as they clearly fall on the side of parable. On page 284, they enter into a brief explanation and history of their categories:

> Importantly, parable and parabolic language can make truth claims. They do
> not simply illustrate something as, for example, one might think of the parable
> of the good Samaritan as an illustration of the importance of being a neighbor

to whomever is in need. Rather, as in the story of the prodigal son, they can make a truth claim: God is like the father who is overjoyed at his son's return from exile in "a far country." God is like that.

So one should not think of history as "true" and parable as "fiction" (and therefore not nearly as important). Only since the Enlightenment of the seventeenth century have many people thought this way, for in the Enlightenment Western culture began to identify truth with "factuality." Indeed, this identification is one of the central characteristics of modern Western culture. Both biblical literalists and people who reject the Bible completely do this: the former insist that the truth of the Bible depends on its literal factuality, and the latter see that the Bible cannot be literally and factually true and therefore don't think it is true at all.[1]

They then say that "parable, independently of historical factuality, can be profoundly true."[2]

I agree with our wise and insightful authors. Parable can most certainly make "truth claims." But I am not inclined to slide without comment over their assertion that it's only since the Enlightenment that Western culture has begun to identify truth with "factuality." Quite frankly, I think that's misleading. It contains too many implications to let pass without objection.

While it seems true that pre-Enlightenment theology or biblical understanding was rich in parable, metaphor, allegory, or whatever forms of explication there may have been besides factuality—although "pre-Reformation" may be a more accurate historical designation—I think it laughable to imply that the great bulk of Christian believers in the early period (a quite long early period) did not assume Adam and Eve were real people, that Cain did not murder Abel, or that a great flood did not once cover Earth (with Noah and his family and all manner of paired beasts safely afloat in a smelly Ark). Biblical "factuality" was so deeply assumed and so thoroughly absorbed in pre-Enlightenment times that other forms of explication were effortless and nonthreatening—something for literate intellectuals who, perhaps like the aristocracy, lived in another world—an inexplicable, imaginary world for the intellectuals, a brutally real but tantalizing material world of the aristocracy. The Roman church, let's remember, only felt profound threat when Galileo's astronomical discoveries and Copernican confirmations confronted the "factuality" of an Earth-centered, God-ordained cosmos. And while the tendency Borg and Crossan identify as a tightening of "factuality" may be represented or symbolized by Galileo's arrest and eventual recanting, this tightening did not invent or create factuality. What it did was accelerate a process of splitting or dissociation between fact and metaphor that has had (and continues to have) great shaping impact, an ever-widening bifurcation, not only on "Western culture" in some vague and generalized way, but on our minds and

1. Borg and Crossan, *Last*, 284.

2. Borg and Crossan, *Last*, 284.

institutions. (Think, for instance, of C. P. Snow's *The Two Cultures and the Scientific Revolution* with its mutually hostile categories of "literary culture" and "scientific culture"—which is only another way of saying "metaphor" and "fact.")

Contemporary fundamentalism and present-day biblical literalism are certainly by-products of the Reformation project and Enlightenment process. That is, literalism is *mythos* asserted as *logos*. That assertion is, I think, indisputable. But fundamentalism's modern strength cannot be explained, dismissed, or glossed over by implying it has no pre-Enlightenment basis or that "factuality" has no roots extending back beyond the seventeenth century. That's simply untrue. Fundamentalism has deep roots in pre-Enlightenment biblical factuality. The multifaceted Reformation (including the Counter-Reformation) was largely a fight—sometimes a quite bloody fight—over contending factualities. What fundamentalism has lost or severed is, in part, an effortless and nonthreatening metaphor process precisely because it was unwilling to see biblical "factuality" blown out of the water. With the rise of scientific scholarship, biblical myth (by refusing to budge) got a terminal case of hardened arteries. It became systematically anti-intellectual, deliberately and consciously so. It rejected a great deal of biblical scholarship precisely because that scholarship began to spring leaks in orthodox creedal assertion. Its ship began to sink. To assert *mythos* as *logos* therefore necessitated tight control of the uses to which *logos* could be put: acceptable Monday through Friday for market procurement and technological inventiveness, unacceptable on Sunday for the exploration of mythological origins. That is, fundamentalism largely cut itself off from the pre-Enlightenment metaphor garden, and it did so, paradoxically, in righteous defense of biblical myth. And although some fundamentalists may search diligently for hidden meaning in symbolic language (in the books of Daniel and Revelation, for instance), they have severe aversion to the eating of metaphoric fruit. Facts, please, nothing but facts, even if those "facts" are divinely packed in obscure biblical symbols.

The irony is that new dimensions of factuality—Copernicus, Galileo, Newton, Darwin, Einstein and Freud, shall we say—are what ignited, triggered, and precipitated a fierce and determined clinging to pre-Enlightenment biblical "factuality." The more science cast doubt on biblical factuality—that is, the "factuality" of religious myth—the more determined biblical literalism became in defense of mythic factuality. If science says "the evidence suggests," biblical literalism insists "God tells us." The scientific conclusion depends on evidence and reason; the literalist relies on a priori assumptions of biblical or church inerrancy, which in turn rely on a conviction (dare we call it "philosophical"?) that the Bible is the true word of God, divinely inspired and divinely guided. Apostolic succession. *Sola scriptura.*

At some point we have to ask what "factuality" is actually about. What's it protecting? If it's not protecting "facts" as such, then what? The protected "facts" must represent something beyond themselves. There may not be a single something that lies beyond: a story or narrative protected, or a standard of morality, or a stance against evil, or even an understandable resistance to troubling doubt and disturbing confusion. But what's really being protected is an image, definition, or understanding of God. At one level, the "factuality" of biblical literalism is both affirmation and defense of the biblical God or, more accurately, the biblical *image* of God.

If *the stories* are factually true, from the Creation account onward, then God is overpoweringly dynamic, powerful beyond our wildest imaginations, intimately involved with human lives, and unpredictably interventionist. *To deconstruct the stories*, fully granting their rich parabolic significance, *is to deconstruct the image of God*. One cannot demythologize biblical stories without demythologizing the image, conception, or understanding of the God who explicates the stories. And, since we can hardly say we know God except through images, to deconstruct image is to deconstruct God. If most Bible stories are not factually true, then the image of God projected through story is called into question. This is where the rubber hits the road. This is where fundamentalists lay claim to the word "conservative," for they feel their conviction links them backward in time to pre-Enlightenment Christian faith. They feel themselves *conserving* traditional conviction. Although there is ambiguity in such a claim, it is not without credibility. It is largely true. Fundamentalists are, largely, orthodox conservatives. To say otherwise seems ridiculous.

Borg and Crossan, meanwhile, for all their brilliant and clarifying scholarship (though it's more spiritually nourishing than mere academic scholarship), sometimes use the name of God like a pea in a shell game. Now you see it, now you don't. When forced by the demands of their analysis, they honestly affirm their disbelief in an overpoweringly dynamic and interventionist God. They don't believe in Anselm's substitutionary atonement. They have seen something more alive, vigorous, and immanent. They have seen (or at least glimpsed) the kingdom of God. They see that the themes of crucifixion and resurrection, unpacked from the one-redemption-fits-all Anselmian narrative, requires a real, basic, personal choice on the part of every would-be Christian: whose "redemption" struggle are you committed to—the bombing of Baghdad by Stealth aircraft or the pouring of blood on the lid of an ICBM silo?

Their God, like Gil Bailie's, is the seemingly powerless God of love and resistance. Although, having said that, I sense they consider it a waste of valuable time to argue over who's got the truer God. Yet they seem to want to gently knock blithe "believers" off their Anselmian merry-go-round for God, this theological whirligig that (like Augustine's doctrine of how God gives and sustains Empire) depends on an image of God as overwhelmingly powerful and interventionist, an image that is, at its core, identical with the contemporary fundamentalists' image of God, an image arrived at through believing biblical stories literally and factually true, *mythos* internalized as *logos*.

The "factuality" of fundamentalism is, in fact, based on a huge *mythological* story that hard-nosed science has largely wrecked: a fifteen-billion-year-old universe; humans evolved from (and with) other primates; civilization as a theft-and-murder protection racket embedded within its own historicized mythology in a manner analogous to how fundamentalism is encased in its historicized mythology. Fundamentalism is a self-constrained quietist rigidity waiting for the God of Genesis and Revelation to crushingly act, to fulfill His master plan as revealed (for those with eyes to see) in prophetic scripture and, in the meantime, holding to Romans 13:1-7 and (wittingly or unwittingly) to *The City of God*, Book IV:33 or Book V:1, upholding and supporting the righteousness of American Christian Empire cleaning up the world for God. In other words, fundamentalism is built on an image of God projected through a literal (i.e., "factual") reading of scripture and the empire rationalizations of Augustine. So we are faced with the somewhat giddy paradox that the dissociation that began with Copernicus and Galileo (insofar as it really began there) has resulted, first, in scientific factuality steadily undermining the "factuality" of Bible stories and, second, in our alarmed and anxious "liberation" from biblical myth, being freed (to some degree forced) into a far deeper and more existentially real encounter with the actual life and teaching of Jesus, compelled to explore a richly complex understanding of the sacred and divine. Either the Jesus story becomes bogus or we are drawn to deeper levels of comprehension.

Borg and Crossan are moving us—if we are willing to be moved—into a more existentially dynamic involvement with the kingdom of God, that is to say with Spirit, who is engaged in the project of dissolving human arrogance, fear, pride, and stupidity in an ever-refreshing yeast sponge of spiritual compassion and ethical humility, of transforming Powers and Principalities into humane agencies fit for radical servanthood and radical stewardship. (Walter Wink insists that Powers and Principalities can be redeemed. I agree. But redemption must be accompanied by repentance, disarmament, and the disestablishment of institutional greed.) The dimensions of global crises seem to indicate that we are, historically speaking, entering a major crisis, a tipping point, an axis of transformation for which End Times is an apt designation. The great and startling discovery is that the cleavage between, let's say, the Vatican and the Catholic Workers, between Pat Robertson and the Open Door Community, is not merely an academic split between pre- and post-Enlightenment theology, but an alignment with either empire or the kingdom of God. Given that it was Empire that (legally) murdered Jesus, this cleavage strikes at the heart of what it means to be Christian, which in turn means that Christianity has been dissociating into two radically different—and opposing—spiritualities: one that's solidly civilized, with both "conservative" and "liberal" branches, and another for those who heed Spirit's call for the resurrection of *pagus*.

How fully Spirit is heeded depends on the energy of people who are ready and willing to recognize Powers and Principalities both for what they are and what they could be, who have undergone conversion from mythology to gospel, from *mythos* to *logos*, who've been born again (or maybe again and again and again), who are ready for what Borg and Crossan call God's Great Spring Cleanup, although I prefer Spirit's Covert Yeasting.

Whatever it's called, I think it's time we got with the apocalyptic project.

16

That Great Unplumbed Pool of Darkness

RECOGNIZING THE KINGDOM OF God as Green, that our spiritual *and* political task
is to help create, to the best of our comprehension and ability, *malkuta* on Earth, is a
thought so contrary to Christian convention that, except for momentary aggravation
or puzzled amusement, it hardly registers as an idea worth internalizing or a project
worth thinking about. Original sin has scotched all possible earthly traction for the
kingdom of God.

If we are church attendees, we may routinely participate in uttering the Lord's
Prayer in unison—your kingdom come, your will be done, on Earth as it is in Heav-
en—but we are unlikely to take those words to heart, much less allow them to lead
us into spiritual transformation or political action. Although Jesus supposedly taught
this prayer to his followers, its this-worldly orientation is opposed to and refuted by
the great bulk of subsequent Christian teaching. The kingdom of God is to happen in
God's good time or (it amounts to the same thing) in the Next Life. So say orthodox
theologians. Normal living in capitalist empire is how Christian believers must live
and prosper, a world in which eutopian sufficiency has been banished in all its preindustrial forms and not deemed likely for revival in any postindustrial formation. The
kingdom of God, it seems, requires an exit visa to be utilized only at the termination of
this earthly life, with miraculous transport elsewhere for those with a ticket of salvation. *Civis* will triumph over *pagus* once and for all.

What's normal for us in the affluent West is a stable, comfortable, middle-class
life—a fairly large and well-kept home, one or both married partners working full-
time in factory or office, the kids in school, cars in the garage, the bills paid, money
saved for retirement and the kids' college, the usual array of electronics in the "entertainment center," various insurance policies, perhaps a pet or two. Church involves
impulses that are powerful but opaque—a need for moral self-confirmation, a desire
to see the next generation shaped by moral certitudes and taught the core religious
stories within the received tradition, a felt obligation to mingle with others (and "worship" with them) in order to confirm that this normality is shared and valued, and,
finally, an underlying hope to be chosen by God for an eternal afterlife in heaven. Or,
if one secretly doubts some or all of the conventional religious teaching, it's important
not to stray too far from the emotions protecting one from pervasive meaninglessness

or a terrifying fear of hell—or perhaps it's only fear of being seen as intellectually skeptical or spiritually odd. Fear is a boundary hard to cross, especially under the moral surveillance we identify as God's.

Politically, we are only superficially informed. Commercial TV networks, perhaps some select religious broadcasts either on television or radio, an occasional dip into AM radio rants—these constitute the "news" shaping our outlook. Throw in an occasional newspaper or magazine. For those who feel obliged to vote—perhaps the most emotionally charged and intellectually assertive act of normal citizenship—the selection of candidates is largely determined by an aura of authoritative "moral values." For normal middle-class religious people, Republicans remain largely the candidates of choice, for they (the Republicans) claim to represent "freedom," "lower taxes," "pro-life" values, "traditional" values and a "strong defense," all juxtaposed against the various Evil Others who apparently are intent on undermining or destroying our "Christian" way of life. Not firmly grounded in Green spirituality, a condition reflective of social and cultural realities, Democrats—as in the mid-term elections of 2014—get pounded. That is, neither decisively conventional nor inspiringly visionary, Democrats are (Revelation 3:15-17) neither hot nor cold, merely lukewarm, fit only for electoral expectoration. To suggest, in such a context, that the kingdom of God is Green, that servanthood and stewardship need a much deeper political understanding and economic unfolding, is a total nonstarter, a big zero, almost as if one spoke a language no one understood or wanted to understand—interesting sounds, perhaps, but sounds devoid of meaning. Reduced consumption, military contraction, *pagus* restoration, and Green socialism appear as complete political losers. They're as dead in the water as the kingdom of God, as incomprehensible as *malkuta*.

What's so ironically interesting, in one respect, is that many who have left the Christian fold and abandoned its core scriptures did so at least in part—perhaps in large part—because "the faith" is dominated and saturated by a vacuous and bland normality, simultaneously cloying in an emotional sense and almost totally devoid of intellectual rigor. (*Mythos* still has *logos* locked in a broom closet.) And that leads us to ask: If Jesus, a lowly country peasant, was so radical and revolutionary that the Powers of his day wanted him dead, and if those who presently call themselves "Christian" claim to be his devoted followers and behavioral disciples, wanting to live as fully "in Christ" as is humanly possible, how did *normal* Christianity get to be so demographically dominant, so complacently affluent and boringly middle class? How did Christians get so utterly misinformed about who Jesus is and remain so willfully uninformed about possible meanings within the kingdom of God proclamation? How did we come to reflexively align ourselves with the strongest expressions of empire and empire entitlements? Why do we consistently vote Republican when that party's top leaders have been major war criminals? (Not that Democrats constitute a flock of angels lusciously preening their gorgeous wing feathers.)

The more I've thought about this, and the more I've read, the more convinced I've become that the deflection of the kingdom of God from Earth to Heaven not only is key to this puzzle, but deflection has probably been operative from the moment Jesus uttered his proclamation, or at least since his brutal crucifixion. Jesus was a spiritual revolutionary whose vision and intent was to initiate spiritual transformation whereby empire would be politically "overthrown" (or simply overgrown) by collectively transformed behavior rendering empire impotent and irrelevant—overthrown or overgrown by the growth of spiritual comprehension, a process by which the "principles" of the kingdom of God proclamation—radical servanthood and radical stewardship—would become so clearly, deeply, and fully part of human consciousness that ethical transformation of "human nature" would result in the dissolving of empire, both its external predatory structure and its internal (or psychological) matrix of compulsive control. (Of course this is precisely what the theologians of original sin say can't be done.) But as Ched Myers puts it in *Binding the Strong Man*, "Mark's concern is not only liberation from the specific structures of oppression embedded in the dominant social order of Roman Palestine; it also includes the spirit and practice of domination ultimately embedded in the human personality and corporately in human history as a whole."[1] The "kingdom of God" therefore constitutes a transformation on multiple levels simultaneously. If the "kingdom of God" is about liberation from domination—whatever else it may be about—then it's obvious that domination in both a political and economic sense creates and reinforces, by the requisite conformity demanded by "society," a correspondingly dominated human personality internalizing domination in the form of insecure righteousness. For the conventionally orthodox who have internalized Romans 13:1-7 and Augustine's dicta regarding the godly origin of kingdoms and empires, the kingdom of God proclamation is, at best, merely a pointer toward an otherworldly heaven, attainable (if one is chosen) only after death.

The first hurdle for my comprehension came as I was pursuing an answer to the puzzling question: Why are small farms dying? This led to the origins and history of horticulture, the early practice of agriculture, and the subsequent economic, cultural, political, and religious impoundment of the agrarian village by a bandit aristocracy in a congealing civilization. That is, I had been taught—implicitly if not explicitly—that civilization was the great upward human thrust out of primitive evil, out of backwardness, barbarianism, savagery, and paganism. Civilization was a metaphysical entity overpoweringly *good*, even God's prize creation in human affairs, a mighty effort that lifted us from creepy jungle to secure city. Therefore to recognize and come to grips with civilization as a "mafia" protection racket, run by a self-selected bandit aristocracy, constituted a real spiritual crisis. I was faced with a hard choice: either I was willfully venturing into perverse evil by believing civilization built on a foundation of violence, greed and theft or, alternatively, I was confronted with the brutal truth that association of the divine with civilization was the key device by which civilizations

1. Myers, *Binding*, 103.

have justified themselves (and civilized theologians have justified civilized oppression) since the rise of the first institutionalized bandit class of nascent aristocrats. That is, I first confronted the *mythos/logos* problem in a theoretically "secular" context, a civilizational-formation context, and I was compelled to recognize that *logos* was revealing a male bandit hiding beneath the *mythos* robes of the "divine" king.

Once I had broken through to this understanding, and it wasn't an easy thing to do, I began to see Jesus in a totally new way. He had, after all, been put to death by the collusion of two aristocracies—the subject Jewish temple authorities of Israel and the colonial overseers of the ruling Roman Empire. That he would've been crucified for advocating private piety and afterlife salvation was transparently ridiculous, even laughable. (Had he been advocating those harmless things, the authorities might even have subsidized his project, at least with tax-exempt status.) He was legally assassinated because he disturbed and threatened the Powers and Principalities. He posed a "dangerous" *pagus* alternative to *civis* domination. And, as I slowly came to realize, his "dangerous" alternative was contained within or expressed by his "kingdom of God" proclamation, a proclamation consisting of radical servanthood and radical stewardship based on trust in the daring depth and compassionate embrace of underlying Spirit and a corresponding conviction that human behavior—human "nature," I suppose—is capable of bold yet humble self-regulation, self-governance, and even ethical transformation.

Here we confront a major aspect of our current theological dilemma. If we say, in regard to Jesus' kingdom of God proclamation, that "the divine" we need to put our trust in is "God" or "Yahweh," we are instantly spun back into an otherworldly, brutally aggressive conception of the divine that has been exploded by modern scientific scholarship or evokes images of triumphant domination and totalitarian holocaust. Ched Myers, for instance, seems to want to dodge this bullet when he says he is "not anxious to enter into 'meta-symbolic' debates" and therefore has "tended to avoid talk about God."[2] But in an earlier passage, where he explains the concept "war of myths," he uses the European conquest of the Americas to illustrate a point:

> On one side were the stories of the indigenous peoples: their legends of creation, their clan genealogies, their gods, their welcoming rituals, all of which reflected a living, concrete, cultural fabric, social organization, a relationship to nature and technology, and so forth. On the other side were the Europeans: their myths of "discovery," ideologies of conquest, the flag they planted as symbol of "ownership."[3]

But note that on the European side, there is no explicit mention of or reference to God as related to or justifying the myth of discovery, ideology or flag, while on the indigenous side we have "gods," without capitalization; therefore "gods" are mere

2. Myers, *Binding*, 37.
3. Myers, *Binding*, 16.

cultural fictions. (They certainly aren't *God* or "gods" would've been capitalized.) At this point I accuse Ched Myers, despite his excellent and compelling analysis of Mark's gospel, of attempting to smuggle God through spiritual customs by keeping Him hidden in an unlabeled gunny sack. (Does Myers not know that Pope Alexander VI, in 1493, issued a papal bull allotting to Spain and Portugal all lands in the newly discovered Western Hemisphere or that this bull expressed the will of God?) That is, Myers is against the brutality of imperialism—except when it comes to God or Yahweh.[4]

If these gropings are more or less accurate, then it seems, at least in some respects, that Global Crisis is related to our historic understanding of the divine. Everything conventional in regard to God is big, male, powerful, interventionist, and totalitarian—at least in the sense of tolerating no other gods—and, God forbid!, any Goddess or goddesses. When Constantine and Augustine welded the Christian God, Yahweh of ancient Israel, to the Roman Empire, there was no longer any reason to decline the "practice of domination ultimately embedded in the human personality and corporately in human history as a whole," as Ched Myers has so well put it. That is, the

4. In the August 28-September 10, 2015, issue of *National Catholic Reporter*, pages 1b-8b, there are two well-written pieces by Vinnie Rotondaro. The first ("Lives carved by trail of history") is largely about Lakota life on the Cheyenne River Indian Reservation in and around Eagle Butte, South Dakota, a life still shaped by "deep psychological wounds" and "unresolved Native American grief" caused by "historical trauma" associated with the crushing of indigenous culture. The second article ("Disastrous doctrine had papal roots") is explicitly about the "Doctrine of Discovery" as generated by a series of papal bulls—*Romanus Pontifex* in 1436 (the taking of the Canary Islands by Castile), *Dum Diversas* in 1452 (instruction to Portugal to enslave Saracens, pagans, and others), another *Romanus Pontifex* in 1454 (the seizure of land and people in Africa), *Inter Caetera* of 1493 (jurisdiction of Spain over most of the New World), and others alluded to but not named—which authorized both slavery and land confiscation on an international and even global scale.

These bulls worked their way, says Rotondaro, into international law and ultimately into American law pertaining particularly to Native people and Native land. Rotondaro goes on to describe in some detail the efforts by some contemporary Catholic communities, especially the Loretto Community, who have asked the Vatican to repudiate the Doctrine of Discovery, requests that have not been successfully responded to.

One person quoted in "Disastrous doctrine had papal roots" is Steven Newcomb, an *Indian Country Today* columnist and cofounder of the Indigenous Law Institute. Much of Rotondaro's second article relies on Newcomb's analysis (inclusive of Newcomb's book *Pagans in the Promised Land: Decoding the Doctrine of Christian Discovery*). But Rotondaro doesn't link the Doctrine of Discovery to the theology that identifies the Christian mission of conquest to the Old Testament construct of Chosen People. (See my reference to Steven Newcomb in "The Superlative Proportions of our Self-Inflation," chapter 17 in *The Kingdom of God Is Green*, especially pages 108-10.) That is to say, the Doctrine of Christian Discovery is not simply a set of egregious errors originating in the fifteenth century, a set of errors for which papal apology is sufficient. Repudiation or revocation is not simple precisely because the Doctrine of Discovery is directly connected to the worship of the Hebrew Yahweh who *commands* the taking of other people's land, the wrecking of their spiritual practices, and even their wholesale murder. To repudiate the Christian Doctrine of Discovery therefore requires the repudiation of the ancient *Hebrew* "Doctrine of Discovery." Such repudiation would remove the religious justification for Christian Discovery, call into question the Constantinian accommodation, and—most powerfully of all—undermine worship of a Father God who unhesitatingly commands conquest and even orders genocide to achieve His aggressive ends. This, in essence, would require the Vatican to repudiate a core set of convictions on which its very existence depends.

Western construction of God, especially in its empire formulations, has vastly accelerated the growth and spread of a kind of human personality that instantly thinks of God as big, male, powerful, interventionist, and totalitarian; and, in turn, this view or understanding of God, by a process of internalization and identification, by religious and secular alignment with God's purpose, justifies the men, nations, and corporations who imitate the traits of God; it empowers aggressively brutal behavior on Earth, including global economic dominance and military conquest. Just as God Almighty tolerates no other gods, so Christian civilization conquers or extirpates other forms of human self-governance, including all other expressions of spirituality. The only good god is a dead god. The only good economy is an aggressive capitalist economy.

So when Sigurd Olson, one of those Wisconsin naturalists (along with John Muir, Aldo Leopold, and Gaylord Nelson) who did so much for the cause that used to be called "conservation," describes how he was inspired to find a boy hopelessly lost in the wilderness—well, let's not get in the way of Olson telling his story:

> Another time when I had lost a boy on a canoe trip through wild country and no amount of searching or trailing seemed to do any good, the same thing happened. The youngster would starve if we did not find him, and in the trackless waste where he had disappeared his body might never be found. I remember vividly the end of the long search when everyone had given up hope how I sat on a windfall wondering what to do. I had covered the country for miles around, crossed and recrossed it time and again, trying to figure out what the boy might have done in his wanderings. I prayed then, long and silently, poured out my hopes and fears in a final desperate attempt to find a solution. Somehow in the process I must have aligned myself with forces, thoughts, and feelings beyond understanding, dipping once again into that great unplumbed pool of darkness involved with the spiritual background of all mankind.
>
> I shall never forget the calm that came over me, a sense of resignation and acceptance of a power beyond me that somehow I had touched. I rose and started off through the woods, following a route as unerringly as though it were blazed. Within three miles over bogs and rugged hills, I found the boy sitting on the bank of a beaver flowage he had crossed, and when I saw him, I was not surprised.[5]

What Sigurd Olson calls "that great unplumbed pool of darkness" seems to me not essentially different than the Cloud of Unknowing alluded to by medieval mystics. But the great bulk of us don't want to go there. It's too insecure, too devoid of comforting assurance, too elusive, and, most importantly, too outside our sense of control and moral self-justification. We are too restless and impatient to sit quietly in any Cloud of Unknowing or Pool of Darkness. In such presence we can only be empty and wait. We may be tugged in directions we've been trained to ignore or avoid. The unplumbed pool of unknowing isn't fit for a civilized mind, for the civilized mind wants clarity,

5. Olson, *Open*, 11-12.

organization, action, and a plan. The civilized mind needs to feel itself in control. In Olson's case, powerful but mysterious confidence came to him precisely as he had given up on clarity, organization, action, and a plan. It is *this* Spirit, in my estimation, in immanent depth below our capacity to cajole or manipulate, who waits on our willingness to let go of our self-important mascot God. Or perhaps Spirit doesn't exactly wait so much as our letting go would enable Spirit to enter into and guide us. And that means it's not that Spirit's waiting; our refusal to let go of Almighty God is precisely the obstruction. We're always looking up and out when we should—and could—be looking down and in.

The problem, of course, is that to cross the threshold from empire to servanthood and stewardship is to confront our sense of vulnerability, anxiety, insecurity, and fear. That is, civilization does not tolerate an alternative governing structure, certainly not one in which aristocrats and the wealthy are asked to become "least," "stewards" or "servants," or trust their wealth to a commonwealth of public good, just as Christian orthodoxy endlessly fights against an Earth-based understanding of the kingdom of God, just as our egos are in the controlling grip of superego constructs that are an odd blend of relentless paranoia and unrelenting possessiveness. Civilized wealth is not created out of thin air but congealed by a process of accumulation under rigorous regimes of control and extraction.[6] To break free of such regimes, or to dissolve them, requires what we might call revolutionary consciousness; but those who own and control wealth-producing economic configurations (or who represent them in formal governance) are not enthusiastic about seeing control dissolved or ownership socialized. They will punish and kill those who attempt or even advocate such audacity. Peasants and craft workers have always known this. Jesus obviously knew this. The open expression of grievance and the articulation of alternative ways of social conduct has always been dangerous business. Therefore the problem of entering the kingdom of God is not simply personal bravery to make do with less or share more fully; but, insofar as such an impulse achieves (or threatens to achieve) larger social traction in the direction of libertarian democratic ecological socialism, it "invites" persecution or suppression by the controlling Powers. And, insofar as we are all inclined to avoid pain and seek—if not pleasure, exactly, at least a relatively pain-free life—we all are party to evasion. This evasion is normative. We can readily explain its realism. Christianity has officially pandered to—and by such pandering has perpetuated—this evasion since at least the Constantinian accommodation. We lack clarity of vision, and our vision is clouded by our lack of bravery. We go with the flow; and the flow, warm and murky, provides us with the comfort of socially sanctioned normality. Our passivity is enforced by doctrine and creed. Original sin and the doctrine of the two kingdoms justify our passivity and complacency.

6. See, for example, "Socio-Economic Tensions," section 2B, in Ched Myers' *Binding the Strong Man*, pages 47 through 54.

One can also see this evasiveness at work in scripture, especially in John's gospel with its twin forms of evasiveness: first its repeated portrayal of "the Jews" in a pejorative and disparaging way—as if Jesus and his disciples weren't Jewish, as if the peasants he lived with weren't primarily Jewish—and then having Jesus repeatedly assert he had "come down from heaven" (John 6:38, etc) and was "not of this world" (John 8:23, etc), thereby implicitly showing why the term "kingdom of God" makes only two appearances in John's gospel.[7] Less than three centuries after Jesus' death, Christianity merged with the Empire that oversaw and compelled his legal murder (see John 11:47-50), and shortly thereafter Augustine rationalizes the "two kingdoms" as God's will, one kingdom under the control of state power and the other guided by the church toward an otherworldly destination, all of it supposedly mandated and sanctioned by God. This is the rationalized regime we live under to this day and whose consequences are dramatically closing in on us.[8] Christianity—certainly *civilized* Christianity—is the tomb in which the peasant Jesus has been buried, and from which he is now resurrecting.

---

7. "The Jews" as a term, almost always used pejoratively, appears nearly sixty times in John, though only once as Jesus gives the long Last Supper discourse to his disciples in chapters 13 through 17. But in chapters 18 and 19, in that emotionally charged section where Jesus is arrested, arraigned, sentenced, flogged and put to death, "the Jews" occurs at least twenty times, leaving little doubt—"Pilate tried to set Jesus free" (John 19:12)—that it was "the Jews" who wanted, demanded, and achieved Jesus' death. The other major theme in John is, of course, that Jesus repeatedly utters otherworldly remarks about himself and his mission. This occurs in many places and contexts in John, but nowhere more emphatically than when Jesus tells Pilate (John 18:36), "My kingdom is not of this world."

8. In an essay entitled "Protestant Support for the Political Right in Weimar Germany and Post-Watergate America: Some Comparative Observations," published in the *Journal of Church and State* in the spring of 1982, Professor Richard V. Pierard is quite explicit about the Protestant Right (the 1920s in Germany and the 1970s in the United States) supporting conservative politicians and authoritarian policies precisely because of the "link between throne and altar," a circumstance that in Germany "reached back to the Reformation, and the power of the crown was regarded as 'sacred' since the office was derived from God's will and grace and was to be exercised according to his command." A democratic republic was a sin because such an invention "struck down an authority sanctified by God and history."

Those passages are from pages 250 and 251. There are more such passages on pages 252, 247, and 255.

Of course, in the U.S. there is no throne, but there were (and are) "parachurch bodies that worked to establish the tie between 'nation and altar,'" and evangelical conservatives who propagated "a popular mythology about America's Christian nationhood." Pierard also says "it is ironic that the American 'free' church tradition provided just as good an opening for rightist ideas to infiltrate the Christian ranks as did its diametrical opposite, the conservative, 'state' church tradition in Germany."

What Pierard doesn't say, however, is that the link between throne and altar reaches back, not just to the Reformation, but at least to Augustine and Constantine. What we have in these rightist tendencies is consistent with predemocratic governing structure and with predemocratic theology. That is, the "modern" world does indeed constitute a revolution; and it is a revolution, even unwittingly, that not simply "challenges" earlier conceptions of throne and altar, nation and altar, but is in process of undermining and dissolving those conceptions. The civilized vertical must dissolve before the truly creative work of neolithic reconstruction can begin, after roughly five millennia of suppression. As eutopian democracy will eventually supplant aristocracy (with contemporary plutocracy operating as an aristocratic holdover while utopian "democracy" sheds its civilized mythology), so immanent Spirit will supersede transcendent God. That means religious rightists are fighting an aggressive rear-guard

Political revolutionaries, envisioning liberation as their goal and objective, frequently developed an enabling ideology of justified violence. (If violence was the means by which the oppressive system had come into being and subsequently sustained itself, it therefore seemed obvious and logical that only violence could break open or undo that system.) But we have lots of examples demonstrating how difficult it is for liberation movements to forego violence and repressive control, even if the revolution was "successful" in the short term. In part—the Soviet Union, say, or Cuba—this difficulty is compounded by intense outside hostility, against which the maintenance of armed force was deemed necessary, as well as an underlying civilizational "archetype" by which the state *always* is in control of armed violence. Mohandas Gandhi may be the greatest practitioner of revolutionary nonviolence in human history; but India, after Gandhi's assassination, became a conventional, civilized state willy-nilly. Therefore the task is not merely the marshalling of successful nonviolent tactics and cooperative strategy during a revolutionary period leading up to "liberation." That, in a sense, is the lesser, even if extremely difficult, part. The creation of a sustained and sustaining culture of cooperative nonviolence *after* the "victory" may be the hardest project of all. But this is also the point where politics qua politics must undergo spiritual conversion and ethical deepening. The kingdom of God isn't attainable without this conversion and deepening.

The "kingdom of God" appears twice in John's gospel, unlike the first three gospels where combined usages add up to about one hundred. Both of those in John occur in the talk Jesus has with Nicodemus, in the third chapter. In both instances, Jesus tells Nicodemus it's necessary to undergo rebirth in order to either see or enter the kingdom of God. That is, there's no way to enter the kingdom of God except by spiritual conviction and emotional conversion. You have to want in and you have to commit yourself to staying in or at least come in like you mean to live there, despite doubts, fears, and lapses. Here, I think, is the doorway, the eye of the needle it's necessary to crawl through if one believes that Jesus is the "Son of God."

Of course, "Son of God" as a concept presents a whole, new problem, for if Jesus "came from above" or was "sent from above," then it was God Above who sent him, and that means "above" is where God abides, and we're back to heaven. If heaven is where God lives, so to speak, then heaven is "above"; and if the promise of "believing in" Jesus is eternal life with him (and God) in heaven, then the goal of any believing person is to be included with the eternally saved above. Not only does such language convey an image or impression of an awesomely powerful God who resides above, it also tells us, at least implicitly, that life on Earth is rather trivial compared to the prospect of eternal life above.

Therefore the kingdom of God, as I've been advocating, and as it conceptually occurs in the first three gospels, is a distraction at best and even a hindrance to attaining

---

action that is both offensive and defensive, "protecting" their image of God, both in the past and for the future.

eternal life above. In other words, John's gospel not only sets the historical stage, with its repeated accusatory term "the Jews," for centuries of anti-Semitic behavior in the Christian world, it also locates our true home "above," not in or of this world, as it radically distances us spiritually and psychologically from Earth and nature. Institutionalized scapegoating and extraterritorial expectation are the building blocks of John's gospel. Is it any wonder why Constantine chose this religion in the early fourth century? There is nothing here, once the kingdom of God is theologically repudiated, threatening to the prerogatives of Empire. But if Jesus had actually said and advocated the things that allowed him to become the savior of the fourth-century Roman Empire, there would have been no reason to nail him to a post a few centuries earlier.

What I'm groping for is an explanation not only of why the dominant form of Christianity in America aligns so easily with empire—in a sense, that's easy to understand as a consequence of all the evasions and compromises historic Christianity made "with the world," certainly including the Constantinian accommodation followed by Augustinian metaphysics—but also why, as we face Global Crises of unprecedented and even lethal magnitude, Christianity's response vacillates between tepid, casual or nonchalant, with (sometimes) a kind of manic glee that not only correlates these crises with approaching End Times catastrophe but does what it can politically to accelerate disaster. It's therefore no wonder why saying the kingdom of God is Green falls not merely on deaf ears but, though they might hear the words, on ears unable to process the meaning in any way that reflects an understanding of what Jesus' spirituality is about. Christians have had the kingdom of God squeezed almost entirely out of their souls. To understand what that squeezing signifies is also to understand the meaning of *civis* squeezing the cultural and evolutionary life out of *pagus*, for the crucifixion story is an icon of how *civis* views and treats *pagus*.

If we can grasp enough of these dynamics to surmise the impact on human psychology—first how the rise of civilization forcibly determined all rural life (peasant and indigenous) to be metaphysically inferior and worthy only of exploitation or extermination, and then how Christianity in its merger with civilizational structure and orientation not only taught that empires are given by God but also that the enemy of Christian salvation is the pagan (i.e., the country dweller, but also, more generally, the state of nature), and then, with the modern industrial liquidation of the peasantry and the annihilation of the indigenous, as a fully civilized, utopian psychology achieves global supremacy—we can begin to realize that civility exterminates its earthy ancestor and rejects earthly cultural corrective, and it does so via both its religious ideology and its traditional utopian governing mythology. Thus we can begin to recognize the depth of our numbed incapacity to respond to crises that might even lead to mammalian extinction, including the death of our own species, as we have been taught to spurn life in this world—except temporarily for the gated First World affluence of civility—in anticipation of eternal life above. We are *civis* possessed and *pagus* averse.

Tolerating no other gods lies at the heart of "conservative" repudiation of multiculturalism, and Abrahamic religions have had the bulk of their respective adherents magnetically aligned in accordance with the polarizing power of a Male God who not only hates all other gods or Gods but who has a special reservoir of boiling rage for any goddess or Goddess. We can therefore say that Green socialism has no chance of becoming our primary political understanding until this monotheistic, magnetic alignment loses its polarizing power and psychological hegemony. And while it's true that civilizational religions of monotheistic construction have been losing and will continue to lose firm adherents (due, in broad terms, to various solvents of "modernity"), it remains true that civilization is a form of power concentration, male in its core structure, needing for its validation the blessing of a god or God who not only approves the core structure but mandates it. So it's not only civilizational structure that obstructs the kingdom of God, but the conventional, orthodox adherence to Almighty God, as well. Christian orthodoxy is a protective moat around *civis*, the City of God shielded from rural wickedness.

If Dorothy Dinnerstein is correct in the broadest and most general way, then the image of God under which our modern civilizational institutions have been built, maintained, and justified is itself based on lopsided sexual and gender arrangements that disappear in the mists of the ancient past. Civilization and God reflect each other's gender deformity and psychopolitical pathology. All these elements—ancient sexual arrangements, civilizational power structure and utopian ideology based on male supremacy, religious understandings of the divine as totally male—are connected, entangled, and essentially inseparable. They merge as myth in which our consciousness floats. That means a successful "revolution"—if there is to be a successful revolution—must deal adequately with all these elements simultaneously: but with an over*growing* far, far more than a mere over*throwing*. This is not just about taking off an old shroud and throwing on a new one. This is apocalyptic shroud dissolvement and reformulation. We need a big mythic picture; but the new myth must be transparent. It must reflect our actual history.

There is no doubt that a strong process of dissolvement is in progress. (I wouldn't be writing this essay if there weren't.) But as dissolvement accelerates, prompted largely by both the positive and negative solvents of modernity, with various shocks jolting and accelerating incremental shifts in understanding and character, there is also a hardening at the core of threatened "conservative" prerogatives. That there is a gradual and incremental "Fabian" change is of course true. Change is constantly occurring. It is in many respects unstoppable. The river of life keeps flowing. But big resistances and big blockages also make for big upheavals that—like the French Revolution—can be terribly messy and very brutal. I somehow cannot get it out of my head that despite (for instance) the largely nonviolent uprisings in Tunisia and Egypt, great turmoil and horrific violence lie ahead in this century, for God Almighty—which is in very large part the massive projection of aggressive male prerogative—will not go down without terrible conflict and breathtaking destruction. To believe in any of the Abrahamic God constructs is to consent to live within the boundaries of those male projections which, in both civil and religious constructions, are empowered and sustained by violence. It would be wonderful to be proven wrong, but, unfortunately, I don't think I will.

17

Stories

THE LATE CATHOLIC THEOLOGIAN Thomas Berry said we're between stories, between biblical story and scientific story. To say we're between stories is true. To say we're between biblical and scientific stories is also true. But that's a narrow and partial truth. Those aren't the only two stories in the world—or even in the West.

Biblical story means not only the stories themselves—the Genesis account of Creation, Adam and Eve in the Garden of Eden, Cain killing Abel, Noah and the Ark, Joshua storming Jericho, etc—but the extent to which those stories, originating in the Middle East, constitute the core cultural narrative of the Western world, which is itself an astonishing phenomenon. Those stories have been at the heart of our world's meaning and purpose, completely overshadowing our own ethnic accounts. Virtually everybody in the larger European tradition (at least since the Middle Ages) knew those stories, to one degree or another. The power of Christianity can be measured by the degree to which its story overpowered and displaced native or indigenous story. Bible stories were the Middle Eastern (religious) backdrop to our Western (secular) lives. In religious terms, America is a province of Greater Israel; Israel's God is America's God. That's why tiny Israel has such disproportionate influence in American politics; it's a mirror image of the importance of the Chosen People in biblical story and the importance of biblical story in the American psyche. (Manifest Destiny is a consequence of Chosen People.) Because of Yahweh, little Israel can even push goliath America around on occasion.

We might say that scientific story begins with Copernicus and Galileo and continues on through Newton, Darwin, Einstein and Freud. Or we might say that Copernicus and Galileo picked up where Aristotle left off. But, however we date or configure it, the cumulative effect of scientific story has been to reveal an expanding universe immensely huge, far more complex and infinitely older than the Genesis world depicted in biblical story. Scientific story has shown biblical story to be composed of accumulated cultural legend and ethnic mythology, poetically (and politically) powerful but empirically fanciful, even as American politics remains tethered to Israel and Israel's God construct. Yahweh now commands the American descendents of the Roman Empire, which is an immense leap of faith. In this sign conquer.

Berry also believed in scientific truth. He realized that biblical story, while densely loaded with rich imagery, was—perhaps for the most part—not factually true. He also knew that Christianity, if it wasn't to die of hardened spiritual arteries, due to *mythos* acting as if it were *logos*, needed to move beyond its literalism. Its spiritual truth had to be true also in a factual sense. It had to get its preoccupation out of Israel, its mind freed from Yahweh.

But there are problems with Berry's biblical versus scientific duality. First, it totally overlooks the abundance and variety of creation stories in both the Old and New Worlds before the steamroller of Western Christian civilization smashed those stories flat. (How many indigenous creation stories were there in North and South America before the coming of Europeans a little over five hundred years ago? Does anybody know? Does anybody care?) Second, it's possible to utilize scientific truth to understand, modify, and enlarge biblical story in a way quite different than Berry's New Universe Story. His way depends on an elusive "Cosmic Christ" theology overlaid onto or injected into a Big Bang cosmology. The other way might be a bit more recently and modestly begun, starting with a twelfth-century Italian monk named Joachim of Floris.

As we have seen, Joachim meshed the Christian Trinity with the Old and New Testaments, and he came up with Three Ages in human history: the Age of the Father, corresponding to the Old Testament, consisting of monarchy, discipline, and law; the Age of the Son, love institutionalized in the church; and the Age of the Holy Spirit, characterized as consecrated anarchy or holy freedom.

Here's where the camel of science sticks its nose under Berry's New Universe tent. In the nineteenth century various archaeologists uncovered the agrarian villages predating the rise of civilization. Among the things discovered were religious figurines of an explicitly female nature. This led (with other evidence) to the conclusion that, prior to the Age of the Father, there was a long, extended, creative, and apparently quite peaceful Age of the Mother. Just as God (as Jack Miles has shown) couldn't stand and wouldn't tolerate any reference or allusion to the Goddess, so the Age of the Father deleted the Mother's Age from the historical record. Mother was banished to the archaeological digs. But by putting the rediscovered Mother in front of Joachim's Father, Son and Holy Spirit, the sequence not only gets enlarged to four (a sequence with historical correlation); but, to make the sequence semantically coherent and prophetically potent, the Holy Spirit reveals Herself as Daughter.

Modification of Joachim's trio creates a quartet of Mother, Father, Son, and Daughter. It's the Daughter's Age we're entering. That's a crucial and vital part of Joachim's modified story. Therefore, we're not so much between stories, perhaps, or in need of a Cosmic Christ leap to outer space, as we are between the phases of an unfinished story, a story in need of modification, an incomplete and truncated story whose proper reformulation provides an astonishing and wonderfully enlarged story with stunning historical and spiritual significance. The story that's unfolding is one of female prestige and feminine influence, of rediscovered and renewed earthiness. Its primary divinity will once again be female, *malkuta* enfleshed .

II

To say this implies an unorthodox enlargement of Christian convention. Thomas Berry, to some extent in the footsteps of Teilhard de Chardin, pushes toward the New Universe Story with Cosmic Christ embedded in the unfolding of the vast universe. But it's crucial that our spirituality become more Earth-centered and Earth-based. The otherworldliness of Christianity, with its odd blend of paranoia and aggressiveness, has been an immeasurably huge contributor to the shaping of our current global crises. Otherworldliness snips the nerves of ecological empathy (and empathy for the indigenous) by insisting that Earth is irredeemably fallen and, probably, doomed to destruction. The New Universe Story essentially perpetuates otherworldliness and, by perpetuation, fails to offer adequate relief to our earthly predicament.

Now Berry recognized the disablement of Mother as a consequence of patriarchal establishments, including religious formations following civilizational consolidation. And he relied on scholarly, scientific work in order to come to that understanding. So it's not that Berry was oblivious to science in the fields of archaeology, anthropology, and religious history. He was not oblivious of the Mother's era. Not at all. But he didn't enlarge Trinity to accommodate Her importance. He failed to grasp the *mythic* constriction of Trinity.

So when Berry says Teilhard was the greatest transformative Christian theologian since Paul the Apostle, and I say Joachim opened the door in an entirely different but wonderfully grounded direction, we have less a competition between theological giants—Teilhard versus Joachim—than a question of whether Christian orthodoxy is or isn't to be breached. By going with Teilhard, Berry stayed within Trinitarian orthodoxy, which enabled the metaphysical etherealization of Christ as cosmic "Word." By modifying Joachim's Three Ages to Four, I am breaking with Trinitarian orthodoxy (while holding fast to Jesus' "kingdom of God" proclamation, precisely because it's so ethically foundational and Earth-based). Berry accepted important elements of critical scholarship, but he apparently never let that acceptance alter his attachment to Trinitarian orthodoxy. The New Universe Story was Berry's means of evading a deeper and more prophetic truth. Trinity is mythically incomplete. The New Universe Story provides Trinity a Milky Way cloud cover.

Mother must be included—fully and equally included—in our understanding of the divine, given what we now know about Her spiritual banishment and historical disablement, and what we also now recognize as the Father's wrathful psychosis. Berry recognized all this—he was no dummy—but he chose to glide above it (if I might put it this way) with a cosmology twinkling with star dust. Thus he was able to remain "orthodox," which meant he confronted neither Trinitarian convention nor the smug and complacent self-image of the church as God's Establishment on Earth.

But the globalization of civilization inevitably brings to lethal culmination the diseases of Class and War, the traumatic institutions that are its interior heritage from its inception. Thus we are increasingly engulfed in intensifying Global Crises precisely as those traumatic diseases have globalized. Male violence (with corresponding presumption of political entitlement) holds this thing together—or as together as its intensifying centrifugal externalities allow. But we have to recognize that all three Abrahamic religions took shape in an atmosphere of consolidated male power. Therefore, as Jack Miles points out, we have a purely Male God who hates the Female Goddess with inexplicable apoplectic rage. To glide away from this raw reality toward a supposedly soothing Cosmic Christ is to evade the core problem. Psychotherapy—including religious psychotherapy—is based on facing the truth, not evading it. Staying within Trinitarian orthodoxy, which Cosmic Christ allows, actually extends and compounds the problem. The solution requires a break with orthodoxy. Affirming Mother and Her spiritual equality opens the hidden door. Keeping Her banished keeps Trinity in control; bringing Mother into Mandala reveals the hidden Daughter.

Joachim, it's true, was a Trinitarian. His room had three doors—one each for Father, Son, and Holy Spirit. But all rooms have four directions; and Joachim's construct, enlarged and clarified by serious scholarship, enables us to perceive a door in his blank wall, a door covered over by centuries of forgetfulness, a forgetfulness caused in part by fear of Father rage, which is part of the nucleus of male domination. To uncover and open this door means to face into and therapeutically resolve our fear of (and political dependence on) the wrathful Father, to first recognize and then abandon violence as the organizing principle of civilizational economic structure and political legitimacy, and to embrace human equality and ecological reverence—servanthood and stewardship—as the ethical underpinnings of our lives in a global Green culture. This is what democracy means. This is the nonviolence democracy requires. Our survival depends on this embrace.

The Age of the Son was unable (to some degree unwilling) to realize in social terms the ethics of the gospels. Some proportion of this failure was a consequence of Christian capture by Roman and Greek civilizational presumption, largely made possible by early Christian failure to adequately embrace "kingdom of God" ethics and instead indulge in nasty mud fights over metaphysical distinctions and theological speculation: gnostics versus the orthodox, in particular. Orthodox Christianity defined itself under the brooding power of a wrathful Almighty God. This is how Christians brought Yahweh to Rome, installed Him as Almighty God of the Roman Empire, and gave Him new continents to intimidate and invade. But we now recognize, thanks to historians like Toynbee and Mumford, how the undergirding principles of civilization are antithetical to gospel ethics. Civilization is based on unlimited taking; gospel ethics are about equitable sharing. Therefore the unfolding of gospel ethics into sustained (and sustainable) human conduct requires the breakdown and shrinkage of civilizational bondage, with male presumption contracting at its core. Therefore the "new" religion—if that's what the Daughter's Age implies—will be far more embracing of gospel ethics than orthodox Christianity ever was. For those who love Truth, for those who know that what makes the Holy Spirit holy is Love, stepping into the Daughter's Age will be a spiritual liberation without compare.

18

Drying Dishes with My Friend Jim

(for Jim Lewis and Carl Nelson)

At a recent Friends Meeting, as we were drying dishes, Jim Lewis asked my thoughts on the "kingdom of God"—that phrase or "concept" (sometimes "kingdom of heaven") appearing close to one hundred times in the first three canonical gospels. Jim and I were immediately interrupted. Our conversation never returned to the subject. So here, in written form, I'll respond to Jim's question. But, first, some general impressions:

1. That the term "kingdom of God" occurs so often in the first three gospels indicates its importance to the overall message of the gospels and, therefore, its centrality in Jesus' teaching.

2. That the term is so little discussed, thought about, or preached on is itself an interesting subject for consideration.

It seems that wrestling with the meaning of the "kingdom of God" has not elicited much interest in Christian thought for the bulk of Christian history. (The conventional explanation is, first, that the "kingdom of God" didn't arrive as Jesus anticipated— God didn't bring it on as He was expected to— and, second, once Jesus was dead, the Second Coming didn't quickly occur; therefore the "kingdom of God" was postponed to Heaven. In the meantime, only pious waiting was possible.) The Anabaptist portion of the Protestant Reformation—especially the rural and lower-class communalistic movement that persists among Mennonites, Amish, and Hutterites to this day—may be, besides celibate monasticism, Christianity's greatest "kingdom of God" response. That is, those folks (the so-called Anabaptists) "rediscovered" the "kingdom of God" in *their* Reformation—a Reformation violently attacked by Catholics and Protestants alike—as they set about arranging their communal lives accordingly, even as they did so from within the constrictions of Trinitarian orthodoxy with its male-dominated and God-the-Father proclivities. (Quakers with their silent gatherings are, one might say, post-Anabaptist Anabaptists or perhaps the first congregational representation of Joachim's Third Age.)

It's my impression that early church controversy—"orthodox" versus "gnostic," for instance, in the second and third centuries—was largely about abstract theological doctrine and metaphysics. Was Jesus God? Are the Father and Son equal and of the same substance? What is the "definition" of the Holy Spirit? Was Mary as "Mother of God" also divine? How is a person saved for eternal life? What constitutes a "sacrament"? The literate church fathers got into enormous controversies over belief and doctrine. Exploring the meaning of the "kingdom of God" was largely lost in sprawling controversies more metaphysical than ethical, more philosophical than spiritual. The merging of Christianity with Empire in the early fourth century perpetuated—even institutionalized—neglect of the "kingdom of God" proclamation.

So I think we not only have to recognize that the "kingdom of God" as a "concept" was neglected early on, we also have to ask *why* it was neglected, given its prominence in the gospels. These are not idle questions.

Oddly enough, I'd like to start by asking who killed Jesus and why. If we go with the gospel of John, it would be "the Jews" (I've counted the references—about sixty) who were responsible for Jesus' crucifixion. Not all sixty pertain explicitly to the arrest, trial, and crucifixion of Jesus; but the tone set by the repeated use of "the Jews" reeks of a scapegoating propensity. (For those who wish to study this scapegoating of "the Jews" more deeply, see James Carroll's book *Constantine's Sword: The Church and the Jews*. It's largely a history of how the church was the carrier of anti-Semitism through the centuries, leading to the Nazi death camps.)

A number of contemporary scholars (I'm most familiar with James Carroll, John Dominic Crossan, Marcus Borg, and Ched Myers) say it was collusion between the Jewish aristocracy and the Roman occupiers of Israel that resulted in Jesus' crucifixion: not "the Jews" in some generic or populist sense, but the male upper or ruling class, the cream of the crop, the best and brightest, the beating heart of civility: it was *those* people who arranged the legal murder of Jesus. That's the view I find plausible: Jewish upper class plus Roman occupier conspiring to smash any semblance of "revolution" from below. I think there's really no adequate explanation for the crucifixion but that Jesus was making ripples in a world—in a governing system—extremely vigilant for any hint of unrest or revolt. Any disturbance was a potential threat to a vastly outnumbered aristocracy, a threat to be dealt with immediately and harshly.

It wasn't "the Jews" who murdered Jesus or wanted him dead. It was the hard-core governing center of civilization that felt he had to go, without delay.

Even though we're groping for the meaning of the "kingdom of God" proclamation, we are aided in our investigation by first inquiring into the nature, function, or purpose of civilization. We might consider, at least tentatively, that civilization has a powerfully hostile attitude toward the "kingdom of God." As a child, I was essentially taught that to be civilized was in the same moral universe as Christian salvation. I suspect all who are reading these sentences were similarly taught. That is, civilization represented a decisive cultural elevation above primitivity and backwardness, while

Christianity offered eternal life to those God found spiritually acceptable. If we were to overlay or superimpose these respective constructs onto social demographics, we would see a classical economic pyramid: primitivity (indigenous people, peasants, the working class) at the base of the pyramid; urban civility (the middle class) would be in the center; and the gated elect (what we now call the one percent) would be at the top. And if we really dare to stretch our minds by utilizing Freud's famous trio of terms, we might say primitivity = id, middle class = ego, and upper class = superego. In that sense, Jesus arose from a huge rural lower class—the id—and was crushed by the gated one percent—the superego. The middle class—the ego—was largely constituted in that historical time and place as retainers of the one percent; as such, they were probably passive and perhaps even indifferent spectators to the centuries-old conflict between peasants and aristocrats. (In that sense, contemporary passive indifference on the part of the affluent West's middle class toward Third World destitution or global climate change is psychologically continuous and historically consistent. Once comfortably under the "security" umbrella of civilization's violently extractive system, it's difficult to voluntarily downsize or leave, much less deliberately examine the violent, predatory nature of such "security.") It was only in my adulthood, and then by an odd path, that I came to a view of civilization radically different than the one I had absorbed as a child. I found this new view extremely difficult to accept, precisely because the earlier teaching had been so firm in its unwavering adoration of civility's nearly divine goodness.

The "odd path" I took was in asking "Why are small farms dying?" This led me to read history, especially the history of agriculture and agriculture's relationship with civilization. This history blew to pieces what remained of my Sunday School fundamentalism. That is, as a child I'd taken Bible stories to be literally true; to come to terms with Stone Age gatherers slowly but methodically developing what we now call horticulture required facing into my childhood beliefs regarding six-day creation and the God who had accomplished this stupendously creative act. To accept cultural evolution required letting go of my childhood beliefs, although to say "beliefs" doesn't begin to convey the power of the protective emotional security fence around those beliefs. Those "beliefs" weren't just lightly stocked packages of "information" on transitional shelves in my brain; they permeated my entire sense of reality and were a huge part of my identity. Letting go meant identity confusion.

Horticulture produced food abundance; that abundance, in turn, facilitated the domestication of an entire set of animals—goats, sheep, cows, chickens, horses, etc—resulting in what we now call agriculture: a blend of plant and animal domestication with fields and pasture. An increasingly complex network of agrarian villages was in a process of vigorous cultural evolution. By "cultural evolution" I mean this horticultural/agricultural village dynamic was unfolding from *within*, by means of its own collective organic intelligence and need; it was not being directed or controlled from *without*. It was certainly a cultural departure from hunting and gathering; but it was a creative, voluntary departure, with no end in sight. We cannot legitimately call this evolutionary novelty by the name "civilization," for "civilization" derives from the same root that gives us "city." Civilization comes with cities and is an entirely different kettle of fish than clusters of villages. Various scholars (including Lewis Mumford) show that the rise of the city occurs simultaneously with the rise of an explicit ruling class or aristocracy (which literally means—*aristokratia*—the rule of the strong or the best). Civilization since its inception has been a process, a system, created by armed coercion for the benefit of a predatory few or dominant minority. Horticulture and then agriculture facilitated a new magnitude of abundance. But civilization is not a "natural" progression or logical outgrowth of the agrarian village. It's not the spontaneous combustion of excessive social size. Civilization is the murderous, institutionalized, overpowering theft of village abundance, intentionally so.

Not only did civilization come into being with the rise of the city, with the emergence of an aristocratic ruling class, but the agrarian village as a whole was coerced by violence and threat of violence into relinquishing its "surplus" so the ruling class might use this "surplus" in ways only aristocrats saw fit. Farmers and gardeners suddenly found themselves a destitute "peasantry," victims of institutionalized theft without apparent end. Cultural evolution of the agrarian village was arrested by systemic violence and unreienting expropriation. The rise of civilization both thwarted the cultural evolution of the agrarian village and, because of violent expropriation, essentially froze village life in a mode of bare subsistence and cultural impoundment. The social consequences of this impoundment became the millstone of "backwardness." That is, oppression produced destitution, and destitution was contemptuously identified as stupid backwardness: another example of the victim blamed by the victimizer. The emergence of civilization may well represent the first instance in human history where folk evolution was not only forcibly suppressed but actually replaced by ruling-class dictatorship. Civilization is a male warrior anomaly that actually claims to be in legitimate—divinely justified—control of cultural evolution.

Jesus was a peasant. (See John Dominic Crossan's excellent book *The Historical Jesus: The Life of a Mediterranean Jewish Peasant*.) It finally dawned on me, after a good decade of reading and rereading the four canonical gospels, that the "kingdom of God" proclamation, with its radical servanthood and radical stewardship, with its repeated and unrelenting attacks on those who "lord it over," was a call for liberation from the ruling dictates (the overarching ruling structures) of civilization. The "kingdom of God" contains the germ of what we might call an alternative organizing principle for human society. That's not to say the "kingdom of God" proclamation was or is purely political as we understand the term "political" in modern usage. It definitely was and is spiritual: but insofar as it "requires" a belief in the divine, it's a belief that has to pass through the eye of an ethical needle. That is, this understanding is achieved by the practice of radical servanthood and radical stewardship, by the abandonment of violence and the relinquishing of security rationalizations within civilizational mythology—including, in the end, the abandonment of belief in a violent God whose episodic use of sacred violence for righteous purposes justifies civilization's monopoly on violence and its use in behalf of civilizational order.

In that sense, the "kingdom of God" proclamation, consciously or unconsciously, deliberately or accidentally, is a call for the restoration of precivilized cultural evolution. No more "lording it over," no more righteous selfishness disguised or rationalized as state necessity or national glory. The "kingdom of God" would dissolve civilization as we know it and restore cultural evolution in a folk mode. That is, civilization instills fear of what we might call organic intelligence; to undo civilization's traumatic institutions is to dissolve our fear of human freedom.

But there's another, unexpected wrinkle in all this. Lewis Mumford (*The Myth of the Machine*), Elise Boulding (*The Underside of History*), Gerda Lerner (*The Creation of Patriarchy*), and many other scholars show that the spirituality of the precivilized agrarian village was overwhelmingly feminine. Its divinity was the Mother. But with the imposition of civilized aristocracy—extractive "government" by violent and predatory male will—spirituality (including divine imagery) was forced toward total maleness. (Which is of course the unifying characteristic of the three Abrahamic religions, all of which arose in a Middle East under civilizational rule for hundreds if not thousands of years, therefore prone to imagine God as King of kings.) A startling piece of information came from Neil Douglas-Klotz, in a book entitled *The Hidden Gospel: Decoding the Spiritual Message of the Aramaic Jesus*. Douglas-Klotz, a scholar of the language Jesus supposedly spoke (Aramaic), says the "word usually translated as 'kingdom' is gendered feminine in both Aramaic (*malkuta*) and Hebrew (*mamlaka*)" and the word "'queendom' would be a more accurate translation." So, if we dare to say "queendom of God," we might as well go all the way and honestly say "queendom of the Goddess." And then we may just as well recognize that this "queendom of the Goddess," when understood in a context of cultural evolution and its subsequent blockages, is the Mother of the precivilized agrarian village. Anything less than this only amounts to inserting a bit of femininity into God, perhaps as a prophylactic inoculation building immunity against greater infection, which seems to be the prevailing form of cautious liberal theological cosmetology.

It seems obvious to the point of being irrefutable that the contemporary bundle of global crises (WMDs, climate change, species extinctions, etc, etc) has burst on the world scene simultaneously with the institutional consolidation of civilized globalization. That is, it's precisely the alignment of civilized globalization with intensifying crises that constitutes the correlation we mostly refuse to recognize. We might take this refusal—especially in the Christian West, where we claim to have a particular propensity to both perceive and tell the truth—as an astonishing indicator not only of how fully the "kingdom of God" proclamation has been neglected to the point of abandonment, but also an amazing lesson on how completely civilized mythology has infiltrated and corrupted Jesus' core teaching—and, finally, why he had to be murdered. That is, the kingdom of God proclamation was abandoned for the same reason as Jesus' crucifixion. Both Jesus and his proclamation challenge civilizational rule. To suppress the kingdom of God is to leave Jesus hanging on the cross. It is to say no to spiritual transformation on Earth. Just as we have *not* been taught that civilization killed Jesus, so our collective enthrallment to the moral and metaphysical sanctity of civilization is so enveloping that we are not permitted to recognize civilization as the root cause of our growing ecological disasters: there's always a scapegoat or an "externality" to blame it on.

Perhaps we can conclude—looking back both on Christian history and on the history of civilization—that the sheer overbearing power associated with aristocratic civilization served to align human consciousness with civilized mythology and its superego proclivities. It suppressed all other stories, all other identities. The only "free" life was to be found within the operating perimeters of civility. Its history was, in the end, the only history that mattered, just as its purpose is the only purpose that matters. Peasants were obliged to be deferential and obedient. "Savages" were to be crushed, with survivors forced to accept civilized ways of living. To be human was to be civilized. All other modes of life were subhuman. Except, perhaps, for a few raw characters who didn't care what anybody thought (the sociopathology of power—the "traumatic institutions"—peopled by real sociopaths), it seems that most rulers felt the need to justify themselves morally and spiritually. To justify themselves they had to have their policies and actions justified; and—probably in virtually all cases—this justification was carried out (or articulated in public) by religious figures in the employ or in mythological confluence with the ruler; therefore sanctification came in the name of God or the divine.

From the position of the common person, leadership is often looked for and needed. We all undergo instruction of one sort or another. Jesus, of course, was an astonishingly clear and bold leader. But what happened after his murder? I think we can see (as early as Paul's letters) that instead of pithy peasant parables and unflinching confrontations with authority that constituted Jesus' way of being in the world, the overall behavior of his followers—down to us in our day—was to slide into metaphysical, doctrinal, or denominational clusters based largely on differences of abstract beliefs regarding the metaphysical nature of God or how we are to achieve life eternal. This process was quite advanced by the time Constantine decided to make Christianity the state religion of the Roman Empire, with Augustine following a bit later as justifier in chief, a role he fulfills to this day.

Gil Bailie, in *Violence Unveiled*, talks about the function of "sacred violence" as disguising both "founding violence" and "scapegoating violence." As regards the origins of civilization, the nature of its myth is becoming clearer and clearer: instead of civilization as the great lifter of torpid humanity out of backwardness and primitivity, it poisoned the fermenting cultural evolution of the agrarian village, just as it demolished countless indigenous communities. With Christianity, "sacred violence" is more complex. That is, it was never hidden that Jesus was crucified as a common criminal or rabble rouser. But the official reasons for his crucifixion slid between the perfidy of "the Jews" (who spitefully set him up or at least cravenly betrayed him) and the "hidden" purpose of God the Father magnificently sacrificing His Only Son for the Redemption of the World, which meant (John 3:16) that "believing in" Jesus as the Only Son of God put one on the path toward eternal salvation in an otherworldly afterlife.

In this smooth unfolding of deflective myth, the "kingdom of God" practically disappears from view. It certainly atrophies as ethical dynamic. Christianity not only became explicitly civilized with the Constantinian accommodation; it became the state religion of the very system that oversaw Jesus' murder. We might even say that Jesus became the "bride" of Constantine as the church became the concubine of the Roman Empire. Together they forged a project known as Christian Civilization, a project that, after a thousand years, more or less, erupted out of Europe on a global-conquering mission. We, in a world of accelerating and intensifying crises, are the children and heirs of that mission whose psychomythic engine is the City of God.

Why are small farms dying? Because with the industrial revolution, civilization had no further use for peasants. The backwardness of the peasant and the squalor of the village were to be done away with. The expulsion and exile of peasants flooded cities with factory wage-slaves. Agriculture was industrialized to maximum "economies of scale." Small farms—as in the "Jeffersonian vision"—filled an intermediate need between an extinguished peasantry and a maximized industrial agribusiness. Small-scale farming got to domesticate the wild landscape before being pushed aside for agribusiness-sized "economies of scale."

There is a direct connection between the fates of the precivilized agrarian village and the "kingdom of God." Both were suppressed by the patriarchal establishment. The manic utopianism of civilization's world conquest project, as Arnold Toynbee says in his *Civilization on Trial*, is based on Class and War, on elite control, and on a standard of living (especially as it has become industrialized and "democratized") that is ecologically ruinous. If we are seriously looking for an alternative organizing principle for society, one based not on Class and War but on servanthood and stewardship, its name in the gospels is the kingdom of God—or, in Neil Douglas-Klotz's translation from the Aramaic, the queendom of the Goddess. Our sincere embrace of this kingdom/queendom would not only allow Earth's ecology to recover some degree of healthy functioning, it would also facilitate a magnificent growth of grounded human (and humane) culture. It would, I believe, do one more thing in regard to fundamental Christian concepts: it would, by restoring the feminine spirituality of the precivilized agrarian village, resurrect the Mother (the divinity of the era) and, in so doing, reveal the Holy Spirit (the divinity of the emerging era) as Daughter. The Christian Trinity—Father, Son, and Holy Spirit—will be transformed into a post-Christian Mandala of Mother, Father, Son, and Daughter.

The irony of saying "post-Christian" is that while the term applies to much of Christian theology and metaphysics from the second century onward, it doesn't apply to the ethics of Jesus or his "kingdom of God" proclamation. Just the opposite: the "post-Christian" world will be the unfolding of gospel ethics, of that "kingdom" or "queendom" Jesus gave his life to initiate.

If this perspective is crudely false, then we might conclude—aside from wishful thinking—there really is no hope for us. That is, if the globalizing of civilization results in the toxic spread of its "diseases of Class and War" (Arnold Toynbee) or the infiltration of its "traumatic institutions" (Lewis Mumford), then civilization is destined to culminate in an absolute whirlpool of death, destitution, and carnage. With Weapons of Mass Destruction and the rampant stupidity that refuses to recognize (much less seriously address) Global Warming and Climate Change and other toxic "externalities" too numerous to itemize, the realities are in place (including a neo-aristocratic concentration of stolen wealth) by which to achieve either some cocktail "Armageddon" or restoration of a vigilant and exceedingly brutal aristocracy which sees to it that democracy dies and stays dead. If Jesus' core proclamation—the "kingdom of God"—could get diluted by metaphysical abstraction as early as the second century (see Elaine Pagels' *Beyond Belief, The Gnostic Gospels*, or *Adam, Eve, and the Serpent*), and if the Christian church could by the early fourth century consent to cohabitation with the Empire that murdered its spiritual inspiration, then what hope is there that the twenty-first century will witness an upsurge in "kingdom of God" consciousness? What makes us think we're so special, smart, or deserving to escape the destructive trajectory?

As far as I can think my way through these thoughts, I see only one basis for hope. That hope rests, not on our smartness and not on our moral superiority, both of which are hugely inflated and dripping with toxic narcissism, but on the infiltrating, consciousness-changing energy of Spirit. But what, then, do I mean by "Spirit"?

To enlarge Trinity into Mandala, to go from three to four divine "persons" or representations, is to realize, first, that Mother absolutely must be restored—*restored*, I say, not invented or contrived—to our gendered understanding of the divine (and, with Her restoration, the cultural resurrection of the life-mode of Her age), and, second, that the Holy Spirit, in order to be gender consistent, must be understood as Daughter. Not only does the enlargement of Joachim's revelation make for four divine figures or "persons," it balances the sacred genders. No longer is "God" totally male. Now we have Mother, Father, Son, and Daughter—or, if we prefer, Goddess/God, each with two revelations. (Goddess = Mother and Daughter; God = Father and Son.) This configuration frees us from the utopian otherworldliness of the male-dominated system known as Christian Civilization—frees us from it and enables us to recognize its pathologies .

Now all this (at least for me) is extremely interesting and very appealing. But if it's not true, it's merely cute. And cute will not save us.

So here's my final thought, although it's a thought with a lot of ignorance in it. By "ignorance" I mean not-knowing. I feel myself here at the extremity of my capacity to understand—or, alternatively, I have not yet sunk deeply enough into the unfathomably deep Inner Silence of Spirit, where greater understanding (and perhaps even some wisdom) might be found.

Spirit is like groundwater, like yeast. (I soaked in the "groundwater" image from John Shelby Spong, who said he got it from Matthew Fox.) "Groundwater" is infiltrating, nourishing, vital, and indispensible for life. But it's also—compared with the usual heroic, supernatural, monstrously powerful and extraterrestrial images of God—quite powerless and vulnerable. (Can "groundwater" be fracked by the utopian mining techniques of Christian Civilization?) Perhaps Spirit is vulnerable the way Jesus was vulnerable or the way the "kingdom of God" has obviously been vulnerable.

What makes Jesus so compelling is that he lived his life in a far fuller embrace of Spirit than the rest of us. He lived in the world as a free and complete human being, and he invited us to join that liberation. He set us an example—a vital, living, incredibly brave example—of what human life could be, of what spiritual courage looks like. The gospels contain valuable nuggets of his spiritual groundedness and profundity. (Not that we are to "imitate" Jesus—that's already a mimetic evasion—but, instead, find the courage and humility to live our own earthy lives of servanthood and stewardship.) But that the "kingdom of God" proclamation suffered such historical atrophy indicates both the tendency of human spirituality to slide comfortably into theological abstraction and the compelling power of murderous civilization to facilitate that political slide. The question for us revolves around the infiltrating and vital properties of "groundwater" and "yeast." Either we humans are being sufficiently "yeasted" by the infiltrating, fungal properties of Spirit—"yeasted" at all possible levels and dimensions of behavior and consciousness—or we are not. If Spirit wants us "yeasted" into kingdom/queendom consciousness, then it's our ethical responsibility to cooperate to the fullest extent of our capacity.

If we are not in process of being sufficiently "yeasted," then dreadful destruction and/or aristocratic restoration are likely outcomes. But if we *are* in process of being sufficiently "yeasted," then the kingdom/queendom truly is at hand, and our world—the one we actually live in—is about to be transformed into a magnificence beyond our imagining.

19

The Deep Ecology of Global Sharing

GREENS HAVE BEEN STUCK in single-digit electoral despondency for a number of seasons and reasons. The commonly accepted explanation for this disheartening condition is a "wasted vote" perception in the context of a two-party system. To vote Green is to throw away your vote, an empty act reserved for the desperate, totally disaffiliated, airhead, or cynical. Of course, if we had a democratic multiparty process of governance, Greens could have a toe (perhaps even a foot) in the legislative door, an opening the "major" parties are obviously not eager to provide. The two industrialist and capitalist parties seem to have no time for ecological socialism. As it is, Greens are mostly huddled under the bridge, holding numb hands over a smoky fire in a can.

All that seems true, even if expressed somewhat fancifully. Yet the problem lies deeper than structural exclusion in an electoral sense. The greening of public consciousness is an immense and—culturally speaking—revolutionary and even transformational task. So much of the habituated planking that has gone into building normal political consciousness is either antithetical to Green culture or impervious to its attractions, at least beyond silent sports, decorative landscaping, or "wilderness" art. Corporate advertising does not encourage Green conservatism. Professional politicians, almost without exception, want nothing to do with serious Green advocacy, in part (is it the larger part?) because to get to Green requires downsizing our gluttonous appetite for utopian commodities and a corresponding downsizing of the weaponry protecting our gluttonous appetite. Confronting utopian bulimia is considered political suicide, an affront to a stock market ascending like Jesus into the sky, with comfortable prosperity for those Left Behind until the Second Coming.

Human beings are obviously capable of believing in and doing self-destructive, stupid, and ecologically disastrous things, even while assuming a happy posture of moral normality. Mutually Assured Destruction may be the pre-eminent emblem of such suicidal righteousness, as we lead busy, preoccupied lives under the ever-present shadow of nuclear extermination, an extermination-in-waiting we seem determined to ignore. Meanwhile, the speed with which globalization has been poisoning Earth and wrecking noncivilized (or, at least, nonindustrial) cultures is awesome, the bulk of that velocity contained within the radiant dynamic of civilized Progress. We are collectively in the grip of something with enormously destructive momentum, something we seem—politically speaking—incapable of recognizing or naming. We are mentally unable to link our way of life and standard of living to this unprecedented crisis. The connection—try as we may—is always beyond our comprehension. Or, for those who can discern the link, disconnecting from the complexity of the overarching system is dauntingly difficult. And, besides, even if I try to disconnect, nobody else will, so what's the point? Why bother?

Yet if we dare apply, even provisionally, the word "evil" to this gripping something—*Webster's* defines evil as causing pain or trouble; harmful; injurious; threatening to bring misfortune; and so on—we are compelled to admit that virtually all the operative specifics within the globalized momentum of Progress are carried forward on the basis of the "good," that is, effective, efficient, beneficial, valid, genuine, healthy, strong, vigorous, honorable, worthy, and happy. The car that speeds me down the winter road, radio playing Bach fugues and heater keeping me summer warm, is subjectively experienced as wonderful and good. Yet the human capacity to technologize and commercialize comfort is, with its protective military apparatus, part of the engine of destructive momentum. Private and corporate good generates public and ecological evil. Thousands upon thousands of people in Iraq have been murdered, had their lives, homes, and neighborhoods ruined, their countryside poisoned, so I can drive warmly down the winter road, esthetically enveloped in baroque audio massage from a technologically amazing and extremely compact sound system, spiritual uplift in a sea of anguish and blood.

The extent to which a successful Green political movement requires a corresponding transformation of cultural and spiritual consciousness is beyond my capacity to express or articulate. Who among us lives deeply enough within transformed Green consciousness to throw open those doors of perception? I grew up on a small, subsistence farm in northern Wisconsin. I remember work horses and threshing crews, kitchen canning and barnyard butchering. I have lived most of my adult life in "voluntary poverty," the bulk of it in homemade buildings in the woods, without electricity or running water, with woodburning cookstove and kerosene lamps. Although these life choices represent a deliberate "retreat" and even a conscious "monasticism" of a sort, I am still groping for adequate immersion in Green consciousness. Since culture is collective, one can only go so far individually. The yearning I feel cannot be satisfied in the absence of Green cooperative culture, and cooperative Green culture exists more in the imagination than it does, as it were, on the ground.

My intellectual journey can be said to have begun in the early 1970s when, living in inner-city St. Louis, missing rural life, I asked people I thought informed and smart to explain to me why small farms were dying. The answers did not satisfy. Eventually I found great insight in the works especially of Lewis Mumford and Norman O. Brown.

What I learned was this: What we so piously and adoringly call civilization came into being roughly five thousand years ago with the ruthless impoundment of a slowly evolved agrarian village, a village culture unable to prevent impoundment.

With impoundment came slavery and militarism. Aristocrats living off peasant labor and peasant production was the modus operandi of civilized conduct until both the industrial revolution and modern political "revolutions" muddied the classical water. Industrial "democracy" threw a "scientific" shroud over the predatory nature of civility. Civilized intellectuals could only see the backwardness of the village; entrepreneurial capitalism would somehow enable rustics to throw off their rusticity and become civilized. We learned that sticking a kinder and gentler label onto capitalism—"democracy"—worked like a magic wand to reduce if not completely eliminate the predatory nature of civilization. Just as civilization went magically from "pagan" to "Christian" with the Constantinian accommodation, so civilization ceased being aristocratic and instead became "democratic" because semantic magic (plus a little capitalist economics) once again did its amazing work. We in this country have been taught that our civilization has been successfully democratized, or at least democratized to the maximum extent possible. All we have left to do is iron out a few wrinkles elsewhere in the world where resistance remains tied to various kinds of stubborn economic backwardness and faulty religious conviction.

But if civilization is based on slavery and militarism, on class division and divine kingship (transformed in our time into the "unitary executive"), then the "democratization" of civilization means we've democratized systemic economic predation. We've become empire "democrats" or "democratic" imperialists not only in terms of corporate and military globalization, but also in terms of our habits of consumption, our political reflexes, and our religious expectations. Empire—like civilization—is not only external apparatus but also internal disposition. We are not merely the passive recipients of empire largesse; we're also its active psychopolitical building blocks. To live normally within its energy field is to participate in its mythic momentum and to internalize its superego superiority.

If civilization in its initial formation impounded the agrarian folk community and thwarted its cultural evolution by forcing it into becoming a destitute peasantry—thus establishing as a civilized convention the endemic "backwardness" of the rural—then the industrial revolution enabled civilized elites, both capitalist and communist, to destroy peasant life and the peasant village altogether by turning agriculture into an industry based, to the fullest possible extent, on a rationalized factory model of maximized scientific production while expropriating its "surplus" via government-controlled commodity pricing.

The destruction of peasant culture proceeded simultaneously with the brutal suppression and even extermination of noncivilized indigenous cultures as Euro-American industrial civilization reached global dimensions. To be civilized was self-evidently superior—so superior, in fact, that it freely generated murderous racism and expounded genocide as public policy. (The only good Indian is a dead Indian.) That which was designated "savage" or "primitive" or "backward" was to be enslaved, converted, or exterminated. Civilization was in a hurry. The missionary wore a watch and carried a pistol. There was no time for hesitation or excuse. We had to destroy the village in order to save it.

The point here is that we've all had our minds and lives profoundly shaped by this process precisely as this process has created, in its own image, a superstructure of overbearing institutions that, in turn, shape our attitudes and perceptions. Virtually every one of us has had his or her consciousness largely contained within the parameters of civilized definition. We were, so to speak, schooled in its meaning. We are conditioned to a constantly modifying, civilized progress. We have learned to crave electronic stimulation and intensely rationalized structure. We fear darkness, manual labor, the unadorned quietness and slowness of nature, or the prospect of life without instant, unlimited energy slaves at our immediate beck and call. We feel a kind of panic if asked to imagine a future with few parking lots and no flashing lights.

We've also been stripped of a folk heritage that knew and embodied the practices of sharing, self-provisioning, and sufficiency. Folk consciousness was ruptured by the replacing of collective folk self-reliance (oikonomia) with individualized (but institutional) dependency on mass consumerism (chrematistics). So as crises reveal themselves around us—now here, now there, often with surprising speed and shocking intensity—we are largely bereft, not knowing what to think or do; and, thus bereft, most people, so far, attribute most of these crises to critical flaws in design. What's needed, therefore, from this point of view, is technofix "greening" of infrastructure: get it right, get it cool, so we can achieve an even higher Standard of Living via "green" nanocivility without all those bothersome externalities.

But nuclear weapons, glacier melting, species extinctions, desertification, etc, etc, tell a very different story. They tell us that the civilized project, with what Lewis Mumford calls its "traumatic institutions" and Arnold Toynbee calls its "diseases of Class and War," has reached a terminal, global crisis. What we are facing demands something far greater and much deeper than tweaky tinkering with technofix corrections in design: nothing less than a complete, sincere, humble reappraisal of the entire civilized project is what's needed.

I believe these are the major options: total devastation; devastation on such a scale that only remnants of human community survive; restoration of explicit aristocracy, with the great bulk of the population—a severely reduced population—forced into explicit peasant servitude; or, finally, the unfolding of transformed Green consciousness with a corresponding Green culture sustaining and upholding a powerfully humble Green political stability.

And that, once again, raises the question of what constitutes Green consciousness. I think we can say, with Jerry Mander, that it involves a warm, repentant embrace of the indigenous. We can say, with Merlin Stone, it involves a similar embrace of the precivilized feminine. With Dorothy Dinnerstein, gender-balanced child rearing. With E. F. Schumacher, the rural. With Wendell Berry, the agrarian. With Maynard Kaufman, an Earth-centered spirituality. With Leopold Kohr, the small-scale. With

Norman O. Brown and Lewis Mumford, the utter transformation of our institutions, both domestic and public.

But that's not all. If we want sailing ships and energy-efficient trains, the internet and some sort of functional power grid, we're going to have to ask who gets to own those things. If, in snooty anticollectivist piety, we insist on private ownership of the large-scale and complex (because anything "socialist" is unspeakably evil and untrust-worthy), we've just thrown the door open to unlimited private wealth and power, and thus, in the long run, to the restoration of aristocracy—and, with it, the complete rehabilitation of civilization's traumatic institutions and diseases. If the small-scale belongs rightfully in private and cooperative hands (a nod here to Leopold Kohr), the large-scale belongs—as R. H. Tawney says—in the public domain. And that means Green socialism. The small-scale and the socialized need to be in dynamic balance.

Green and Red need to get their acts together, get married, make babies. They can be as indecent as their imaginations permit, making political love on park benches, in coffee shops or cafes, on the beach, or while waiting for the police during sit-ins at the local congressman's office. But it's time they got it on. There's no time to lose.

Beyond all this, there's the matter of religion. As far as I can tell (I'm not Huston Smith), all religions are built of two fundamental elements—creedal mythology and spiritual ethics. The ethics are remarkably universal—compassion, forgiveness, mod-esty, humility, love, and so on—while the creeds and mythologies are distinct and unique, even incredible and bizarre. Religious conflict is almost entirely rooted on the creedal side, in the mythology of whose gods are favored, of whose saint is going to beat the crap out of the other guy's saint, of whose *mythos* qualifies as *logos*.

It's not incidental that the three Abrahamic religions have been, and are, seriously at each other's throat. If civilization, as a system of slavery and militarism, has reached its globalizing terminus, we shouldn't be shocked to discover that the Father religions which have risen to massive global influence during the reign of traumatic institu-tions, drunk with notions of mythological exceptionalism and creedal supremacy, are also busy breaking each other's heads.

Perhaps we can more accurately say that conflict *within* religions is largely creed-al, that is, such conflict involves dispute and contention over points of core doctrine, while conflict *between* religions is primarily mythological, that is, aggressively and even contemptuously dismissive of the other guy's sacred story. Neither the Crusades nor the Thirty Year War was organized by overflowing love or sustained by super-abundant forgiveness. Protestant versus Catholic (or Protestant versus Protestant) is almost entirely an issue of creed, while Christian versus Moslem or Moslem versus Jew has to do with which sacred story God favors mythologically. Are Jews divinely chosen by Yahweh for the re-establishment of a Greater Israel? Was Jesus born of a Virgin and did he rise from the dead, thus signaling his sole godly Sonship and, therefore, the total superiority of Christianity? Is Mohammed the greatest and final Prophet whose religion is destined to become global and universal? Is it irrelevant that the final book (Revelation) in the Christian New Testament is about the disastrous clash of armies at Armageddon? Should we be surprised that the unfolding of fundamentalist "reality" follows a fairly strict (if also extraordinary) rendition of mythological script? But we should be clear here. Apocalypse does not produce End Times. End times forces us to uncover the roots of End Times causation. Disclosure of root causes constitutes the apocalyptic.

When the toxic dust settles, it'll be massive devastation, a reconstituted aristocracy, or a bravely humble Green world with, at minimum, an Earth-centered spirituality, or, perhaps, a new eco-feminist religion strong with ethics grounded in servanthood and stewardship: the deep ecology of global sharing. That we are so collectively stupid and politically stubborn about making the obvious and necessary choices is a sobering commentary on the power of inherited mythology and collective illusion, our willful disinclination to acknowledge our righteous sins or embrace the humility of repentance. The world is in process of undergoing a religious cerebral hemorrhage, a civilized stroke. We'll either come out of it dead, crippled, or astonishingly renewed. Only one thing is certain: we'll never, ever, be the same again.

20

Trinity as Symbol of Historic Crimes and, with Modification, of Transformative Fulfillment

The intellectual question that looms over our time is whether the current state of profound metaphysical and epistemological irresolution is something that will continue indefinitely, taking perhaps more viable, or more radically disorienting, forms as the years and decades pass; whether it is in fact the entropic prelude to some kind of apocalyptic denouement of history; or whether it represents an epochal transition to another era altogether, bringing a new form of civilization and a new world view with principles and ideals fundamentally different from those that have impelled the modern world through its dramatic trajectory.

Richard Tarnas, *The Passion of the Western Mind*, page 410

THERE ARE MANY WAYS of looking at and understanding Christian Trinity. In that construction, God is Three Persons—Father, Son, and Holy Spirit. But we can easily identify four variations in how Trinity is understood. These are 1) Trinity as divine fact, 2) Trinity as elusive theological symbol, 3) Trinity as concocted religious nonsense, and 4) Trinity as historical construct rich in unexplored psychomythological and undeveloped psychoanalytical meaning.

The first of these (Trinity as divine fact) corresponds to traditional Christian orthodoxy and is near the hub of "conservative" conviction, both Catholic and Protestant. The second (Trinity as elusive theological symbol) is descriptively protean, open to all manner of metaphysical shape shifting, a kind of conceptual First Responder employed to prevent symbolic collapse, and it falls largely in the "liberal" camp, both Protestant and Catholic. The third (Trinity as religious nonsense) is most clearly represented in outspoken secular irreverence, finding nothing in "Trinity" that a good dose of hard science wouldn't cure. And with the fourth, the shaggy, unkempt, out-of-wedlock child of folk evolution and the Enlightenment—Trinity as a richly psychomythological (if also somewhat smudgy) window into human history and the human future—we have a "point of view" that is literally none-of-the-above and therefore treated, for the most part, with disapproving, aggravated, and disbelieving grimaces by one, two, and three above.

In broad outline, the first position is what we might call "conservative" or "fundamentalist," and it claims a firm grip on true Christian faith, on the real Christian heritage. The second position is composed of "liberal" churches and religious persons who use Trinitarian language in liturgy, hymnody, and creedal recitation because it's the venerable linguistic inheritance of their religious tradition; but the actual conviction of those who utilize Trinitarian language in this prophylactic way seems mushy, cloudy, and subject to intellectual awkwardness (if not open embarrassment) if such folks are pressed for clarity or explanation. The third position we might say is areligious, unreligious or antireligious, probably "atheist" in a flat-footed and uncompromising sort of way, materialist rather than idealist or spiritualist, hardheaded about science in a narrow and factual sense. The fourth position is a lonely one, treated with contempt by those of the first position, anxiously shunned by those of the second, held in a permanent state of cynical condescension by the third: hated by the first, embarrassing to the second, and seen as simply stupid by the third.

Since most literate persons, even the most pedestrian, have an elemental grasp on and recognition of the first three positions—conservative, liberal, atheist—it's the ragamuffin fourth (clown, comedian, magician, poet, prophet) that's of interest here. We'll see what jokes or tricks or prophecies—perhaps even some quirkish wisdom!—we might elicit from these quixotic quipsters.

II

I have no idea how many saints there are in the Roman Catholic canon, but I don't think Joachim of Floris (or Fiore or Flora) is among them. He apparently never made the holiness grade. Perhaps his miracles weren't up to snuff. Perhaps he got on the wrong side of the apostolic fence. Perhaps he wandered too close to the kingdom of God and got his otherworldliness singed. But Joachim is claimed (I'm claiming him) as a saint of the fourth position, an early (twelfth-century) Italian monk of consecrated psychoanalytical eutopianism.

Isn't that a mouthful? Let's chew it into smaller bites.

III

Joachim (however he arrived at it) provided a critical construct by which to reconfigure or reconceptualize not only the Christian depiction of divinity, but also that depiction's relationship to core dynamics within civilization. Once we understand Trinity for its mythological meanings and exclusions, we see its operative male supremacy pertains both to Abrahamic religions and to civilization, and that the religions themselves (whatever else is in them, some of it spiritually profound) were shaped as divine rationalizations for male warrior energy controlling the *Realpolitik* heart of civilization. The remainder of this essay will be an attempt to demonstrate the relevance of Joachim's construct—with a crucial modification—regarding our circumstance of deadly global crisis.

But, first, a little personal background mixed with a provisional explanation of how this modification of Trinity came to me.

IV

I was raised on a small homestead farm in northern Wisconsin. Literate working class. One-room rural elementary school without running water. A compulsory, dull high school and nearly two unfocused years at a state university. United Church of Christ Protestant—an affiliation that began to wither before I left high school—but with an exposure to Sunday School Bible stories and Christian doctrine that was deep and persistent.

Estrangement was threaded into ever-enlarging skeins of compulsory schooling from elementary on. A home life gripped by never-enough economics. My mother's cancer and death. A brief factory job. Immature college floundering. A relentless Selective Service, an escalating war on Vietnam, and an enforced facing of institutionalized moral murder in the names of God and Country. An uninspired marriage. Anomie in a big city. Jobs with little joy and no future.

The flickering light at the end of this unhappy tunnel came with a growing awareness of how deeply I was missing rural life and by asking why small farms were dying. Pursuit of an answer to that question began to guide and shape my life. Nearly fifty years later, I'm still directed by its force and flow.

It's not so much that I realized God's not who He's cracked up to be (we have to be very careful about blithely demolishing inherited religious images, as if we've discovered they're simply obsolete and therefore to be casually discarded and replaced with new images more compatible with current temperament), as that atheism in its bleak and sterile expression is only a psychic way station, an intermediate time zone of mythological sterile void, on the way to an unexpectedly rich and exhilarating complexity of understanding—and even on the way, if I might dare employ the word, to an embracing revelation, perhaps even *apokalypsis*.

V

Since nobody I knew could, with any degree of competence or coherence, tell me why small farms were dying, I realized that to try to answer this question on my own, I'd have to know a lot more than I did (which was next to nothing) about agriculture's history and its relationship to civilization.

So, next up: what I learned about the history of agriculture—and what I learned about myself as I learned about the history of agriculture.

VI

Well, history and religious "history" collided inside me. Here's how it happened. In *The City in History*, Lewis Mumford gave a tour of agriculture's origins. He said, as the ice and snow receded at the end of the last Ice Age, gatherers by their attentive diligence (over many generations) developed what we now think of as plant domestication or horticulture. This level of concentrated plant development led, eventually, to the domestication of a few animals and then to agriculture. All that took several thousand years. But empathy-deficient warriors arrested the open-ended cultural evolution of the agrarian village by violently imposing on villagers and village food production an unrelenting expropriation, and that expropriating imposition forced into being a two-character economic and political dynamic of aristocrat and peasant lasting thousands of years. It is the primal structure of civilizational inheritance.

Right away there were two serious problems. First, I had never learned anything substantial about evolution, cultural or otherwise; although I had learned that God created the entire world—the whole universe—in six days. Emotionally this meant that by "consenting" to "believe in" evolution (including the cultural evolution of the agrarian village) I was trespassing biblical boundary having to do with the sacred nature of time and, more importantly, the credibility of sacred scripture itself; and I discovered in myself a rather fearful and aggravated fundamentalist—a biblical literalist—a believer in Genesis—who radiated a certain fierce resistance to the idea of open-ended evolution and who said "Evil afoot! Back off!" Oh my goodness gracious! We don't seem to realize what a load of conviction we carry until we disturb sacred memory, memory with deep emotional and moral power.

The second problem was that everything I'd learned about civilization had come dressed in upper-class dinner clothes and was wrapped in impeccable moral authority. Now I was being asked to believe the founding of civilization was a brazen, brutal, and bloody act of criminal armed robbery? First I'm asked to voluntarily enter the precivilized time zone of "pagan" evolution and then take a long, hard look at civilization's origins from the peasants' point of view? Is this what happens when my teddy bear gets confiscated? All because I want to know (am determined to know) why small farms are dying? What's my world coming to?

VII

As hard as it was emotionally to accept an understanding of time and cultural evolution emerging from a far distant past, and to realize how directly and powerfully that distant past was responsible for shaping contemporary life, it was in some ways even harder to accept the core criminality of civilization—although, I have to say, my recent exposure to the U.S. military machine, with its transparent political self-righteousness (perhaps even its mythic psychosis—we're talking mass murder, after all, plus sadistic ecological devastation), had provided me a raw body of brutal experience by which to overcome my induced indoctrination. I'd just been manhandled, as it were, by the collective male will of the male-run political and economic governmental system, threatened with prison if I refused to be trained in organized invasion and state-sanctioned murder. It was not a subtle lesson. PTSD is not for sissies.

Mumford had more or less postulated a core aggressive rigidity (kingship) rising from within the agrarian village itself, with explicit human sacrifice playing a bloody and complicated role in the transformation of peaceful agrarian villages into expansive and controlling aristocratic kingdoms and empires. There were other scholars (I came to side with them) who said aristocracy and kingship arose when nomadic warrior/raiders decided to stay and rule rather than just pillage, loot, rape, and burn before riding off to wait for the village to sufficiently recover so the fun and excitement could be indulged in all over again: nomad raiders, it needs to be said, who brought with them the worship of a fiercely aggressive Sky God of the steppes whose forced installation in the village overpowered and incrementally supplanted reverence for the village divinity—the Mother Goddess.[1]

But there's a crucial footnote to this violent take-over of the agrarian village. Its gist can be stated ever so briefly, but its historical impact lasted roughly five thousand years. I mean the core dynamic of traditional civilization: ten percent (at most) hereditary aristocracy, ninety percent (more or less) expropriated peasants. This pattern, with variations, lasted until the early modern period when kingship was terminated (sometimes with a sharp blade) and an ersatz aristocracy of bourgeois/industrial/corporate wealth boldly took its place. Civilization, with no substantial change in its

---

1. Riane Eisler, on pages 44 and 45 of her *Chalice and Blade*, talks of "nomadic invaders" who gradually "imposed much of their ideology and way of life on the peoples they conquered": "The most famous of these are a Semitic people we call the Hebrews, who came from the deserts of the south and invaded Canaan (later named Palestine for the Philistines, one of the peoples who lived in the area). The moral precepts we associate with both Judaism and Christianity and the stress on peace in many modern churches and synagogues now obscures the historical fact that originally these early Semites were a warring people ruled by a caste of warrior-priests (the Levite tribe of Moses, Aaron, and Joshua). Like the Indo-Europeans, they too brought with them a fierce and angry god of war and mountains (Jehovah or Yahweh). . . .

"These striking similarities between the Indo-Europeans and the ancient Hebrews have led to some conjecture that there may here be some common origins, or at least some elements of cultural diffusion. But it is not the bloodlines or cultural contacts that cannot be found that are of such interest. It is what seems most definitely to unite these peoples of so many different places and times: the structure of their social and ideological systems.

"*The one thing they all had in common was a dominator model of social organization*: a social system in which male dominance, male violence, and a generally hierarchic and authoritarian social structure was the norm. Another commonality was that, in contrast to the societies that laid the foundations for Western civilization, the way they characteristically acquired material wealth was not by developing technologies of production, but through ever more effective technologies of destruction."

core predatory values, was commercialized and "democratized." We could all become raiders of the lost ark. Capitalism is the current name of the game by which we raid.

With industrialization, the peasantry (more or less simultaneously with most of the remaining indigenous cultures) underwent what we might call cultural genocide. The newly victorious middle class, strutting with self-righteous religious confidence and civilized self-assurance, may have continued to harbor secret awe of aristocracy (an awe fully discernible in its imitative "aristocratic" lifestyle and perpetual deference to the King of kings), but its embarrassed, angry contempt for the "backward" contained no mercy. Subsistence was sloth, and sloth was sin. Enclosure of the commons—the death of the peasantry—swiftly accompanied the victory of the middle class. The neolithic died with the death of the commons, subsistence, and self-provisioning. Sloth was banished with the backwardness in which it had luxuriated. (See Josef Pieper's stimulating little book *Leisure: The Basis of Culture*.)

We seem to like the cozy comfort of the word "democracy," but we blithely gloss over the extermination of those classes and cultures closest to Earth, much as we've blithely internalized the supposedly wholesome mission of democratic civilization. Isn't it grand that now, at long last, we're all so civilized, all so middle class—even if we had to destroy the village in order to save it? Even if we have to wreck Earth's ecology in order to preserve our Standard of Living?

VIII

Well, one more footnote. It's important not just to recognize but to deeply take in the fact that all three Abrahamic religions—Judaism, Christianity, and Islam—were founded in a social world of explicit empire, kingdom, and kingship. Unflinching male rule. The respective depictions of God as stand-alone Male within the three Abrahamic religions (what the late religious scholar Marcus Borg called the monarchical model) perfectly reflect the power dynamics of the period. The core power projection of each religion—its depiction and understanding of God's absolute male power—remains at the heart of each orthodoxy: a singular God, a jealous God, a God who looks just like a king. There shall be no other gods before me. God the Father is in each instance sovereign and supreme. Therefore each respective religion sees itself as the true carrier, the true conveyer, of the highest supremacy and the truest sovereignty—quite aside from any ecumenical suggestion of equality. Liberals may want to hold hands and say we're all sailing in the same general direction. Different sails, maybe, the same direction. Conservatives, meanwhile, remain in a strictly one-sail/one-boat navy with all hands on deck, ready for impending engagement and some truly vigorous action.

IX

There is another path of analysis that helps focus our minds. This path (to the best of my knowledge) was opened by the French anthropologist of archaic religion René Girard and made accessible to English speakers by Girard's American disciple Gil Bailie. The core thought has to do with how "founding violence" gets robed in religious or quasi-religious holiness. This robing not only sanctifies founding violence retroactively, it also institutionalizes the violence as an ongoing moral and sacred monopoly of deadly force by which evil is deterred, obstructed, and ultimately defeated. Victims of this violence become *scapegoats* on whom suppression or even extermination is justified. (The only good Indian is a dead Indian.)

Gil Bailie's *Violence Unveiled* is, at heart, an unusual expression of Christian apologetics. It should be taken seriously at that level. But its analysis—or, perhaps, the tools of its analysis—are more fundamental. For instance, its focus can be directed toward the Joshua account of Israel's founding violence—the genocide visited on the city of Jericho at Yahweh's command—as well as toward the violence of civilization's founding, a founding that created and sustained a system of economic exploitation based on slavery and militarism that, although modified in recent times by upsurges in "democracy" and the global spread of industrialization, is still very much with us and continues to be at the heart of how we justify not only our nuclear weaponry but also our "standard of living" and "lifestyle." Everyone now is to achieve a "civilized" standard of living and behave as we do. Our current and perhaps terminal Global Crisis is a direct outgrowth of these violent foundings and their merged moral sanctification: one as Civilization, the other as Christianity: fused first as Christian Civilization and now as utopian commercialization.

Bailie's book helps us understand how and why Jesus was legally murdered by this system of moral sanctification, a conspiracy between the Jewish temple authorities (the national aristocracy) and the Roman occupier (the colonial aristocracy). But we can walk this analysis into even deeper waters. The Jesus who proclaimed the "kingdom of God," the peasant who challenged both the system and the practitioners of moral violence and who paid for that challenge with his life, was, three centuries later, installed as the Otherworldly Savior in the State Religion of his primary murderer (the Roman Empire), with "the Jews" as an ethnic group now collectively designated his killers. Instead of obvious collusion between self-interested aristocracies (one bent on self-preservation, the other on political control), the agents of Jesus' crucifixion were now identified as Jewish rabble, a mob, and—dare we say it?—a *pagan* upsurge of raw and irrational hatred. This shift of emphasis from viciously vigilant superego (Jewish temple and Roman fortress) to irrational idish upsurge from below is itself a perfect illustration of the Girard/Bailie thesis, of how evil is both projected and deflected onto a scapegoat. (There may have been a murder here, but *we* didn't do it. *They* did. Or, if *we* carried it out, it's only because *they* made us do it.) By the time we get to Augustine's elegant rationalization of Christian Civilization, we find Jesus transformed from a Jewish revolutionary spiritual peasant to an unfairly crucified urban prince now (somewhat belatedly) under the loving protection and fatherly jurisdiction of a Roman Empire God. The Holy Roman Empire rescued Jesus from the Christ-killing Jews and the religion of the Son began beating up on the religion of the Father.

The orthodox mission eventually congealed as the determined conquering and forced conversion of paganism the world over. And here—pagan from *pagus*, country district or country dweller, peasant's Latin root as well—we have the perfect semantic scapegoat by which urbanized Christianity merged with civilizational empire, a powerful and deadly fusion in which the City of God takes as its civilizational mission the conversion (or suppression) of the entire *pagus*: godly *civis* in planetary mission to uproot, convert, or destroy all possible forms of demonic *pagus*. This has been (and it remains) the most concentrated body of fiercely aggressive psychic energy within our current (and intensifying) Global Crisis. It is *this* concentrated energy that must be identified as fully as possible and transformed as completely as possible. We need to get inside the Right of Christian Discovery to see what's made it a ticking genocidal and ecocidal time bomb. Our survival depends on just this identification and transformation.

X

Gil Bailie's *Violence Unveiled* was published in 1995. René Girard's most recent book (that I know of) is *Battling to the End*, published in English in 2010. Here Girard openly reveals himself a loyal Roman Catholic. He believes in the divine mission of the church and in the overarching virtue of the papacy, including papal infallibility. He's utterly positive about the Judeo-Christian heritage and he's skeptical if not hostile toward Islam. Girard gives every indication of believing the "Judeo-Christian revelation" *exempt* from the dynamics of founding violence. With the explicit case of Jesus, one can certainly make the case that here is the clear countertendency, even the remedy, to founding violence: what Gandhi would call *satyagraha* or "self-suffering." (As we have seen, Ched Myers makes just this claim.) But to assert, even implicitly, that Jesus therefore removes the Judeo-Christian heritage from the list of founding-violence actors is so staggeringly naïve as to qualify for an award in magical thinking.

That doesn't mean there's nothing of value in Girard's construct. Far from it. But it does suggest caution. (There's no Index reference in his book for Civilization. None for Jericho.) Founding violence, for Girard, is totally about "archaic" religion. He says, however, that he has "the impression that this religion [Islam] has used the Bible as a support to rebuild an archaic religion that is more powerful than all the others . . . , an archaic religion strengthened by aspects of the Bible and Christianity. Archaic religion collapsed in the face of Judeo-Christian revelation"—tell that to all the "pagans," "infidels," "savages," and "perfidious Jews" who've been persecuted and killed over the centuries—"but Islam resists. While Christianity eliminates sacrifice wherever it gains a foothold, Islam seems in many respects to situate itself prior to that rejection."[2] Christianity *eliminates* sacrifice wherever it gains a foothold? Has Girard not heard of the Crusades, the Inquisition, or the Right of Discovery? Or that the only good Indian is a dead Indian? Or that the village, to be saved, must first be destroyed?

Girard's useful and even profound formulations about founding violence and scapegoating turn in on themselves when he essentially scapegoats everything outside the "Judeo-Christian revelation." If Mumford and Toynbee are accurate with "traumatic institutions" and "diseases of Class and War" as core dynamics within civilization, and if the founding of Israel as a nation was based on Yahweh's *command* of genocide on the inhabitants of Jericho (see Joshua 6), then how in the world can one *not* apply Girard's analytical tools to the "Judeo-Christian revelation" itself, as well as to the construct of "Christian Civilization" with its wars, crusades, inquisitions, state violence, and ecocidal End Times justifications?

I have before me The Jerusalem Bible, open to the "Introduction of Joshua, Judges, Ruth, Samuel and Kings." It says: "The Fathers of the Church saw in him [Joshua] a foreshadowing of Jesus: both bore the name 'savior' and both led their followers through the waters (the one of Jordan, the other of baptism) to a promised land, while the conquest and division of the territory [Israel] are an image of the progressive expansion of the Church."[3] Joshua foreshadows Jesus. The conquest of Jericho is an image of the progressive expansion of the church. So says The Jerusalem Bible.

The crucifixion of Jesus inverts our understanding of violence. We see unmistakably in his case how the scapegoat mechanism works precisely because Jesus is a scapegoat. That part is absolutely clear and true. But the use to which the orthodox narrative has been put is both a misuse and an analogous falsehood. That is, if Jesus took the wrath of God (Yahweh) upon himself, then Jesus is not to be compared with Joshua but with Jericho: for it was *Jericho, not Joshua*, upon which Yahweh's earlier (founding) wrath was concentrated. If genocidal violence "created" the nation of Israel, or if such violence was the "sacred" portal through which the wandering Hebrew tribes entered the "promised land," then the crucifixion of Jesus—the new "Joshua" who both atones for the immense sin of the first Joshua and defies the genocidal wrath of the Father God—this crucifixion *dissolves* the glue that binds the beneficiaries of genocide into national/religious identity. To use the "conquest and division" of conquered territory as a template for "the progressive expansion of the Church" (so says The Jerusalem Bible, complete with *Nihil Obstat* and official *Imprimatur* on the copyright page) is totally (and willfully?) to miss the core and crucial point—a point, it seems, René Girard also missed.

If Jesus undoes the efficacy of sacred violence, he undoes not only "Jericho" as the means and rationale—the template—by which Israel comes into existence, he also

2. Girard, *Battling*, 214.

3. Jerusalem, 269.

undoes the "founding violence" of civilization: including the "progressive expansion of the Church," insofar as that expansion was or is based or dependent on armed conquest. (The Right of Christian Discovery absolutely depends on the orthodox assertion as expressed in The Jerusalem Bible.) Jesus undoes the scapegoating of "pagan," for *pagan* is the core scapegoat term of Christian civilization, its "archaic" Other deserving suppression if not extermination: godly *civis*—the City of God—righteously overpowering and, if necessary, brutally crushing wicked *pagus*.

Perhaps the single biggest clue as to the accuracy of this analysis is the extent to which the "kingdom of God" proclamation has been almost entirely absent from Christian discourse for centuries. In *A Whole Which Is Greater: Why the Wisconsin "Uprising" Failed*, religious scholar James Veninga says that "social gospel" theologian Walter Rauschenbusch insisted that the "idea of the Kingdom of God shriveled in Western civilization as the idea of the Church moved forward; the latter supplanted the former."[4] According to Lewis Mumford, in his 1944 book *The Condition of Man*, the "Christian Church itself replaced the promised Kingdom of the Lord."[5] In other words, the "progressive expansion of the Church" not only took political precedence over the spiritual internalization and cultural articulation of the "kingdom of God" proclamation; that expansion also proceeded with ethical/spiritual oblivion in regard to the deep transformative meaning of the "kingdom" proclamation. Therefore it was necessary to identify *Joshua* as the "foreshadowing" of Jesus rather than recognizing that the Father murdered the Son in a fit of divine masculine rage (or dispassionate political calculation) and, by so doing, He undid the efficacy of sacred violence. The Father, by His impulsive rage, undid the sacred rationale for founding violence. That's what the story means. That's its mythic lesson. The Son was innocent of wrongdoing and the Father demonstrated his uncontrollable rage and heartless *Realpolitik*. We might say (crudely paraphrasing Thomas J. J. Altizer) that the Father electrocuted Himself, that He continues in an ongoing state of divine shock. Jesus undoes all justification for male supremacy. With male supremacy dissolved, so go the gender prerogatives of the raging Yahweh. *That* is the psychoanalytical understanding of this religious mythology, even as we realize "Father" is largely a symbolic projection and stand-in for overarching superego, the established political and religious systems, created under civilizational conditions, whose collusion resulted in Jesus' murder. The murder of Jesus represents Yahweh's involuntary suicide.

This is a far more consistent application of Girard's founding insights than his muddled effort to protect "Judeo-Christian revelation" from the humiliating implications of his own analysis. Scapegoating, after all, is the projection of the undesirable or unwanted onto an innocent entity. If the mimetic is crucial to Girard's explication of scapegoating and founding violence, and if he identifies himself as an orthodox Christian Catholic, then one has to recognize that "orthodox" means (according to

---

4. Veninga, *Whole*, 176.

5. Mumford, *Condition*, 75.

Webster's) a "conforming to the usual beliefs or established doctrines . . . proper, correct, or conventional." That is, "orthodox" is also mimetic. I think we can see Girard stuck precisely in this "divine" mimetic glue. His religious loyalty constitutes the glue. His religious identity blinds and binds him to the church's sins.

It's not Joshua who foreshadows Jesus; it's Jericho. Yahweh creates Israel by means of sacred violence at Jericho, and Yahweh destroys Israel—murders his Son—by means of another burst of sacred violence, the historical consequence of which was a new religion of the Son that, at least in the ensuing orthodoxy passing down through centuries, was never strong enough or mature enough to face the psychoanalytical meaning (which is also the deeper ethical meaning) of its own mythology, never capable of recognizing the "divinization" of male authoritarianism in the imagery of the Father, too psychologically timid and spiritually weak, too reflexively deferential to authoritarian male power, to enter the ethically and spiritually liberating "kingdom of God." That the "kingdom of God" *shriveled* in Western civilization correlates tightly to the church's refusal to recognize the conquest of Jericho as a foundational act of genocide as commanded by Yahweh, God Almighty. The Global Crisis is, perhaps paradoxically, forcing us to re-examine, at a far deeper level, the meaning—and the promise—of the "kingdom of God" or *malkuta*. Servanthood and stewardship are no longer optional or laughably fanciful ethical considerations. They're the only viable paths out of our predicament. Without repentance, there's no pathway to right relationships, either human or ecological. But to take this path requires facing into what has obstructed *malkuta's* unfolding for most of the last two thousand years. Orthodoxy is the owner/operator of these obstructions—in collaboration, that is, with civilizational empire. Here is the deeper (and more deadly) meaning of the Constantinian accommodation.

XI

If 1492 is a wonderfully magic or merely convenient date on which to hang the crossing of a global threshold, we can certainly say that the official doctrine of Christian Taking or Right of Discovery—all lands not held by Christian believers were considered legitimately available for Christian confiscation—meshed perfectly with Western European military organization, cannon, commercial interests, and sailing ships. The entire world rightfully belongs to Christians acting in God's behalf. Nature—wilderness—global ecology, all this is the repository of demonic paganism, subject to systematic interrogation by Christian inquisition. Christian imperialism was in process of producing scientific imperialism, whose offspring are Weapons of Mass Destruction, Climate Change, and even the proposed geoengineering that now offers to technologically mitigate Climate Change.

XII

If the sudden and violent expansion of European Christian civilization into the Western Hemisphere may be likened to the advance of a glacier—though a glacier with an amazingly powerful mythic engine—then to be born a white kid in northern Wisconsin in 1946, whose parents were only a generation or two removed from immigrant German-speaking forebears, and whose father homesteaded a piece of logged and burned-over rocky land that was a tiny portion of a vast tract ceded by Native occupants (Ojibwe under threat of armed confiscation) barely a hundred years previous, then I too was born in the momentum of that glacier. Occupier colonist. Land usurper. Child of empire. Imperialist dirt farmer.

I knew no Native kids. My English-language culture (my mother's family largely spoke *Plattdeutsch*) consisted of hard physical work, a one-room elementary school, Sunday School in town, 4-H, and, later, high school by yellow bus. (My father was the driver.) If the glacier's thrust was to overpower, confiscate, and colonize the land (in which process the making of small farms was part of the domesticating effort, before they too were rubbed out in favor of industrial agribusiness), we children were brought up officially—in both a secular and a religious sense—in the ideological, mythological, and religious glide-path of that glacier. We post-World War Two children were to move out of and beyond the glacier's small-farm domesticating edge—which had become, apparently, the cutting edge of obsolescence—and turn our attention and energy toward more mentally challenging glacial projects involving science, finance, law, and industry. Progress was to be our most important product. Chemistry for better living. Energy too cheap to meter. Such were the chief commercial slogans of our childhood.

Well, living in the late 1970s in a poorly built shack in a wooded portion of the farm I'd grown up on, emotionally battered, culturally estranged but increasingly focused intellectually ("Why are small farms dying?" was my mantra), I had already read Norman O. Brown's *Life Against Death: The Psychoanalytical Meaning of History* and was into Michael Harrington's *Socialism* when the latter introduced me to Joachim, who somehow had the impulse to mesh the Old and New Testaments of the Christian Bible with the construct of Trinity, and he came to the conclusion (the insight? the revelation?) that there were/are Three Ages to human history. (Remember Joachim was operating within the conviction, as I had as a child, that the Genesis account of Creation was, in its core elements, factual history. The sequential unfolding of Joachim's ages reflects that literal understanding.)

So, Joachim proclaimed (said Michael Harrington) Three Ages to human history: the Age of the Father (corresponding to the Old Testament, characterized by monarchy, discipline, and law), the Age of the Son (corresponding to the New Testament, involving the life and death of Jesus, characterized as love institutionalized in the church), and—soon to come—the Age of the Holy Spirit (corresponding to the

Third Person of the Trinity, whose manifestation will result in consecrated anarchy or holy freedom). This vision (if that's what to call it) was apparently, at first, received with openness, wonder, and joy. But it didn't take long for church authorities to realize Joachim's Third Age would, if true, surpass and supplant the Roman Catholic Church; and, since that scenario was an institutional nonstarter, the answer is No, your vision (or whatever you want to call it) is a fraud and it will be suppressed. Apostolic succession will not be toyed with, thank you very much.

But I'd been reading history. I'd fought my way, so to speak, beyond the orthodox/fundamentalist electronic dog collar into a range of history the authors of the Bible knew nothing about or, at least, didn't seem to be interested in. Perhaps it was willful disinterest. (Did those who contemplated the past really know nothing of the precivilized world? Was such ignorance a consequence of trauma? Was it deliberate amnesia? Was it not so much turning the cheek as averting the gaze?) But I had come to know about gathering and horticulture and settled villages and the domestication of animals and agriculture and the agrarian village. And I knew that the spirituality of this village culture was oriented toward the feminine or the female, fully reflective of the social prestige and cultural influence of the horticultural garden. It was an Age of the Mother. Female energy and gardening creativity were at the heart of village culture. And that was not merely my undereducated opinion. I'd read my Johann Jakob Bachofen and Elise Boulding.[6]

So, you know, playing with concepts, toying with constructs, I nudged Mother in front of Father, thinking Joachim (like myself a few years previous) knew nothing of the Mother's Age. And then—I'd also been pondering the historical meaning of the women's movement—I looked again at Joachim's modified configuration, now with Mother in the first position, in first place. Let's see: Mother, Father, Son, *Holy Spirit*—?

Well, let's just say that lots of thoughts and discoveries have seriously impacted me over the decades (learning, for instance, that civilization is built on the violent expropriation of agriculture, that *pagus* is the common root of both pagan and peasant, that *apokalypsis* means disclosure not End Times), but sliding Daughter in the place of Holy Spirit nearly made my hair stand on end. Nothing had ever come close to that all-embracing impact. *The Age of the Holy Spirit had just revealed itself as the Age of the Daughter.* I was stunned, frankly and astonishingly stunned. With the restoration of Mother to Her rightful place, Daughter openly revealed Herself. Holy smokes! And I don't know how I would've ever come to that realization had it not been for that twelfth-century Italian monk, Joachim of Floris. Thank you, Michael Harrington. Thank you very much. Joachim, I kiss your tonsured head.

6. See chapter 3, "Roots," pages 24 through 34, in my *Nature's Unruly Mob: Farming and the Crisis in Rural Culture.*

XIII

We bright, intellectually liberated Westerners have little difficulty seeing how the gods and goddesses of other, earlier times and places were mass psychic projections of human emotions and gender dynamics. To see that now is child's play. It's a sort of mythological theater, intellectual Sesame Street. But when it comes to *our* religious constructs, watch out! We tend to whistle a different tune if *our* convictions are even remotely threatened with such scrutiny or critical understanding. Here's a sober and sobering assessment from biblical scholar Burton L. Mack:

> The disclosure of a myth is deemed academic as long as the myth belongs to somebody else. Recognizing one's own myth is always much more difficult, if not downright dangerous.
>
> The reason for this is the way myths work their magic. Myths are guardians of cultural identity and work best when taken for granted. Left undisturbed, a myth makes it possible to assume that others agree in advance on the rules that govern the daily round. Should a myth ever be named and questioned, the collective agreements basic to a society's well-being come unglued and people feel unsettled.
>
> The Christian myth is particularly vulnerable to unsettling questions. Most myths take place once upon a time in an irreal world. Like all stories, they allow the listener to suspend judgment while watching the story unfold. Christian myth claims to be history and asks its adherents to believe that it is true. As long as there is no other data from which to construct a different account of the same chapter of history, the Christian myth can work much the same way as other myths. Christians can simply bracket the story of Jesus from the rest of human history and treat it as an exceptional moment, realizing that the events recorded are fantastic but allowing the story to stand. If, however, the history yields to other explanations and the fantastic features of the gospels are explained as mythic, the Christian gospel will be in very deep trouble, and Christian mentality will have to renegotiate both its real and imaginary worlds.[7]

If we're orthodox, "conservative," and perhaps fundamentalist, our core religious constructs are the articulation of divine fact. God *is* Three Persons, and that's that. Those constructs are not to be examined mythologically, much less—God forbid!—psychoanalytically. That would be sacrilegious to the point of utter blasphemy. If we're orthodox and "liberal" (certainly not fundamentalist—God forbid!), we might be willing to toy with mythological or psychoanalytical interpretations—we are, after all, intellectually curious and professionally open-minded—but such interpretations, while certainly novel and even provisionally interesting, have lots of substantial competitors in the field of symbolic understanding; and nothing, after all, is to be

---

7. Mack, *Lost*, 237-38.

taken too seriously, for concentrated enthusiasm is an obvious characteristic of intellectual inexperience and scholarly immaturity. Conclusions are for amateurs. If we're scientific atheists, such mythological interpretation may be of obscure (and quite harmless) interest somewhere in the university's Humanities or Religious Studies Departments—if anybody's still there, if there still are such departments—but anything psychoanalytical—? You've got to be kidding! Really! How very nineteenth century. So charming. Now go play in traffic.

So that allows us (for those who haven't left the room) to ponder the fourth position, the shaggy, disheveled and unkempt, the clowns, poets and prophets, the slimy bottom of the barrel of perception. Once we're willing to *look* through Joachim's eyes and have our historical vision corrected and clarified by the scholarly ophthalmology of recent centuries, once we're even provisionally *willing* to ground Trinity in a historical and psychoanalytical field of perception (seeing *through* the eyes rather than *with* the eyes, as the seer William Blake advised), then we can recognize with embarrassing ease the role the Maleness of God has played in Christianity's civilizational glaciations, how the simple but profound enlargement of Trinity to Mandala (Father, Son, and Holy Spirit to Mother, Father, Son, and Daughter) has the capacity to transform heavenly utopian hubris into earthly eutopian humility: Mother rescued from Her traumatic historical banishment; Father mandated to a shrink specializing in the treatment of compulsive megalomania; Son liberated from his gilded tomb; Daughter freed of her ghostly wrappings, now dressed for joy in the garden. Such a modest reformulation of our dominant myth, but what an amazing and wholesome release of impounded energy!

XIV

Let's briefly revisit our four basic groups: "conservative," "liberal," atheist, and bohemian poet. The first may be somewhat fascinated with the analysis presented above, shake itself free of that fascination, and find fascination (which, for a moment, felt strangely compelling) replaced with boiling rage. The second, always more sophisticated, overstimulated to the point of weary satiation if not surfeit, turns away not so much because of explicit rejection but because surfeit has bluntly dulled the capacity for astonished discovery. The third is so incredibly smart, well-informed, and cutting edge that nothing so patently stupid could possibly pass the crap detection sniff test.

But I and mine, said the shaggy Walt Whitman, convince not with words but with our presence. Well, maybe beneath all the sentimental crucifixion scenes, golden fascist garb, and gentle idiot Sunday School portraiture, that's why we can't seem to shake free of Jesus the eastern Mediterranean Jewish peasant. There's just something about his *presence* that keeps turning our heads and humming in our hearts. But if this *presence* is to prevail, along with the revolutionary and transformative ethics of the "kingdom of God" proclamation, it (or they) will do so only as the radical eutopian presentness of that Jewish peasant infiltrates our hearts, transforms our minds, and reveals to us the essential criminality of civilization's founding violence, and how its violence has played out over time. And, since we really sort of are at the end of history, what with Weapons of Mass Destruction, Anthropocene Climate Change Extinctions, and whatever else we might add to this End-of-the-World list of End Times woes, it's sort of really time to consider the path not (yet) taken, the denied and suppressed truths, the set of humble choices that free us from our staggering arrogance and the literally unimaginable ecological consequences of our staggering arrogance. The clock is ticking quite loudly. If End Times is incapable of provoking *apokalypsis*, we are indeed doomed.

I'm not saying this will be the name we finally settle on, but let's—at least for the time being—call it democratic ecological libertarian socialism. On a global scale. One Earth. One severely and seriously chastened humanity. Radical stewardship. Radical servanthood. This is where apocalyptic disclosure leads.

But please don't think I'm promoting a Four Person God instead of a Three Person God. Psychomythological honesty unhesitatingly points out that "ages" are human-created masks for historical periods of cultural transformation imbued with spiritual significance. These "ages" may be *personifications*, but they are not "Persons" in any meaningful spiritual sense. Spirit—whoever and whatever Spirit may be—can wear these masks if She wishes. But Spirit—whoever and whatever Spirit may be—was here long before these masks were formed, and She will be here long after they may be no longer needed.

Our stubborn and stupid arrogance is beyond belief. Yet only a humility that's brave enough to abandon the hubris of founding violence and the self-serving mythological rationalizations that accompany founding violence is big enough and strong enough to save us. The grand paradox is that it's *vulnerability* that saves us from the consequences of our security obsessions. That, too, is one of the core messages of Jesus. To lose our precious identity is to find out who we are. But to bring Mother out of Her dungeon, Son out of His crypt, Daughter out of Her airless closet—and face down the stupendous arrogance and righteous sadism of Almighty Father before rehabilitating the Old Man as Gentle Baba (for Father, too, is here to stay)—is to find some ecological peace and humanitarian quiet in the divine—and, yes, anthropocentric—family. Without which I think we are doomed.

21

Crashing the Jesus Seminar with
My Friends *Pagus* and *Apokalypsis*

THIS ESSAY—DESPITE ITS NEXT-TO-LAST status—is the final contribution to *Picking Fights*. This is where "Crashing the Seminar" seems to fit, one last squabble before calling it quits.

In early September 2015, with a half-dozen publishing deadlines already missed, and fresh from the library where, having used the noninternet computer to put corrections into the manuscript, I wandered into St. Vinnie's thrift store, drawn as usual to the used book section, and there, for a mere two dollars, was a pristine paperback copy of Robert W. Funk's *Honest to Jesus*. How could I resist?

I'd known of Funk for years, knew of the Westar Institute and the Jesus Seminar, was familiar with several books each by Marcus Borg and John Dominic Crossan (both Fellows of the Seminar), but I'd never read anything by Robert Funk. The blurb on the bottom of the front cover—a quote from *The New York Times Book Review*—said Funk was a "scholarly curmudgeon" which, considering the source, seemed high praise. (*Webster's* says "curmudgeon" means "a surly, ill-mannered, bad-tempered person.") Well, Funk on occasion reveals a sharp and pointed pencil. He doesn't mince words when it comes to the stubborn, willful ignorance of conventional Christian believers or to the institutions and clergy who allow such ignorance not only to persist unchallenged but to dominate religious life at the congregational level. (Spiritual comprehension may have moved on since the sixteenth century, but please don't shock the children.)

Funk's sharpness connects closely to a confrontational side of Jesus that's mostly ignored or overlooked in the gospels. It's easier, it seems, to cozy up to a Jesus who's been drugged and domesticated, all happy smiles at the petting zoo. All in all (although I know only a fraction of its work), the Jesus Seminar—certainly the work of Crossan and Borg—has struck me as spiritually alive, even prophetic and apocalyptic. They, like Robert Funk, are after the Real McCoy.

Well, to say the Jesus Seminar—or Borg, Crossan, or Funk himself—dips into the apocalyptic presents a bit of an etymological problem, for Funk uses "apocalypse" and "apocalyptic" fairly often in *Honest to Jesus*, but he always employs the terms in the usual end-of-the-world way, typically as criticism of conventional belief, both in our time and in first-century Palestine. Yet the etymology doesn't support Funk's usage.

As we have seen, "apocalyptic" has nothing intrinsically to do with End Times or its religious anticipation. *Apokalypsis* has to do with (perhaps shocking) disclosure of what's hiding in the mythic closet. End Times is what happens when apocalypse is ignored, obstructed, or prevented from coming into clear consciousness. End Times is the interior logic of traumatic institutions externalized as Global Crises, an externalization that mimics the externality of God.

Parallel to this is Funk's conventional use of "pagan" or "neopagan." Just as apocalypse has come to mean its opposite (predestination, we might say, rather than open-ended revelation), so civilization—which may well qualify as the biggest Powers and Principalities criminal in human history—has demonized *pagus* in order to magnify its apotheosis by cloaking its guilty fear in a shroud of accusation against the victim of its theft. Neither of Funk's usages—neither "apocalyptic" nor "pagan"—breaks through to *apokalypsis*, revelation or disclosure, which is why I'm crashing the party with my rough and ragged friends in order to pick yet another fight with the gods.

The purpose of the Jesus Seminar is, to the best of intensive scholarly effort, to get as clear and fresh a glimpse, a view, an understanding of Jesus as is humanly possible, by means of scholarship embedded in spiritual integrity. Well, these scholars not only want to see a real, living Jesus, they also want to know what's meant by "kingdom of God" or (as Funk seems to prefer) "God's domain." ("*Malkuta*" does not make an appearance in *Honest to Jesus*.) The twin spiritual objectives of the Jesus scholars are seeing Jesus as clearly as possible and understanding the meaning of the kingdom of God proclamation as fully as possible.[1]

Funk is unhesitating in saying that Jesus was a peasant—possibly illiterate and perhaps illegitimate, killed by the collusion of Jewish temple authority and Roman occupier. But Funk doesn't seem to realize that such powerful comprehension—*civis* powers executing a spiritual revolutionary from the *pagus*—arouses the spiritual nerve endings of *apokalypsis*. It's true that Funk and his brilliant colleagues have fought their way through a huge array of creedal barriers and dogmatic obstructions to reach the precincts of the living Jesus, but the final steps require something different than scholarly aptitude and intellectual drive. (I can't help but think here of Zeno's Paradox in regard to scholarly process: there's always another half-distance to go to reach the target, ad infinitum. But getting to Jesus requires a leap right through Zeno's Paradox.) The Jesus Seminar can clear away a lot of obstruction—and apparently it has actually

---

1. For a similar effort to plunge through accrued Buddhist doctrine to founding person and primal intent, see Stephen Batchelor's wonderfully lucid *Confession of a Buddhist Atheist*, especially chapter 8, "Siddhattha Gotama." Batchelor's book also reveals (although unintentionally) the acute difference between Buddhism and Christianity in their core personages. That is, Gotama was an aristocrat who attempted to work from the top down, with a powerful emphasis on "mind," while Jesus was a peasant whose effort was bottom up, with primary emphasis on "heart." On page 110, Batchelor says Gotama "saw his teaching—the Dhamma—as the template for a *civilization*." (Batchelor's emphasis.) Jesus, on the other hand, with his *malkuta* construct, was sowing the ethical and spiritual seeds for *village culture* transformation. Perhaps these dialectical efforts, as East and West absorb each other's spirituality, are in process of historical and spiritual synthesis.

done so—but entering into "God's domain," involving the whole body and not just the mind, is an existential act involving risk, adventure, and a powerful sense of trust. And that leads immediately to the question: trust in what or whom? And that instantly involves questions about the sacred or divine or what's meant by God or Spirit.

Funk uses "God" a lot, but "God" no longer works. "God" is—perhaps paradoxical if not contradictory—so vastly extraterritorial (God the Creator of the Universe) and so pathologically tribal (Yahweh the commander of genocide) that it's impossible—at least it's impossible for me—to say "God" when I mean Spirit. Spirit has intense Earthlife energy. God has a well-deserved reputation for despising *pagus*. To close this loop, one would be compelled to say that God hates Spirit. (Well—Jack Miles again—if God hates Goddess, if Spirit may be designated as She, then God's hatred of the feminine is obvious.)

Here's where *pagus* shuffles in—one foot bare, the other in a dusty sandal. An important—even crucial—aspect of *apokalypsis* is realizing how *pagus* became the spiritual enemy of civilized Christianity, and what it means spiritually and ecologically to undo that vicious attribution. It's time to undo the supremacy of a theology that takes its civility as normative. Such undoing amounts to revelation and disclosure. I have tried in these essays to explore some elements of that *apokalypsis*.

II

Funk says Hermann Samuel Reimarus (1694-1768) was the first of the modern gospel scholars, an assessment Jaroslav Pelikan essentially supports in his Afterword to *The Jefferson Bible* (see page 157). But Funk also says "The first quest [for the historical Jesus] ended with the publication of Albert Schweitzer's famous work, *The Quest of the Historical Jesus*, in 1906. This was followed by a long period when the quest was dormant as a consequence of the domination of neo-orthodoxy."[2] Funk goes on to say that the "neo-orthodox framework was supplied by Karl Barth," a framework lasting roughly until 1975.[3]

The Jesus Seminar began its work in 1985. (We might say that World War One was used by "conservatives" to demolish the legitimacy of the social gospel—as if World War One wasn't the bloody half of the two kingdoms exercising territorial prerogative. That is, the murderousness of Powers and Principalities gets blamed on the alleged naïveté of the social gospel!)

In the Epilogue to *Honest to Jesus*, Funk says "neo-orthodoxy is dead," the "dying gasp of creedal Christianity." "Creedalism is a religion that supersedes Jesus, replaces him, or perhaps displaces him, with a mythology that depends on nothing Jesus said,

---

2. Funk, *Honest*, 62-63.

3. Funk, *Honest*, 63.

or did, with the possible exception of his death."[4] Later Funk says "We will have to abandon the doctrine of the blood atonement":

> The atonement in popular piety is based on a mythology that is no longer credible—that God is appeased by blood sacrifices. Jesus never expressed the view that God was holding humanity hostage until someone paid the bill. Nor did Amos, Hosea, or other prophets of Israel. In addition, it is the linchpin that holds the divinity of Jesus, his virgin birth, the bodily resurrection, and a sinless life together in a unified but naïve package: God required a perfect sacrifice, so only a divine victim would do.[5]

If blood atonement is near the heart of the mythical matter—and we might bear in mind here René Girard's work on scapegoating and sacred violence; that is, blood atonement is a perfect example of the scapegoating construct—and if creedal Christianity is a religion built on myth—if "God" is mythical while Spirit is living and alive—then we need to examine the meaning of this myth rather than just reject it as meaningless or opaque ornament. What does Christian myth signify? What does "blood atonement" say about the relationship of Yahweh to Jesus or king to peasant or *civis* to *pagus*?

III

Well, let's go back to Funk's assertion about abandoning the doctrine of blood atonement. This is a tricky proposition, for myth is neither true nor false in the usual empirical sense. Yes, blood atonement needs to be let go of as a creedal assertion purporting to be religiously factual. In that sense we can say no to blood atonement. But if blood atonement as a religious construct was believed to be true, we have to ask about its mythic significance. What did it depict that accrued such massive acceptance? What social reality was it reflecting? What collective psychic fear does it represent?

Here we have to look at myth as psychic projection, and we have to examine that projection via "divine" "Persons." Christian blood atonement has two such Persons in play: God the Father and Jesus the Son. Jesus as God's Son is sacrificed to appease God the Father's wrath. God the Father does to Jesus what Abraham *almost* did to Isaac in Genesis 22:1-18, what Joshua (at God's command) *actually did do* to the people of Jericho, as described in Joshua 6. This calls for a psychoanalysis of patriarchal authority—a psychohistory, a psychomythology, a spiritual psychoanalysis of civilization's superego. What's the meaning of all this Father wrath?

To demythologize the Jesus story is not so simple as to say, "Well, we no longer believe all that stuff about blood atonement or virgin birth or bodily ascension into heaven." Disengaging from literal belief—getting some distance and breathing room

---

4. Funk, *Honest*, 304.

5. Funk, *Honest*, 312.

from its oppressive weight—is of course necessary as an initial step toward achieving transformed understanding. That's obviously true. But to stop there, to just repudiate mythology as false, to renounce it as worthless claptrap, is a really big mistake. This mythology has operated as the cultural superego of the Western world for most of the last two thousand years; that should be reason enough to pay it close attention. If the work of the Jesus Seminar is to uncover the historical Jesus and penetrate the meaning of the kingdom of God proclamation—yes to all that—a comparable work is to understand creedal myth for what it actually signifies. But as Funk himself says:

> The principle deficiency in biblical scholarship currently is its lack of a myth criticism. We have developed historical criticism to a high art, but we have been unable to conceive a critical relation to the stories that undergird our tradition and limit our vision. In the next phase of our work, we must remedy this fundamental deficiency.[6]

I don't pretend to know the many pathways in and out of myth criticism, but psychoanalysis—certainly Norman O. Brown's *Life Against Death* and Dorothy Dinnerstein's *Mermaid and Minotaur*—are exceptionally promising rows to hoe. But once again: myth criticism is not myth demolition; it's not the wanton destruction of religious artifacts, such as was indulged in by zealous Christian reformers in the sixteenth century and now practiced by Islamic zealots in present-day Syria. Myths need careful deconstruction not brutal demolition. Burton Mack obviously sees this.

As I attempted to show in the preceding essay, Trinity must be included in the project of mythic deconstruction. To do this entails (Funk again) "setting the Bible in the larger context of Western history"[7]—that is, recognizing that civilized history chopped the agrarian village out of its narrative just as Judaism and Christianity chopped Mother out of their theophanies. These are parallel and reciprocally reinforcing removals. The restoration of Mother—and this is both redemption of *pagus* from its scumbag cellar and liberation of *apokalypsis* from its End Times captivity—should, in my estimation, provide the Jesus Seminar with a wonderfully enlarged field of exploration and understanding. It's here where the Jesus Seminar needs to take a closer look at Joachim's construct.

IV

Setting the Bible in a larger context of Western history by means of psychoanalytical comprehension is to conceive a critical relation to the stories that undergird our mythic tradition and to radically enlarge that vision. The fundamental deficiency has been breached. The remedy has begun. To refuse Mother because She's not a

---

6. Funk, *Honest*, 309.

7. Funk, *Honest*, 24.

notarized, ecclesiastical revelation is to remain an obedient child of the institutional church with its ingrown two kingdom orthodoxy.

But there are a few more things—difficult things—to wrestle with here. One is that Funk repeatedly alludes to Jesus' attention "riveted on his Father's will" and that this "Father is not a cosmic bully."[8] Or, as he says later, "Jesus had utter confidence in his Father and in the essential goodness of humanity."[9] But Funk never squares this good and gentle Father with Yahweh the genocidal tribal chieftain. (Shades here of Michael Lerner's Left and Right Hands of God.) That problem—and it is the gorilla in the room—is simply not addressed. So if Jesus' Father (we might presume) is not the genocidal Yahweh, who is He? From Funk we get only silence, and it's not an edifying silence. Perhaps this silence is connected to the lack of myth criticism in biblical scholarship.

Another problem involves the kingdom of God or God's domain. There are elements of this problem all the way through *Honest to Jesus*, but let's start with chapter Thirteen, "Domesticating the Tradition and Marketing the Messiah." In brief, Funk describes how Jesus was, after his death, transformed from iconoclast to icon, how emphasis moved from vision to visionary. Or, in Funk's words: "The focus of Jesus' words was imperceptibly but steadily shifted away from his glimpse of the kingdom to a story in which Jesus himself was the center of attention."[10] As Funk goes on to say: "With the shift in focus from Jesus' vision of God's domain to Jesus himself—from the proclaimed to the proclaimer—Jesus becomes the one who authorizes the kingdom, who guarantees that it is God's will. In addition, he also becomes the future bringer of the kingdom that has not yet arrived."[11] Here's a longer passage:

> The mythical Christ gradually replaced the Galilean sage as the gospels grew. Jesus' fantasy of the kingdom was embedded in a larger picture that had Jesus himself as the center of attention. Jesus' vision of the kingdom became his followers' vision of him. Having given Jesus the leading role in the story, they then wrote a part for themselves into the drama. The result was the disenchantment of God's kingdom.
>
> The enchantment that had cast its spell over Jesus meant that God's dominion was immediately and powerfully present for him. With disenchantment, that kingdom was pushed off, first into the immediate future and then into the indeterminate future. If the kingdom was to come in the future, there would be a delay, and a delay required a second coming of the messiah—of Jesus—to achieve what his first coming had not. In other words, the overpowering vision of Jesus was translated back into the ordinary apocalyptic expectations of that time: God was expected eventually to interfere directly in all human affairs. The vision of Jesus was thereby domesticated. The fantastic

8. Funk, *Honest*, 160.

9. Funk, *Honest*, 243.

10. Funk, *Honest*, 248.

11. Funk, *Honest*, 250.

reality of the kingdom of God for Jesus had been reduced to something to be looked for and hoped for at some future date.

Fascination with Jesus' vision fades as realism sets in. The disciples are unable to maintain the enchantment. Times stretches out. The kingdom is no longer present; it will come, it was believed, at some future date. The chronology of the long run replaces the bewitchment of the present.[12]

So by the time Christianity is appropriated by Constantine three centuries later, "The original iconoclast—the subverter of the primary world—has been replaced by an icon who belongs to the popular expectations and hopes of that world. The enchanting immediacy of his secondary world—the kingdom of God—has been replaced by the political realism of Constantine's empire."[13]

These two problems—God as gentle daddy or genocidal Father and the loss of immediacy for the kingdom of God—are not resolved, and their irresolution is connected. Let's just say that a perpetually postponed kingdom needs a king or a prince to eventually usher in that kingdom. That is, a kingdom that's waited for and for which there is no alternative but to wait is a construct that needs a royal actor whose timetable is inscrutable. Those who wait are essentially passive. There's nothing they can do to make royalty hurry. Their enchantment is in the cooler. But did Jesus believe or teach that understanding? Funk certainly seems to say or at least imply that he did not.

Well, if no outside actor—at least in conventional theistic understanding—is needed, then how does the "enchantment that had its spell over Jesus" get transferred to the rest of us? What is that enchantment? How do we become empowered by or with his vision? (The alternative—that the kingdom is an objective eschatological condition into which we all will be eventually thrust irrespective of our volition—puts us back into the God-will-do-it-to-us-someday position, with no enchanting leap needed on our part, except to get on the right side of God's disposition.)[14] I understand that the Jesus scholars, by the nature of their procedure, have to accept as authentic the story or image or terminology that's at the end of their scrupulous winnowing process, and this may include Jesus saying abba or Father. I am in no position to challenge such scholarly conclusion. But does historical scholarship get the last word here? Are we, in the final analysis, captives of the written word?

---

12. Funk, *Honest*, 254.

13. Funk, *Honest*, 256.

14. Paul Tillich, on page 218 in *The Protestant Era*, says "We cannot bring it about by willing and acting. It occurs, or it does not occur. But, if it occurs, it is not only revealing for our time but also illuminating for the past, making its concepts and words contemporary, pointing to their depth and reality." Well, maybe we can't make "it" occur by willing and acting. In this respect, we might even say Jesus also failed. But such a view must never lead to ideological passivity, for such passivity has a tendency to be obstructive and negative, capable of thwarting what it otherwise—in an otherworldly sense—claims to revere and believe in. Yet—pay attention!—if it does occur, it will be revealing not only for our time but also illuminating for the past. Perhaps its time has come.

Isaac Asimov with his Second Foundation construct (see the original *Foundation* trilogy) and his later construction of Gaia (see *Foundation and Earth*) is pointing us, for all the technological glitter and clapboard plot lines, in the right direction: the Second Foundation as a (overly psychologized) kingdom of God enchantment depiction and Gaia as personification of Spirit. Spirit is earthly and immanent. Spirit is (for lack of better comprehension) the consciousness of matter, nature, and life on Earth. Spirit is growing and evolving. And some people (who can say how or why?) have waded deeply into this enchanting pool of spiritual comprehension. When push comes to shove, we are obliged to say Jesus went in over his head and came up from Spirit's pool fully enchanted, his face radiant with happiness and his eyes alive with vision.

I believe Jesus said "Here's enchantment, people. Dive in." And mostly what he got—besides summary execution—was quizzical looks. Virtually everyone felt something powerfully alive, invigorating, and even intoxicating in his presence—how else to explain how we even know of this obscure peasant? To embrace or swallow or dive into this enchantment felt unbelievably exhilarating and completely terrifying. (Big Daddy is not going to like this one little bit, and there'll be hell to pay.) And since Robert Funk doesn't explore or deconstruct "God" or "Father," he can wander—even if it's briefly, as in pages 169 and 170—into God's domain as frontier, as "dividing line between civilization and the wilderness,"[15] which leads him to reference American pioneers, mountain men and cowboys, with no mention made of the indigenous people whose lifeways were crushed or the prairie farmers who tried mightily (but unsuccessfully) in the late nineteenth century to transform American culture toward what we would now call Green socialism. That is, Funk essentially operates within the intellectual convention of the Christian Right of Discovery, with all its "chosen people" baggage, with a pagan "frontier" into which the cutting edge of civility penetrates. This does not get us out of and beyond fatherland. This is still Yahweh, Joshua, and Jericho. We are left entangled in prevailing myth.

V

At one point while trying to get direction for this little essay, I pulled off the shelf my dusty paperback copy of Joseph Campbell's *Myths to Live By* and popped open the Index to see if there might be an entry for "Myth, definition of." No such luck. But under J, there was "Joachim of Floris, 255–56." I had no idea Joachim was tucked inside myths to live by. Here's the paragraph:

> But to return, finally, to the mythological, theological aspect of this moment: there was a prophetic medieval Italian abbot, Joachim of Floris, who in the early thirteenth century foresaw the dissolution of the Christian Church and dawn of a terminal period of earthly spiritual life, when the Holy Ghost, the

---

15. Funk, *Honest*, 169.

Holy Spirit, would speak directly to the human heart without ecclesiastical mediation. His view, like that of Frobenius, was of a sequence of historic stages, of which our own was to be the last; and of these he counted four. The first was, of course, that immediately following the Fall of man, before the opening of the main story, after which there was to unfold the whole great drama of Redemption, each stage under the inspiration of one Person of the Trinity. The first was to be of the Father, the Laws of Moses and the People of Israel; the second of the Son, the New Testament and the Church; and now finally (and here, of course, the teachings of this clergyman went apart from the others of his communion), a third age, which he believed was about to commence, of the Holy Spirit, that was to be of saints in meditation, when the Church, become superfluous, would in time dissolve. It was thought by not a few in Joachim's day that Saint Francis of Assisi might represent the opening of the coming age of direct, pentecostal spirituality. But as I look about today and observe what is happening to our churches in this time of perhaps the greatest access of mystically toned religious zeal our civilization has known since the close of the Middle Ages, I am inclined to think that the years foreseen by the good Father Joachim of Floris must have been our own.[16]

Of course, milling around in Joseph Campbell's *Myths*, I happened upon his four "functions normally served by a properly operating mythology." These functions are, in order: "to waken and maintain in the individual a sense of awe and gratitude in relation to the mystery dimension of the universe, not so that he lives in fear of it, but so that he recognizes that he participates in it, since the mystery of being is the mystery of his own deep being as well"; "to offer an image of the universe that will be in accord with the knowledge of the time, the sciences and the fields of action of the folk to whom the mythology is addressed"; "to validate, support, and imprint the norms of a given, specific moral order"; and, finally, to guide every person "stage by stage, in health, strength, and harmony of spirit, through the whole foreseeable course of a useful life."[17] Joachim provided us with the core template; the enlargement of that template—Trinity to Mandala—meets all of Joseph Campbell's required functions. Trinity enlarged—engendered—to Mandala satisfies the hungers of a properly operating myth.

The Holy Ghost or Holy Spirit is Daughter, Mother is restored before Father, and beneath the sequential masks of Mandala—Mother, Father, Son, and Daughter—is Spirit, who is Living Presence. It's She whose pool of enchantment Jesus dove into. Fully clothed or buck naked, it's the pool into which we all need to plunge. Eutopian therapy consists of daring each other to dive in and then acting as each other's happy lifeguard. The Jesus Seminar folks can help us reach the (Zeno's Paradox) edge of this pool, but we'll never know who Jesus is—or what his vision was—until we're willing to dive headfirst into the wild flowing river of his eutopian enchantment. When enough of us do just that, this world will be transformed.

16. Campbell, *Myths*, 255-56.
17. Campbell, *Myths*, 221-22.

22

Who or What's the Radical?—An Afterword for Dorothy Day

Is Christianity dying? Is the religion that gave morals, courage, and art to Western civilization suffering slow decay through the spread of knowledge, the widening of astronomic, geographical, and historical horizons, the realization of evil in history and the soul, the decline of faith in an afterlife and of trust in the benevolent guidance of the world? If this is so, it is the basic event of modern times, for the soul of a civilization is its religion, and it dies with its faith.

Will and Ariel Durant, *The Age of Reason Begins*, page 613

DOROTHY DAY, COFOUNDER WITH Peter Maurin of the Catholic Worker movement, was an emblem for the Sermon on the Mount. Her "houses of hospitality" continue to embrace the kingdom of God proclamation. But what, exactly, does her Catholic Worker life say about the human condition, about America and democracy, about the relationship between the genders and the races? About apocalypse?

Dorothy Day's historical significance (perhaps like that of Joan d'Arc) is less about the historical particulars of her accomplishment than the power of her image that, at some level, reflects an exceptional radiation of both person and purpose. Dorothy Day's accomplishment was to reveal, to anyone with the wit to see or the sensibility by which to pay attention, what the American social underbelly looks like—the battered woman, the frightened child, the sloppy drunks and vacant drug addicts, the homeless, hopeless, and destitute. She in essence said, "Here, take a good look. This is what we think of the kingdom of God."

The broader Catholic Worker movement has carried on this energy by creative protests against war and the ecocidal weapons of war, against the punitive and sadistic legal system, against the nearly total overpowering of evolutionary human economy by the massive commercialism of corporate industrialization, against a global system that—the more it succeeds—the deeper become the attendant ecological, cultural, and spiritual fractures and crises.

Can we shake some policy specifics out of this Catholic Worker energy field? What would its achieved world look like? What would its radiant kingdom of God look like? And can we do this shaking by utilizing as a constructive framework the old categories—particle and wave—of Works and Faith? That is, if the collective Catholic Worker energy field ramifies as Works in the direction of Green culture—radical servanthood and radical stewardship, in short—what's the Faith or collective spiritual consciousness holding Green culture in sustainable coherence? Is it Christian orthodoxy taken more seriously? Or is it something wonderfully transformative?

If human culture always and inevitably contains (or is contained by) an appropriately accompanying collective consciousness, this collective consciousness also saturates prevailing religious sensibility and may even be primarily lodged in it and expressed by it. Religious consciousness is supposedly ideal consciousness, the highest and fullest expression of our being. If that's so, then transformation to Green culture requires a corresponding transformation of spiritual sensibility, of how the spiritual is understood and experienced. If we're to have new wine, we need new wineskin (Luke 5:37-39). And, since Catholic Workers are in the historical stream (or at least within the troublesome undercurrent) of Roman Catholic Christianity, with a strong element of Reformation scriptural scholarship thrown in, it's not a surprise that of all Christian formations—excepting, perhaps, various branches of Anabaptism—the Catholic Workers have most fully rediscovered the primary importance of the kingdom of God proclamation and have tried to live it out. But how we understand and internalize *malkuta's* meaning—its Earth-centered spirituality and its corresponding ethics of radical sharing—is a huge part of how or with what groundedness the collective consciousness of Green culture can and will take shape.

It's my impression that the Catholic Worker movement is transformative and radical, not merely in the repair and reform mode. (These need not be either/or so long as repair and reform doesn't get to retard transformation by an inveterate dragging of orthodox feet.)

The question is: Who or what is the transformative radical?

To go right to the psychoanalytical heart of the matter—and, if it's not too precious, the psychomythological heart of the matter—it's this: If Jesus was and is divine (and with "divine" one cannot say *was* without meaning *is*), then divine resides in body and blood, skin and bones, ovary and testicle. If we are in the stream of evolved Creation, then Life-as-particle lives a half-life, so to speak, with Life-as-wave. If body lodges or generates consciousness, so Life lodges or generates Spirit. Or they cogenerate one another. But this compels reconsideration of the Gaia Hypothesis, whether or not "Gaia" is the name or dynamic to be settled on. The only life we really know, despite all the star gazing, is Life on Earth. All else is metaphysical spacecraft.

Earth groundedness brings us smack up against the immanent as pagan, which is what orthodoxy has taught us to fear and hate. Our collective alienation from earthy life is the product of utopian civility combined with otherworldly religion. It's this fear and hate we need to fully face, get inside of and resolve. That is to say, the radical transformation of our collective spiritual consciousness requires a complete reappraisal of orthodox, Constantinian, Augustinian Christianity—Catholic, Protestant, the whole kit and caboodle—with the monarchical God who oversees the City of God recognized for the civilizational and utopian male construct that it is—that they are—and the civilizational and male purposes they have so faithfully served.

That's what we have to recognize and find the courage to get beyond. It's time for catholic workers of all persuasions to let go of Trinity, for it's this construct above all that keeps aggressive male energy (and our deference to it) in "divine" rigidity. Trinity concentrates maleness into divine supremacy. Male domination is home free with such a construct. To leap beyond Trinity requires the simple, short, revolutionary step of restoring Mother to Her rightful historical position and spiritual disposition, a restoration instantly revealing the Daughter. What makes this leap possible for all us frightened children—anxiously wanting to be boldly radical, not content to be timidly reformist—is that the peasant divinity of Jesus redeems *pagus*, and redemption of *pagus* enables us to recognize Spirit as Earth Wave to the Particle of Life.[1]

This transfiguration frees us to achieve a far fuller embrace of our human and evolutionary past, including—always a reverent word for Joachim's great achievement—the Mother we left behind and who we now welcome home, and of whom we ask deep historical and spiritual forgiveness.

If Self is what occurs when id, superego, and ego happily integrate rather than remain in tense layers of unresolved separation, then we might say that Daughter is what happens as the finest aspects of Mother, Father, and Son congeal. If so, we will enter spiritual transformation as we are brave enough and *sufficiently trusting of Spirit* to begin acting as Selves redeemed: not thereby disdainful of renunciation as renunciation is discerned spiritually needful or ecologically necessary, but cognizant that Life seeks and needs fulfillment; and, to be as fully alive as Life permits, we too are creatures in need of earthly fulfillment.

God the Extraterrestrial Father drove an otherworldly spike through the agrarian village heart of the Goddess of Earthly Life. Feral males strutting as marauding warriors created the diseased and traumatic institutions of Class and War. Folk evolution was violently thwarted and culturally constrained. Utopia overcame eutopia. *Civis* overpowered *pagus*. But the peasant Son loved the eutopian Mother with such tender conviction that he died for Her—in nonviolent defiance of the utopian Father. That's the mythic story to be read between the lines of the civilized Christian narrative. These psychodynamic energies have now reached culmination in Global Crisis and End

---

1. On page 262 in his *Christian Mystics*, Matthew Fox quotes Nicolas Berdyaev on the "divinization of all creatures": "The central idea of the Eastern Fathers was that of *theosis*, the divinization of all creatures, the transfiguration of the world, the idea of the cosmos and not the idea of personal salvation. . . . Only later Christian consciousness began to value the idea of hell more than the idea of the transfiguration and divinization of the world. . . . The kingdom of God is the transfiguration of the world, universal resurrection, a new heaven and a new earth." Well, even if we are more modest and concentrate on the transfiguration of human behavior and human intelligence, let's be grateful for what we get.

Times. To uncover and disclose these dynamics constitutes our apocalyptic moment. Daughter is the emerging face of Spirit. It's She who will heal our riven souls.

Bibliography

Adler, Margot. *Drawing Down the Moon: Witches, Druids, Goddess-Worshippers, and Other Pagans in America Today*. Boston: Beacon Press, 1986.

Alter, Jonathan. "The Ideological Divide." In *The New York Times Book Review*, October 24, 2010.

Altizer, Thomas J. J. *The Gospel of Christian Atheism*. Philadelphia: Westminster Press, 1966.

———. *The New Apocalypse: The Radical Christian Vision of William Blake*. Lansing, MI: The Michigan State University Press, 1967.

Aristotle. *On Man in the Universe*. Edited with Introduction by Louise Ropes Loomis. New York: Walter J. Black, 1943.

Armstrong, Karen. *The Battle for God*. New York: Borzoi Books, 2000.

Arntz, William, Betsy Chasse and Mark Vicente. *What the Bleep Do We Know!?* Deerfield Beach, FL: Health Communications, Inc., 2005.

Asimov, Isaac. *Foundation*. New York: Avon, 1951.

———. *Foundation and Earth*. New York: Doubleday & Company, Inc., 1986.

Bacevich, Andrew. "Twilight of the Republic?" In *Commonweal*, December 1, 2006.

———. "Who Runs the Pentagon?" In *The Nation*, February 8, 2016.

Bachofen, Johann Jakob. *Myth, Religion, and Mother Right: Selected Writings of J. J. Bachofen*, translated by Ralph Manheim. Princeton: Princeton University Press, 1992.

Bailie, Gil. *Violence Unveiled: Humanity at the Crossroads*. New York: Crossroad, 1995.

Batchelor, Stephen. *Confession of a Buddhist Atheist*. New York: Random House, 2010.

———. *Living with the Devil: A Meditation on Good and Evil*. New York: Riverhead Books, 2004.

Bennett, John C. "Reinhold Niebuhr's Social Ethics." In *Reinhold Niebuhr: His Religious, Social, and Political Thought*, edited by Charles W. Kegley and Robert W. Bretall. New York: The Macmillan Company, 1956.

Berry, Thomas and Thomas Clarke. *Befriending the Earth: A Theology of Reconciliation Between Humans and the Earth*. Mystic, CT: Twenty-Third Publications, 1991.

Berry, Thomas. *The Dream of the Earth*. San Francisco: Sierra Club Books, 1990.

———. *The Great Work: Our Way Into the Future*. New York: Bell Tower, 1999.

Berry, Wendell. *What Matters? Economics for a Renewed Commonwealth*. Berkeley: Counterpoint, 2010.

Blake, William. "A Vision of the Last Judgment." In *The Complete Writings of William Blake*, edited by Goeffrey Keynes. New York: Random House, 1957.

Boff, Leonardo. *Cry of the Earth, Cry of the Poor*. Maryknoll, NY: Orbis Books, 1997.

Borg, Marcus. *Evolution of the Word*. New York: HarperCollins, 2012.

———. *The God We Never Knew*. San Francisco: HarperSanFrancisco, 1997.

Borg, Marcus and John Dominic Crossan. *The Last Week: A Day-by-Day Account of Jesus's Final Week in Jerusalem*. New York: HarperLargePrint, 2006.

Boulding, Elise. *The Underside of History: A View of Women through Time*. Boulder, CO: Westview, 1976.

Bradley, James. *The Imperial Cruise: A Secret History of Empire and War*. New York: Little, Brown and Company, 2009.

Brown, Norman O. *Life Against Death: The Psychoanalytical Meaning of History*. Middletown, CT: Wesleyan University Press, 1959.

———. *Love's Body*. New York: Vintage Books, 1966.

Buckberry, Seedy. *A Windfall Homestead*. Eugene, OR: Resource Publications, 2013.

———. *Get Poor Now, Avoid the Rush*. Eugene, OR: Resource Publications, 2011.

Caldwell, Christopher. "The Ideological Divide." In *The New York Times Book Review*, October 24, 2010.

Campbell, Joseph. *Myths to Live By*. New York: Bantam Books, 1972.

Capra, Fritjof. *The Web of Life: A New Scientific Understanding of Living Systems*. New York: Anchor Books, 1996.

Caputo, Philip. *A Rumor of War*. New York: Ballantine Books, 1977.

Carroll, James. *Constantine's Sword: The Church and the Jews*. Boston: Houghton Mifflin, 2001.

Cassier, Ernst. *The Myth of the State*. Garden City: Doubleday & Company, 1955.

Cayley, David. *The Rivers North of the Future: The Testament of Ivan Illich*. Toronto: House of Anansi, 2005.

Chittister, Joan. "A Conversation with the Speakers." In *God at 2000*, edited by Marcus Borg and Ross Mackenzie. Harrisburg, PA: Morehouse, 2000.

Chomsky, Noam. *Failed States: The Abuse of Power and the Assault on Democracy*. New York: Metropolitan Books, 2006.

———. "Howard Zinn's Legacy in Words and Action." In *Howard Zinn's Legacies*, edited by Davis D. Joyce. Madison, WI: *The Progressive*, 2014.

Cobb Jr., John B. "Preface." In *The Christian Future and the Fate of Earth*. Maryknoll, NY: Orbis Books, 2009.

Cox, Harvey. *The Secular City: Secularization and Urbanization in Theological Perspective*. New York: The Macmillan Company, 1965.

Crossan, John Dominic. *God and Empire: Jesus against Rome, Then and Now*. New York: HarperCollins, 2007.

———. *Jesus: A Revolutionary Biography*. San Francisco: HarperSanFrancisco, 1994.

———. *The Historical Jesus: The Life of a Mediterranean Jewish Peasant*. San Francisco: HarperSanFancisco, 1991.

———. *The Power of Parable: How Fiction by Jesus Became Fiction about Jesus*. New York: HarperCollins, 2012.

Daly, Herman E. "Foreword." In *What Matters?* by Wendell Berry. Berkeley: Counterpoint, 2010.

Davis, Wade. "Introduction." In *Book of Peoples of the World*. Washington, D.C.: National Geographic Society, 2007.

de Castillejo, Irene Claremont. *Knowing Woman: A Feminine Psychology*. New York: Putnam, 1973.

de Riencourt, Amaury. *The Coming Caesars*. New York: Coward-McCann, 1957.

Delio, Ilia. *The Emergent Christ: Exploring the Meaning of Catholic in an Evolutionary Universe.* Maryknoll, NY: Orbis Books, 1999.

Dinnerstein, Dorothy. *The Mermaid and the Minotaur: Sexual Arrangements and Human Malaise.* New York: Harper & Row, 1976.

Douglas-Klotz, Neil. *The Hidden Gospel: Decoding the Spiritual Message of the Aramaic Jesus.* Wheaton, IL: Quest Books, 1999.

Durant, Will. *The Reformation: A History of European Civilization from Wyclif to Calvin, 1300-1564.* New York: Simon and Schuster, 1957.

Durant, Will and Ariel. *The Age of Reason Begins: A History of European Civilization in the Period of Shakespeare, Bacon, Montaigne, Rembrandt, Galileo and Descartes, 1558-1648.* New York: Simon and Schuster, 1961.

East, Elyssa. "Criminal Mind: The psychopath who roamed belle epoque France." In *The New York Times Book Review*, October 24, 2010.

Ehrenreich, Barbara. *Blood Rites: Origins and History of the Passions of War.* New York: Metropolitan Books, 1997.

Ellsberg, Robert. *All Saints.* New York: Crossroad Publishing, 1997.

Ellul, Jacques. *The Technological Society.* Translated from the French by John Wilkinson. New York: Vintage Books, 1964.

Erikson, Erik H. *Gandhi's Truth: On the Origins of Militant Nonviolence.* New York: W. W. Norton & Company, Inc., 1969.

Etzioni, Amitai. "Needed: A Progressive Story." In *The Nation*, May 24, 2010.

Fikes, Jay C. *Reuben Snake, Your Humble Serpent: Indian Visionary and Activist.* "Foreword" by James Botsford and "Afterword" by Walter Echo-Hawk. Santa Fe: Clear Light Publishers, 1996.

Fox, Matthew. *Christian Mystics.* Novato, CA: New World Library, 2011.

———. *Original Blessing.* Santa Fe, NM: Bear & Company, 1983.

———. *The Reinvention of Work: A New Vision of Livelihood for Our Time.* San Francisco: HarperSanFrancisco, 1994.

Frankl, Viktor. *Man's Search for Meaning.* New York: Simon & Schuster, 1984.

Funk, Robert W. *Honest to Jesus.* San Francisco: HarperSanFrancisco, 1996.

Gilk, Paul. *Green Politics Is Eutopian.* Eugene, OR: Wipf and Stock, 2008.

———. *Nature's Unruly Mob: Farming and the Crisis in Rural Culture.* Eugene, OR: Wipf and Stock, 2009.

———. *Polemics and Provocations: Essays in Anticipation of the Daughter.* Eugene, OR: Wipf and Stock, 2010.

———. *The Kingdom of God Is Green.* Eugene, OR: Wipf and Stock, 2012.

Girard, René. *Battling to the End.* Lansing: Michigan University Press, 2009.

Gonzalez, Justo. *The Story of Christianity: The Early Church to the Dawn of the Reformation.* New York: HarperCollins, 1984.

Goodman, Paul. *Growing Up Absurd.* New York: Vintage Books, 1960.

Goodwyn, Lawrence. *The Populist Moment: A Short History of the Agrarian Revolt.* New York: Oxford University Press, 1978.

Grandin, Greg. "The Kissinger Effect." In *The Nation*, September 28/October 5, 2015.

Greider, William. "The GOP Crack-Up." In *The Nation*, November 9, 2015.

Harrington, Michael. *Socialism.* New York: Saturday Review, 1970.

Harvey, Andrew. "Rebirth through the Wound." In *Gay Soul.* San Francisco: HarperSanFrancisco, 1995.

————. *Son of Man: The Mystical Path to Christ*. New York: Jeremy P. Tarcher/Putnam, 1998.

Hedges, Chris. *Death of the Liberal Class*. New York: Nation Books, 2010.

Herbert, Bob. "Tone-Deaf in D.C." In *The New York Times*, November 5, 2010.

Hofstadter, Richard. *The Age of Reform: From Bryan to F. D. R.*: New York: Vintage Books, 1955.

Jackson, Wes. "Between Soil and Soil." In *The Progressive*, December 2010/January 2011.

Jensen, Derrick. *Endgame: The Problem of Civilization*. New York: Seven Stories Press, 2006.

Jerusalem Bible. Garden City: Doubleday, 1966.

Johnson, Elizabeth A. *SHE WHO IS: The Mystery of God in Feminist Theological Discourse*. New York: Crossroad, 1995.

Jung, Carl. *Memories, Dreams, Reflections*. Recorded and edited by Aniela Jaffé. Translated from the German by Richard and Clara Winston. New York: Vintage Books, 1965.

Kaplan, Justin. *Walt Whitman: A Life*. New York: Simon and Schuster, 1980.

Kaufman, Maynard. *Adapting to the End of Oil: Toward an Earth-Centered Spirituality*. Xlibris, 2008.

King, Richard. *The Party of Eros: Radical Social Thought and the Realm of Freedom*. Chapel Hill: The University of North Carolina Press, 1972.

Klein, Naomi. *This Changes Everything: Capitalism and the Climate*. New York: Simon & Schuster, 2014.

Kohr, Leopold. *The Breakdown of Nations*. New York: E. P. Dutton, 1978.

Kurlansky, Mark. *1968: The Year That Rocked the World*. New York: Random House, 2005.

Lakoff, George. *Don't Think of an Elephant!* White River Junction, VT: Chelsea Green Publishing Company, 2004.

Lasch, Christopher. *The True and Only Heaven: Progress and Its Critics*. New York: W. W. Norton & Company, 1991.

Latourette, Kenneth Scott. *A History of Christianity: Beginnings to 1500*. New York: Harper & Row, 1975.

Leopold, Aldo. *A Sand County Almanac*. New York: Sierra Club/Ballantine, 1974.

Lerner, Gerda. *The Creation of Patriarchy*. New York: Oxford University Press, 1986.

Lerner, Michael. *The Left Hand of God: Taking Back Our Country from the Religious Right*. New York: HarperCollins, 2006.

Lewis, C. S. *That Hideous Strength*. New York: Macmillan, 1968.

Loomis, Louise Ropes. "Introduction." In *Aristotle: On Man in the Universe*. New York: Walter J. Black, 1943.

Mack, Burton L. *The Lost Gospel: The Book of Q and Christian Origins*. New York: HarperCollins Publishers, 1993.

MacMillan, Margaret. *Paris 1919: Six Months that Changed the World*. New York: Random House, 2001.

Mander, Jerry. *In the Absence of the Sacred*. San Francisco: Sierra Club Books, 1992.

Manning, Richard. "Against the Grain: A Portrait of Industrial Agriculture as a Malign Force." In *The American Scholar*, Winter 2004.

Marx, Leo. *The Machine in the Garden: Technology and the Pastoral Ideal in America*. New York: Oxford University Press, 1964.

Mayer, Arno J. "Lower Middle Class as Historical Problem." In *Small Comforts for Hard Times: Humanists on Public Policy*, edited by Michael Mooney and Florian Stuber. New York: Columbia University Press, 1977.

McCabe, Mike. "Who's Awake in Clark County." In *A Whole Which is Greater: Why the Wisconsin "Uprising" Failed*, edited by Paul Gilk and David Kast. Eugene, OR: Wipf and Stock, 2012.

McFague, Sallie. "A Square in the Quilt: One Theologian's Contribution to the Planetary Agenda." In *Spirit and Nature: Why the Environment Is a Religious Issue*, edited by Steven C. Rockefeller and John C. Elder. Boston: Beacon Press, 1992

McNeill, William H. *The Rise of the West: A History of the Human Community*. Chicago: The University of Chicago Press, 1965.

Merton, Thomas. "Introduction." In *The City of God* by Saint Augustine. Translated by Marcus Dods, D.D. New York: Random House, 1950.

Miles, Jack. *God: A Biography*. New York: Alfred A. Knopf, 1995.

Minutes of the Lead Pencil Club: Pulling the Plug on the Electronic Revolution, edited by Bill Henderson. Wainscott, NY: Pushcart Press, 1996.

Monbiot, George. *Feral: Rewilding the Land, the Sea, and Human Life*. Chicago: The University of Chicago Press, 2014.

Morwood, Michael. *Is Jesus God?* New York: The Crossroad Publishing Company, 2001.

Mumford, Lewis. *The City in History: Its Origins, Its Transformations, and Its Prospects*. New York: Harcourt, Brace, and Jovanovich, 1961.

———. *The Condition of Man*. New York: Harcourt, Brace and Company, 1944.

———. *Interpretations and Forecasts: 1922-1972*. New York: Harcourt, Brace & Jovanovich, 1979.

———. *The Myth of the Machine*. New York: Harcourt, Brace & World, 1967.

———. *The Pentagon of Power*. New York: Harcourt, Brace & Jovanovich, 1970.

———. *The Transformations of Man*. New York: Harper & Row, 1972.

Myers, Ched. *Binding the Strong Man: A Political Reading of Mark's Gospel*. Maryknoll, NY: Orbis Books, 2008.

Nasr, Seyyed Hossein. "Islam and the Environmental Crisis." In *Spirit and Nature: Why the Environment Is a Religious Issue*, edited by Steven C. Rockefeller and John C. Elder. Boston: Beacon Press, 1992.

Nearing, Helen and Scott. *Living the Good Life*. New York: Galahad-Schochen Books, 1970.

Newcomb, Steven T. *Pagans in the Promised Land: Decoding the Doctrine of Christian Discovery*. Golden, CO: Fulcrum, 2008.

O'Brien, Tim. *The Things They Carried*. New York: Broadway Books, 1990.

Olson, Sigurd F. *Open Horizons*. New York: Alfred A. Knopf, Inc., 1969.

Oreskes, Naomi and Erik M. Conway. *The Collapse of Western Civilization: A View from the Future*. New York: Columbia University Press, 2014.

Pagels, Elaine. *Adam, Eve, and the Serpent*. New York: Random House, 1988.

———. *Beyond Belief: The Secret Gospel of Thomas*. New York: Random House, 2005.

———. *The Gnostic Gospels*. New York: Random House, 1979.

Pal, Amitabh. "The Toll of Overreaching." In *The Progressive*. November, 2010.

Pelikan, Jaroslav. "Afterword." In *The Jefferson Bible*, with an Introduction by F. Forrester Church. Boston: Beacon Press, 1989.

Perlstein, Rick. "That Seventies Show." In *The Nation*. November 8, 2010.

Pieper, Josef. *Leisure: The Basis of Culture*. Translated by Alexander Dru and with an Introduction by T. S. Eliot. New York: Random House, 1963.

Pierard, Richard V. "Protestant Support for the Political Right in Weimar Germany and Post-Watergate America: Some Comparative Observations." In *Journal of Church and State.* Spring, 1982.

Riesman, David with Nathan Glazer and Reuel Denny. *The Lonely Crowd: A Study of the Changing American Character.* Garden City: Doubleday Anchor Books, 1953.

Rockefeller, Steven C. "Keeping Faith with Life." In *Spirit and Nature: Why the Environment Is a Religious Issue,* edited by Steven C. Rockefeller and John C. Elder. Boston: Beacon Press, 1992.

Rotondaro, Vinnie. "Lives carved by trail of history" and "Disastrous doctrine had papal roots." In *National Catholic Reporter.* August 28-September 10, 2015.

Rynne, Terrence. *Gandhi and Jesus: The Saving Power of Nonviolence.* Maryknoll, NY: Orbis Books, 2008.

Sale, Kirkpatrick. *After Eden: The Evolution of Human Domination.* Durham, NC: Duke University Press, 2006.

———. "Foreword." In *The Breakdown of Nations* by Leopold Kohr. New York: E. P. Dutton, 1978.

Schumacher, E. F. *Small is Beautiful: Economics as if People Mattered.* New York: Harper & Row, 1973.

Schweitzer, Albert. *Out of My Life and Thought: An Autobiography.* Translated by C. T. Campion. New York: Henry Holt and Company, 1949.

Seeger, Pete. "Introduction." In *Rise Up Singing,* edited by Peter Blood-Patterson. Bethlehem, PA: Sing Out Corporation, no date.

Slattery, W. Michael. *Jesus the Warrior? Historical Christian Perspectives & Problems on the Morality of War & the Waging of Peace.* Milwaukee: Marquette University Press, 2007.

Smith, Huston. *The Religions of Man.* New York: Harper & Row, 1965.

Smith, Paul. *The Countrywoman.* New York: Penguin Books, 1989.

Spong, John Shelby. *A New Christianity for a New World.* San Francisco: HarperSanFrancisco, 2001.

Stone, Merlin. *When God Was a Woman.* New York: Harcourt Brace & Company, 1976.

Suzuki, David (with Amanda McConnell). *The Sacred Balance: Rediscovering Our Place in Nature.* Vancouver: Greystone Books, 2002.

Swomley, John M. *American Empire: The Political Ethics of Twentieth-Century Conquest.* New York: The Macmillan Company, 1970.

Tarnas, Richard. *The Passion of the Western Mind.* New York: Ballantine Books, 1991.

Tawney, R. H. *The Acquisitive Society.* New York: Harcourt, Brace & World, 1948.

———. *Religion and the Rise of Capitalism.* New York: Mentor Books, 1953.

Teilhard, Pierre de Chardin. *Man's Place in Nature.* Translated by René Hague. New York: Harper & Row, 1966.

———. *The Phenomenon of Man.* Translated by Bernard Walt. New York: Harper & Row, 1959.

Thoreau, Henry David: *Faith in a Seed: The Dispersion of Seeds and Other Late Natural History Writings,* edited by Bradley P. Dean. Washington, DC: Island, 1995.

Tillich, Paul. *The Protestant Era.* Translated by James Luther Adams. Chicago: University of Chicago Press, 1957.

Toynbee, Arnold. *Civilization on Trial.* New York: Oxford University Press, 1948.

Tuchman, Barbara. *The Proud Tower: A Portrait of the World before the War, 1890-1914.* New York: The Macmillan Company, 1966.

Tucker, Mary Evelyn and John Grim. "Introduction." In *The Christian Future and the Fate of Earth*. Maryknoll, NY: Orbis Books, 2009.

Veninga, James. "Can Religion Help Revive the Progressive Tradition?" In *A Whole Which Is Greater: Why the Wisconsin "Uprising" Failed*, edited by Paul Gilk and David Kast. Eugene, OR: Wipf and Stock, 2012.

Wain, John. *Samuel Johnson*. New York: Viking Press, 1975.

Waite, Robert G. L. *The Psychopathic God: Adolf Hitler*. New York: Basic Books, 1977.

Wills, Garry. *Papal Sin: Structures of Deceit*. New York: Doubleday, 2000.

Wink, Walter. *The Bible in Human Transformation*. Philadelphia: Fortress Press, 1973.

———. *The Powers That Be: Theology for a New Millennium*. New York: Doubleday, 1998.

Zinn, Howard. *A People's History of the United States*. New York: Harper & Row, 1980.

Zizek, Slavoj. *Living in the End Times*. Brooklyn, NY: Verso, 2010.